C0-AZH-197

Bernhard Klausnitzer

INSECTS

Their Biology and Cultural History

Photos by Manfred Förster

UNIVERSE
BOOKS
New York

Translated from the German
by Sylvia Furness

Published in the United States of America in 1987
by Universe Books
381 Park Avenue South, New York, N.Y. 10016

87 88 89 90 91/10 9 8 7 6 5 4 3 2 1

Design: Traudl Schneehagen
Printed in the German Democratic Republic

Library of Congress Cataloging-in-Publication Data

Klausnitzer, Bernhard.
Insects: their biology and cultural history.

Bibliography: p.
Includes index.
1. Insects. 2. Insects—History. I. Title.
QL463.K62 1987 595.7 87-5853
ISBN 0-87663-666-0

Contents

Half-title
Female Bush Cricket, *Leptophyes albovittata*, from Central Europe.
Note the sabre-shaped ovipositor and the absence of wings.

Frontispiece
Male Common Blue *(Polyommatus icarus)* from Central Europe.

Title page
Male Stag Beetle, *Lamprima adolphinae*, from New Guinea.

Copyright page
Syrphids (Hover-flies) *(Episyrphus balteatus)*. The larvae live predaciously on aphids.

Introduction

From the earliest times, man's attitude to insects has been determined primarily by the extent to which they are useful or harmful to him. Numerous documents bear witness to a very ancient knowledge both of the usefulness of certain species of insects and also to the frequent devastation of food stores by insect pests. At the same time, insect form and colour have long been admired and insects have served as models to inspire a wide range of artistic activity.

Today, the study of insects has become so diversified and also so vitally important that an independent branch of zoology has developed in entomology, the science of insects. Entomological Societies exist in many countries, some with well over a century of tradition behind them. Scientists working in Institutes of Entomology constantly reduce the number of unanswered questions; international congresses bring together thousands of entomologists who confer in specialist study groups—specialization is a marked feature of the science of insects. Some 30,000 articles appear each year in almost a thousand journals dedicated exclusively to entomology.

Of the many relationships existing between man and insect, there is space within this book for only a few examples.

First one might recall that two species of insects were among the earliest animals to be domesticated by man: they were the honey bee and the silk-worm. At first, wild insects were used, later domestic forms were developed. In contrast to vertebrates, they retained their independence of form and changed less as a result of domestic breeding. Various scale lice were used in early times as a source of colouring matter, varnishes and waxes. At times, they had considerable commercial significance.

Although insect protein is very suitable for human consumption, it has been little used in Europe. Thousands of years ago, however, people included insects frequently in their diet. They are still eaten in considerable quantities today in many countries, especially in tropical regions. The eggs, larvae, pupae and imagines of many of the larger species, particularly certain grasshoppers, termites, bugs, cicadas, ants, beetles and butterflies were, and are still today, used as food. The relevant literature contains a wealth of specialist recipes.

The consumption of insects was very often associated with a belief in an effect going beyond their simple nutritional value, in particular, the idea that they could increase sexual potency. The transition to the use of insects to cure a wide variety of illnesses was a logical one, and we know that remedies of this kind already existed in Ancient Egypt. In this sphere, needless to say, superstition and reality did not necessarily coincide. Many of the medicaments recommended can at best have had a psychological effect. But the undoubted efficacy of cantharidine, the active principle of the Blister Beetle or Spanish Fly (Meloidae), is well-known; we are also familiar with the action, curative and lethal, of the poison of bees and wasps. Poisonous Leaf Beetles (genus *Diamphidia*) can be highly dangerous, even as dried museum specimens. For many scientific discoveries in the field of genetics, we are indebted to laboratory insects, bred and killed in millions, in particular to Fruit Flies of the genus *Drosophila*. By their death, they benefit human life.

Proturans (Protura), first discovered by Filippo Silvestri, an Italian zoologist, as recently as 1907, are only 0.6–2.4 mm long and live in the upper layers of the soil. They are the only known insect in which antennae are absent, while the anterior legs have a sensory function.

Numerous species of insects attack dead vegetable matter physically and chemically and so play a decisive part in breaking down organic material into its inorganic components. Work of this kind goes on secretly and silently; we scarcely notice the disappearance of such things as tree stumps, dead branches and fallen leaves. The removal of excreta is also largely the work of insects. We only appreciate the value of their myriad activity when suddenly it ceases. Australian Dung Beetles failed to colonize initially unfamiliar cattle dung, and so over a period of time, thousands of square kilometres were lost as pasture land. With carrion, the situation is similar. Here too, it is the insects, especially flies and beetles, that make use of this organic material in their everyday activity.

In their utilization of dead organic matter, insects contribute significantly to soil biology. By helping to form humus, break down the soil and distribute nutriments, they exert a beneficial influence on the soil.

One hundred and twenty-five million years ago, angiosperms and many groups of insects began their common development. An important result of this parallel and consecutive evolution is the series of reciprocal adaptations associated with pollination. To cultivate many species of plants, we depend today upon the pollinizing activities of insects. The value of honey bees as pollinating agents is immensely greater than the profits that arise from keeping them to provide honey and other products.

Certain insects are also very useful to us as the enemies of other insects. Many species live as predators or parasites on others. One need think only of the many predacious beetles, Hymenopterans, flies and bugs as well as the various parasitical "ichneumon flies" (in the widest sense), tachinid flies and other parasitic Dipterans. As links in food chains, they all make a vital contribution in maintaining the stability of ecosystems. Certain phytophagous species are used for the biological control of weeds.

Just as diverse as the usefulness of insects is the damage they can cause to man, indeed, here they can justifiably be ranked as a "world power". In this context, one probably thinks first of those species that are pests on plants. The practice of monoculture and intensive farming proves so favourable to the insects that feed on the particular crops, that the threat of their propagation on a huge scale and complete devastation of the crop is a very real one. Massive crop failures have been caused not only by migratory locusts—insects dreaded by farmers for thousands of years—but also by the caterpillars of various species of butterfly. It is still true today that we "harvest what the insects leave behind". In addition, it must be said that destruction of living plant material

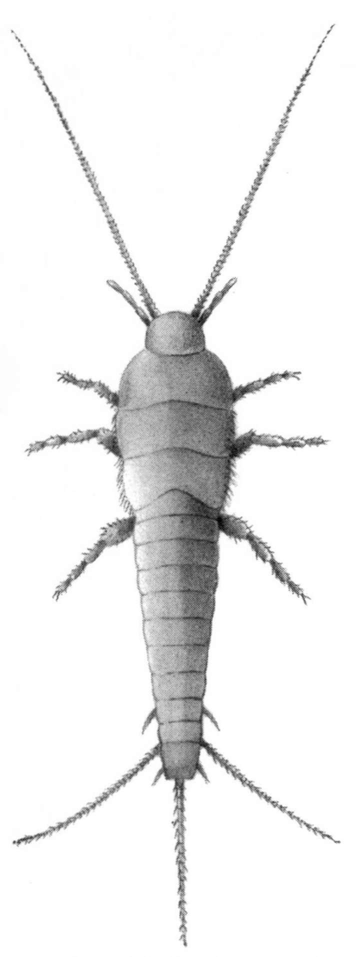

The Silverfish *(Lepisma saccharina)* is a cosmopolitan, typical representative of the order Zygentoma. The earliest reference in literature to this species of insect occurs in the *Erh Ya* (about 500 B.C.). The renowned microscopist Robert Hooke (1635 to 1730) devoted a chapter of his *Micrographia* (1665) to the Silverfish: "To the small Silvery Bookworm".

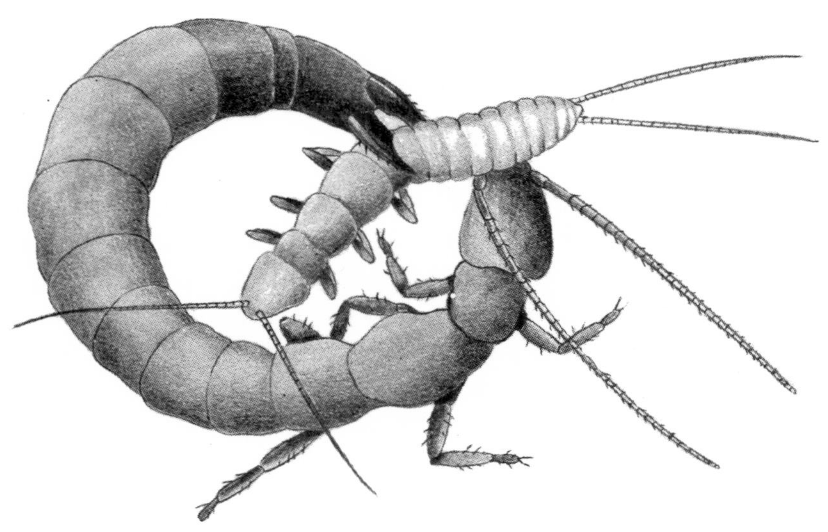

Among Double-tails (Diplura) there are some species with long, many-segmented abdominal appendages *(Campodea)* and some with short, force-like cerci *(Japyx)*. Here, one of the forceps-tailed Japygidae that has seized and is devouring a Campodeid.

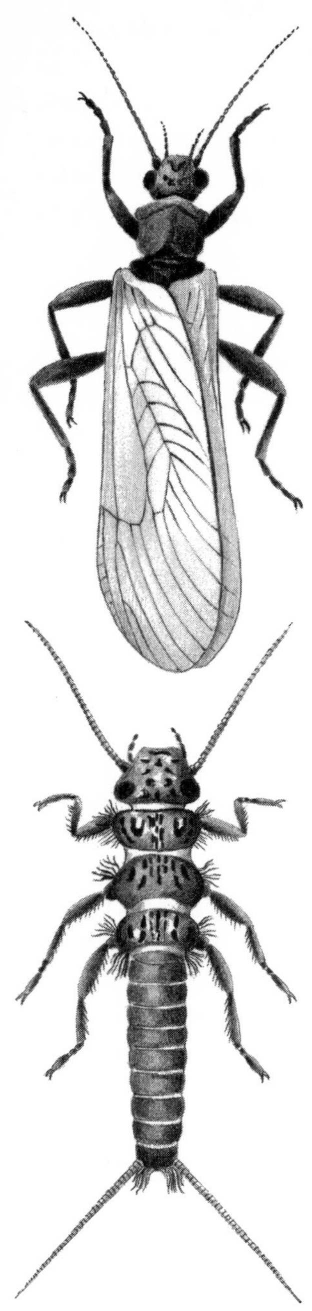

Above an imago, below a larva of *Perla marginata*, a representative of the order of Stoneflies (Plecoptera), a distinctive feature of which is the presence of two long abdominal filaments and the development of the larvae in water. Caspar Schwenckfeld mentions a species of Stonefly: "Musca caudata. A tailed fly. A quite large, grey fly with narrow, elongate abdomen, from the end of which two long hair-like caudal appendages protrude."

and damage caused by feeding are not the only disadvantages. Many species, particularly aphids and cicadas, transmit plant diseases, viroses for example, and so cause considerable crop damage. A glance at the specialized literature shows that throughout the world, the lists of pests are very long. But there are always a few "major pests" that are responsible for the greater part of the destruction; something like 10 per cent of the species can be blamed for 90 per cent of the damage. Wood and other organic materials (fabrics, wool, furs) are also damaged or destroyed by certain species of insects. Of particular importance is the large number of wood pests (many beetles, termites). Even in very early times, insect pests in stored food commanded attention, and recommendations for their control are numerous. Then as now, it was grain stocks in particular that were seriously at risk from insect attack (by corn weevils, corn moths and other pests), but in addition, almost all other kinds of stored food—whether cheese or flour, biscuits or smoked meat, fruit or chocolate—are often infested by insects.

Particularly tiresome are the many flies that pester domestic animals or humans, without causing them any direct harm by stinging. Their effect on humans cannot be measured precisely but may well manifest itself in ill humour or the absence of a sense of achievement. Cows troubled in this way may show a reduced milk yield.

It is a short step from insects that are troublesome to man and beast to those that transmit disease. Flies and wasps can spread large numbers of bacteria. The causative organisms of malaria that are carried by mosquitoes (*Anopheles*) are still today among the most feared agents of disease. In 1981 there were 215 million cases of chronic and 140 million of acute malaria in 107 countries. 1.8 thousand million people are at risk of infection. Consider also the dreadful pictures of the doomed victims of sleeping sickness, a disease of the central nervous system, caused by unicellular organisms and transmitted by Tsetse Flies (*Glossina*). In the Middle Ages, plague carried by fleas wiped out half the population of Europe. Other species of insects are themselves the agents of disease, for example, warble flies, deer botflies and horse botflies on domesticated and wild animals. Humans also suffer occasionally from fly larvae in the eye or in wounds. Larvae bred in sterile conditions were used especially during the 19th century to remove diseased tissue from suppurating war wounds.

Finally mention should be made of one more relationship of the greatest diversity: the artistic confrontation between man and insect, that has its roots in part in ancient cultic beliefs. One need think only of Scarabaeus and Psyche, of dances and songs based on insect-linked themes, or in the belief in predictions of good or bad fortune, wealth or poverty, that are very widespread features in most cultures and in which species of insects of striking appearance play an important part.

Poets have sung of insects, musicians have set their activity to music, painters, fascinated by their beauty, have used every available technique to represent them, and sculptures of insects abound. Various insects have also served as models for other branches of art and craft, including, for example, glyptography, coin manufacture, postage stamp printing, porcelain painting and design, and of course, photography, both scientific and artistic. A wide variety of jewelry and household goods are modelled on insects or use insect bodies in their manufacture.

Beginning with the cabinets of natural history specimens in the days of feudalism, insects were increasingly collected. Then as now, the motives of the collector varied greatly. Aesthetic appreciation and delight in colour and form may be just as decisive as a passion for collecting or scientific interest. But whatever the reason for their creation, valuable collections were built up by enthusiasts from a wide variety of professional backgrounds; today, they are among the treasures of many museums and an indispensable aid to scientific research.

The fundamental literary work of Fritz Simon Bodenheimer on the history of entymology of the pre-Linnaean period has lost nothing of its importance even for present-day research in this field. He traced the literary sources of Antiquity and the Middle Ages and interpreted the material excellently.

He was born on June 6, 1897 in Cologne and died in London on October 4, 1959. He studied in Germany and it was here that he wrote his standard work on entomology. In 1928 he became a staff member of the University of Jerusalem and continued his scientific work in the field of entomology there, for instance on topics such as the role of insects in human nourishment, locust plagues, manna, honey bees and scale insects. Bodenheimer wrote fifty books and more than four hundred articles.

It is impossible for the author to say how many books about insects have been written throughout the world in the course of centuries. Anyone wanting to add a new one must endeavour to introduce some originality. The fundamental concept of this present book is to introduce to the reader references to insects dating from early and recent times, and by commenting on the examples, to show how knowledge has developed to the state in which it exists today, how ancient much of that knowledge is, and the point of view from which man regards certain species of insects, while leaving others largely ignored. More material on the cultural history of insects has found its way into the manuscript than had originally been intended. Attempts at judicial pruning served rather to emphasize the fundamental intention than to efface it. Finally I gave up the attempt, cherishing the modest hope that perhaps it is precisely in this aspect that the book's individuality lies. From this point of view, it is difficult to achieve complete unity of text and illustration. Many of the pictures and captions provide additional information that is intended to heighten the impression of the infinite diversity of the insect world. Since it was in any case impossible to achieve completeness, I have selected what is rare and fascinating. The photographs taken by my colleague Manfred Förster contribute even more: they show the beauty of insects; they are intended to clear away a small part of the mountain of vilification that has accumulated over centuries.

Globular Springtails *(Sminthurides aquaticus)* before mating. The male has modified gripping antennae; allowing himself to be carried by the female, he directs her to a position over a previously deposited spermatophore. Springtails, which make up the order Collembola, are present in such large numbers in the upper layers of the soil, that 400,000 individuals have been found in one square metre. The occurrence on a massive scale on snow was reported by Spielenberger, a Warsaw physician, in 1683 and by Rudolph Jacob Camerarius of Tübingen in 1697. The first detailed descriptions of Springtails were by Carl de Geer (1740).

For the book's organization, several possibilities existed. I decided to treat important systematic groups in succession, and to introduce minor orders that are otherwise hardly mentioned, in at least one illustration, so that the book gives a certain insight into altogether 35 of the world's orders of insects. A text book might well be organized in this way. But I am convinced that the book has nothing in common with a school textbook, apart from one important aim: that of imparting knowledge.

Another aspect was of importance to me and it is one to which entomological textbooks have rarely devoted themselves: that of inspiring real affection for insects, an animal group that has been living in the world for 500 million years.

Insect Diversity

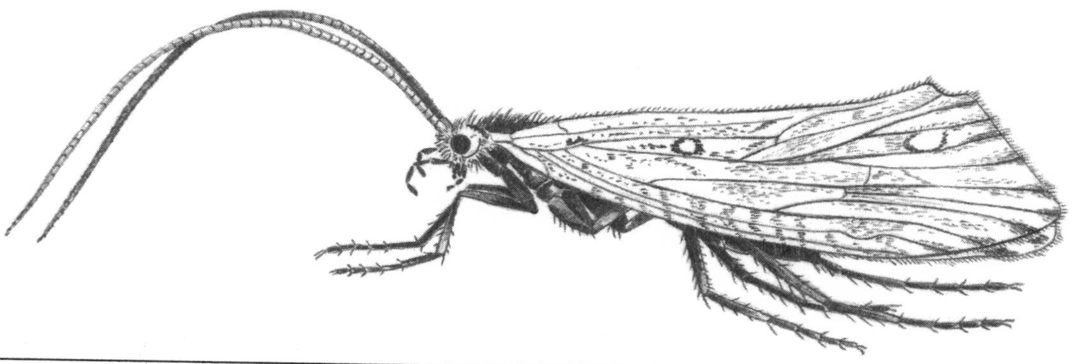

A multiplicity of species

Speculation and knowledge about the number of species of insects living on the earth have been subject to great change. In those writings of Aristotle that have been handed down to us, 47 species of insect are mentioned, in Pliny 61. The following Table shows the insects with which these two great writers of classical Antiquity were familiar:

	Aristotle	Pliny
Grasshoppers (Ensifera and Caelifera)	3	4
Beetles (Coleoptera)	6	9
Hymenopterans (Hymenoptera)	12	11
Butterflies (Lepidoptera)	6	6
Dipterans (Diptera)	8	8
Bugs, aphids (Heteroptera, Homoptera)	5	7
Other orders	3	3
Defined species	43	48
Undefined species	4	13
Total	47	61

For more than two millennia, there was no change in the total range known to classical antiquity. Johann Sperling, in his *Zoologia physica* published in Leipzig in 1661, speaking about zoology as a science, says: "It requires much work, both because of the abundance and because of the delicacy of the objects. It is extremely laborious to work through all the animal species. After all, we know at least 40 species of beetles, 50 of caterpillars, 70 of flies and more than 100 of butterflies. Nevertheless there is a series of excellent authors in this field. What is demanded is less memory in learning facts than judgement in distinguishing between the species."

As a result of the work of the great collectors and systematists in the years that followed, there was an enormous growth in knowledge about various insect species. In 1701, John Ray in London was able to write: "Butterflies and beetles are such numerous groups that I believe we have 150 or more species of each in England. Together with larvae and pupae, that makes 900 species. But

Above:

Caddis Flies (Trichoptera). Here, one of the largest European species *(Phryganea grandis)*. The first detailed description of this insect is found in Caspar Schwenckfeld's *Theriotropheum Silesiae* and a little later in the writings of Leonhard Baldner.

we exclude larvae and pupae from the concept of species, and count them in with the relevant insect . . . The number of insect species in the whole world, on land and water, must be in the region of 10,000, and I would think more rather than less.

"Note: Since then (i. e. since 1691), in my neighbourhood alone, I have bred 200 species of butterfly and now believe the total of insects in Britain to be some 2,000, and that of the whole world some 20,000."

Today, we have reached something like a million species, and there are many entomologists who consider the true total of insect species in the world to be much higher: four to five million.

Classifying the diversity

It is surprising that many of the ideas on insect systematics and particular groupings were comparatively clearly defined right from the start, and have remained constant, while other groups, usually the same ones, have changed repeatedly over the centuries. Bodenheimer (1928) provides a summary of Aristotle's ideas on the classification of insects: "Within the group of Entoma, Aristotle unites various groups: in addition to the true insects there are also arachnids, myriapods and worms. As systematic sub-groups within the insect group in our sense, only Coleoptera, Hymenoptera (Aphids, Vespids) and Diptera can be recognized with certainty. Bloodless winged insects (Pterota) are either Coleoptera, which have their functional wings under a wing cover, such as the Scarab Beetle and the Blister Beetle, or they have no wing covers and are therefore either Diptera or Tetraptera. The latter are particularly large or they have a sting at the back. The Diptera are small and have a sting at the front, like flies, botflies and crane-flies. Apart from these, butterflies, cicadas, grasshoppers and lice stand out as indefinite small groups. Whereas butterflies, cicadas and lice are not defined in detail—they are clearly too well known—characteristics that define grasshoppers are the posture of the jumping legs and the female ovipositor."

Aldrovandi's system

The system of insect classification drawn up by Ulisse Aldrovandi contains important observations. For the first time, an author describes the principles on which his system is based:

"First I distinguish between the insects according to the place in which they live and are born, then according to their physical characteristics such as colour, size, body parts, their feeding habits, the manner of their birth, locomotion, coitus. 1. According to the place in which they live and are born: some live in simple media, such as in water, air, earth or fire (like Pliny's pyrausta), but most of them in mixed media like the snow-worms or the worms that inhabit stone, plants, animals or animal excreta. Some live in homogeneous media, for example, in meat, bone, nerve and so on; others in heterogeneous ones like tongue, liver, spleen, etc. The animal products that serve as media are in part solid, like wool, in part fluid, like cheese, butter, wax. Best-known of all are the water insects. Of these, some live in the sea, others in marshes, torrents, springs, ponds and reservoirs. 2. According to bodily characteristics: particularly in the case of butterflies and caterpillars, colours are very important in distinguishing species. Ants and "worms" on the other hand are more or less uniform in colour. And then, whether they are large or small; round, angular or oval: smooth, rough or hairy. The upper half is different from the lower. But to all of these, three parts are common: head, thorax and abdomen."

In Aldrovandi's division into habitats (although no insects live in fire and scarcely any in the sea), we can recognize the preliminary stage in an ecological approach, and one which undoubtedly represents progress for that time.

Although the tripartite division of the body into head, thorax and abdomen defines an important character of all insects, Ulisse Aldrovandi's taxonomic system, like that of Aristotle, contains a number of groups of non-insects: Millipeds, Isopods, Arachnids, "worms", Echinoderms and even fish (sea-horses). It is not possible here to discuss the identity of all the insects mentioned.

On right:

1 *Dilta hibernica*, a representative of the Cliff or Coast Bristletails (Archaeognatha) on tree bark. Note the large maxillary palps (sensory structures on the lower jaw) which consist of seven segments—the largest number of any insect—and the three long abdominal appendages.

2 Springtails *(Orchesella villosa)* from Central Europe. In two of the specimens shown, the forked springing organ or furca is released. By means of this organ, which is characteristic of the Collembola, some species can jump a distance of up to 25 cm.

On left:

3 Above left: The larvae of many species in the family Rhyacophilidae of Caddis Flies build nets and other silken structures in flowing water in which they capture prey, while others move about freely in search of food (Central Europe).

4 Above right: In contrast to almost all other Caddis Flies, the larvae of *Enoicyla pusilla* (Central Europe) do not live in water but in the moss and leaves at the base of deciduous trees in woods, where they feed primarily on fallen leaves. They pupate at a depth of about 5 cm. In autumn, the pupa moves to the surface and the imago hatches. Whereas the wings of the male are fully developed, those of the female are reduced to short rudimentary stumps. The eggs are deposited in the upper layer of humus in clusters consisting of 30–90 eggs enclosed in gellatinous mucilage.

5 Below: The larvae of most species of Caddis Fly live in water inside transportable cases. Depending upon the nature of the body of water, the caddis cases differ considerably in form and in the material of which they are constructed. Here, a representative of the Limnophilidae living in standing water in Central Europe.

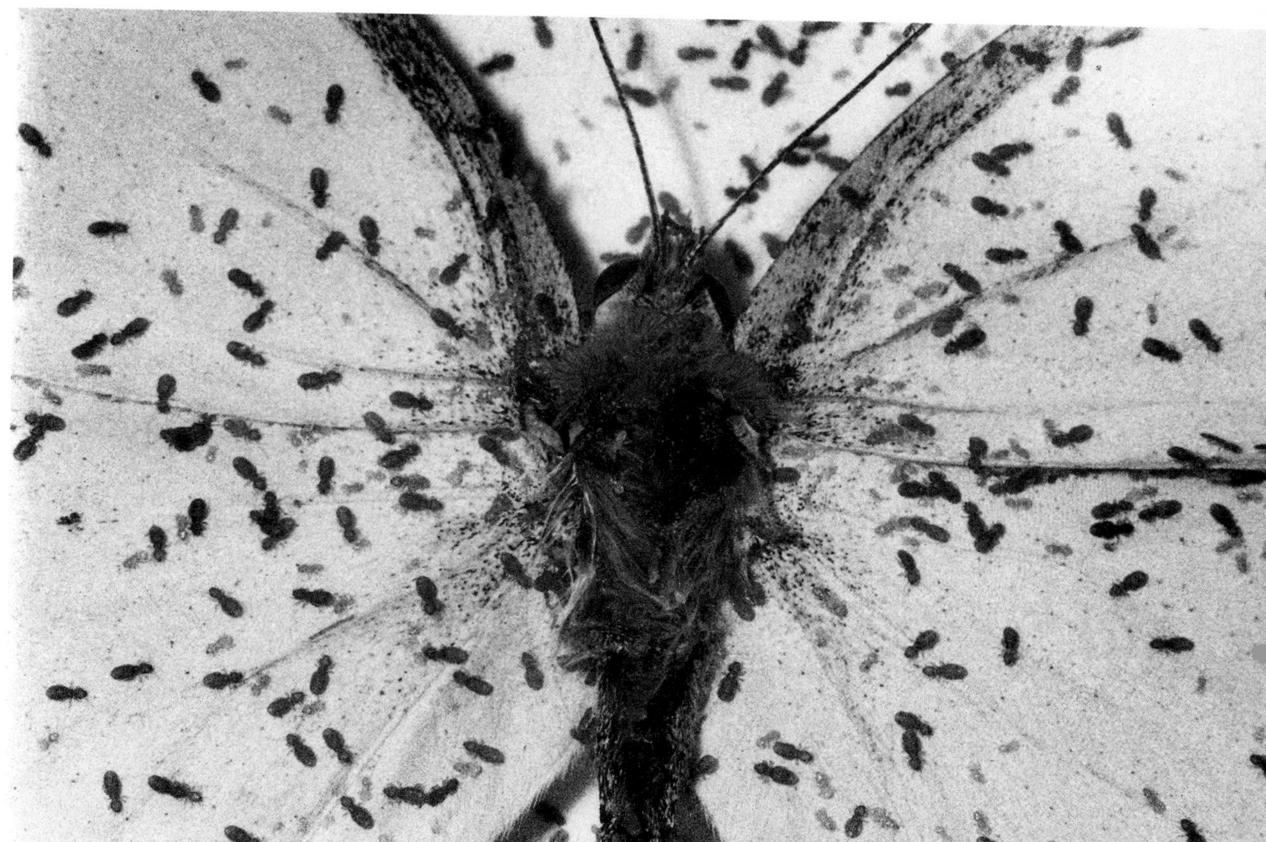

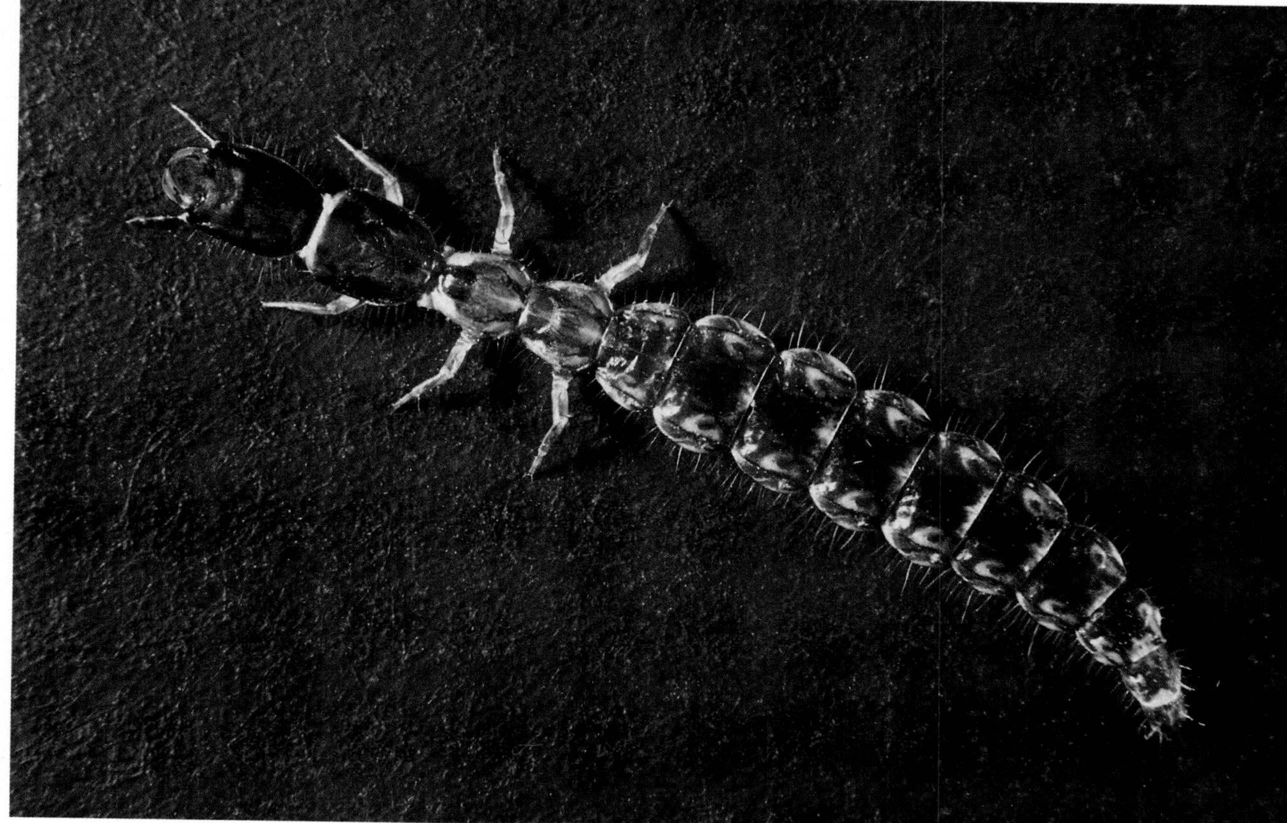

6 Above: Psocids (Dustlice or Booklice) are often found in large numbers in insect collections, especially *Liposcelis* species. This example shows a heavily infested White (Pierid butterfly).

7 Below: The larvae of most Snake Flies (Raphidioptera) live under bark where they prey upon other insects. Illustrated here, the European species *Inocellia crassicornis* that lives mainly on conifers.

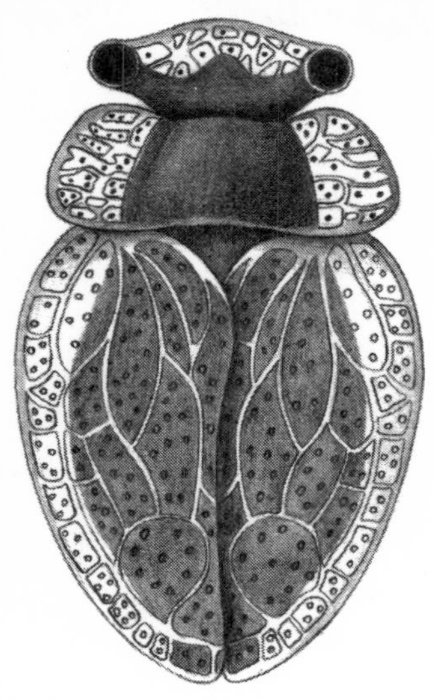

Hemiodoecus fidelis is one of the small number of species in the order of Coleorrhyncha; it lives on certain mosses in forests of Southern Beech *(Nothofagus)* in the south of Chile and Argentina, in New Zealand, Australia and Tasmania.

The definition of the individual groups is, however, a substantial advance, and the introduction of a dichotomous key for identification has proved its value and is still retained to this day. The credit goes to Aldrovandi for having first put forward an identification key of this sort for insects.

Let us now look at his system of classification, which is at the same time an identification table.

1. Land insects
1.1. With legs
1.1.1. With wings
1.1.1.1. Without elytra
1.1.1.1.1. With four wings
1.1.1.1.1.1. With hyaline wings
1.1.1.1.1.1.1. Wax producers: Honey Bee, Wild Bee, Bumble Bee, Wasp, Hornet
1.1.1.1.1.1.2. Non-wax producers: Cicada, Perla, Rhynchota heteroptera, Orsodacne
1.1.1.1.1.2. With squamous wings: Butterflies
1.1.1.1.2. With 2 wings: Flies (Muscidae), Tabanidae, Culicidae, Ephemeridae
1.1.1.2. With elytra: Grasshoppers, Crickets, Beetles, Cockroaches
1.1.2. Without wings
1.1.2.1. Few legs
1.1.2.1.1. With 6 legs: Ant, Bedbug, Louse, Tick, Flea, Lens cossus, Mole Cricket, Earwigs
1.1.2.1.2. With 8 legs: Scorpion, Spider
1.1.2.1.3. With 12 and 14 legs: Loopers, Caterpillars
1.1.2.2. Multipeds: Millipeds, Isopods, Centipedes, Julus
1.2. Apods: Worms that come into being in humans, animals, plants, stone, metal, Teredo, Earthworms, Snails, Moths, Otips

2. Water insects
2.1. With legs
2.1.1. With few legs: Phryganide larvae, Musca fluviatilis, Cantharis aquatica, Viola aquatica, Tipula alata and Aptera (probably mostly Water Fleas; the Author)
2.1.2. Multipeds: Scrophula seu Tinea, Pulex marinus, Pediculus marinus, Oestrus sive Asilus marinus, Scolopendra marina, Vermes in tubulis delitescantes [probably mainly marine Annelids; the Author]
2.2. Apods: Worms, Echinoderms, Sea-horses.

Moufet brings scarcely any progress

A somewhat different system, perhaps more formal, is that drawn up by Thomas Moufet and published in 1634 in his book *Insectorum sive minimorum animalium theatrum*:

1. Winged insects
Bees, Wasps, Hornets and Bumble Bees, Flies (including Neuroptera, Ichneumon Flies, Tipulidae), Mosquitoes, Butterflies, Glowworms and Fireflies, Grasshoppers (Acrididae, Tettigoniidae and Mantidae), Cicadas and Crickets, Cockroaches, Beetles (Buprestis and Cantharis, Scarabaei, minor beetles, Meloe and Water Beetles), Mole Cricket, Pyrigonus, Water Skippers, Earwigs, Winged Scorpions, Bugs and Lice, Flower Bugs.

2. Wingless insects
2.1. Terrestrial creatures
2.1.1. With legs
2.1.1.1. With many legs (Caterpillars, Cockchafer larvae, Staphylinus and Julus)
2.1.1.2. With 8 legs (Scorpion, Spiders)

8 One of the principal recognition features of the Scorpion Fly (Mecoptera) is the curious prolongation of the head into a "beak". The vernacular name refers to the habit of the male of carrying its large organ of copulation at the end of the abdomen curved upwards, giving it an appearance somewhat reminiscent of a scorpion. Here, *Panorpa germanica* (Central Europe).

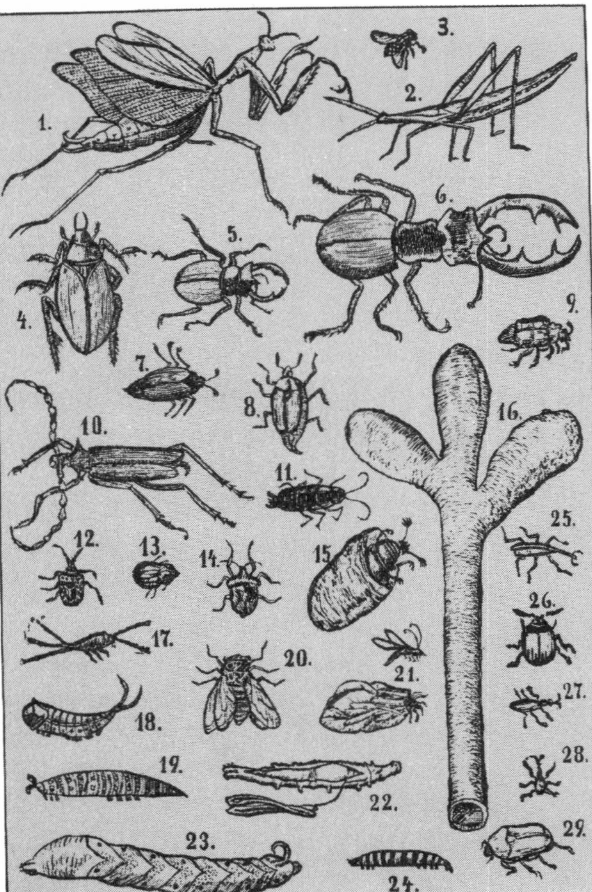

Woodcut plate from *De Animalibus insectis* by Ulisse Aldrovandi.

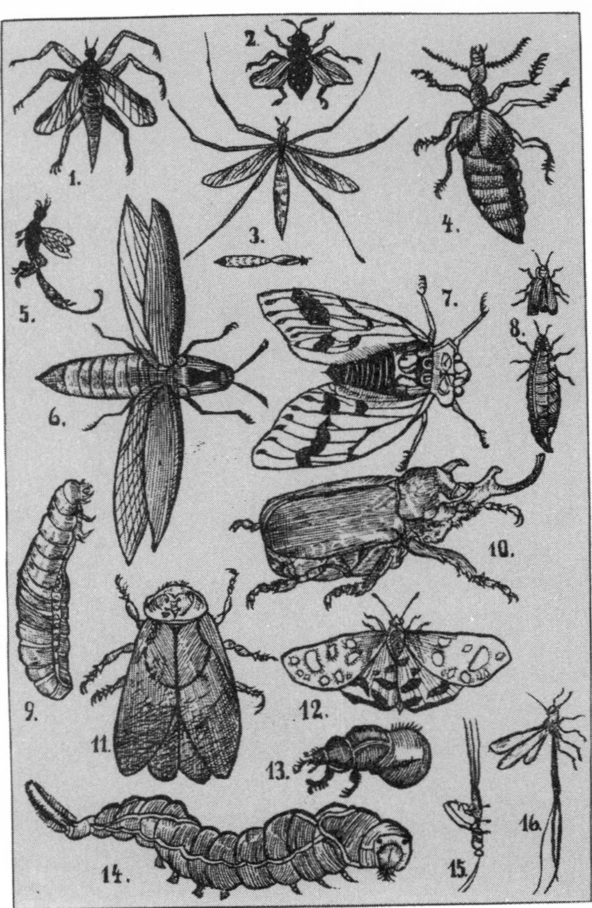

Plate from *Insectorum sive minimorum animalium theatrum* by Thomas Moufet.

Grylloblatta campodeiformis (♀) is a representative of the insect order Notoptera that contains only a small number of species. They live in the Arctic-Alpine zone of North America and Asia on the surface of the soil under stones and moss. They are well adapted to the extreme conditions of the biotope by a low temperature preference and specifically timed development.

2.1.1.3. With 6 legs (Ants, females of Cicindela and Meloe, Worms that live in wood, trees, fruit, clothes, beds etc.)
2.1.2. Without legs (Worms)
2.2. Aquatic creatures
2.2.1. With legs
2.2.1.1. With 6 legs (Beetle larvae, Notonecta, Dragonfly larvae etc.)
2.2.1.2. With many legs (Marine Centipedes)
2.2.2. Without legs (Leech, Horsehair Worm)

The scheme shows little improvement on the work of Aldrovandi, except perhaps that fewer non-insects are included. His "winged scorpions" probably refer to Water Scorpions (Bugs). One retrograde step is the absence of a subdivision within the winged insects. Clearly the "wingless insects" prove the most difficult. The category of "multi-legged" probably proved confusing at first. Caterpillars, for example, in addition to the 6 thoracic legs, have additional legs on the abdomen, while Cockchafer grubs do not. So it is not at all clear why Moufet placed them among the many-legged insects, particularly since his illustration of a May Beetle larva correctly shows it to have only thoracic legs.

If by "Staphylinus" we are to understand a representative of the Rove Beetles (Staphylinidae), this insect has 6 legs and no more. His "Julus" is a millipede with "many legs", but other features show it not to be an insect at all. The eight-legged creatures are Arachnids, and octopody is a fundamental characteristic of this animal group.

Swammerdam takes account of metamorphosis

Quite different ideas on the classification of insects, which are fundamentally still valid today, are those developed by Jan Swammerdam, on the basis of his own thorough studies of insect metamorphosis, which appear in his *Bijbel der natuure*, published in 1737, fifty-two years after his death, by Boerhave.

"The first order is that in which the creature emerges from the egg directly with all its limbs, gradually grows to its full size, thereupon becoming a nymph, which can no longer moult.

"The second is that in which the creature emerges from the egg with 6 legs, and gradually, by means of a number of fully-developed *calveulorum*, that is, small sacs or buds, acquires complete wings, and finally becomes a nymph.

"The third is that in which a small worm or caterpillar without legs, or with 6 legs, or with even more legs, emerges from the egg, its limbs grow imperceptibly under the covering skin which it finally casts off and becomes a pupa or aurelia.

"The fourth order, finally, is that in which the worm again emerges from the egg without legs, or with 6 or more legs, and grows imperceptibly within its skin, does not however cast the skin, but in it, takes on the form of a nymph."

Swammerdam's views on a system of classification are based on exceptionally meticulous and skilful work typical of a difficult personality heavily burdened with problems. In addition to his fundamental research into metamorphosis, we are indebted to him for his extremely thorough studies of honey bees and a number of valuable findings, particularly in the sphere of insect anatomy.

The first of his four orders corresponds approximately to that known as the Ametabola, a group still retained in many taxonomic systems today. Its typical features are the smooth transition between individual stages of development and the ability of the imagines to moult. There is no distinctly separate larval stage, so we can speak of direct development. Typical representatives of the "Ametabola" are the lowest, primarily wingless orders of insects that are summarized as primitive insects. Our Hemimetabola (insects with incomplete metamorphosis) can be seen as belonging to the second order. Every school child hears about them in his biology lessons. The third order is

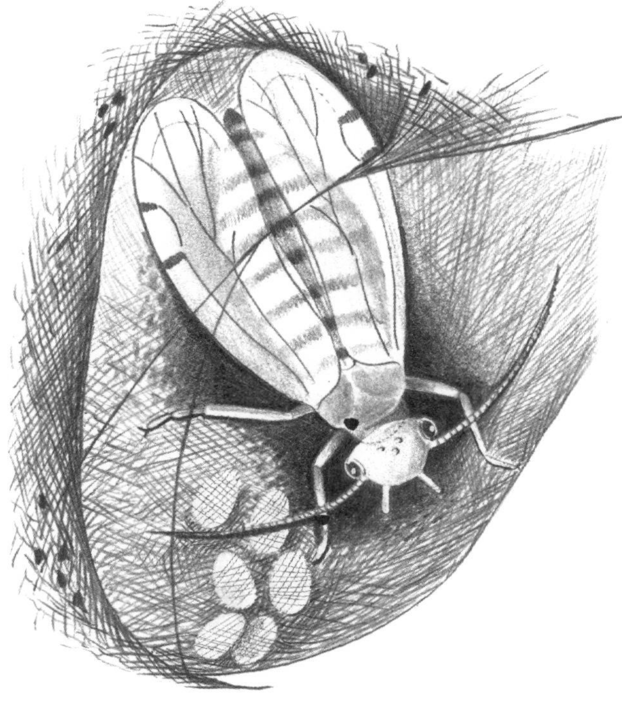

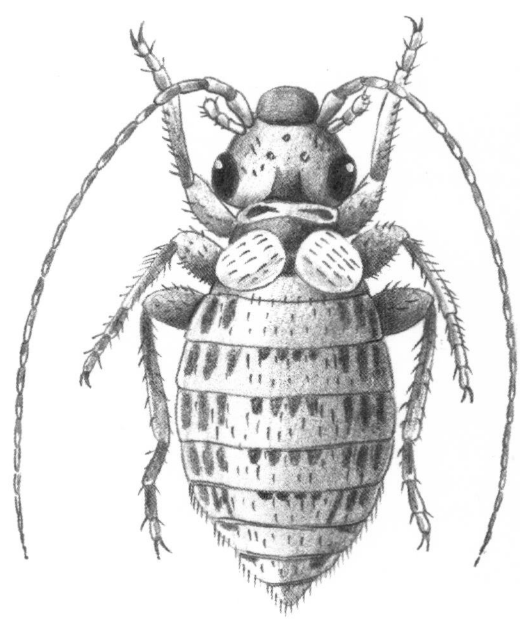

The Psocoptera have various vernacular names indicating the considerable variety of their modes of life: Barklice, Lichen-lice, Booklice, Dustlice. There are both winged and wingless forms. Left: female of *Ectopsocus briggsi* spinning a silken web over a clutch of eggs. A second, looser gauze above the insect contains balls of excreta.
Right: *Trogium pulsatorium*; the female of this Psocid produces a tapping sound by striking the abdomen against a hard surface, leading to a variety of superstitious misinterpretations.

also widely-known: the Holometabola, insects with complete metamorphosis. Swammerdam himself describes his fourth order as coordinated with the third. Its main feature is the retention of the penultimate and the final larval skin for use as a protective covering or case (puparium), in which the pupa lies freely. Pupal cases are characteristic of many flies (the group of Cyclorrhapha).

A classification system for the insects of Britain

Because Swammerdam's findings remained dormant for a long time in the form of a manuscript, the possession of which had become the subject of a lengthy dispute, it is not surprising that, in the meantime, other systems had become established, which took metamorphosis much less into account. One such was the work of a very acute observer of nature, Martin Lister (1638–1711), who was the personal physician to the Queen of England. He classified the insects of Britain as follows:

1. Insects that come from round eggs, and in all respects apart from size, are already in their definitive form when they hatch.
6-legged: Lice
8-legged: Spiders, Scorpions

Multi-legged: Millipeds
Without legs: Worms and Molluscs

2. Insects that hatch from elongate eggs as worms and later become pupae. These two stages are simply growth phenomena of the adult insect.
With elytra: Beetles, Grasshoppers
Without elytra
With 4 wings: Butterflies, Dragonflies, Bees, Wasps
With 2 wings: Flies, Mosquitoes, Horse-flies

Lister also numbers certain groups of creatures among the insects which should not be included there: spiders, scorpions, millipeds, worms, molluscs. Some advance is seen in his establishment of Group 2, which from the definition he gives, clearly comprises the Holometabola (insects with complete metamorphosis). Of course, neither grasshoppers nor dragonflies belong there. Nevertheless, today's order of Diptera is clearly characterized by its prime feature of possessing two wings.

Vallisnieri's ecological system of classification

The Italian physician Antonio Vallisnieri was probably the first to establish an ecological system of insect classification. His manner of distinguishing between the four groups had a lasting influence upon the study of insect ecology of his time. It is by no means easy to set up a system of classification for animals on the basis of ecological data, yet environmental demands are important characteristics of every group of animals and therefore of systematic significance. Valisnieri was probably the first to bring out clearly important associations and groups based on life-form.

"The first group comprises all insects that subsist upon or live in plants or in any way obtain nourishment from them.
The second group comprises all aquatic insects.
The third all those insects living in the soil and in hard substances.
The fourth, all epizoa and endozoa together with all insects that feed on meat."

As an example of his system, let us consider some of the 41 sub-groups within the first major group, to illustrate Vallisnieri's manner of observation.

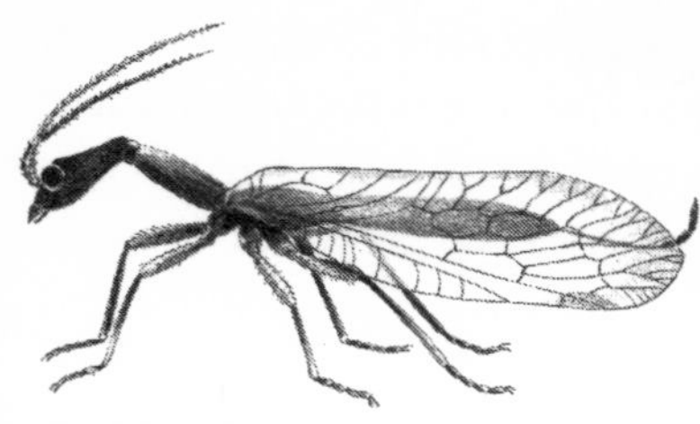

Important recognition features of Snake Flies (Raphidioptera) are the "neck-like" elongation of the prothorax and the characteristic posture.

"1. First I deal with those insects that for the most part hide themselves in the hearts of plants, build their nests in reeds and the hollow stems of other plants or that feed on plant juices. Included here are certain small woodland bees, a number of ichneumon flies, some ants etc.
2. The second group is made up of those which themselves hollow out the pith of plants in order to lay their eggs there.
3. Less ingenious insects lay their eggs on the stem or branches, and the larvae themselves must eat their way into the pith.
4. Those insects that eat into plants with such force that the latter wither or fail to come to fruition.
5. Those that eat only as much of the plants as is essential for their development. The plants do not die but become weakly.
6. Those insects that produce galls (on branches and stalks).
7. The very widespread group of insects that eat only the leaves, leaving behind the leafless plant damaged.
8. Those insects that lay their eggs on the underside of leaves, frequently causing the leaf to curl slightly, and which are content with a little sap or exudate.
9. Leaf-miners.
10. Those that lay their eggs in the central rib of a leaf without thereby destroying it, and whose larvae feed between the individual leaf veins."

John Ray sets new standards

John Ray (1628–1705) is one of the most important systematists. Son of a smith, he was assisted by scholarships to study theology and languages, and later held posts as lecturer, preacher and tutor at Cambridge. Reactionary upheavals after the death of Oliver Cromwell (1658) obliged him to sever his connections with the university. Together with Francis Willughby (1635–1672), a

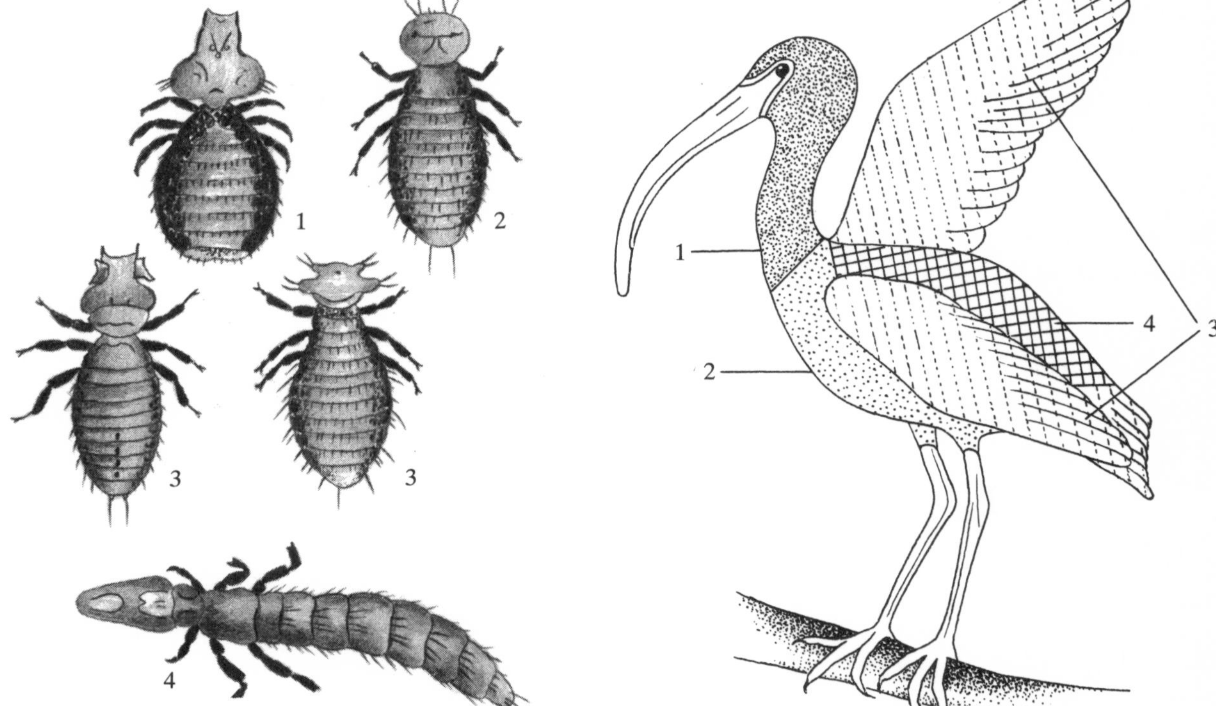

The order of Animal Lice (Phthiraptera) includes Biting Lice and Bird Lice (Mallophaga). Each species is restricted to a quite particular area of the host's body, as shown in this diagram of an ibis.
1 *Ibidoecus*;
2 *Menopon*;
3 *Colpocephalum* and *Ferribia*;
4 *Esthiopterum*.

Characteristic features of Thrips (Thysanoptera) are the reduced area of the wings, which are fringed with long, marginal bristles, and a protrusible vesicle on the extremity of the tarsus that serves as an organ of adhesion. Here, *Liothrips setinodis*. The earliest detailed descriptions of Thrips are those of Carl de Geer (1744).

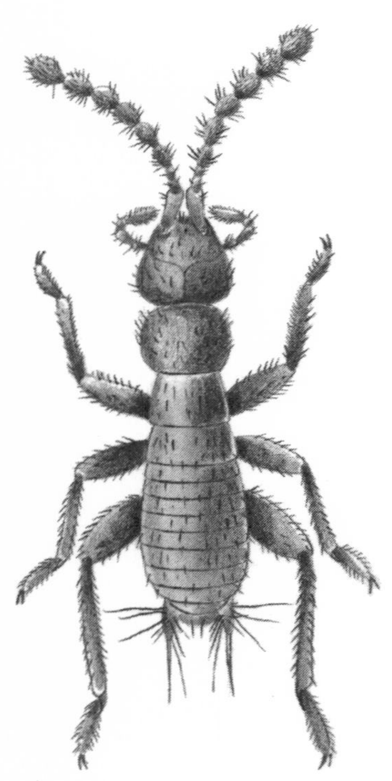

Zorotypus guineensis, 2 mm long, a representative of the few species in the insect order of Zoraptera (Soil Lice). They occur on the surface of the soil among decaying fragments of vegetation in all zoogeographical regions except Europe.

wealthy pupil who shared his enthusiasm for natural history, he undertook many tours, on which he amassed comprehensive collections of botanical and zoological specimens. After Willughby's early death, Ray published extensive botanical works and volumes on zoology, based on his own research and on material bequeathed to him by his friend. He was responsible for vital preliminary work on the binary nomenclature of organisms and the use of a hierarchical type of system; credit for these was later ascribed so persistently to Linnaeus that, still today, he is accepted without reservation as their founder. Ray also established six principles of systematic classification which remain apposite to this day.

1. Immutability of names
2. Exact definition of characteristics
3. Easy determination of characteristics
4. Retention of generally recognized groups
5. Only related forms can be assigned to the same classification.
6. The use of no more characteristics than are necessary for reliable recognition.

In Ray's *Historia insectorum*, we find the following system (commentaries by Bodenheimer, 1928):

1. Without metamorphosis ("Ametamorphata")
1.1. Without legs
1.1.1. Terrestrial creatures
1.1.1.1. Living in the soil: Lumbricus

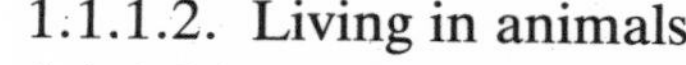

1.1.1.2. Living in animals
1.1.1.2.1. In humans: Eelworms, Tapeworms, etc.
1.1.1.2.2. In animals: Roundworms, thick and short worms (Oestridae larvae)
1.1.2. Aquatic creatures
1.1.2.1. Larger forms: Hirudo (Leech)
1.1.2.2. Smaller forms
1.1.2.2.1. Round
1.1..2.2.1.1. Black: with two small horns on the head, in mountain streams (larvae of Simulium (?))
1.1.2.2.1.2. Red: on the bottom of lakes and ponds (Chironomidae larvae?)
1.1.2.2.2. Flat: certain Flatworms (including the Liver Fluke)
1.2. With legs
1.2.1. With 6 legs
1.2.1.1. Land insects
1.2.1.1.1. Larger
1.2.1.1.1.1. Body flat: Worms in rotten wood and in the soil (indefinable, probably beetle larvae)
1.2.1.1.1.2. Body spherical: Mealworms (Tenebrio?)
1.2.1.1.2. Smaller
1.2.1.1.2.1. They attack animals
1.2.1.1.2.1.1. Evil-smelling: Cimex
1.2.1.1.2.1.2. Not evil-smelling: Bird Lice, Pulex, Pediculus
1.2.1.1.2.2. Do not attack animals: Book Lice; Springtails and others, which cannot be interpreted with certainty
1.2.1.2. Aquatic creatures: Fish Lice
1.2.2. With 8 legs
1.2.2.1. Body with tail: Scorpio
1.2.2.2. Body without tail: Araneus (Spiders); Opilio; Ticks; Mites
1.2.3. With 14 legs: Asellus (Isopods and Amphipods)
1.2.4. With 24 legs: Bristletails (?)
1.2.5. With many legs
1.2.5.1. Terrestrial: Julus, Scolopendra
1.2.5.2. Aquatic: Sandworm; Marine Scolopendra

2. Subject to metamorphosis ("Metamorphumena")
2.1. No dormant pupal stage: Dragonfly; Cimex silvestris; Locusta; Gryllus; Gryllotalpa; Cicada; Blatta; Tipulidae aquaticae (= Hydrometridae); Scorpius aquaticus (= Nepa); Muscae aquaticae (= Notonecta); Hemerobius (= Ephemera); Forficula
2.2. A dormant pupal stage

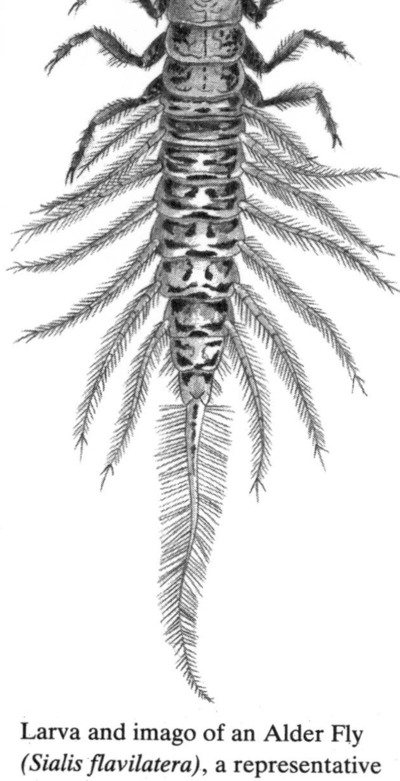

Larva and imago of an Alder Fly *(Sialis flavilatera)*, a representative of the order of Megaloptera. The eggs (numbering up to 2,000) are laid upon plants growing close to water, frequently on reeds. The young larvae fall into the water and live on the bottom of the stream or pond. They breathe through seven pairs of segmented tracheal gills and are actively predacious. Pupation takes place on land. Leonhard Baldner, a fisherman from Strasbourg, first described the biology of the insect, which he called the "fire thief".

Mating pair of Scorpion Flies, *Panorpa communis*. During copulation, the female consumes a drop of secretion deposited by the male.

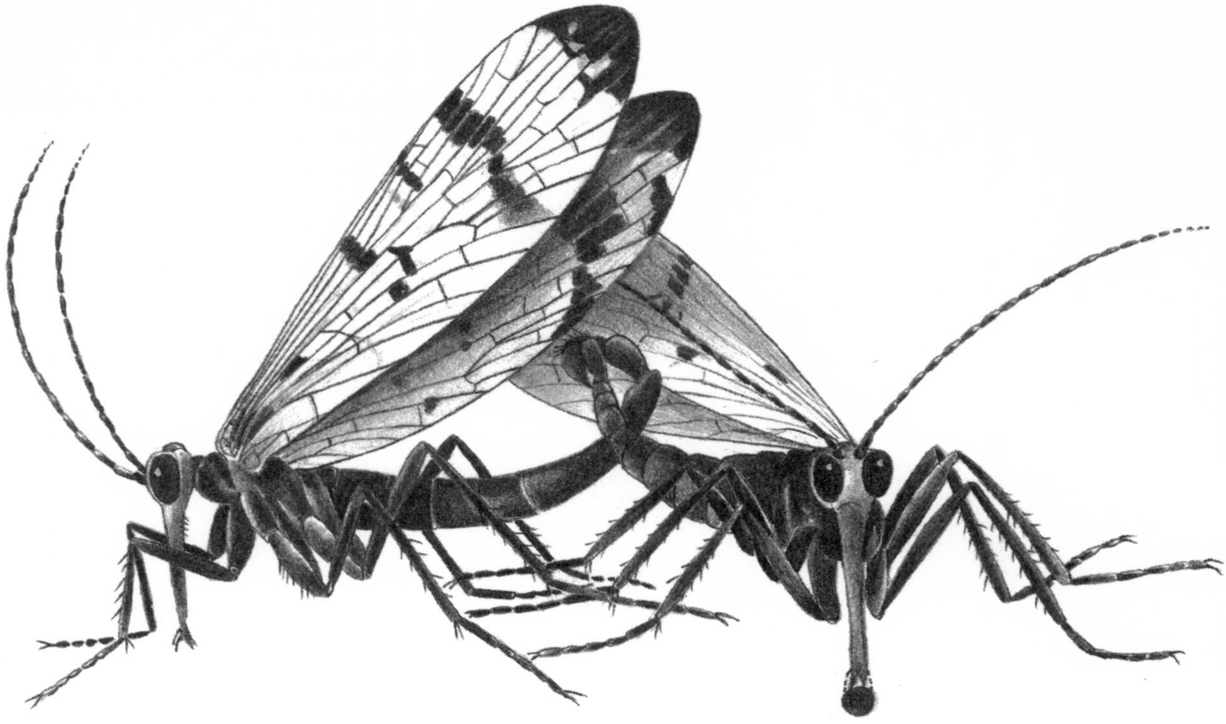

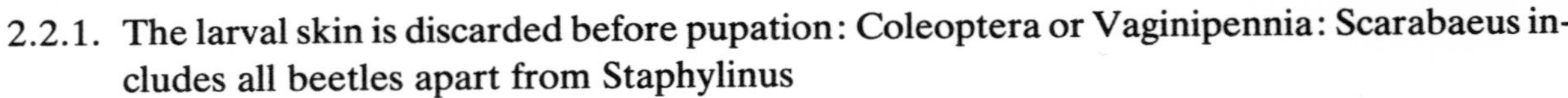

2.2.1. The larval skin is discarded before pupation: Coleoptera or Vaginipennia: Scarabaeus includes all beetles apart from Staphylinus
2.2.1.1. Wings covered
2.2.1.2. Wings not covered: Anelytra
2.2.1.2.1. Wings mealy: Papilio and Phalaena
2.2.1.2.2. Wings membranous
2.2.1.2.2.1. Wings 4
2.2.1.2.2.1.1. Live in colonies and build celled combs
2.2.1.2.2.1.1.1. Collect honey: Apis, Bombylius (Bumble Bees)
2.2.1.2.2.1.1.2. Collect no honey: Crabro; Vespa
2.2.1.2.2.1.2. Do not live in colonies: Muscae vespiformes (= Sawflies); Muscae ichneumones (= parasitic Wasps); Papilioniformia (= Phryganids); Seticaudae (= Ephemerids)
2.2.1.2.2.2. Wings 2: Culex
2.2.2. The larval skin is not discarded but used as a covering inside which the pupa develops (Muscae)

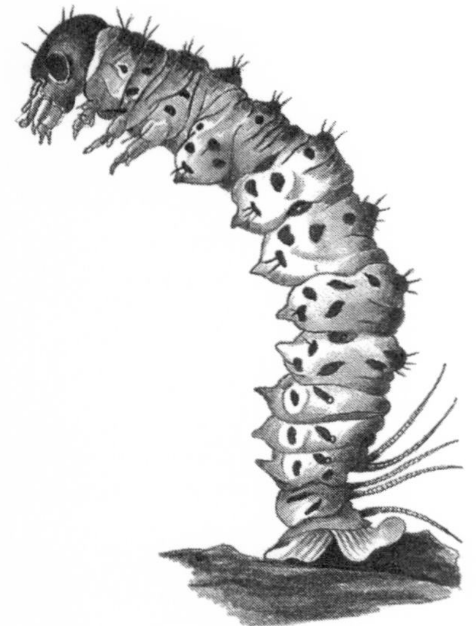

The larva of the Scorpion Fly *Panorpa communis*, like other species of the genus, lives among dead vegetable matter, such as in the pens of small domestic animals.

In addition, precise differential-diagnostic descriptions are given, as well as the first definition of species. "Whichever forms are different according to species, they retain their specific nature without change, and the one cannot come into being from the seed of the other and vice versa." This means that Ray includes within a species all animals that derive from like progenitors: still today a fundamental aspect of species definition. Although there is much real progress, his system also still includes a large number of non-insects.

The insects in Linnaeus's *Systema Naturae*

A glance at Linnaeus's system of classification shows that even for the "Father of Systematics", the concept of insects was still not an entirely clear one, for under "Aptera", he includes both spiders and Crustacea. In the first edition of his *Systema Naturae*, he subdivided insects into four major groups:

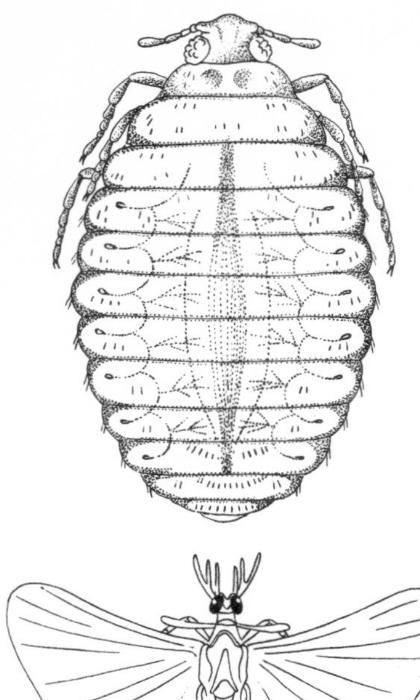

Stylopids or Twisted-wing Insects (Strepsiptera) are parasitic upon other insects, especially cicadas and various bees and wasps. The females are entirely wingless; in the males, the forewings are reduced, but the hind wings are well developed.

1. Coleoptera: Wings covered by 2 elytra
2. Angioptera: Possess wings but no elytra

Here he includes the present-day orders of Ephemeroptera, Odonata, Raphidioptera, Planipennia, Hymenoptera, Lepidoptera and Diptera.

3. Hemiptera: wings without elytra

A conglomeration including Ensifera, Heteroptera, Coleoptera (Lampyridae), Hymenoptera (Formicidae).

4. Aptera: Without wings

Phthiraptera and Siphonaptera together with the above-mentioned non-insects.

The famous *Editio decima* of 1758—Year Zero in the chronology of present-day systematics—brings various alterations and improvements. The Coleoptera are extended to include the Dermaptera, Blattariae and Ensifera. A real advance is the subdivision of the Angioptera into

1. Lepidoptera
2. Neuroptera (by this Linnaeus means Ephemeroptera, Odonata, Raphidioptera, Planipennia, Trichoptera and Mecoptera)
3. Hymenoptera
4. Diptera

Categorization of the "Neuroptera" came much later and very hesitantly. Now, in addition to the Heteroptera, the Hemiptera also comprise the Cicadina, Aphidina, Coccina and as an extraneous element, the Thysanoptera. The Aptera remain a conglomeration: Collembola, Zygentoma, Isoptera, Phthiraptera and Siphonaptera. It was a long time before the excessive preoccupation with the apterous or wingless state ceased to cloud the view of the systematist. The great value of the Linnaean system of classification is the keenness of its perception of kinship groups. Many of the 65 genera, into which Linnaeus subdivided the 2,000 species known to him, still exist today as families or as other groups, many of which are considered to be monophyletic.

Insect classification today

To attempt to describe here the further growth and knowledge in the sphere of insect phylogenesis and its embodiment in systems, would go beyond the scope of this book. We shall therefore present here, in simplified form, the system of insects that is probably the best substantiated in ex-

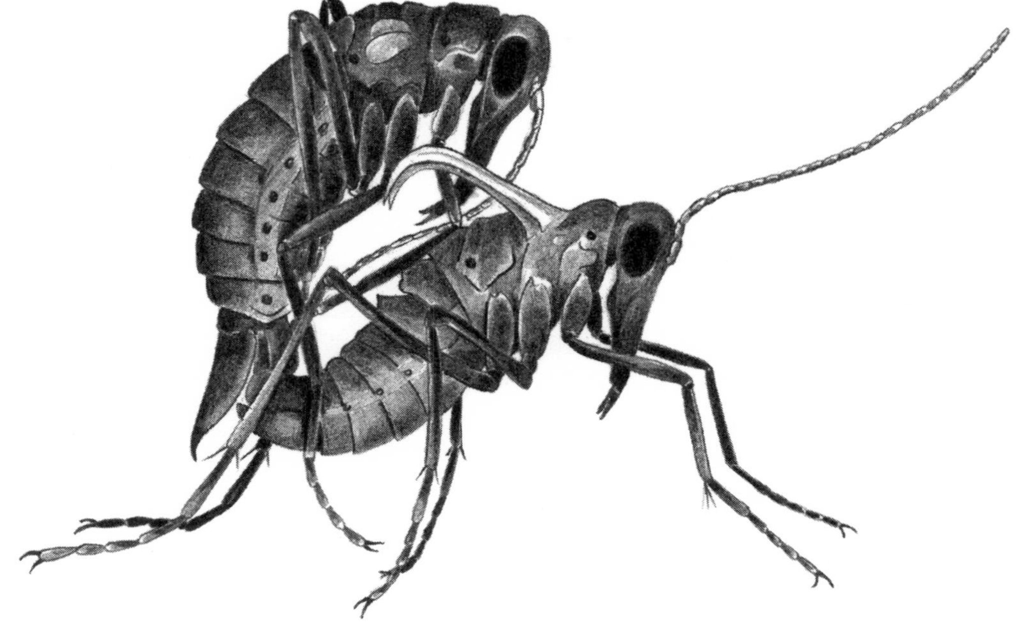

Pair of Snow Scorpion Flies *(Boreus hyemalis)* mating. These insects are active in winter and can leap a distance of 20 cm; this jumping ability is responsible for their popular name of Snow Fleas. The wings are vestigial.

istence today, and for which we are indebted to the eminent phylogeneticist Willy Hennig (1913–1976).

The Scorpion Fly (*Bittacus* spec.) hangs by its forelegs from a blade of grass and waits to capture prey. The raptorial middle and hind legs seize small insects which are instantly devoured. The terminal tarsal segment snaps shut like the blade of a clasp-knife, holding the prey fast.

Sub-class 1:	Entognatha	
Order 1:	Diplura (Two-pronged Bristletails)	500 species
Order 2:	Protura (minute soil-living insects)	250 species
Order 3:	Collembola (Springtails)	3,000 species
Sub-class 2:	Ectognatha	
Order 4:	Archaeognatha (Bristletails)	220 species
Order 5:	Zygentoma (Silverfish)	280 species
Order 6:	Ephemeroptera (Mayflies)	2,000 species
Order 7:	Odonata (Dragonflies)	4,700 species
Order 8:	Plecoptera (Stone-flies)	2,000 species
Order 9:	Embioptera (Web-spinners)	220 species
Order 10:	Notoptera	12 species
Order 11:	Dermaptera (Earwigs)	1,300 species
Order 12:	Mantodea (Mantids)	1,800 species
Order 13:	Blattariae (Cockroaches)	3,500 species
Order 14:	Isoptera (Termites)	2,000 species
Order 15:	Ensifera (Grasshopper—long antennae)	8,100 species
Order 16:	Caelifera (Grasshopper—short antennae)	7,100 species
Order 17:	Phasmatodea (Stick and Leaf Insects)	2,500 species
Order 18:	Zoraptera (Soil Lice)	25 species
Order 19:	Psocoptera (Booklice or Psocids)	1,000 species
Order 20:	Phthiraptera (Lice)	3,700 species
Order 21:	Thysanoptera (Thrips)	4,000 species
Order 22:	Coleorrhyncha	19 species
Order 23:	Heteroptera (Bugs)	30,000 species
Order 24:	Homoptera (Plant-feeders)	43,000 species
Order 25:	Coleoptera (Beetles)	350,000 species
Order 26:	Strepsiptera (Twisted-wing Insects/Stylopids)	400 species
Order 27:	Raphidioptera (Snake Flies)	200 species
Order 28:	Planipennia (Lacewing flies)	7,000 species
Order 29:	Megaloptera (Alder Flies)	50 species
Order 30:	Hymenoptera (Bees, Wasps and Ants)	100,000 species
Order 31:	Trichoptera (Caddis Flies)	5,400 species
Order 32:	Lepidoptera (Butterflies)	110,000 species
Order 33:	Diptera (True Flies)	85,000 species
Order 34:	Mecoptera (Scorpion Flies)	350 species
Order 35:	Siphonaptera (Fleas)	1,600 species

Eighteen out of the total of 35 orders of insects are considered in detail below. They are the most striking and the largest, and those towards which man has turned his attention for centuries. The remaining 17 orders have attracted less general interest, in some cases quite unjustifiably. Usually they consist of only a few species, often they are small and live in seclusion. But typical representatives of all these orders are illustrated and discussed briefly in this book.

Mayflies

(Ephemeroptera)

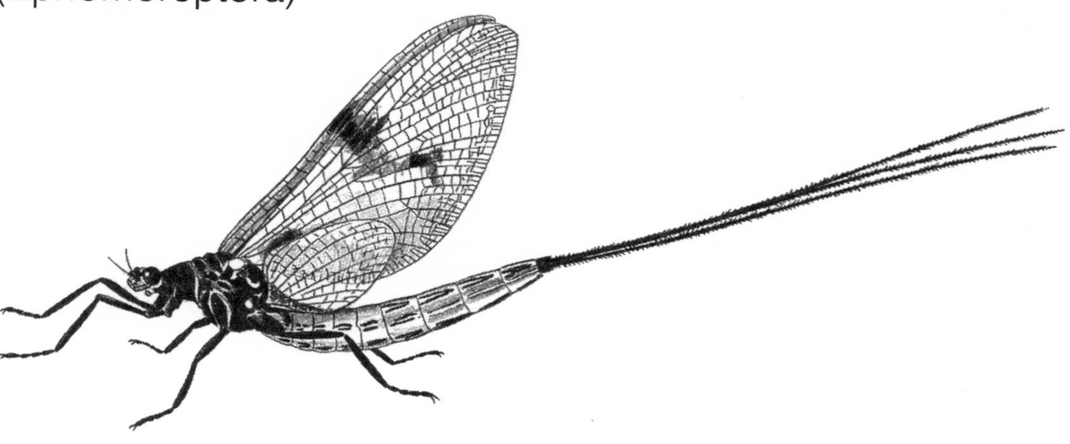

Aristotle—founder of entomology

Aristotle (384–322 B.C.) is rightly called the founder of entomology. With infinite diligence and unsurpassed genius he elaborated a system of thought that retained its dominance for more than fifteen centuries. There is scarcely any scientific discipline that does not have its roots in the work of Aristotle (although, as we shall see, entomology is even older). In the *peripatos*, the covered walk within the Lyceum, where Aristotle held his school (from 335 B.C. until the death of Alexander the Great in 323 B.C.), and where his principal scientific work came to fruition, there must have been an abundance of insects. The song of cicadas and grasshoppers, the colourful diversity of beetles and butterflies all surrounded him. He would not have been Aristotle if he had remained indifferent to all this splendour. The spirit of enquiry already awakened in him by his family and later by Plato (429–347 B.C.), whose pupil he was for some twenty years, must also have led him to a study of insects.

Early knowledge about Mayflies

Aristotle writes that Mayflies feed exclusively on moisture in the form of dew, and live for only one or a few days. And indeed, the mouth parts are reduced so that, at most, a small quantity of liquid can be taken up (e.g. in *Cloeon*). The intestine is without function and contains air, as a result of which specific gravity is reduced, which facilitates flying and hovering. The life span of the imago is indeed very brief, as its ordinal name implies, ranging from one hour to a few days. This period is devoted entirely to reproduction; there is no time to feed. Elsewhere in Aristotle, we read:

"On the river Hypanis in the Cimmerius Bosporus, about the time of the summer solstice, there are brought down towards the sea by the stream what look like little sacks rather bigger than grapes, out of which at their bursting issues a winged quadruped. The insect lives and flies about until the evening, but as the sun goes down it pines away, and dies at sunset having lived just one day, from which circumstance it is called the ephemeron."

It is curious how, time and again, existing knowledge is forgotten or misinterpreted. We read, for example, in the late Roman writer Claudius Aelianus: "There are creatures called Ephemera (living only for a day) that take their name from their span of life, for they are generated in wine, and when the vessel is opened they fly out, see the light, and die. Thus it is that Nature has permitted them to come to life, but has rescued them as soon as possible from life's evils, so that they are neither aware of their own misfortune nor are spectators of the misfortune of others."

Above:

Male of the Common Mayfly *(Ephemera vulgata)*.

Mayfly nymphs

One of the earliest references to Mayfly nymphs is found in the writings of Guilelmus Rondeletius (1555), a professor of medicine from Montpellier. "It is small and has approximately the form of the letter T, three pairs of feet, a tail that ends in three green appendages. Using these together with its legs, it is able to swim."

Mayfly nymphs live in water, and individual species may be adapted to quite different types of bodies of water. Speed of flow, oxygen content and type of food available are important factors. The three "appendages" he mentions are very typical of Mayflies: a pair of lateral cerci (arising from the extremity of the 11th abdominal segment) and a median caudal filament. The latter is wanting in the first nymphal instar, and in many genera, it never occurs (e.g. *Cloeon*). The nymphs breathe by means of tracheal gills that grow out from the post-abdominal segments. The form, number and position of these respiratory organs vary from species to species, and also represent adaptive modifications to the specific type of water inhabited. In many cases, the gills are moved rhythmically, creating a flow of water over the body's respiratory surface. There is also considerable diversity in the diet of individual species. Food includes:

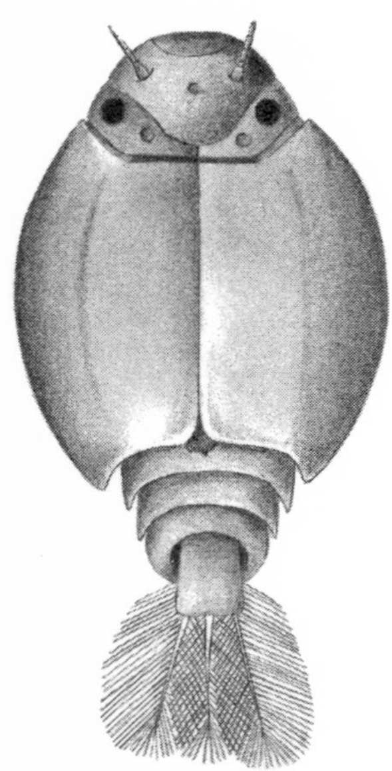

Mayfly nymphs of the genus *Prosopistoma* are found attached to stones in flowing water, although they can also swim rapidly with their fan-like tail filaments. Their tracheal gills are situated inside a branchial chamber which is covered by the dorsal tergites of the pro- and mesothorax. Other chitinous elements contribute to form a perfect respiratory chamber into which water enters through a pair of lateral apertures, and streams out through a central opening.

- plant debris
- animal detritus
- growth on stones (by grazing)
- soil substrate (burrowing forms)
- micro-organisms (filtered out of running water by means of the long fringes of setae on the mouth parts and the forelegs, with the body held against the direction of flow).

In the Congo region, there is one species that tunnels out passages in freshwater sponges. The action of swimming, already being mentioned by Rondeletius, is produced by rapid upward and downward movements of the abdomen supported by the fanning action of the caudal filaments. In many species, swimming is further aided by movements of the tracheal gill lamellae and in certain cases, also by the expulsion of water from the rectum. Other species scarcely swim at all, but merely move along on the ground under water or on aquatic plants. Mayfly nymphs living in flowing water are usually adapted to the current by some degree of flattening of the body. They move in a sideways direction on the underside of stones. Swimming would entail the danger of their being swept away. Burrowing species live in mud or concealed in river banks, and their forelegs have developed into more or less powerful fossorial limbs. Mayfly larvae moult some 12 to 20 times. Depending upon species, they live for one to three years. Within this time, they store up within their body sufficient food, and therefore energy, for the fully developed Mayflies to be able to live and reproduce. Strictly speaking then, the lifespan of a Mayfly is not only some hours or days, but years.

Mass emergence

Leonhard Baldner (1612–1694), a fisherman from Strasbourg, took a keen interest throughout his life in observing the fauna of his native region. He provided clear descriptions of birds, fishes, mammals, amphibia, molluscs, insects and other creatures, accompanying them with hand-coloured copperplate engravings carried out by leading artists of the day. He described five Mayflies which are illustrated in fine detail. Baldner was well aware of the two-year period of development of many species. Of *Polymitarcis virgo*, he writes: "In summer, at harvest-time, when nights are warm, they hatch from the pods and there are so many of them flying together that they are like a dense mist. They are food for fishes. They do not live until the morning, but all die in the night. People say the fruit has flown the box, and it is not every year that they take wing."

The occasional occurrence of *Polymitarcis virgo* on a massive scale is a well-known phenomenon. The species which is particularly conspicuous on account of its whitish wings, frequently

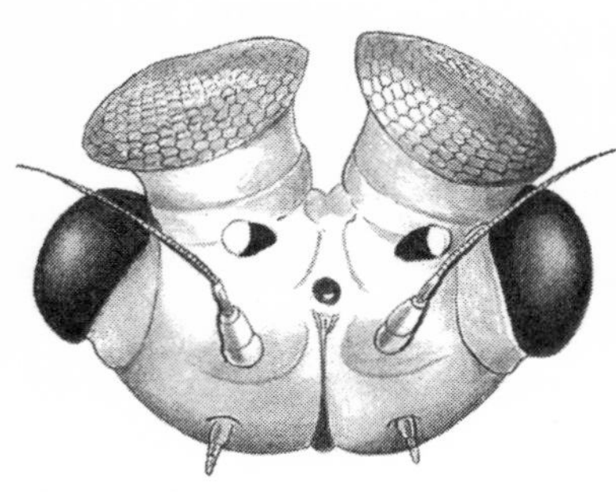

The males of many species of Mayflies have eyes that function particularly efficiently and are used mainly in locating the female. In *Cloeon dipterum*, the eyes are divided, the upper halves, the "turban eyes", are separate from the lower compound eyes, the facets are enlarged and therefore especially efficient.

swarms in vast numbers in August or September along large rivers, and is known to fishermen as the "white worm" or "spinner". Gleiss (1954) describes such a swarm:

"When it is swarming time for the white worm, also known as the "Theiss blossom", it is still the practice today for people living along the rivers Elbe, Moselle and Theiss, and many other rivers, to light large bonfires. Local families take up their long-accustomed place along the river banks and spread out large cloths, awnings, sheets or blankets over the ground. The corners of the cloths are weighted with stones to prevent the wind from catching them. The flies, drawn from far and wide, singe their wings in the leaping flames and fall on to the cloths laid out ready for them. The next day, the wingless bodies, sheltered from the wind, are allowed to dry in the sun, later to be sold as winter food for cage birds and as dried food for aquarium fish, under the name of "White-worm" or "Theiss Blossom". Fish bait can be made by mixing the insect bodies with clay or paste and forming pellets. The entomologist Scopoli (1723–1788) reports that in June every year, the farmers along the river Laz (southeastern Alps) use the accumulated bodies as fertilizer on their fields."

As a noteworthy curiosity, one might mention Schönemund's report for August 1928, when there was such a massive occurrence of *Caenis horaria* on a bridge across the Elbe at Dresden that passers-by complained of being pestered by the flying sub-imagos which brushed against them in an attempt to discard their old skins. Today, however, with the increasing pollution of rivers, phenomena of this kind are rare.

Other species have also been known for their appearance in vast numbers. Probably best known is that of the largest species in Central Europe, *Palingenia longicauda* (length of body 35 mm, the male with 80 mm long abdominal appendages) which occurred from July to September, mainly in Hungary, and was known as "Theiss blossom". Réaumur reports one such "fall of manna" on August 18, 1738, between 8.15 and 10 o'clock in the evening. In 1757, Jacob Christian Schaeffer (1718–1790) considered the appearance of this species in vast numbers as "melancholy heralds and silent prophets of an even greater misery and calamity". On the Rhine and various of its tributaries, *Oligoneuriella rhenana*, locally known as the "Rhine midge" or the "August midge", used to fly in massive numbers every year in July and August.

Reproduction

In many species, the males fly together in swarms into which the females fly. In this way, the union of the sexes during the brief life span of the imago is ensured. In the swarms, that are frequently of considerable size (particularly in the family Ephemeridae), the males repeatedly fly actively upwards to a height of a few metres, then allow themselves to sink down with wings and tail appendages held diagonally upwards. Females flying into the swarm are seized by the males and mating takes place in the air. The compound eyes of the male, often greatly developed, are crucial to the recognition of the female. In the family of Baetidae, the eyes are particularly large, the light-sensitive upper parts are cylindrical in shape and are known as "turban eyes". In the year 1954 Gleiss writes:

"In the American species *Campsurus segnis*, extreme adaptation to the brief span of life spent in the air has resulted in the reduction of all the female's legs to mere small stumps. Only in the male of the species has one pair of long clinging legs been retained. This curious species cannot tolerate any contact with hard ground. If nevertheless it comes about, the creature falls on one side and dies in this helpless position. Such extreme adaptation to a life style as to have caused the reduction of legs to rudimentary stumps emphasizes the fact that—as imagines—Mayflies are in fact nothing but flying reproductive organs."

In mating, the male seizes the female, usually from below, with the abdominal gonopods and the very elongate forelegs. The male's back is laid against the abdomen of the female. There are also species which copulate in flight "belly to belly". In a very few cases, the Mayflies settle and mate. The entire process lasts only a few seconds to minutes.

Oviposition begins immediately after copulation. Frequently the eggs are ejected as the insect flies over water. In other species, the female dips the end of the abdomen into water in order to deposit the eggs. In certain species of the genus *Baetis*, the females crawl into the water and attach the eggs to the substrate. *Cloeon dipterum* must be seen as a rare exception. As long as 10 to 14 days after copulation, the female drops several hundred eggs into the water, from which the small larvae hatch within a minute (ovivivparity).

The eminent anatomist Marcello Malpighi gave a detailed description of the Mayfly's heart and its function. Just as meticulous and of equally outstanding quality is Antony van Leeuwenhoek's monograph on the *Hafft oder Uferaas (Ephemera vulgata)* and Jan Swammerdam's *Ephemerae vita* on the subject of the Oeveraas.

One unique peculiarity of the Mayfly deserves to be mentioned: the sub-imago (known to the fisherman as the *dun*). A flying form, having completed its development in the course of a few seconds to several minutes, emerges from the last nymphal skin; the wings of this sub-imago have a dull appearance and the tail appendages are relatively short. After a certain period of time, depending upon species, this winged form moults again and the sexually-mature imago emerges. This is the only known example among insects of the second moulting of a flying form.

Rhithrogena mimus mating. The male approaches the female from behind and flies under her, initially grasping her behind the head at the wing root with his unusually long forelegs. The accessory organs at the end of the abdomen assist the introduction of the penis into the female's genital aperture. Copulation lasts only about 20 seconds. During mating, the pair lose height and separate before reaching the ground.

Dragonflies

(Odonata)

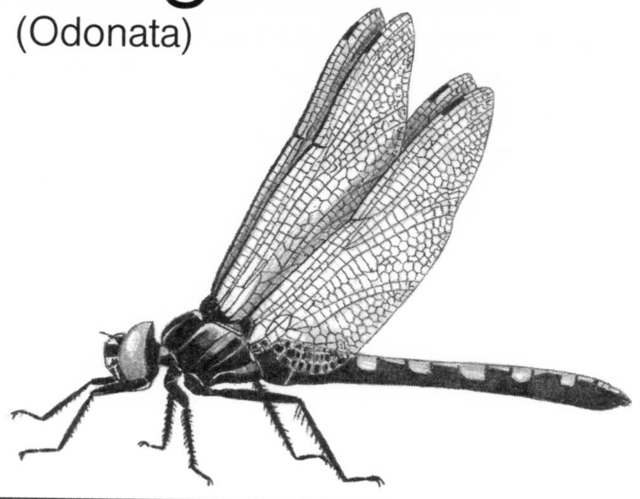

Ulisse Aldrovandi

Today we consider the Italian Ulisse Aldrovandi (1522–1605) to be the founder of scientific entomology. In 1602, after fifty years of study, he published the first literary work devoted entirely to insects: *De Animalibus insectis libri VII* (Bologna, 1602).

Aldrovandi was born in Bologna into a distinguished patrician family of considerable renown in that city. For reasons that remain obscure, he twice ran away from home, first to Rome and then to Spain. But he returned and at the age of seventeen, began to study law and philosophy at Bologna and Padua. Like many of his contemporaries, he fell foul of the Inquisition. On suspicion of heresy, Aldrovandi was arrested and taken to Rome, but was fortunately released. Later, in 1553, he obtained his doctorate in Bologna and began to lecture. He travelled widely throughout Italy, collecting specimens everywhere he went. In 1568 he founded the Botanical Gardens in Bologna. Aldrovandi was a keen collector and set up a museum of his own; his herbarium consisting of 4,000 folios with several thousand species, still exists today. There were also collections of fossils and minerals. In addition, he amassed a considerable library. Unfortunately, scarcely anything has survived of his zoological collection. Aldrovandi's financial situation enabled him to commission watercolours and woodcuts of individual specimens in his collection. It was this varied collection that was the foundation for his great work on natural history, most of which was not published until after his death: it comprised seven volumes on insects, three on birds, two on plants.

With Aldrovandi, a new era dawns for entomology. As was the usual practice in his day, he too carefully included all the views of earlier authors available to him on every insect, which in many cases proved an unnecessary additional burden to his own text. Yet his books on insects are rich in personal observations, and much that he says had not been stated before. The text displays the liveliness of his observations of natural phenomena, again a characteristic by no means universal at that time. Even though Aldrovandi follows Aristotelian teaching on many points, he is nevertheless able, from his own findings, to correct a number of false assumptions that had prevailed until then. Of particular significance is the comprehensive, almost encyclopaedic character of his insect books.

Aldrovandi's books include dragonflies, of which he depicts 21 (?) species. It is a considerable total for that time. Today, some 75 species are known in Italy; throughout the world there are about 4,700.

Above:

Giant Dragonfly (Aeshnidae) has settled to rest during flight.

Characteristics, systematic subdivision and classification

Within the order of Dragonflies, two major sub-orders can be distinguished: the Zygoptera (Damselflies) and the Anisoptera (True Dragonflies).

Character	Damselflies (Zygoptera)	True Dragonflies (Anisoptera)
form of fore- and hind wings	almost identical	different
eyes	widely separated	usually contiguous dorsally
position of wings at rest	held vertically together over body or partly spread diagonally	outspread horizontally
body (imagines)	slender	somewhat stouter
body (larvae)	long, slender	stout
post-abdomen (larvae)	3 terminal processes	5 spinose processes (anal pyramid)
tracheal gills	caudal gills within the terminal processes	in cavity of the hind gut
abdominal terminalia ♂	2 pairs of pincer-like anal appendages	2 paired, 1 un-paired pincer-like appendage
pre-copulative behaviour	♂ seizes back of neck of ♀	♂ seizes pro- or meso-thorax

The earliest finds of dragonflies date from the Upper Carboniferous period, so they are some 250 million years old. They include the largest insects by far that have ever lived, the "dinosaurs" among insects. The Giant Dragonfly *Meganeura* had a wing span of about 70 (up to 75) cm and a body length of 30 cm. It can be assumed that it was a poor flier (the largest recent species is 18 cm long and lives in South America). In the Mesozoic, the True Dragonflies developed, which we know to have existed in a great wealth of forms in the Jurassic: there were 21 genera of Anisozygoptera (a third sub-order) of which only a single species, *Epiophlebia superstes* (the specific name means literally "the remaining one"), still exists in Japan.

We can get an impression of the views of earlier systematists from Thomas Moufet who assigns dragonflies together with lacewing flies, ichneumon flies and Mayflies to the group of Flies and Mosquitoes. And this even though Aristotle and later Aldrovandi even more clearly had defined and circumscribed the Diptera. Moufet deals with dragonfly nymphs and imagines in quite different chapters, and is clearly still unaware of their connection. This is surprising, since the imaginal moult of the dragonfly is a conspicuous natural process, easily observed, indeed, one which is today a popular motif of photography and film. Particularly remarkable is the abrupt transition from aquatic predator to flying predator. Whereas the nymph caught its prey in the specially adapted prehensile "mask", now the imago flies through the air, sometimes at considerable speed, using its legs to catch small insects in flight. Some species take their prey on plants on which they walk or sit in wait.

Even in Caspar Schwenckfeld's book published in 1603, dragonflies are still called Musca (= fly). He writes: "Musca grandior oculata: known as parson, wild horse, camel, water sprite, naiad, water vicar. This is a large fly with four wings. On either side of the enormous, round, lustrous head are two greatly protruding eyes. The thorax is thick and short. The body slender and narrow, terminating in two points. Four hairy legs. The four wings are elongate, strong and with abundant veining. They copulate as flies do."

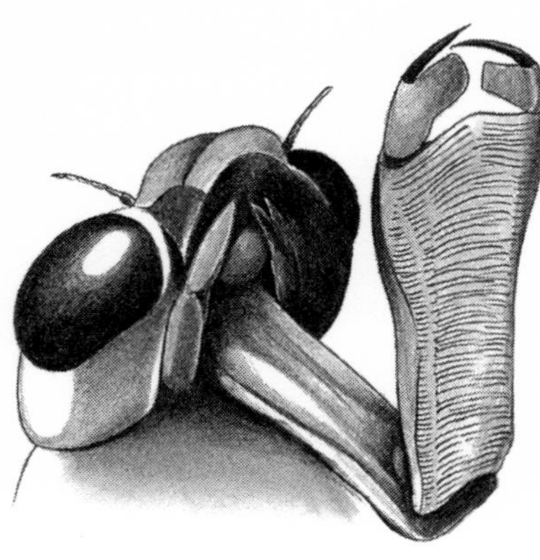

The nymphs of Dragonflies (Odonata) are characterized by modification of the labium or lower lip into a prehensile "mask". This mask can protrude very rapidly to capture prey.

Some of the basic morphological characteristics are correctly described. The compound eye may be made up of as many as 28,000 facets (it can probably detect movement even at a distance of 40 m). The observation on copulation is a misunderstanding, as we shall see, and of course, all dragonflies have six legs. The vernacular names he gives are interesting. We cannot assign Schwenckfeld's description to a particular species, but it undoubtedly refers to one of the large dragonflies (Zygoptera).

Leonhard Baldner also devoted particular attention to dragonflies. Referring to *Libellula depressa*, he writes: "Such insects live in the water in cases, hatch at the end of April and hold their wings widely extended. This genus eats May midges and all kinds of small gnats . . . They live for only one summer and are food for birds, they do no harm or damage to anyone. They fly over the meadows and in reeds on bodies of water. The young come into being from eggs which they attach to vegetation within water. This species has various colours, the males are mostly blue, as far as I have observed, for the blue ones always hang on the green ones."

Baldner's lively description of his own observations is particularly welcome in an age much given to complicated, scholastic mannerisms. By "cases", Baldner meant the larvae. The only point at variance with current knowledge is that in *Libellula depressa*, the eggs are deposited by the female dipping her abdomen into the surface of the water.

Nowhere among early authors is there any reference to dragonflies "stinging". It is not clear how this ineradicable but mistaken notion arose. Only recently a newspaper, in answer to the perennial question "Can dragonflies sting?" stated "Yes, in principle, but they do so rarely". The only answer that can be given is: they can sting no-one, not even those who maintain that they can do so. The ancients provided us with many myths, perhaps this is a present-day fairy-tale. Certain vernacular names, some originating from America, express a belief in the ability to sting: "sewing-needle", "darning-needle", "horse-sting". Some tribes of North American Indians used the motif of the segmented abdomen of the dragonfly in artefacts carved in wood, such as spoon handles.

Reproductive behaviour

Antony van Leeuwenhoek began a close examination of the reproductive process in dragonflies. As a violent opponent of the theory of spontaneous generation, he was particularly interested in proving the existence of spermatozoa. He writes: "At various times I also examined the Juffertyes which are found in July on the rushes along the banks of our canals, for the presence of spermatozoa. In their semen, I found many spermatozoa, but could not at first detect life in them. I decided to continue this examination, because I considered the semen to be immature. In the morning, one frequently sees these insects linked together, flying or settled. I took this to be copulation, and all the more so when I discovered an opening on the back of the female, and there . . . also numerous eggs. Inside the many eggs that I found here, I observed various stages of development, and decided that these insects develop out of the waterworms that we call uvltjes . . . They flew linked together in the way described. At the time of copulation, I saw without difficulty many live spermatozoa in the male semen. They progress in a manner similar to that of snakes, curving the body six to eight times at once . . . I had a sketch made of one of them which still retained this position when it was dead."

Jan Swammerdam gives a particularly accurate description together with excellent illustrations of metamorphosis in dragonflies, which he knows as "schillebolde". Describing the reproductive process, he writes: "The male has its penis situated well forward in its belly. The female, on the other hand, has the genital opening right at the back of the tail . . . And however wonderful a creature the dragonfly is and however curiously its reproductive organs are situated in its body, the manner of its mating is more remarkable still. For the male, as it whirls in the air in a series of rapid turns, is able to extend its tail to the female with dexterity beyond all measure. The latter seizes it to the point between her head and eyes, pushing it to the back of her neck, and grasps it with her legs very eagerly and avidly. Once she has a firm hold on the tail, she curves her abdomen forward to the male copulatory structures that lie at the front on its breast. Consequently, union occurs during flight as they swarm in the air. The extremity of the female's tail is curved up against the mid-part of the male body where the latter conceals his penis. This penis penetrates the genitalia of the female that are situated at the end of the female tail. And in order that the female can reach as far as the breast of the male, she contracts her body and curls her tail in a marked curve. After fertilization has been achieved in this way, the female finally dips her tail into water and rapidly deposits her eggs there."

Scarcely any essentials remain to be added to Swammerdam's meticulously accurate description. The male copulatory organ on the ventral side of the second abdominal segment is a secondary development. In most species, the pre-copulatory stage is initiated in flight. The male seizes the thorax of the female with his six legs. Then he curves his abdomen across the back of the female downwards and forwards, filling his copulatory apparatus with sperm. He then pushes the tip of his abdomen through between the legs, over the thorax of the female, and still further forward to seize her in the region of the prothorax or neck, using his anal appendages. Then he abandons the hold with his legs, stretches out again, and the two creatures fly in tandem, linked as a mating pair. In most species, actual copulation occurs with the insects settled on grass, reeds or other aquatic plants, but in many Anisoptera, it can occur in flight. In many species, the pair separate following transmission of the semen. In others—that is, in the majority of the Zygoptera and the Anisoptera genus *Sympetrum*—the male does not relinquish his hold on the female, but remains linked with her during oviposition (post-copula).

In some species, such as the common *Libellula quadrimaculata*, the entire process of pre-copulation and copulation lasts no more than 5 to 15 seconds, but in other cases, it may be more than half an hour. In many species, particularly in those of the genus *Aeshna*, the males often fight fiercely among themselves for possession of a female, not infrequently with the result that one of them falls into the water with torn wings. In other dragonflies, especially the Coenagriids, various kinds of "aberrations" have been observed. Sometimes a male will seize a female of another species. Usually it is unable to secure a firm hold with its abdominal appendages. Copulation is unlikely to be achieved because the construction of the inferior pair of anal appendages in particular is peculiar to each species, and because the female, upon contact, can recognize heterospecific males by means of tactile stimuli and rejects them. Sometimes a male will seize another male of the same species, occasionally while the latter is already flying in tandem with a female. It is by no means rare to see such a triple chain. In some species, copulation is repeated several times. Sometimes males mate in rapid succession with several females, or females with several males.

Migratory flights

In many respects, migratory flights of dragonflies on a massive scale such as are observed from time to time, still remain a puzzle to us today. Observers report unanimously that such flights consist exclusively of recently matured insects. In the vast majority of cases in Europe, the species involved has been *Libellula quadrimaculata*, but other *Libellula* species as well as certain species of the genera *Sympetrum*, *Somatochlora*, *Aeshna*, and even *Calopteryx* and *Coenagrion* species (that is, Zygopterans) have been found on migratory flights of this kind. The insects—including the Anisopterans—fly remarkably slowly, often individually, and at a height of 2 to 10 m. Lack of food can certainly be ruled out as the reason for the formation of these swarms. Probably the primary cause is the simultaneous development of masses of insects at a single site, after which the effect of "suggestion" causes other insects to join the flying throng. Weather factors that have

Nun hat der müde Sylphe
sich unters Blatt gesetzt,
und die Libell am Schilfe
entschlummert taubenetzt.

Friedrich Rückert (1788–1866),
from: "Abendlied"

Beneath the leaf the sylph now
All drowsily has gone
And on the sedge, dew-sprinkled,
The dragonfly sleeps on.

often been held responsible for swarming, can indeed exert a considerable effect, for example, when a sudden rise in temperature causes the simultaneous hatching of large numbers of imagines from the larvae.

As intermediate host of a parasitic flatworm *Prosthogonimus pellucidus* (Plathelminthes, Trematoda), dragonflies can cause indirect harm to poultry, particularly hens, and more rarely to geese and ducks. The primary intermediate hosts are mussels and snails. The second are the larvae of dragonflies, and especially frequently those of *Libellula quadrimaculata*, in which the cercariae (the larval stage of the trematode) live enclosed in a cystic membrane. The cysts also survive in the imago. If poultry then eat this dragonfly, the cyst casings dissolve in the intestines and the young flatworms move from the cloaca into the oviduct where they cause serious inflammation. The hens, geese or ducks lay shell-less eggs, known as "wind eggs". If infestation is heavy, and as many as 40 to 50 worms have been found in one bird, the disease can be fatal. In nature, the definitive hosts are probably curlews. The life cycle of *Prosthogonimus pellucidus* has been known only since 1928. But long before that time, there was wide recognition of a link between swarms of dragonflies and oviductal worm-disease in poultry; in Holland and along the sea coasts where such swarms are not uncommon, a warning went out, and still does today, as soon as the first insects of such a swarm are observed: "Hide the hens! The dragonflies are coming."

Dragonfly migrations are observed relatively frequently in the north. The creatures will even fly across the sea. Mass flights have been seen, for instance, several times on Heligoland which lies 50 km from the mainland. Large-scale migrations have been reported from the mouth of the Oder (1850), from Warsaw (1880), Belgium (1900), the Saale Valley in Germany (1917) and Berlin (1922, 1923). In Warsaw, the insects are said to have pounded against the windowpanes of a school with such violence that teaching had to be interrupted for a number of hours.

In a publication of the *Academia Naturae Curiosorum* (1673/1674), Friedrich Lachmund records an unusual mass flight of dragonflies (probably *Libellula quadrimaculata*): "Our forefathers believed that large-scale migrations of birds or insects presaged disease or war. On May 18, 1673, just such a vast, evil-boding swarm of dragonflies flew across Hildesheim. Never for a moment was the air free of them, but the whole time, several thousands were in sight. Some flew high, some low, and the boys were able to catch large numbers of them. All belonged to a single species and were dark yellow. On their wings there were black specks. Their direction of flight was from south to north. The insects that were caught were exhausted as after a long migration."

In flight, dragonflies can achieve a speed of 50 km/h for a short period, and their manoeuvrability is exceptional. One species, known as the "globetrotters", was observed from a ship flying in a swarm at a distance of 1,400 km from the coast of Australia.

Earwigs

(Dermaptera)

Writing about earwigs, Thomas Moufet says: "These creatures often live on cabbages, in trees or in the galls of elm leaves. They come into being in garden cabbage and cast their skin every year, after which they are left with a snow-white skin. But in time, they regain their former colour. Englishwomen fear them greatly, for they destroy and devour the gillyflowers. Therefore they spread old rags and the like on the ground to provide the insects with a shelter against the inclemency of the weather. In the morning, they take up the cloths, and the earwigs beneath them can easily be crushed underfoot."

Caspar Schwenckfeld provides further information, particularly the tale of how they creep into the ear: "Earwig, ear worm. A long, flat, ungainly worm, chestnut-brown in colour, whose tail

Above:

Female of the European Earwig *(Forficula auricularia)* in the soil taking care of the eggs.

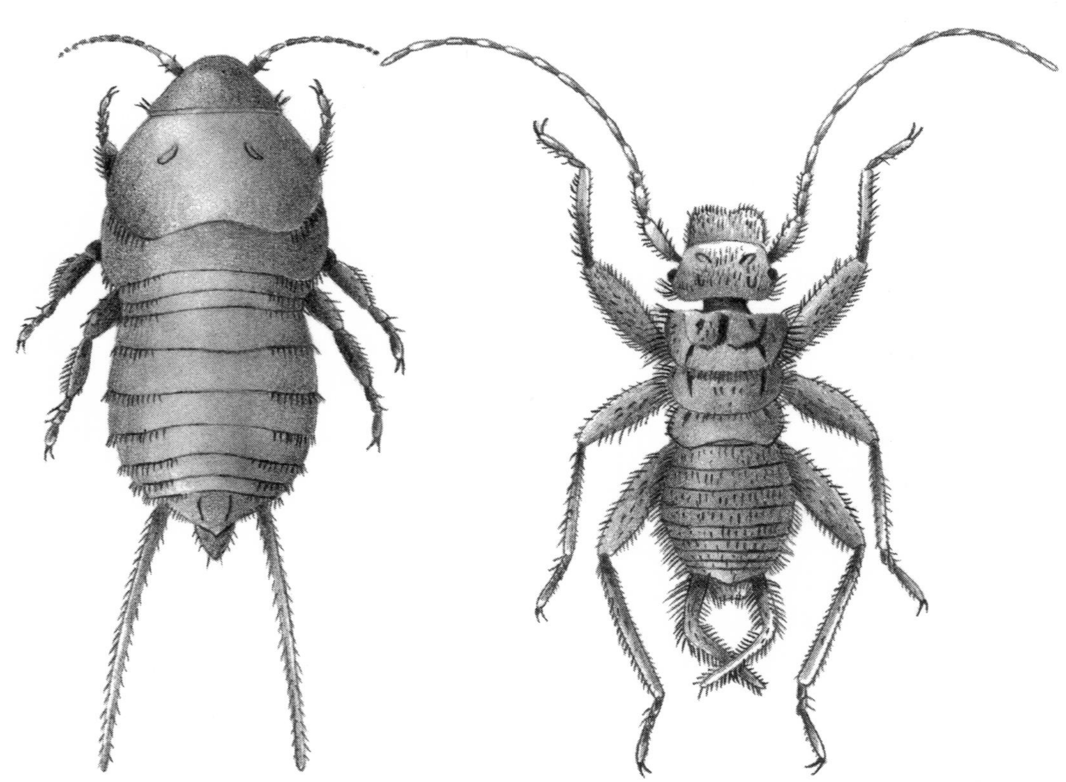

It is not widely known that certain Earwigs live with mammals. *Hemimerus talpodes* with a length of about 12 mm (left) lives ectoparasitically in the fur of African Hamster-rats *(Cricetomys gambianus)*. It is viviparous, apterous and devoid of eyes. *Arixenia jacobsoni*, ♂ (right) occurs on pellets of a bat species in caves on the Sunda Islands. This species is also viviparous and apterous, and the eyes are greatly reduced.

"How limited and unrefined
The working of the earwig's mind,
As through the moss he meekly creeps
A single thought in mind he keeps:
To find a dark and narrow vent
Will make him utterly content.
In answer to his wish most dear,
His eye lights on the poet's ear.
In this enclosure warm and cosy
His future looks distinctly rosy.
But if he thinks that here he may
Continue acting in this way,
Then he is wrong—as one hard blow
From Bählamm's leg did clearly show,
Destroyed the form, by action firm
Which typifies this insect worm,
And his existence here related
Had for the nonce its aims truncated."

Wilhelm Busch (1832–1908), from: Balduin Bählamm

terminates in two points. Close to the eyes, antennae extend like exploratory filaments. They live under the bark of trees. They climb the trees and eat from pears and apples. They like to creep into the human ear, and can be destroyed there by wine vinegar, juniper oil and bitter almond liquor."

Among earwigs, there are both winged and wingless species. In the winged species, including the Common European Earwig *Forficula auricularia*, the forewings (tegmina) are much shortened and cover the hind wings that lie beneath them pleated longitudinally and folded transversely in an elaborate way. A striking feature of the Dermaptera are the cerci modified into stout forceps at the hind end of the body, which differ in form between the sexes. They are longer and more curved in the males. In many species (e. g. the genus *Anisolabis*) the forceps of the male are asymmetrical. The forceps are used in defence, in catching prey, during copulation and for unfolding the wings. Among European species, only the smallest, *Labia minor*, is capable of flight.

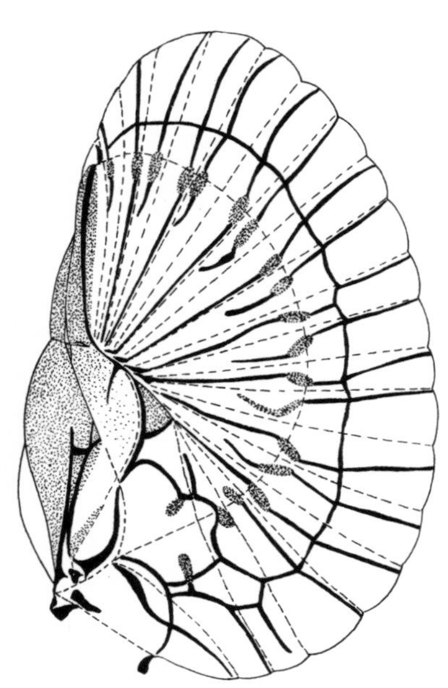

The hind wings of Earwigs (Dermaptera) have an enlarged anal area which can be folded elaborately like a fan, allowing the wings to be housed neatly under the small, strongly chitinized forewings. Though *Forficula auricularia* has fully developed wings, it is hardly ever seen flying.

Mating occurs in early spring. The male inserts the end of its abdomen that it has turned through 180° beneath the female, lifts her with his pincers and introduces the penis. The pair then take up the final position with their heads turned away from one another. The maternal care displayed by the female is interesting and has been examined in detail in the Common European Earwig *Forficula auricularia*. The female excavates a gallery 5 to 8 cm deep, running diagonally into the soil, where, in a hollow, she deposits some 50 eggs. The mother repeatedly "licks" the clutch, removing fungus spores and other harmful germs. If in spite of this, one dies, the female eats it immediately, preventing the spread of infection to the rest of the clutch. In addition, the eggs are re-arranged and defended against enemies. In another species *(Anechura bipunctata)*, the female places fragments of plant material close to the eggs to serve as food for the larvae, which hatch in 3 to 8 weeks, depending upon temperature. At first, the young stages are tended by the female, but not for long; soon she dies and is consumed by her "grateful" progeny. The larvae remain in possession of the maternal home for some time, returning there repeatedly, early in the morning, after their nocturnal excursions. It is only at the imaginal stage that they finally disperse.

Occasionally *Prolabia arachidis* is introduced into greenhouses on plants brought from the tropics. The females of this species of earwig lay eggs that are ready to hatch, but in which the embryos are not capable of breaking through the casing and emerging by their own efforts. So the mother turns her body round and, using her mouth parts, removes the covering from the individual egg, then keeps the still curled embryo covered until it begins to stretch and move. Only then is the next egg laid and the process repeated. In all, it is 8 or 9 hours before the clutch or "litter" is complete. The larvae remain close together for another 3 days, and are cared for by the mother. Only later does the small community break up and the brood care instinct fades.

Mantids

(Mantodea)

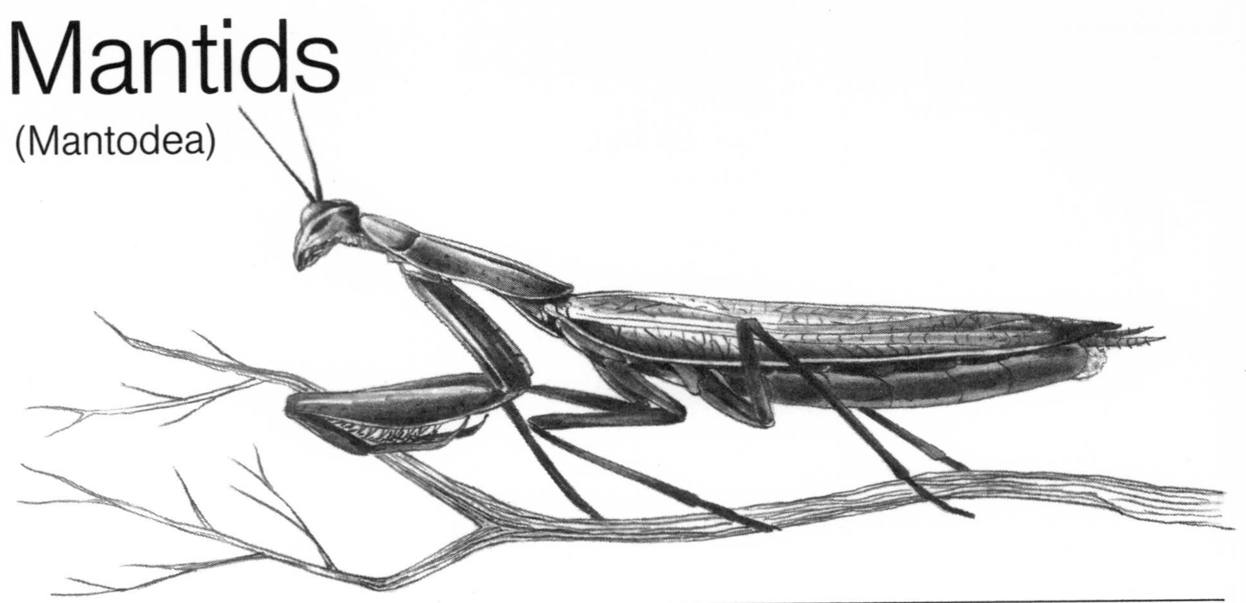

A very early illustration of the larva and imago of a Praying Mantis appears in the Ancient Chinese *Erh Ya*. And of the creature it says: "It eats cicadas and possesses knives (=raptorial arms). In poetry, it is used to represent courage and fearlessness." Certainly the most typical feature of the Mantodea is the forelegs, which have undergone a change of function. While still being used for locomotion, they also serve as raptorial legs, and are extremely well adapted to this additional purpose. The femur is thickly spinose with a ventral groove into which the tibia, furnished with shorter spines, can fit. Considerable mobility has been achieved in the raptorial leg by elongation of the coxae. Once prey is impaled, it is impossible for it to escape.

On the subject of mantids *(t'ang-lang)*, there is a remarkable mixture of fact (observations on biology and morphology) and fiction (medical applications), in the *Pen ts'ao*, the classical Chinese pharmcological writings of about 1108. "The nests are found on the mulberry tree. The Praying Mantis is used to cure goitre. The peasants roast the nests and give them to the children to eat, so that the latter will not wet the bed in the night . . . These nests are not found only on mulberry trees but on all trees, although those on the mulberry tree are the best. At the end of the spring or in early summer, the young hatch from the nests. Each nest produces several hundred larvae . . . The arms of the t'ang-lang give it a very severe look. The neck is long and narrow, the belly large. The head is dark yellow. It has 2 hands and 4 legs, and is very skilful and quick in climbing. Its moustache is its nose. It hides under leaves in order to catch crickets . . . Inside the nests, there are several cells, and in every cell eggs. All these eggs become larvae by the time of mung-chung . . . In the second month, the nests are gathered and roasted on the fire. If they are eaten unroasted, they cause diarrhoea. The nests from other trees should not be used. The twigs should be taken from the east side of the mulberry tree and washed seven times in boiled water, afterwards boiling off the water until none remains. Any other preparation is fruitless . . . The t'ang-lang is good for convulsions in children, particularly those that take a rapid course. The t'ang-lang also eats away warts on the skin. Arrows and knives that cannot easily be removed from wounds can be extracted without difficulty by means of the t'ang-lang. Pound together a t'ang-lang and a croton bean and place them on the wound. The site becomes 'ticklish', and when this itching becomes intense, the foreign body can be withdrawn.

"The nests have a taste between salty and sweet, and they are not poisonous. They are a good remedy for belching and impotence, effective in semen production and for begetting children eas-

Above:

A Mantid (Mantodea) in characteristic posture. The forelegs are raised ready to seize any suitable prey in a flash.

Detail from a page of the *Pen ts'ao*. Mantid with egg pouch.

ily; when women have failure in menstruation; for pain in the hip, gonorrhoea, for the retention of urine, for asthma, nocturnal emissions, bedwetting, etc. the nests should be eaten on an empty stomach."

The construction of the egg packages, the development cycle and even the anatomical details are correct, as is the olfactory function of the antennae. *Mang-chung* is a festival celebrated in the middle of the summer. The second month is the time of April and May.

Mating in the mantids is an interesting process. The smaller, less powerful male approaches the female from behind and tries to spring upon her back. If the female notices the male beforehand, or if the leap is unsuccessful, she does not treat the male as a sexual partner but as prey, and sets about devouring him. Even if the male's leap is successful, the female will sometimes spread her wings suddenly, throw him off and eat him. Large numbers of males are used up in this way. A female has been seen to eat as many as seven males before copulation finally came about. Mating is possible only when the mounted male is able to maintain a secure hold with the middle and hind legs on the female's wings. By continually stroking the female's antennae with its own, the male arouses in her the readiness to mate. After copulation, which lasts for several hours, the male is frequently eaten by the female. Sometimes she even starts to feed on him during mating. It has been observed that copulation can continue even when the head of the male and part of the thorax have been devoured. In mantids, the head is not necessary for the copulatory movements, since they are under the control of the last abdominal ganglion.

A few days after copulation, the female mantids begin to lay their eggs. Using its cerci, the mantid seeks out an appropriate site where it applies a secretion produced from the accessory glands of the female genital organs; using its short gonapophyses, it whips the secretion into a frothy foam which soon hardens. Into this secretion, it places a layer of longish eggs standing upright; it then adds another chamber which it fills with eggs in the same way. It continues until it has completed a packet containing about 100 to 300 eggs. In the course of its life, a female constructs several such oothecae, each of which is some 4 to 6 cm long and 2 to 3 cm wide.

The writings of Ulisse Aldrovandi contain a section on mantids which clearly refers to the species *Mantis religiosa*, the Praying Mantis, that was common in his native region; it is obvious that Aldrovandi was not familiar with the feeding habits of the species. "It is found among herbage in largely uncultivated hilly districts. To anyone who catches it, it delivers a powerful bite which is considerably painful. One such mantid I observed bore countless eggs, of which I do not think all will develop. For if they were to do so, their numbers would be uncontrollably vast, and they would consume the entire year's harvest. It flies more than it jumps: for this reason, nature gave it particularly large forelegs, so that after flying, it can obtain a hold on something. I can find no other cause for it, for in all other species, it is the hind legs that are particularly large and strong, the better to leap with . . . The head resembles the dragonfly's rather than that of the other grasshoppers, which have a somewhat horse-like shape of head . . . The powerful forelegs terminate in scissors and are serrated."

The description of the biology and morphology of *Mantis religiosa* given by August Johann Roesel von Rosenhof (1705–1759) shows a degree of beauty and accuracy rare at that time. His *Insekten-Belustigungen* (Insect Entertainments) have long been a source of pleasure and information to entomologists and others. This is true not only of his work on mantids but of all the illustrations and texts prepared by Roesel. Here, however, our quotation comes not from him, but from an earlier scholar, the Italian physician and naturalist Antonio Vallisnieri, another brilliant and acute observer. "The female constructs an intricate nest, of varying size depending upon her age and the form of her abdomen. It is oval and is attached to hedges or branches. The colour resembles that of drying tobacco or of a withered leaf. The material of which it is constructed is dense,

Die Gottesanbeterin hatte
ihr Männi zum Fressen gern.
Sie schlang eine Portion Gatte
und lobte mit Rülpsen den Herrn.

Wilhelm Pleger, "Kleiner Weltzirkus"

For Madam Praying Mantis
Her mate was a tasty reward.
She swallowed a portion of husband
And burping, gave praise to the Lord.

tough, cartilaginous, but very light. Opened, it reveals the various eggs lying separately in individual cells . . . They begin to build nests in September and continue to do so until the end of October. The young larvae hatch in May or June; they are delicate, white and have the form of their parents. Like all insects, they moult several times during growth. Construction of the nest takes eight hours."

William Piso, a Dutch physician, who together with Georg Marcgrave (1610–1644), a native of Saxony and one of the most outstanding naturalists of his time, undertook a number of journeys of exploration, mentions a mantid in a report from South America. "Because they place the two forelegs together like arms and generally raise them to heaven like hands, they are called *louva dios* by the Portuguese, and *prèque dieu* by the French. And not only savages but Christians in particular believe a great deal of superstitious nonsense concerning them. As if, constantly wasted by consumption, they were teaching man how he should stretch out his hands humbly towards heaven."

"Among the Bushmen, animal worship is especially highly developed. Of the remarkable rock paintings made by the Bushmen of the Cape, the representations of mantids are of especial interest to us here. The Praying Mantis is a figure of legend and power to the Bushmen. The mantid can take various forms, sometimes that of a hartebeest, sometimes human form. One wall painting shows running mantids, half-man, half-mantid, with raised or swinging arms. Striking in appearance is the great Mantis figure standing upright in an attitude of menace, its penis the symbol of strength, creativity and fertility." (Schimitschek, 1977)

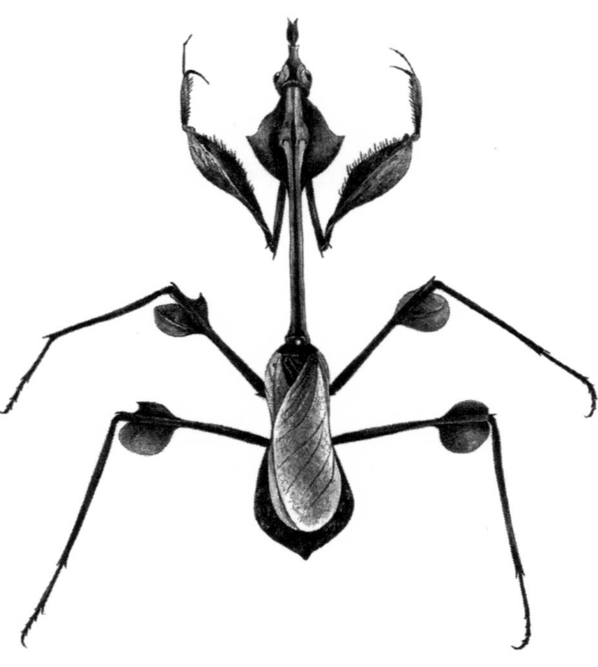

The curious body form of the Southeast Asian Mantid of the species *Gongylus gongylodes* has earned for it the name of the "walking fiddle".

Cockroaches

(Blattariae)

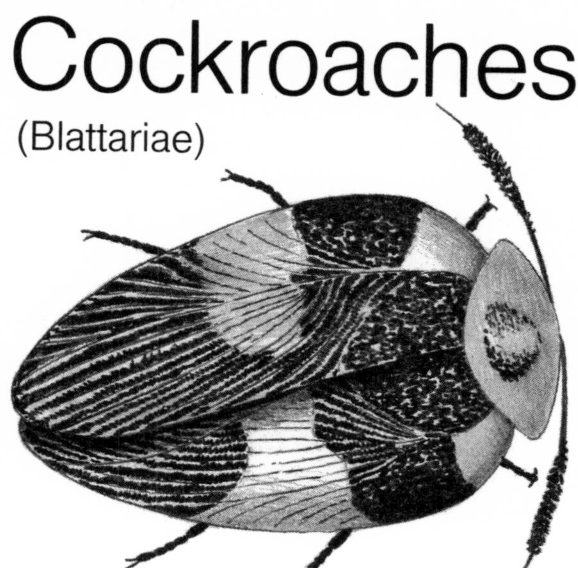

"The innards of those cockroaches found in bakeries, pounded with oil or boiled and poured in drop by drop, relieves earache." In these words, Pedanius Dioscorides (middle of the 1st century A.D.), in his *De Materia Medica*, shows there is at least one useful aspect to the otherwise universally ostracized cockroach.

Kamal al-Din al-Damiri was also familiar with this remedy, but quotes Aristotle as his source, and adds: "This oil is also useful for wounds of the leg and of all limbs."

A Persian scholar, Abu Hanifa ad-Dainuri (died *c.* 895) also recommends the pharmaceutical application of cockroaches. "Pulverized or ground in oil for ulcers of the leg, earache, gynaecological disorders and renal disturbances."

Like mantids, female cockroaches construct an ootheca (egg pod), usually within a single day, but in contrast to the former, they carry it about with them, protruding from the abdomen, finally to drop it. On the subject of reproduction in cockroaches, al-Damiri writes: "After mating, she lays an oblong egg." *Blattella germanica*, the German Cockroach, which is distributed worldwide and found in kitchens, bakeries, zoos, hotels, even on board ships, takes 25 days at a temperature of 22°C, other species only one day. Finally the purse-shaped container splits along a preformed line of weakness along its dorsal edge, and the larvae hatch. Only at this point does the female drop the ootheca. The number of eggs contained in two rows inside the capsule varies between 15 and 20. In *Blattella germanica*, the average number is 30, in *Blatta orientalis* (known in England as the "Black Beetle") usually only 16, and in *Periplaneta americana* (the American Cockroach) 15 to 20. In the course of her life, the female may construct several oothecae; *Blattella germanica* about 4, *Blatta orientalis* about 8 and *Periplaneta americana* 22 to 50. The number of nymphal instars ranges from 5 to 7 or 9 to 10 depending upon species. The duration of development of the domestic species is determined not by the season but entirely by the environmental conditions within the building. In the German Cockroach, it varies between three and nine months.

Cockroaches are omnivores. Nothing that they can possibly bite through with their powerful mandibles is safe from them: bread, cheese, fruit, potatoes, meat and, if nothing better is available, paper, book bindings, clothing material, even leather. They avoid the light, are timid, and because they move rapidly, are difficult to catch. Because they urgently require warmth, the domestic species like to live in kitchens and bakeries. It is embarrassing for a baker if cockroaches are found in bread he has baked, just as bad for the host who serves food with a cockroach in it. The

Above:

Eushelfordia pica. Some cockroach species have brilliant forewings.

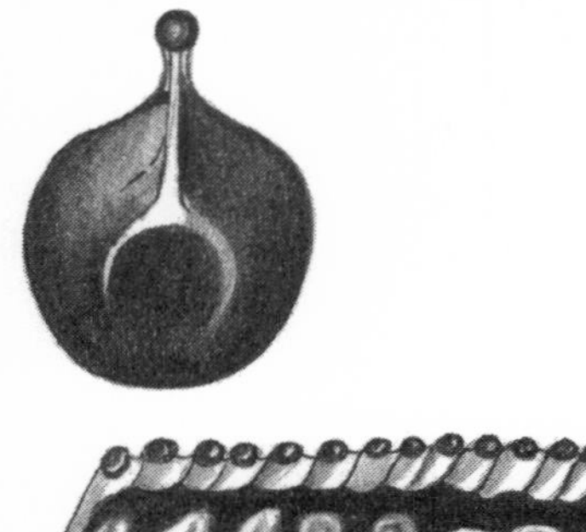

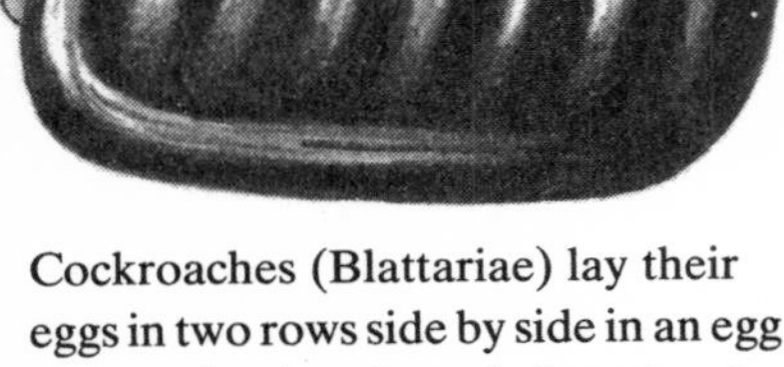

Cockroaches (Blattariae) lay their eggs in two rows side by side in an egg cocoon (ootheca) made from hardened glandular secretions.
Above: End view of ootheca.
Below: Side view.
The Large American Cockroach *(Periplaneta americana)* has been chosen as an example.

creatures are particularly offensive since they often contaminate food, stocks of flour, bread and confectionary with their excreta.

All the species now settled in the immediate vicinity of humans undoubtedly lived originally outdoors in open country. Little is known about the transition to a synanthropic way of life; it is often associated with commercial transportation. Today, the principal domestic species are cosmopolitan. The cockroach was known in Ancient Rome. It is illustrated in the works of Ulisse Aldrovandi and Thomas Moufet. Peter Osbeck writes in his *Reise nach Ostindien und China* (Journey to the East Indies and China; 1750–1752): "Roaches, Blatta orientalis, arrive every year from the East Indies on ships. I have been told that in 1745, when the steamship Gothenburg, returning from China, ran aground and was destroyed on rocks not far from the fortress of Elfsborg, and the wet tea was dried in the ovens of the municipal bakery, this pest also found its way there, along with the tea, and since that time, has often been found in that and several other places. This vermin, which hides during the day, but emerges at night, eats shoes and other garments that are greasy. It is said that bedbugs are their special favourite, so anyone who is inclined to exchange one domestic pest for another, might perhaps be able to confirm my report."

The mating behaviour of cockroaches is interesting, and shows us that these creatures are by no means as dull and monotonous as is widely assumed. The females of many species secrete a sexual attractant which draws the males and initiates courtship behaviour. Using their antennae, the males first arouse the females by tactile stimulation. But their principal attraction lies in pheromones secreted from tergal glands. The male exposes these dorsal glands by spreading its wings and then, moving backwards, pushes itself under the female which immediately begins to lick up the secretion. The male moves his body progressively further under the female and finally copulation occurs with the abdomens joined and the heads of the partners turned away from one another.

Termites

(Isoptera)

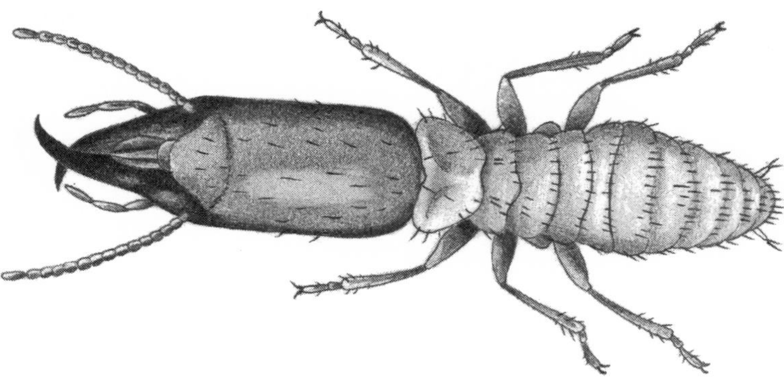

There is a curious story behind the name "termite". It goes back to Pierre André Latreille (died 1833), who in 1802 set up the family of Termitina, in which he placed the species of *Termes* which Linnaeus had assigned to the Aptera in 1758: Linnaeus had given the name Termes to *Termes fatale* (a True Termite) and *Termes pulsatorium* (a Booklouse). It produces knocking sounds in wood, which superstitious people believe to be a warning that their end is near ("termes" means end).

The caste structure

The striking principle of the division of labour has led to the development of morphologically distinct forms that are known as castes (polymorphism). There is, however, a fundamental difference between termites and other social insects such as bees and ants (Hymenoptera). In the latter, the "workers" are always exclusively females in which the reproductive organs have not developed and which are incapable of mating. But in termites, there are both males and females which are non-reproductive sterile castes with reduced or inadequately developed genital organs, and which, together with larvae, are involved in the working activity of the colony.

These individuals are either "workers" or "soldiers". They have the task of foraging for supplies, building up stocks and distributing food, constructing the nest and galleries, caring for the reproductive castes and the brood, cleaning the whole structure and, in the case of the soldiers, defending it primarily against invasive ants. In addition to the primary reproductives responsible for propagation, there are also supplementary reproductives that develop only when they are required, and which can be distinguished from the others, by, for example, the absence of wings.

The armature of the soldier termites shows considerable diversity. Most of them have powerful mandibles with pointed teeth, dentition frequently being more or less asymmetrical. In many genera of the family Termitidae, especially in the genus *Capritermes*, the mandibles of the soldiers are differently constructed and function in a quite different way from normal insect mandibles. The left mandible is twisted into a spiral and is longer than the right one. By means of the latter, which is very powerful, the former can be pressed down and "tensed" or "braced". If the right mandible is then slid across the left one, the latter springs upwards with great force. After locating an enemy by touch, the blind *Capritermes* soldier inserts his mandible underneath his opponent and tosses him in a high arc a distance of 20 to 30 cm. Inside the narrow galleries of the stone-hard termitarium,

Above:

Soldier Termite of *Reticulitermes flavipes*, a species that was introduced into Europe.

Soldier (1) and Worker (2) of *Reticulitermes flavipes*. Note the large head and powerful mandibles of the soldier. The mandibles of *Neocapritermes opacus* (3) are an effective instrument of defence and attack (see text). The soldiers of *Trinervitermes* (4) and of certain other species, known as nasute soldiers, direct against an enemy a spray of liquid secreted from the frontal glands, consisting of several components, which both startle an intruder and hinder him by adhering to his mouthparts.

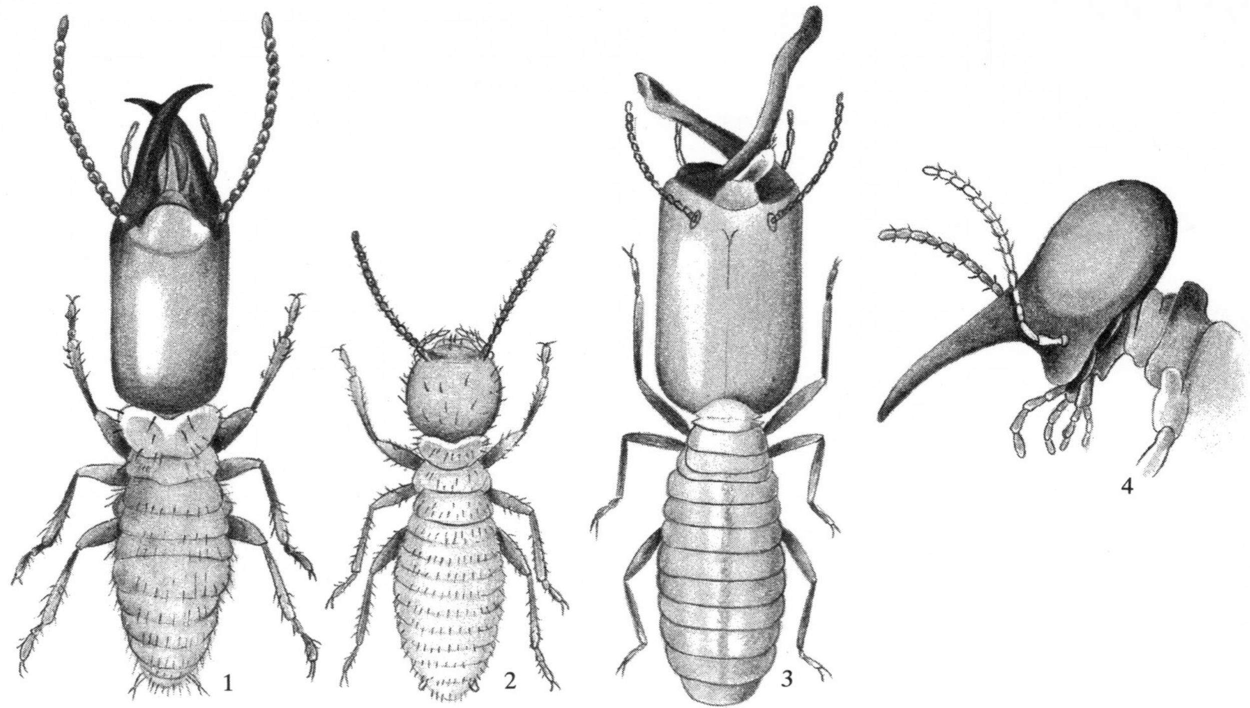

the weapon is even more destructive. *Capritermes* soldiers have been placed inside narrow glass tubes and soldiers of different termite species have been introduced into the other end. In seven out of ten experiments, the latter had its head severed from its trunk. Because mandibles of this kind are unsuitable for feeding, the soldiers as well as the reproductive castes are fed by the workers. In other genera, and most extremely in the many species of Rhinotermitinae, the mandibles are reduced to varying extents or may be merely vestigial. In their place, these soldiers have a different weapon: a frontal gland with an enlarged frontal pore. The gland produces an adhesive secretion which, directed defensively against enemies, rapidly incapacitates them. Such soldiers are known as nasute forms. Some species of termites also have mandibulate-nasute soldiers in which both weapons are functional. In the South American genus *Rhinotermes*, both large mandibulate and small nasute soldiers exist simultaneously.

Reproduction

Among termites, only the reproductive creatures possess wings, and that only during the early imaginal period during which they swarm. The swarming flight of termites serves exclusively as an opportunity for distribution. In neither of the sexes are the gonads fully mature at this time. After swarming, the wings are shed, fracturing along a preformed basal suture, leaving only the stump of the wing, known as the scale. The abdomen broadens out after the wings are shed, to expose scent glands. Only now do the sexes come together in a "mating parade". Pairing is very loose at first. Sometimes a male will pursue another male and a female another female, even though the female is believed to secrete a specific pheromone. An exchange of partners has sometimes been observed. Finally a pair with back turned to back, burrow into the soil. Here the nuptial chamber (or perhaps better, the "foundation chamber") is constructed. Wood-feeding species excavate a chamber in wood. By this time, the reproductive organs have become fully mature, in a process using natural materials made available when the flight muscles are assimilated.

The habitations of termites

An early account of termite nests is given by Smeathman (1781), who reports that in the region of Senegal, that is, in tropical West Africa, there were "white ants which construct dwellings out of soil that they carry in their mouth. They set up their houses, 100 or 150 in one place, like towns, in such a way that when they are completed, they resemble the ovens used in this country for baking bread."

The tallest nests, 6 to 7 m, even 10 to 20 m in height, are constructed by species of the family Termitidae. The nests of other species are simpler and not so tall. The principal feature of all the nests is to create a suitable micro-climate that remains constant within certain limits. Termites are markedly stenothermic, that is, they require a constant temperature in a restricted area, and they cannot tolerate wide fluctuations in humidity.

Building materials include wood, sand, earth, excrement and saliva. There are "concentrated" and "non-concentrated" nests. In the latter, the queen is not immured, but can move freely within the galleries. In the "concentrated" nest, the king and queen remain enclosed within the royal cell.

A termite commonly found in the Cameroon and Congo regions, *Cubitermes fungifaber*, constructs a mushroom-shaped termitarium which it then extends to produce pagoda-like towers. The internal honeycomb structure of the towers extends well down into the ground beneath. This unique method of construction allows rainwater to drain off very rapidly. Equally skilled in building are the *Apicotermes* species, which are also native to the Congo region and members of the sub-family Termitinae. Their nests, only a few centimetres in diameter, are found in primeval forest some 30 to 60 cm deep in the ground. The material used in construction is sandy earth mixed with faecal matter. The nest itself is surrounded by a spongy layer about 1 cm thick consisting of pre-masticated material. Because of its porosity, it surrounds the subterranean nest with a layer of air. The walls of the nest are some 5 to 7 mm thick. Within this wall, there are circular galleries with a diameter of 1.5 to 1.8 mm. At regular intervals, very fine pores, at most 0.5 mm wide, lead from these galleries into the spongy outer envelope; opposite these pores, or in some species off-set from them, similar pores lead into the interior of the nest. The latter is divided into storeys by thin horizontal walls connected by small vertical pillars, and the storeys are linked by stair-like structures. The diameter of the stairways is only just sufficient to allow one termite through. The process by which such complicated subterranean structures are built by termites remains a subject for conjecture.

Nests of Australian Compass or Meridional Termites *(Amitermes meridionalis)*. The nests are disposed with the wider frontage facing east full into the sun, while the narrow end faces south (illustrated above). As a result, the morning sun is exploited to the full, while overheating at noon is avoided. The nests of Compass Termites reach a height of 4 to 5 m.

Early accounts

From what has been said, it is not surprising that termites were a focus of man's attention in very early times. Kamal al-Din al-Damiri writes from Cairo: "This insect informed the spirits of the death of King Solomon. The ant, although smaller than the termite, is its natural enemy. The ant approaches from behind, raises the termite high and flings it into its nest; but if it approaches from the front, it cannot overpower the termite. They build wonderful nests like spider webs, from twigs they gather; the nests are smooth and regular inside from top to bottom, and on one side they have a rectangular door. The entire nest is like a coffin, and from it, the ancient peoples took the idea of a sarcophagus for the dead . . ."

He uses the phrases "More voracious than a termite" and "Liveliev than a termite". But no controversy exists about the relationship with ants which, in fact, are the chief enemy of termites.

In *Curiosities of Creation and Created Beings*, another great Arabian scholar, al-Qazwini writes: "The termite is a small white worm which constructs an arch above itself, similar to an underground cellar, doing so from fear of its enemies such as the ant and others. After a year, two long wings grow, with which it flies . . . If the vaults are destroyed, they all assemble to build them up again; if they are partially destroyed, they all assemble to repair the holes and put the house in order again as rapidly as possible. The termite has two sharp lips with which it pierces wood, brickwork and stones . . . When the termite grows wings, it provides ample food for sparrows . . . It is said that termites can be driven out with sulphur ores and cattle dung."

In 1658, the French traveller César de Rochefort also mentioned termites in his *Historical Description of the Islands of the Antilles*: "In these places there is also a species of ant which has a small black spot on the head but otherwise a completely white body. They come into being in rotten wood, and for that reason, are called wood lice by the French. They have a softer body than our common ants, yet their pincers are so sharp that they eat through the wood and into any chests that are standing on the ground; because they follow one another closely in line, if they are not killed, they assemble there within a few days in such large numbers that they eat through and spoil all the linen, clothes, paper and whatever is in there. They also gnaw at and eat away the corner supports of the simple huts, which finally fall to the ground, unless suitable measures are taken."

The Reverend Mr. Griffith Hughes, in his *Natural History of Barbados*, shows equal concern for the well-being of the residents: "The Wood-Ants are the most pernicious of all others, being so very destructive to Timber of most sorts, that, if not prevented, they will in a few Years time destroy the whole Roof of an House, especially if it be soft Timber. They have likewise caused great Losses to Shopkeepers, by boring Holes through whole Bales of Linen, as well as Woolen Cloths. They are very expeditious in building their Nests, which are long hollow Tubes, the Outside being an Incrustation of a gritty clayey Matter. The Method of destroying them is, to make a small Hole near the upper End of the Nests, and pour into it a little Arsenic, which generally kills those that are present; and the rest, that follow, eat up the Carcases of the slain, and almost instantly swell, burst, and die."

One house was so heavily infested by termites that a party of guests celebrating a wedding was plunged through two storeys into the cellar. In 1814, the magnificent palace of the Governor of Calcutta collapsed because it was infested by termites.

The strangeness of the termitaria, which were unknown in Europe, particularly drew the attention of explorers such as the French traveller Adanson, who reported from Senegal in 1757: "But of all the extraordinary things I observed, noting struck me more than certain eminencies, which, by their height and regularity, made me take them at a distance for an assemblage of Negroes' huts, or a considerable village: and yet they were only the nests of certain insects. They are round pyramids, from eight to ten feet high, upon nearly the same base, with a smooth surface of rich clay, excessively hard and well built. The inside is a labyrinth of little galleries, interwoven

The African species *Cubitermes fungifaber* builds mushroom-shaped nests near trees which are up to 60 cm high.

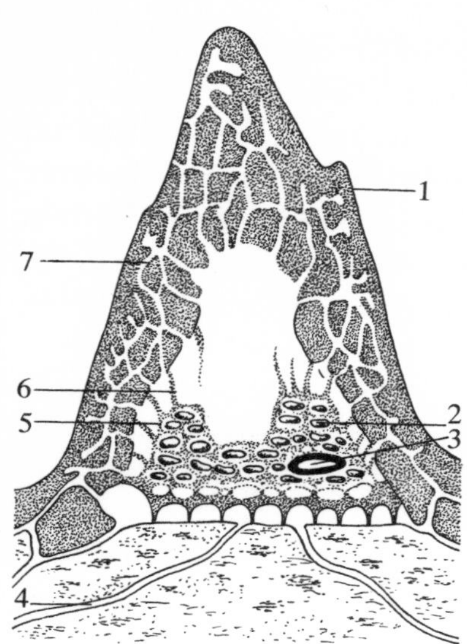

Diagram showing a section through a 3 m high termitarium constructed by *Bellicositermes natalensis* from tropical Africa. The outer covering layer is a hard, brick-like substance (1) with air passages (2). From this, the nest is suspended on lamellae (3). Also marked are the royal cell (4), the fungus gardens (5), store of comminuted woody material (6) and the subterranean entry passages (7).

one with the other, and answering to a small opening, which gives ingress and regress to the insects that inhabit it."

Further on, Adanson writes: "The earth hereabouts was all filled with a species of white ant, called vag-vague, different from that which I have elsewhere described. This, here, instead of raising pyramids, continues buried under ground, and never makes itself known but by small cylindrical galleries, of the thickness of a goose quill, which it erects against the several bodies it designs to attack. These galleries are formed of earth with infinite delicacy of workmanship. The vag-vagues make use of them, as of covert-ways, to work without being seen: and whatever they fasten themselves to, whether it be leather, cloth, linen, books or wood, it is surely gnawed and consumed. I should have thought myself pretty well off, had they only attacked the reeds of my hut; but they pierced through a trunk which stood on trestles a foot above the ground, and gnawed most of my books. Even my bed was not spared and though I took care every evening to beat down the galleries, yet they were frequently erected again, in the middle of the night, up to my bolster; and the vag-vagues got into the bed, where, after cutting the linen and mattress, they came to my flesh and bit me most cruelly."

The termites impressed not only African explorers but also those in Asia. Robert Knox, a Captain in the service of the English East India Company, after twenty years imprisonment, reports in his *Historical Relation of Ceylon, in the East Indies. Together with an Account of the Detaining in Captivity of the author and divers other Englishmen now living there; and of the author's Miraculous Escape*, London, 1681, of which a German edition was published in Leipzig in 1689 and subsequently followed by translations into Dutch, French and Singalese: "They eat and devour all that they can come at; as besides Food, Cloth, Wood, Thatch of Houses and every thing excepting Iron and Stone. So that the people cannot set any thing upon the ground within their houses for them. They creep up the walls of their houses, and build an Arch made of dirt over themselves all the way as they climb, be it never so high. And if this Arch or Vault chance to be broken, they all, how high soever they were, come back again to mend up the breach, which being finished they proceed forwards again, eating every thing they come at in their way. This vermin does exceedingly annoy the Chingulays, insomuch that they are continually looking upon any thing they value, to see if any of these Vaeos have been at it. Which they may easily perceive by this Case of dirt, which they cannot go up any where without building as they go. And wheresoever this is seen, no doubt the Ants are there.

"In places where there are no houses, and they can eat nothing belonging to the people, they will raise great Hills like Butts, some four or five or six foot high; which are so hard and strong, that it would be work enough to dig them down with Pick-Axes. The Chingulays call these Humbosses. Within they are full of hollow Vaults and Arches where they dwell and breed, and their nests are much like to Honeycombs, full of eggs and young ones. These Humbosses are built with a pure refined Clay by the ingenious builders . . . This sort of creatures as they increase in multitudes, so they dy in multitudes also. For when they come to maturity they have wings, and in the Evening after the going down of the Sun, (never before) all those that are fledged and ripe, will issue forth in such vast numbers, that they do almost darken the Sky, flying to such an height, as they go out of sight, and so keep flying till they fall down dead at last upon the Earth. The Birds that tarry up late, and are not yet gone to roost, fly among them and make good Suppers of them."

Mammals as enemies of termites

The massive numbers and the regular occurrence of termites have allowed the development of a specific fauna of termite predators even among mammals. In the order of Monotremata, there are some species that eat termites (as well as ants), such as the Spiny Anteaters (Tachyglossidae), and they display the frequently recurring features typical of this mode of feeding (an example of convergence): long, extensible tongue, powerful burrowing claws, reduction of the teeth. Five species of this animal are widespread in Australia, Tasmania and New Guinea. Mention should also be made of an Australian marsupial, the Numbat or Banded Anteater *(Myrmecobius fasciatus)*, which specializes largely in a diet of termites and which also has an elongate tongue, reduced dentition and strong foreclaws.

Most of the representatives of the order of Edentates (Xenarthra) are well-known termite feeders. Their dentition is degenerate or simplified, the forelegs modified into fossorial limbs, and a long tongue, enlarged salivary glands and muscular protuberances in the stomach to break up the food are effective adaptations to the specific diet. The Antbears (Myrmecophagidae), members of this order living in South America, are highly specialized as ant and termite feeders by the complete absence of teeth and a complicated tongue structure.

Other specialists occurring in Africa are the Pangolins (Pholidota), an order of mammals that is largely termitophagous. Here again, absence of teeth, length of tongue, the presence of horny denticles and grinding plates inside the stomach, and powerful fossorial claws are appropriate adaptations.

Finally there is the Aardvark or Anteater *(Orycteropus afer)*, a species found in Africa, and the sole representative of the order of Tubilidentata (tubular-toothed). The forefeet are furnished with fossorial claws, the curiously constructed teeth and the narrow, flattened and highly extensible tongue that is abundantly supplied with saliva from especially well-developed salivary glands of the lower jaw, are specific adaptations to a diet of termites. They eat primarily species of the genera *Trinervitermes*, *Cubitermes* and *Macrotermes*. The aardvarks break open termite colonies, but the insects they are able to catch in this way do not provide sufficient food for their requirements. So they prefer to seek out columns of termites that are out foraging.

One representative of the carnivores, the Aardwolf *(Proteles cristatus)*, a native of South and East Africa, has adapted largely to a diet of insects, particularly termites. Its dentition is similar in function to that of insectivores. The aardwolf is nocturnal and licks up grass-eating termites of the genus *Trinervitermes* which occur in vast swarms.

In some countries, the primary reproductive castes are eaten at swarming time in considerable quantities by humans, and the thick-bodied queens are considered to be an especial delicacy. They are considered to be sexual stimulants and to possess curative capacities.

Grasshoppers, Locusts, Crickets

(Ensifera and Caelifera)

Swarms of migratory locusts, numbering in some cases 100 thousand million individuals and weighing up to 80,000 tons, can cover an area of up to 210 km in length and an average 20 km in width (4,200 km^2). Because of their habit of appearing suddenly on a tract of land and destroying all growing things, and because there was no effective defence against them, man has feared them ever since he began to cultivate plants, equating them with plague and war. The devastation of his crops caused starvation, poverty, disease and death. It is not surprising then that some of the earliest written records contain accounts of migratory locusts.

Early reports of locusts

Representations of locusts are not rare in Ancient Egyptian art, indicating that in those days, the creatures were already known and feared. Figures of locusts carved in stone on the tombs at Saqqara date from the period of the 6th Dynasty (about 2250 B.C.). In various papyri (1350–1200 B.C.), crop losses are lamented; in addition to locusts, "worms", mice, sparrows and hippopotami are blamed.

The descriptions in Exodus of locust attacks as one of the plagues of Egypt—that can be dated at about 1550 B.C.—are graphically vivid and clearly based on experience.

"–And Moses stretched forth his rod over the land of Egypt, and the Lord brought an east wind upon the land all that day, and all that night; and when it was morning, the east wind brought the locusts. – And the locusts went up over all the land of Egypt, and rested in all the coasts of Egypt; very grievous were they; before them there were no such locusts as they, neither after them shall be such. – For they covered the face of the whole earth, so that the land was darkened; and they did eat every herb of the land, and all the fruit of the trees which the hail had left; and there remained not any green thing in the trees, or in the herbs of the field, through all the land of Egypt."

Expressing the feeling of utter helplessness, the Prophet Joel writes on this same theme: "– Awake, ye drunkards, and weep; and howl, all ye drinkers of wine, because of the new wine; for it is cut off from your mouth. – For a nation is come up upon my land, strong, and without number, whose teeth are the teeth of a lion, and he hath the cheek teeth of a great lion. – He hath laid my vine waste, and barked my fig tree; he hath made it clean bare, and cast it away; the branches thereof are made white. – Lament like a virgin girded with sackcloth for the husband of her youth . . . – The field is wasted, the land mourneth, for the corn is wasted: the new wine is dried up, the oil languisheth. – Be ye ashamed, O ye husbandmen; howl, O ye vinedressers, for

Above:

The species of *Rhaphidophora* (Ensifera) illustrated here inhabits caves in North America. It is wingless, the antennae are extremely long and the body has a hump-backed shape.

Heuschreckenheere kamen hergeflogen,
Unübersehbar siedeln sie in Auen,
und Lager sind an Lagern rings bezogen,
wo irgend Laub und Gras war zu erschauen.
Die Saaten wurden und die Rebenbogen
von ihrer Sichel sogleich abgehauen.
Bald finden sie kein Hälmchen mehr zu zehren
und müssen dann in neue Länder kehren.

Swarms of locusts came flying;
In countless numbers they settle in meadows
And occupy site after site all round,
Wherever foliage and grass is to be seen.
At once the crops and arching vines
Are cut down by their sickle.
Soon not a blade remains to be eaten
And they must move on to new lands.

Abraham Emanuel Fröhlich (1796–1865),
from: "Sermon of the Locusts"

the wheat and for the barley; because the harvest of the field is perished. – The vine is dried up, and the fig tree languisheth; the pomegranate tree, the palm tree also, and the apple tree, even all the trees of the field, are withered: because joy is withered away from the sons of men . . . – The seed is rotten under their clods, the garners are laid desolate, the barns are broken down; for the corn is withered. – How do the beasts groan! the herds of cattle are perplexed, because they have no pasture; yea, the flocks of sheep are made desolate."

For us today, these descriptions are documents of cultural history. They are an impressive, lively and accurate representation of events, which, in spite of all measures for combatting locusts by poison and fire, can still be observed even today.

In Homer's *Iliad* (8th century B.C.), there is a passage which refers to the use of fire against locusts. "As when at the rush of fire locusts take wing to fly unto a river, and the unwearying fire flameth forth on them with sudden onset, and they huddle in the water; so before Achilles was the stream of deep-eddying Xanthos filled with the roar and the throng of horses and men."

We are told more about migratory locusts and means of controlling them in Pliny: "They fly with such a noise of wings that they are believed to be birds, and they obscure the sun, making the nations gaze upward in anxiety lest they should settle all over their lands. They pass over immense tracts of land and cover them with a cloud disastrous for the crops . . . gnawing away everything with their bite, even the doors of the houses as well.

Italy is infested by swarms of them, coming principally from Africa. In the district of Cyrene there is actually a law to make war upon them three times a year, the first time by crushing the eggs, then the grubs and last the fully grown insects. Also they keep jays for this purpose, which meet them by flying in the opposite direction, to their destruction. In Syria as well people are commandeered by military order to kill them."

Aurelius Augustinus (Saint Augustine, Bishop of Hippo; A.D. 354–430) writes in his *De civitate Dei* (City of God): "One may also read that Africa, which had by that time become a province of Rome, was visited by a prodigious multitude of locusts, which, after consuming the fruit and foliage of the trees, were driven into the sea in one vast and measureless cloud; so that when they were drowned and cast upon the shore the air was polluted, and so serious a pestilence produced that in the kingdom of Masinissa alone they say there perished 800,000 persons . . . At Utica they assure us that, of 300,000 soldiers then garrisoning it, there survived only ten." The helplessness in face of locusts also finds expression in Bodenheimer's account (1928): "In the middle of the 16th century, the areas immediately round the town of Arles were devastated by locusts. So the latter were summoned before the court of justice, with the court ushers out in the fields loudly proclaiming the summons. Those charged, failed to appear, so they were given a defending counsel in the person of the distinguished advocate Martin. In his speech for the defence, he spoke to this effect: 'The Creator makes use of animals in order to punish men when they refuse to pay a tithe to the Church. The locusts that are accused, are tools in God's hand, which he is using to lead men back to the path of salvation, repentance and the payment of taxes. Therefore one should not curse them, but must endure the damage they cause until it pleases God to order things differently.' The prosecuting attorney took a different view. 'God,' says he, 'has created animals solely for the benefit of man, and the earth bears fruit only for the cultivation of religion and the enjoyment of man. But since the locusts devour these fruits, they must be cursed by man.' Bitter arguments followed, which were concluded by the court of justice cursing the pests and demanding that they leave the area. The defending counsel lodged an appeal against this sentence, but in the meantime, the locusts beat a retreat from the field of battle. They could no doubt have tolerated the curse, but they could not hold out against the horror of a court case with all its attendant chicanery and stages of appeal."

Locusts as food and as medicine

A well-known Ancient Assyrian sculpture (about 1800 B.C.) from Nineveh in Mesopotamia shows servants carrying locusts as a delicacy to be served at a banquet held by King Sennacherib of Assyria (reigned 705–681 B.C.). Also well-known is an Ancient Babylonian seal showing the God Marduk with locusts.

Leviticus lists the laws of clean and unclean meats, and contains the passage: "Yet these may ye eat of every flying creeping thing that goeth upon all four, which have legs above their feet, to leap withal upon the earth; – Even these of them ye may eat; the arbeh after his kind, and the solam after his kind, the chargol after his kind and the chagab after his kind."

It is remarkable to find a distinction drawn between four species of locusts and grasshoppers, which, although difficult to interpret today, led the internationally renowned director of the former German Entomological Institute, Walter Horn (1871–1939), to describe Moses as the founder of systematic entomology.

The eating of locusts was widespread. John the Baptist is reported to have survived in the wilderness on a diet of locusts and wild honey. Diodorus Siculus (1st century B.C.) tells of one group within the population of Ethiopia—he called them acridophagous—whose staple food was locusts, which they preserved in salt to last all the year.

In our own time, Reisch (1954) talks of the diet of the Bedouins: "Locusts, cured by salting, will keep for years, and are much appreciated in times of scarcity." Herodotus (484–425 B.C.) writes that after the creatures are killed, they are first dried in the sun, then ground to powder and finally mixed with milk.

Food carrier with grasshoppers. Ancient Assyrian sculpture in the Palace of Sennacherib in Nineveh.

Aristophanes (445–386 B.C.) describes a method of preparation by roasting, then adding aromatic vinegar and pepper. It is said that when the Municipal Council of Frankfurt am Main met in session after a plague of grasshoppers, this insect was served to them to eat. In many African countries, locusts are considered a delicacy and are eaten roasted, grilled and smoked, or used as a preserve.

A different use to which grasshoppers and locusts have been put is seen in *De Materia Medica* of Pedanius Dioscorides, a native of Anazarbus in Cilicia, who lived in the middle of the 1st century A.D. "Locusts, in the smoked form, are helpful in cases of urine retention, particularly in women. The flesh is unfit for use. The locust known as asirakos or onos is wingless in its juvenile stage and has long legs. Dried and taken in wine, it is very efficacious for scorpion stings." Similar information is given in 1534 by Paulus Aegineta in his *Opus de re medicina*. "In cases of difficulty in urination; taken ground without the wings, in wine, for scorpion bites."

Needless to say, prescription of this kind have importance for us today only as interesting and curious documents of the period they represent. Only in a very few cases is it possible to show any beneficial effects on the health of the patient.

Grasshoppers and locusts in art

A drawing of a grasshopper scratched on a bison bone has survived from the Neolithic cultural epoch of the Middle Magdalenian period (*c.* 20 000 B.C.) in the Trois Frères Cave in the Ariège Department. The insect represented is probably a member of the genus *Troglophilus*; as a cavernous form, they are widespread in Europe today.

"The grasshoppers appear in the Egyptian Book of the Dead as a religious symbol. This is clear from texts in the pyramid of Neferkare, 6th Dynasty (2180 B.C.). In another pyramid: 'I was born in the land of locusts' (18th Dynasty, 1500 B.C.). In the pyramid of Merenre (Antyemsaf I., 6th Dynasty, about 2272 B.C.): 'He rose up in the form of a locust'."

"The ancient Sumerian cuneiform symbolism contains the first character denoting the locust. Locust standing upright, body in a vertical position, saltatorial legs, head with antennae to the right. – According to Unger (1940), the interpretation is: 'locust—negation—non-existence —destruction—image. The locust was considered the symbol of destruction'; engraved on a golden dagger from Ur, as a symbol of death to the enemy. For Unger, the fact that the locust symbol also had the meaning of an 'image', indicates an early form of animal worship. As the symbol of destruction, the locust appears on Sumerian and Cretan-Egyptian dagger-blades, for example, the blade from the Ah-hotep tomb." (Schimitschek, 1977)

Schimitschek continues: "A stater from Metapontion (400–350 B.C.) bears on its reverse an ear of corn and a locust. The locust symbol was considered capable of averting ill-fortune. It is often depicted with an ear of corn or a cluster of grapes, or else on the back of an animal or even of a human being. Gems show it as an Amazon with shield and battle-axe. On a Roman gem, there is a figure of a man with a locust on his back almost overpowering him . . .

Among the Greeks, locusts are found on coins and gems; it was a symbol used to ward off evil. A bronze locust was found in the Didymaion ruins, the shrine of the Oracle of Apollo Philesius in the region of Miletus. In about 500 B.C., Pisistratus had a bronze locust placed on the Acropolis at Athens to avert evil. Vergil is said to have attached a bronze locust to a tree near Naples to keep locusts away . . .

According to Lipffert (1964), in Christian iconology the grasshopper is a symbol for the soul because it casts its skin four times and frees itself from the burden of earthly things. In Dürer's work, it is found in the paintings 'Madonna with a Multitude of Animals' and 'The Holy Family with a Grasshopper'."

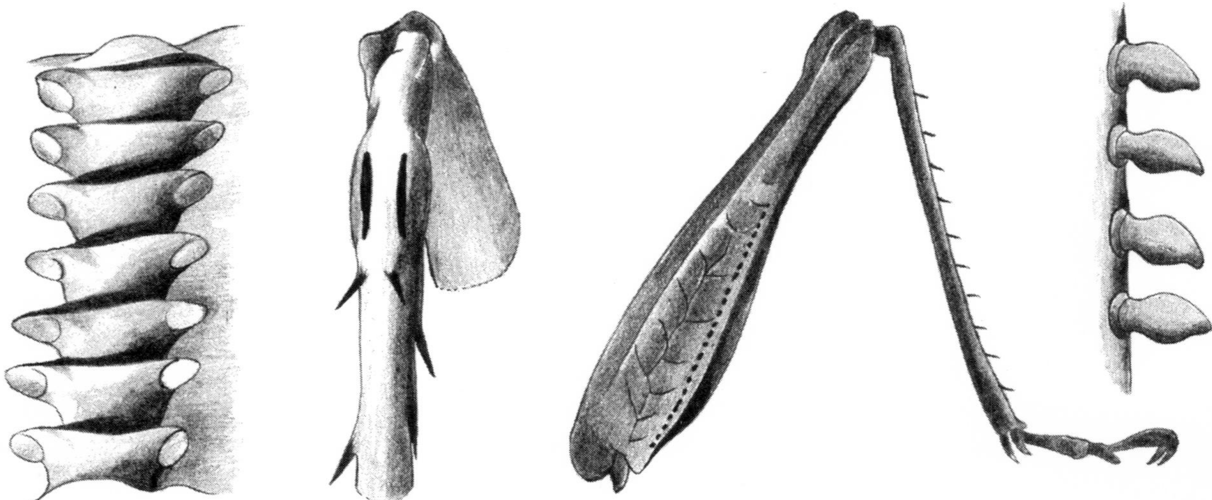

Left: The stridulatory file of the Field Cricket *(Gryllus campestris)*. Centre: The fore tibia of a Great Green Bush Cricket *(Tettigonia viridissima)* with the openings of the tympanal organs. In the Indian species *Despoina superba*, there are even auriculate appendages that serve to channel sounds. Right: Hind leg of a Short-horned Grasshopper (Caelifera) showing the stridulatory ridge, together with a magnification of some of the peg-like projections.

Ensifera and Caelifera

The group of Orthopterans (grasshoppers, locusts, crickets), which for a long time was known as the Saltatoria, because of the ability to leap on saltatorial legs, can today be considered as two orders of insects, the Ensifera and the Caelifera.

Characteristics	Ensifera (long antennae)	Caelifera (short antennae)
antennae	longer than the body (at most 9 times as long and composed of 500 segments—cavernicolous forms)	shorter than body
female ovipositor	sword-like	short but capable of telescopic extension
tympanal or auditory organ	on the fore tibiae	on first abdominal segment
stridulation	right and left forewings are rubbed together	hind femur is rubbed against the forewing
diet	insect prey, also plants	plants
examples	Long-horned Grasshoppers, Bush Crickets, Gryllids, Ground Crickets, Field Crickets, House Crickets, Mole Crickets	Short-horned Grasshoppers, Acridids, Migratory Locusts, Common Grasshoppers, Grouse Locusts

Stridulation

A striking characteristic of grasshoppers and locusts is their ability to produce sound. Aristotle made some early observations on sound production by insects. Of grasshoppers, he writes: "The noise made by grasshoppers is produced by rubbing or reverberating with their long hind legs." In most cases, it is only the males that produce sound by stridulation. In the short-horned grasshoppers, the females also possess stridulatory organs, but they are less highly developed. Both sexes are able to hear.

In both orders, sound is produced on the principle of friction between a stridulatory vein furnished with peg-like projections (80 to 300) and a sharp stridulatory edge, much in the manner of drawing a file across the cutting edge of a knife. In the long-horned grasshoppers, the sound thus produced is further amplified by means of the "mirror", a very fine membrane on the first forewing or tegmen, close to the stridulatory edge, which is thrown into vibration and acts as a resonator. If the forewings are so greatly reduced that they are no longer capable of sound amplification, a resonant area may be developed on the abdomen, as in the South African species *Trachypetrella anderssonii*. In another South African species *Bulla longicornis*, the abdomen is inflated into an air-filled blister which amplifies the sound.

In the short-horned grasshoppers, stridulation has been found to take place in seven different ways. But not all methods are employed by a single species, nor are they always clearly distinct from one another. "Common song" is that most frequently heard. It is assumed to be an indication of well-being and to have no further biological significance. "Seeking" song is that produced by males when they are attempting to locate a female. If at this time, two males meet, "rivalry song" follows immediately, which is characterized by a particularly sharp accentuation of the individual sounds. Frequently one male stridulates in the pauses made by the other male. "Disturbance song" is even sharper than rivalry song, and can be interpreted as an expression of anger. Once a male has found a female, "courting song" begins. Initially this is somewhat softer than common song, but increases as excitement grows, then falls away to "reduced song". This is followed by the mating sounds that consist of short, disconnected notes.

There are also some unusual examples of sound production. The grasshopper *Calliptamus italicus* produces a mandibular sound by rubbing together the toothed edges of the jaws (a kind of gnashing of teeth). *Oedipoda* species stridulate during flight, using the hind wings which are especially heavily veined. The Creaking Locust *(Psophus stridulus)* makes particularly loud stridulatory sounds with its gleaming red hind wings.

In his tale "Das Haidedorf", Adalbert Stifter (1805–1868) writes: "There was one of his favourites, a noisy purple-winged hopper, which flew up in dozens in front of him and settled again as soon as he had passed through its territory—there were its countless cousins, the larger and smaller grasshoppers, like so many Hungarian haiduks, clad in strident green, merrily and restlessly chirping, so that on sunny days there was a vibrant singing along the whole length of the heath."

The auditory range in short-horned grasshoppers differs from that of humans. The lower auditory threshold is about 300 Hz (ours about 16) and the upper about 21,000 (ours between 17,000 and a maximum of 20,000).

Reproduction

Aristotle was the first to summarize the grasshopper's life cycle. "The Acridids copulate in the same way as other insects; that is to say, with the lesser covering the larger, for the male in general is smaller than the female. The females first insert the hollow tube, which they have at their tails, in the ground, and then lay their eggs: and the male, by the way, is not furnished with this tube. The females lay their eggs all in a lump together, and in one spot, so that the entire lump of eggs resembles a honeycomb. After they have laid their eggs, the eggs assume the shape of oval grubs that are enveloped by a sort of thin clay, like a membrane; in this membrane-like formation they grow on to maturity. The larva is so soft that it collapses at a touch. The larva is not placed on the surface of the ground, but a little beneath the surface; and, when it reaches maturity, it comes out of its clayey investiture in the shape of a little black grasshopper; by and by, the skin integument strips, off, and it grows larger and larger. The grasshopper lays its eggs at the close of summer, and dies after laying them . . . The male grasshoppers die about the same time. In spring-time they come out of the ground; and, by the way, no grasshoppers are found in mountainous land or in poor land, but only in flat and loamy land, for the fact is they lay their eggs in cracks of the soil. During the winter their eggs remain in the ground; and with the coming of summer the last year's larva develops into the perfect grasshopper."

Attracted by the chirping of the male, the female of many species crawls on to the back of the male, where in some cases, especially among cavernicolous forms, she finds a pleasant-tasting secretion that is produced from glands in the male's first abdominal tergite. If the male were to assume the upper position, the sword-like ovipositor would make contact between the external genitalia difficult. As it is, the male effects copulation merely by curving the abdomen upwards. Other species have other mating positions, such as our own Great Green Bush Cricket *(Tettigonia viridissima)*.

Sperm is transmitted by means of a spermatophore of highly elaborate construction. Only a small part is introduced into the sexual opening of the female. Osmotic processes force the spermatozoa slowly into the vagina. Immediately after copulation, the female begins to eat the spermatophore. The male, however, has covered the latter with a spermatophylax (or "spermguard") consisting of a gall-like mucous substance which must be consumed first. By this time, the spermatophore itself has been emptied and is finally consumed as an empty case.

Knowledge about locusts and grasshoppers in the Middle Ages

Arabian authors writing in the Middle Ages frequently mention locusts. The Arab countries are still today one of the principal areas susceptible to locust attack. Al-Qazwini writes: "The locust occurs in two forms. One which flies high in the air, called the horseman; the other jumping form is known as the walker. When the days of spring arrive, the locusts seek out good, soft earth, settle there and dig a hole with their tail. Into this they deposit their eggs and fly away. They are killed by birds or by the cold. Once their metamorphosis is complete and the spring has passed, they burst the buried egg and appear as small creeping creatures on the surface of the soil. It is said that each locust lays many eggs. When they emerge from the eggs, they eat whatever crops they happen to see, until they are adult and capable of flight. Then they rise from the ground and migrate to another area where they deposit their eggs. Such is their custom; it is ordered thus by the sublime being, the knowing one." Of husbandry, the author says: "If locusts are seen approaching a village, the people of the village hide so that nobody is to be seen. If the locusts see no people, they pass by that place and none settles on it. Where people burn locusts in that place, they go away if they perceive the smell, otherwise they die and fall to the ground."

Medieval scholasticism added nothing new to what was known about locusts, as we see in an extract from the *Little Compendium* written in the 13th century by an English Franciscan friar Bartholomaeus Anglicus. "The locust gets its name from its long legs which are as long as a lance shaft. They have no king, yet move in well-ordered flocks. Their mouth is square-shaped, and they have a sting instead of a tail. They have bent and folded legs."

With the renascence of Aristotelian zoology, all that was known about grasshoppers was summarized. The English physician Edward Wotton (1492–1555) wrote a compendium in which he repeats transmitted knowledge on the subject, without adding any new observations of his own. "Grasshoppers come into being from creatures of their kind and copulate as all insects do, the male above the female, the female with her tail turned up to the male, and they separate only slowly. The females give birth by piercing the ground with their ovipositor, and place their young there as in a cell. Egg-like small worms develop which, in the ground, are enclosed in a delicate membrane. The young grasshoppers cut through it and emerge. The young are so delicate that the slightest touch destroys them. They are not laid in the upper levels of the soil but rather deeper, and remain in the soil throughout the winter. Towards the end of the next spring, small, black, creeping grasshoppers emerge, without legs and wings. Soon they begin to grow. They lay their eggs at the end of the summer and then die, because at that time, worms are engendered in the region of the neck which throttle them. So most of them die, but some seize the murderous serpents with their mandibles and kill them . . . It is said that in India, they are three foot long, and the peasants there use their legs as harrows." This text, of course, contains a number of inaccuracies. The Indian giant grasshoppers do not exist. The "worms" referred to may perhaps be parasitic roundworms (Nemathelminthes, Mermitidae), which often infest grasshoppers.

Caspar Schwenckfeld acquaints us with an orthopteran he calls "Locusta": "This grasshopper is a field insect, weak in the wing and usually flying low, which is extremely harmful to all herbs and crops. Like all insects, its body is segmented. On either side, it has two wings attached at the shoulder. Of these, the upper ones are of a single colour with blackish or reddish spots, the lower delicate and whitish. The wings move in a broad sweep like a bird's wings or a ship's sail. It flies by using the latter. Close beneath the back, a membrane is stretched, by means of which they stridulate . . . Instead of lungs, they move the long, soft abdomen in a circling motion, distending it to take in air. During copulation, the male sits on the back of the female. Bending and twisting the end of its body, the male inserts two pointed processes at the end of the abdomen into the female genitalia. Eggs are deposited in level and fissured ground. The eggs hibernate and the young grasshoppers emerge in the following spring."

Migratory locusts in medieval Europe

Let us return to migratory locusts. A clearly-marked phenomenon in Europe, especially in the Middle Ages, was the occurrence of distinct "locust years" that are associated with particularly favourable weather conditions. A broadsheet concerning migratory locusts in Lusatia, published in 1542, entitled *True and Fearful Tidings . . . of outrageous Locusts / and the Damage they have wrought / and are continuing to do. 1542 on 15th August*, is historical evidence that a plague of locusts was not unknown even in European countries. It reads: "On the Day of Saint Aegidius / there came into the land between Prebitz and Goerlitz / vast hordes of locusts / which feasted on and consumed every thing there was / all round the villages Weigessdorff / Aarnt / Canewitz Buchwalde / Klux / Malschwitz / for a length and breadth of three and a half miles / After that they divided and one part moved towards Loeben / the other part towards Witgenau / the third remained in the country.

"The following Monday in the afternoon / at about three o'clock / I was travelling with good friends towards Gorgk / to my meadows / that lie a mile away from the town / when they came flying dense and thick / as if it were snowing great snowflakes / they fell upon the foremost meadows / the hindmost meadows were consumed and completely devastated / the forward ones suffered the same fate. You could not put a foot down / without crushing one / two / three or four / they squeaked and champed noisily in the grass / like titmice. The largest are grey and blackish / at least as thick and long as a man's little finger / in appearance very strange / they have four small sharp teeth / like a little pike / the others are yellow and green. I was overcome by horror and dread / as I walked in among them. The after-grass in little stooks / and the cut grain was consumed / as well as the standing crop / On that day Bastian and his wife were on the road from Cotbus / At Wittgenau the other swarm met him / The distress, worry and trouble he had / he will acquaint you of himself."

Bodenheimer (1929) reports on the species that was significant for Europe, *Locusta migratoria*: "Today its home is in the reed-covered flood-plains of southern Russia, but in earlier times, it was equally at home in regions with similar topography and vegetation on the lower Danube, especially in Romania and Hungary. Some reports indicate that even within historical times, Poland and the land east of the Elbe might well have been counted among the permanent breeding sites of this species . . . Two migratory routes lead across Hungary or Poland respectively to Germany and Austria.

In favourable years, namely dry and hot, the eggs laid by these swarms produced secondary swarms which in the following year or even years, caused immense damage in those sites, and which finally perished as they continued their migration westwards. In historical times, the lands along the east of the Elbe and the Rhine Valley have been the place of origin of secondary swarms of this kind. As land was increasingly put under cultivation, even larger areas became unsuitable for the mass development of locusts. At first they disappeared in the territory east of the Elbe, later in Poland and Hungary. With increasing river regulation and reclamation work, they will probably disappear finally as massive invasions in southern Russia, and then, after centuries of hard work, man would have succeeded in driving out of Europe one of his most dangerous enemies . . . The question of the origin of the swarms that caused devastation in Germany has not yet been completely settled. It is known that in the years 1336, 1475, 1693, 1747 to 1749, that is, the most important years for locust attack, the swarms came originally from Hungary and Poland. In Germany itself, three migratory paths can be seen: Austria—Danube, Bohemia—Saxony—Main and Silesia—Brandenburg. But these locusts went on breeding for years within the country itself, to some extent even in Brandenburg, before finally becoming extinct in their migratory form. This was certainly the case in the locust years of 1752–1754, following the insects' arrival in 1747–1749. In 1747, the swarms began to move into Romania and laid their eggs in Transylvania.

On right:

9 Mating of the Damselfly *Lestes sponsa* (Central Europe). Male (above) and female (below).

10 Male Mayfly *Ephemera vulgata* (Central Europe).

11 Larva of the Mayfly *Cloeon dipterum* (Central Europe).

On right:

12 Above: A Skimmer, *Libellula fulva* (Central Europe), alights for a brief pause during flight.

13 Below left: Pair of Dragonflies of the species *Enallagma cyathigerum* which is widely distributed in Europe. The male (above) initiates copulation by seizing the female in the region of the neck with the cerci.

14 Below right: Larva of the Common Meadow Dragonfly *(Sympetrum vulgatum)* from Central Europe.

15 *Sphodromantis lineola* from West Africa, copulating.

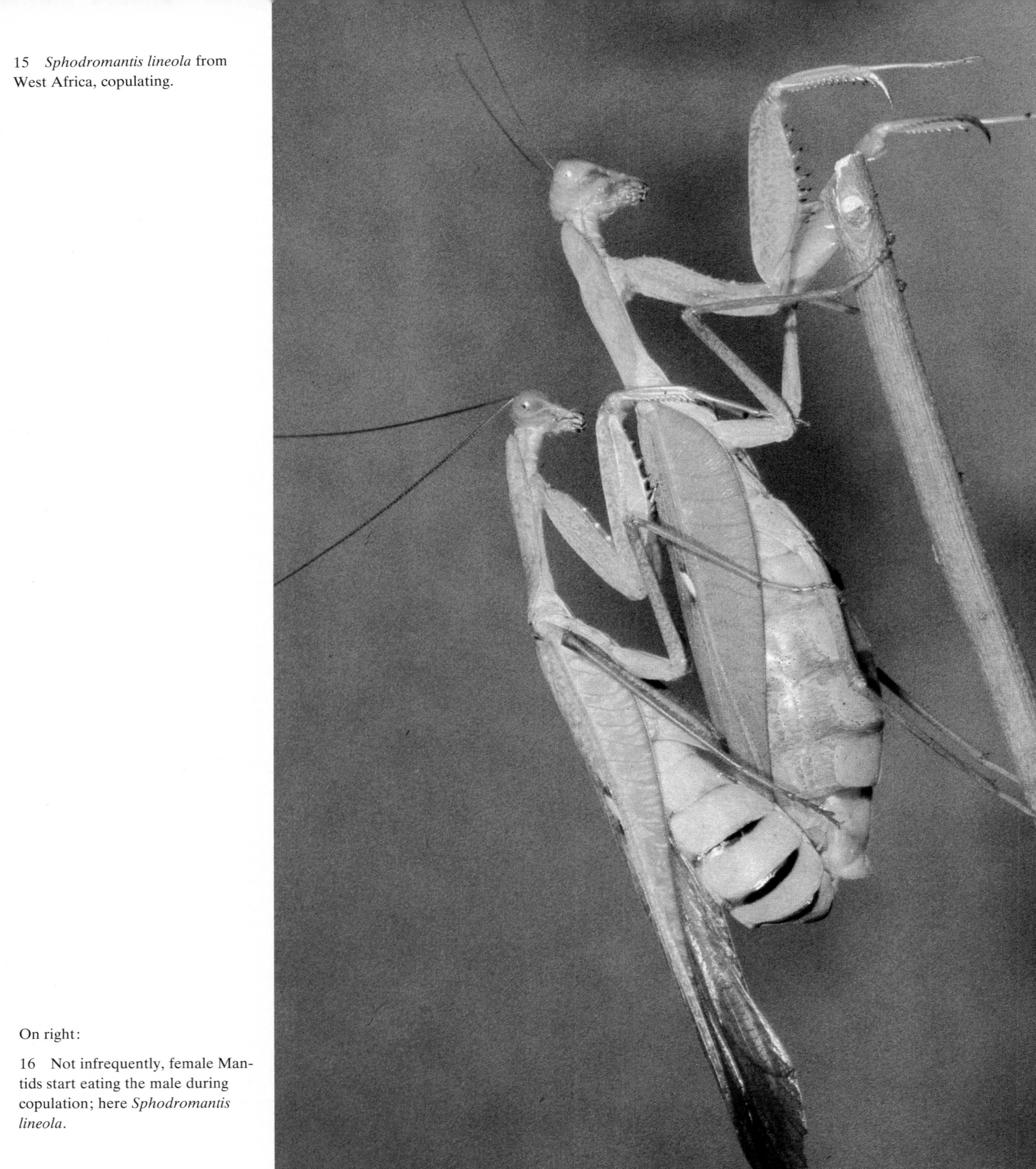

On right:

16 Not infrequently, female Mantids start eating the male during copulation; here *Sphodromantis lineola*.

On left:

17 The ootheca (egg cocoon) of the Praying Mantis *(Mantis religiosa)* from southern Europe is made from a frothy glandular secretion which hardens rapidly and is produced by accessory glands (the colletorial glands) which are part of the female reproductive system. The eggs, numbering about 100 in a clutch, are protected by this spongy covering from the rigours of the winter weather.

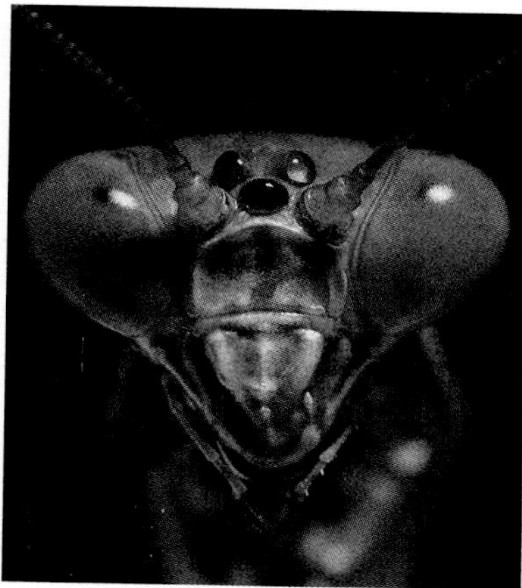

18 The head of the Mantid, here *Sphodromantis lineola*, is furnished with well-developed and functionally effective compound eyes, and in addition, three simple eyes (ocelli).

19 Raptorial legs are a typical feature of Mantids (Mantodea). The photograph shows the forelegs of a male *Sphodromantis lineola* from West Africa.

20 Above: A species of cockroach commonly found living freely in Central Europe as a non-domestic species is the Forest Cockroach (*Ectobius silvestris*). The wings of the female are reduced.

21 Below: The Madagascan Hissing Cockroach *(Gromphadorina portentosa)* is remarkable for the hissing sounds it produces when disturbed. Immediately after moulting, the cockroaches are almost white, and at first very soft.

On right:

22 One of the largest species of cockroach is the Giant Cockroach *(Blabera craniifer)* from South America which can be up to 6 cm in length.

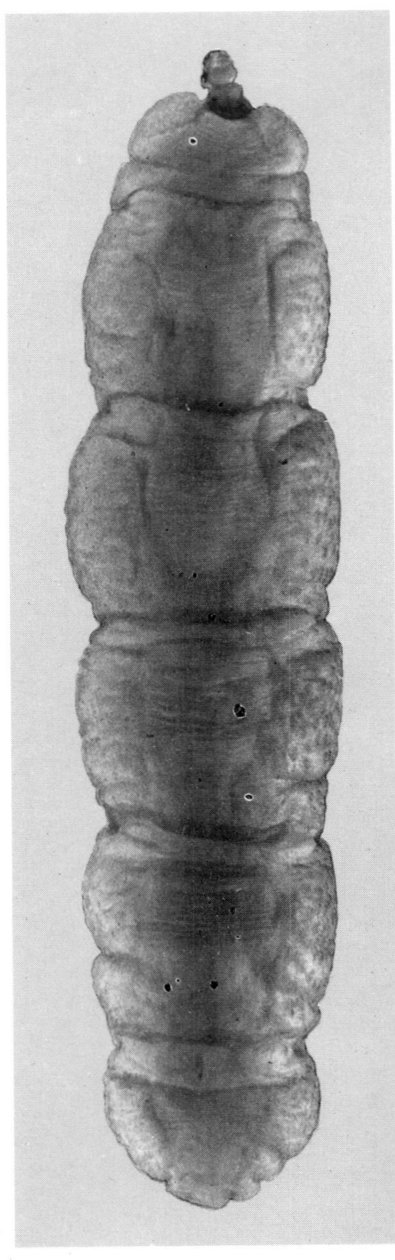

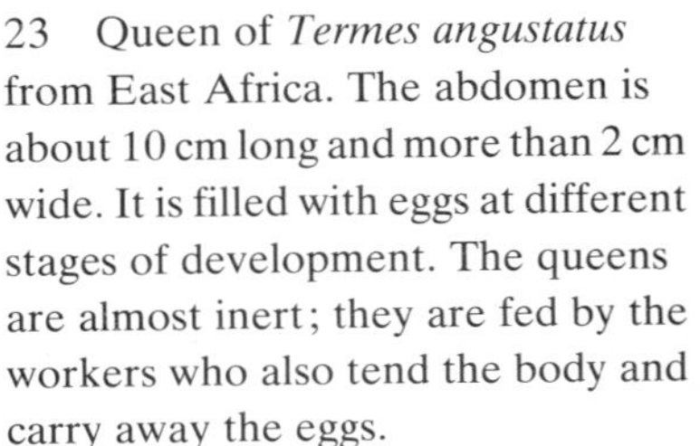

23 Queen of *Termes angustatus* from East Africa. The abdomen is about 10 cm long and more than 2 cm wide. It is filled with eggs at different stages of development. The queens are almost inert; they are fed by the workers who also tend the body and carry away the eggs.

24 A nest, several metres in height, built by an African species of termite.
Photo: Tierbilder Okapia, Frankfurt/Main.

25 The Southern European Cricket *(Gryllus bimaculatus)* bears a close resemblance to the indigenous Field Cricket. It is often kept as a pet or as food for terrarium animals.

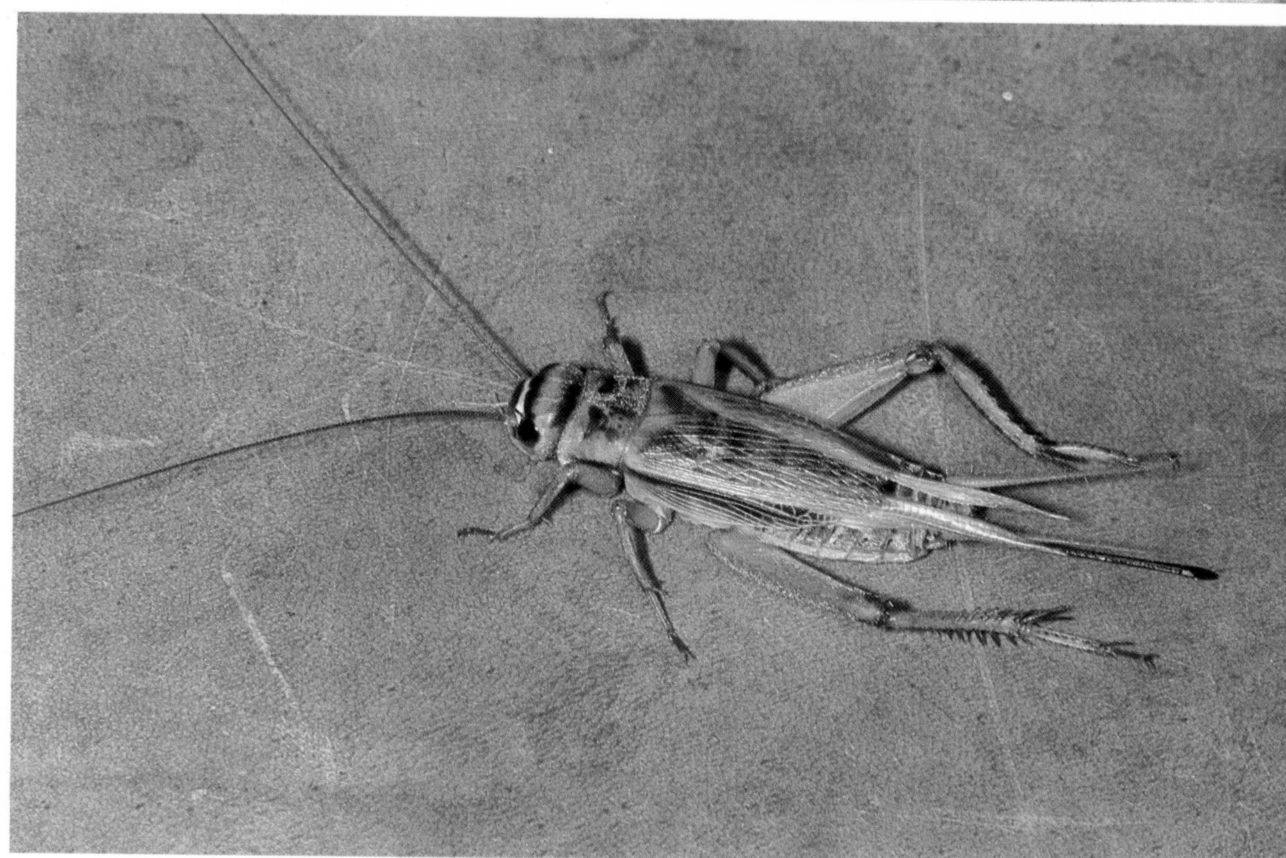

26 The House Cricket *(Acheta domesticus)* lives in close proximity to man. It is found primarily in towns, also on rubbish dumps and even on ships.

27 Above: *Trachyzulpha fruhstorferi* (Ensifera) from Java is remarkable for the battery of spines covering its pronotum.

28 Belove: *Schizodactylus monstrosus* (Ensifera) from Bengal inhabits deserts and loose sandy soils. The involuted wings are a conspicuous feature of this species.

29 Above left: *Dysonia melaleuca* (Ensifera) from North America is characterized by its lichenose markings and form.

30 Below left: *Typophyllum lunatum* (Ensifera) comes from Brazil.

31 Above right: A Bush Cricket with curiously long antennae is *Sasima spinosa* (Ensifera) from the Bauda Islands.

32 Below right: Male Bladder Crickets (Pneumoridae) have an inflated abdomen and normal wings. Illustrated here, *Pneumora ocellata* (Caelifera) from South Africa. The females are elongate, short-winged, and in contrast to the males which are predominantly green, have strikingly bright colourings.

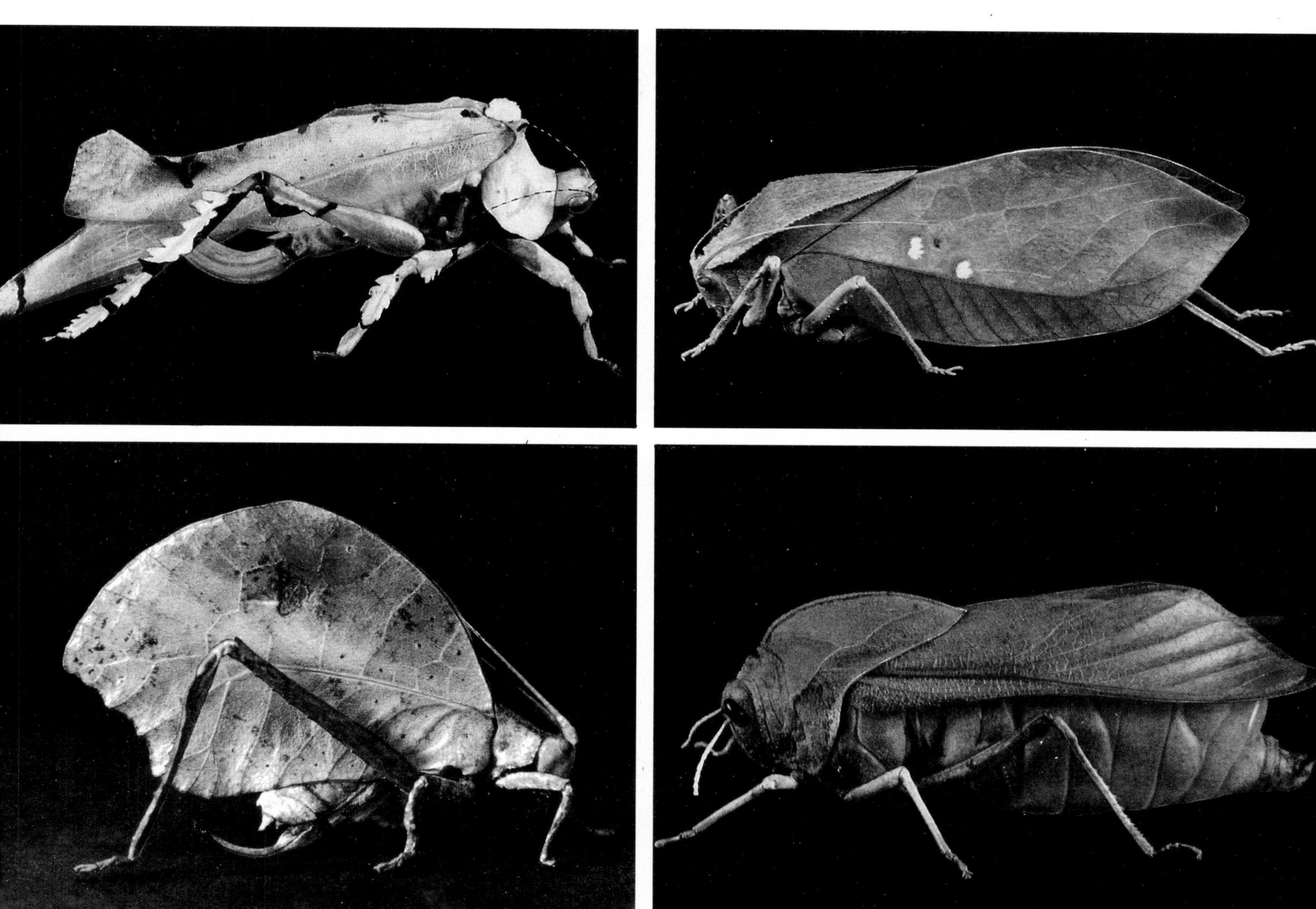

On left:

33/34/35 The three photographs show a male Wart-biter *(Decticus verrucivorus)* from Central Europe in various stages of its grooming process.

36 The Towered or Nosed Grasshopper *(Acrida ungarica)* from southeastern Europe, is remarkable for its curiously elongated head (Caelifera).

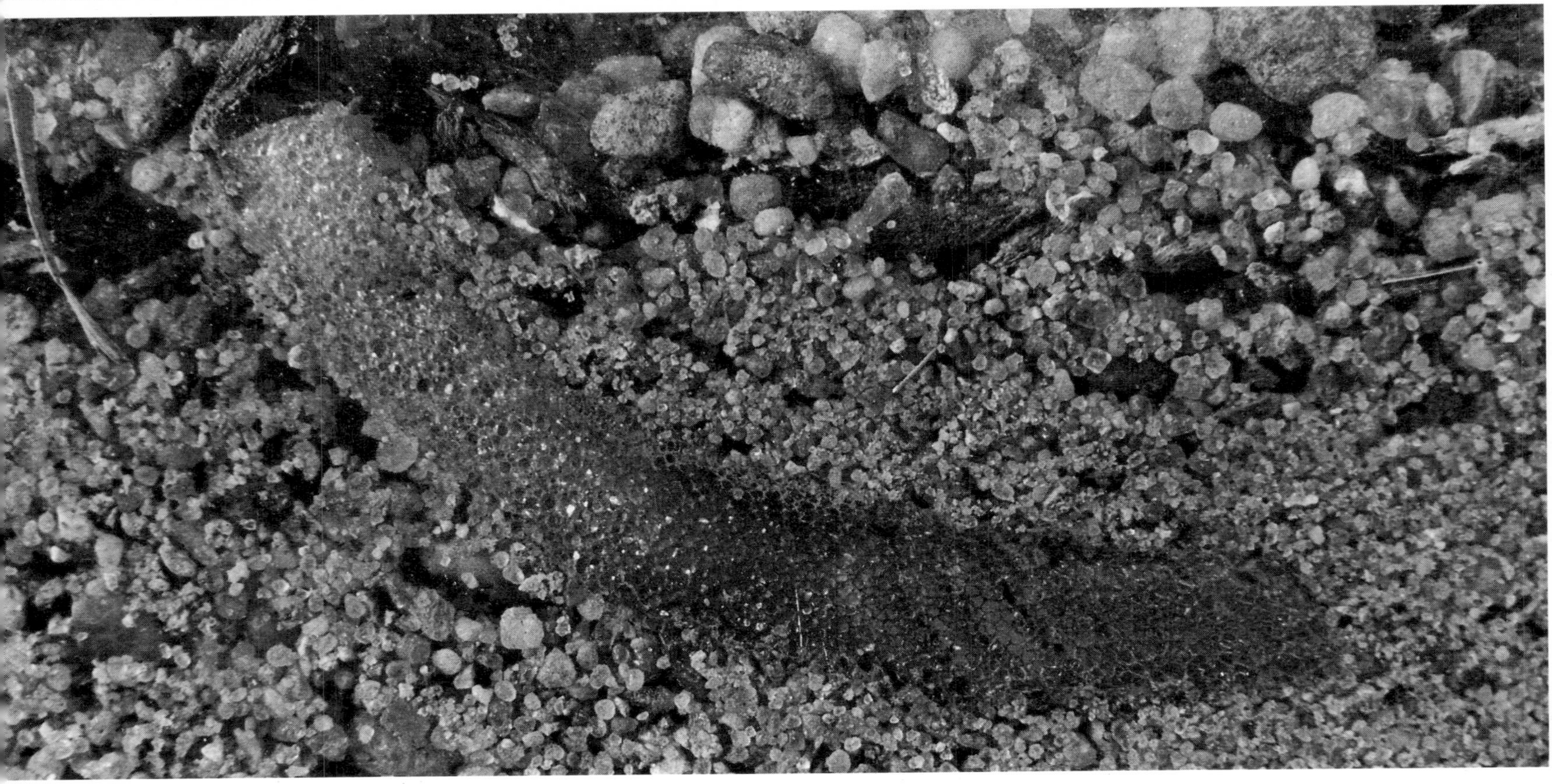

On left:

37 Above: Pair of Migratory Locusts *(Locusta migratoria)*.

38 Below: The egg clutch of a Migratory Locust *(Locusta migratoria)*. The eggs are deposited in the ground in rows.

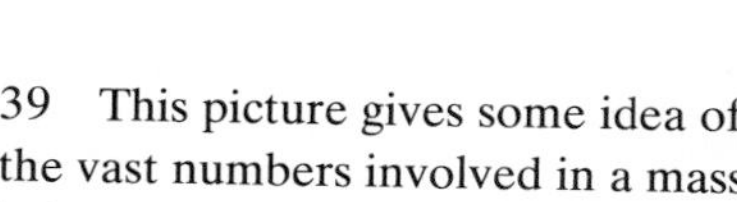

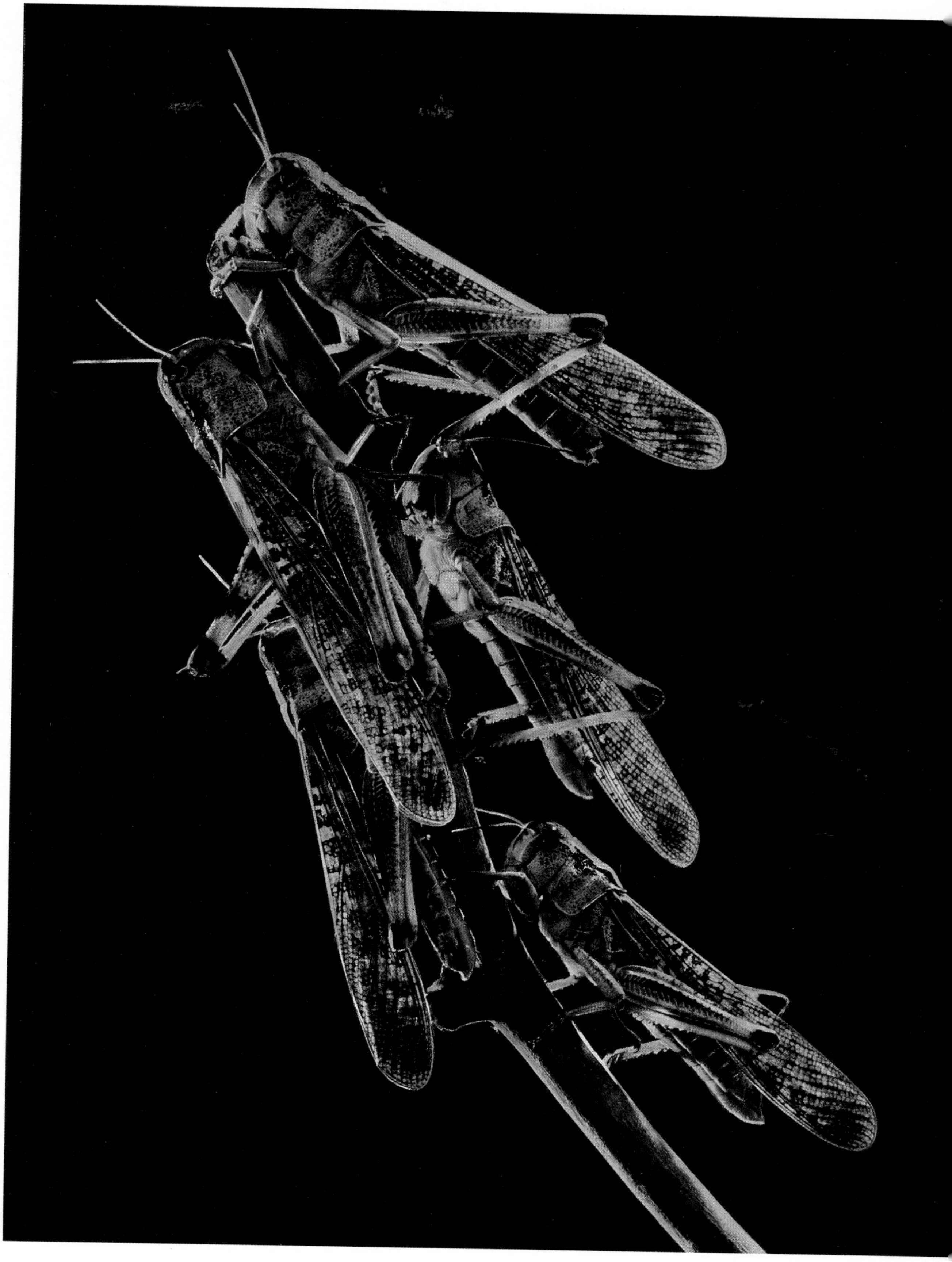

39 This picture gives some idea of the vast numbers involved in a mass infestation of Migratory Locusts.

Following pages:

40 The larva of a locust *(Locusta migratoria)* moults to become an imago (from left to right). At first the dorsal skin tears apart and the moulting locust emerges, then by increasing pressure of the body fluid the wings begin to unfold and stiffen.

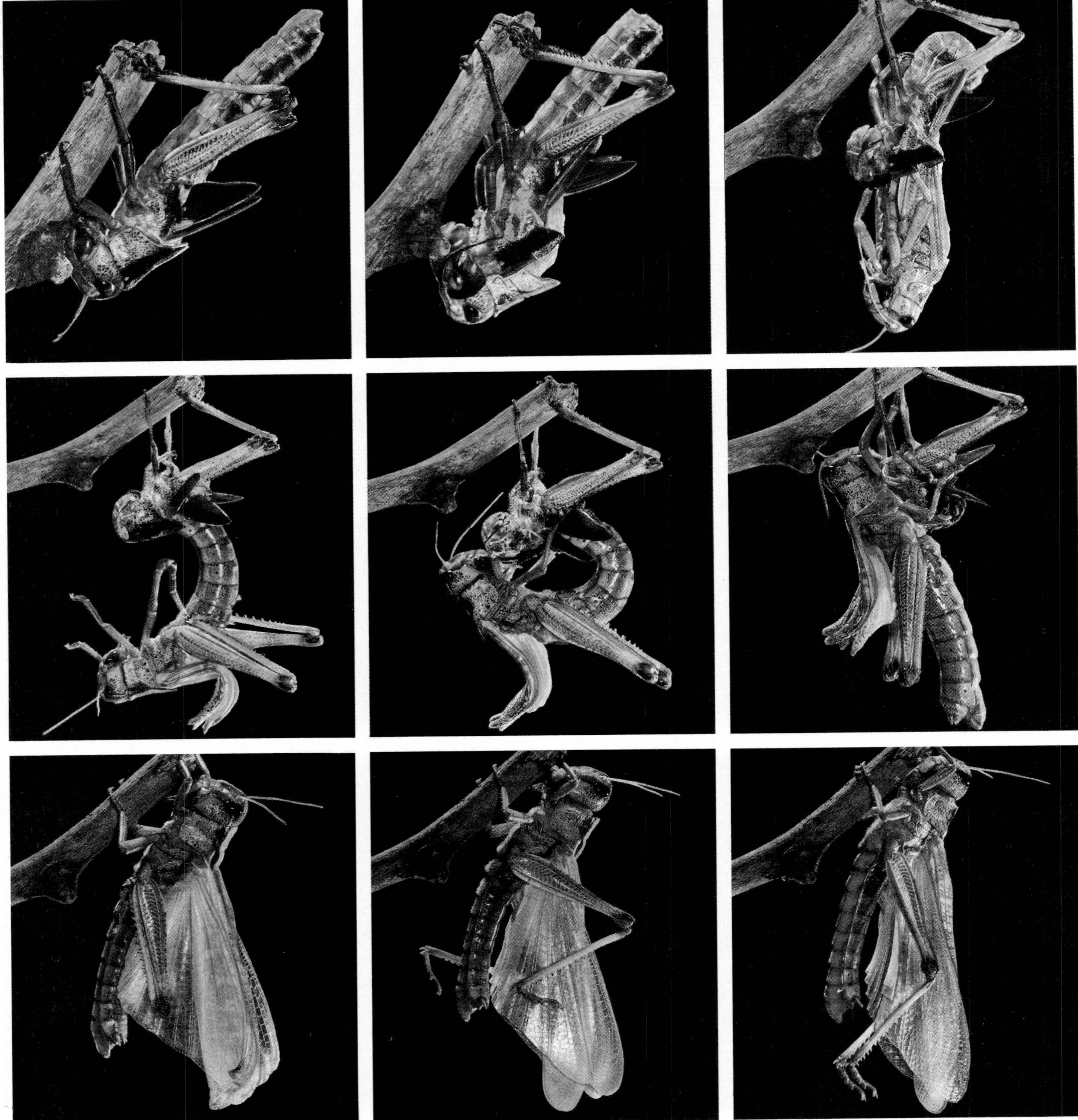

41 Pressed close to the branches are two female Common Stick Insects *(Carausius morosus)* from India. In this species, reproduction is almost exclusively parthenogenetic. Males are seen very rarely.

42 *Baculum extradentatus* of Farther India is a species of Phasmidae with males (left).

On right:

43 Above: Head of *Extatosoma tiaratum*.

44 Below: *Extatosoma tiaratum* is a Leaf Insect (Phasmidae) about 15 cm long, from New Guinea.

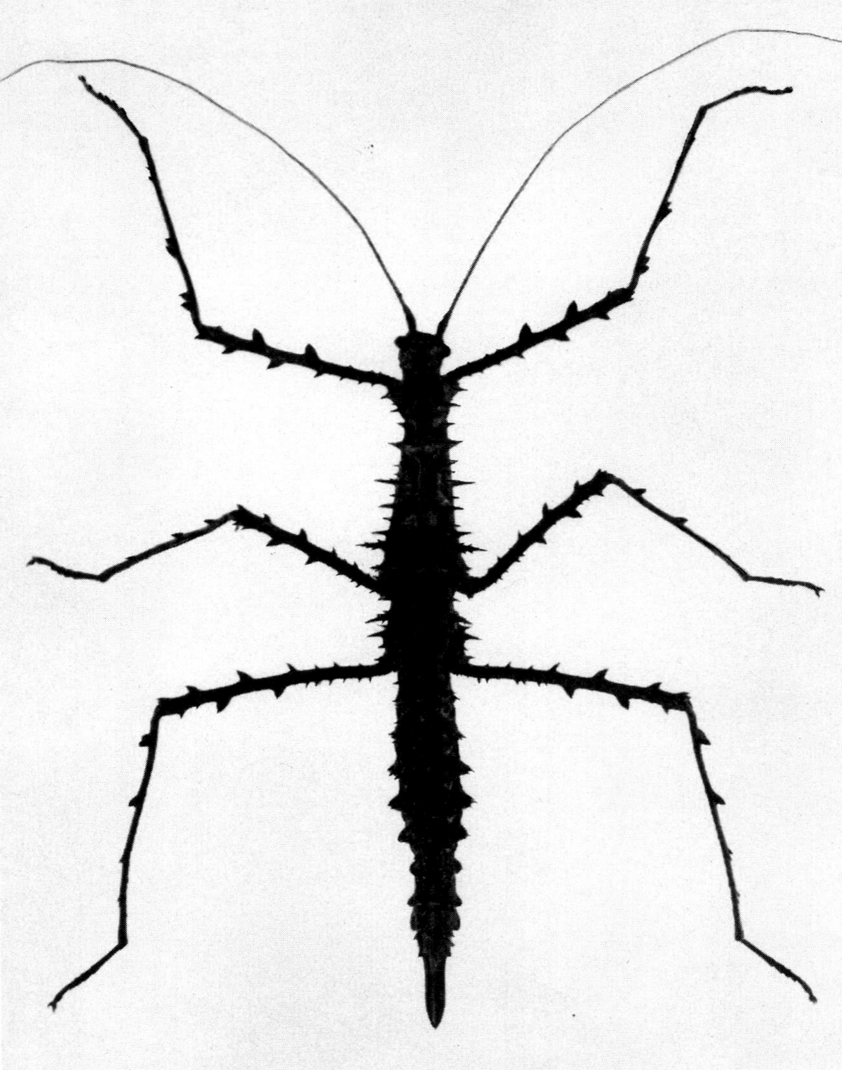

45 Above left: *Eurycantha calcarata* from New Guinea (here a pair of them) is wingless and is distinguished by its many spine-like growths.

46 Above right: The body of *Neopromachus flabellatus* of New Guinea is beset with bizarre cuticular processes.

47 Below: The Moving Leaf *(Phyllium vidifolium)* from East India.

On right:

48 *Phasma reinwardi* from New Guinea is a particularly large Stick Insect. The small wings do not permit free flight. The longest of the Stick Insects, indeed, the longest of all insects, is *Pharnacia serratipes* which can be up to 33 cm in length.

The swarms produced by these eggs began the notorious migration of 1748 which carried them across Hungary and Poland to Germany, on to Holland, England, Scotland and even to the Orkney Islands. Local mass infestations have occasionally developed in the original site, one example of which is the infestation in the Swiss Canton of Valais in the last century."

A passage taken from Dalla Torre describes a swarm in 1338 that was mentioned in at least thirty chronicles. "In the same year, locusts flew from Tartary through Hungary, Austria and all the other German lands. They came into the valleys of the Inn and Adige at Bozen and Innsbruck on August 24. They flew for fourteen days. Their flight began at the hour of the tierce, and ended at the close of the working day. Then they settled and devastated all the fields and pastures, even the vineyards. Sometimes they flew so densely that one could scarcely see the seedlings in the field even in broad daylight. On the Adige, the following happened: the eggs of the locusts were left behind between Bolzano and Kaltharen, so that in the following year, many locusts were seen again."

A report from 1547 runs: "There were so many of them flying that they blotted out the sun; and so many crawling that you could not see the ground; and they have the appearance such as you see here. People caught those on the ground, and citizens and peasants throughout the whole land were ordered to catch them. And that went on for three weeks, and every day, two thousand *sesters* were gathered up, which is the equivalent of a thousand *malters* [a *malter* is an old German corn measure ranging from 1.5 to 12.6 hectolitres]; along a quarter mile of road, there were three hundred people, both women and men, and every hundred people gathered up the quantities described above, and that went on every day for three weeks. May the Lord God be gracious and merciful to us, for the way things are going in the world now, it is like the days of King Pharaoh. Know too, that in Innsbruck, they came across the bridge in such numbers, moving like an army, and tried to force their way in. Then the city authorities gave orders for them to be swept with brooms away from the town into the water, until they covered the whole water. And this also went on for three weeks on the bridge."

On November 30, 1753, Frederick the Great (1712–1786) issued a "Renewed Edict concerning the Destruction of Locusts". Bodenheimer (1929) summarized it thus: "First of all the egg-laying sites should be recorded carefully in autumn and spring. Pigs are to be kept there until the late autumn. Before the onset of winter, they are to be shallow-ploughed with care, and then the pigs are to be put back on them. In addition, every countryman, according to his status, must collect and deliver half to one measure [approximately 3 quarts] of locust-eggs. Eggs handed in over and above the compulsory quantity are to be paid for at 2 groschen per measure. Inhabitants of towns and the neighbouring country district must also participate in all these measures. In the spring, herdsmen and foresters must keep a sharp look-out for emerging young hoppers. Where they appear, ditches are to be dug, in the direction of the prevailing wind, 20–25 strides in length, $2\frac{1}{2}$ foot wide and $1\frac{1}{2}$ foot deep, in which, in turn, pits $1\frac{1}{2}$ foot in depth are to be made every 4–5 strides, across the width of the ditch. At sunrise, a start must be made on driving the hoppers into these ditches . . . 4. As soon as the sun rises and the hatched insects spread out, my subjects must begin to drive the locusts where they are lying scattered about, all the time noting well in which direction they themselves show an inclination to go, since it has been observed that they move not only from east to west, but also with the wind; so the run of the ditch and the direction of driving must be adapted accordingly, otherwise no progress will be made with the drive, and the locusts would rather let themselves be trampled underfoot than be forced to take a different direction. In the ditches, they collect in the prepared pits or are swept together there, stamped down and covered with soil. New pits are hollowed out in between the old, and the drive is continued. The organization of these groups of drivers is set down in detail. In order to combat the flying locusts,

49 The first larval instar of *Extatosoma tiaratum*.

particularly on overcast days, pigs and turkeys are to be put into the field . . . 14. Furthermore, we require that, in accordance with the Edict of November 24, 1752, the mayors of those villages in which locusts have been seen should report to the District Administrator every 14 days, informing him whether eggs have remained lying on their land, whether progeny have been left on their fields, whether and for how many days our subjects have searched for progeny, how many young have been found and to whom they have delivered them. Similarly, how much land they have ploughed up because of infestation, how much fallow land they have broken and how much cultivated or fallow land they intend to plough up before winter for the purpose of eliminating the insects. All of this will be examined by the District Administrator when he visits the area, and should it be discovered that all those measures that were ordered have not been everywhere carried out, he must immediately report the same to the Office of the Commissioners of War and of the Domains, so that contraventions may be punished accordingly."

The swarms of locusts even made their way to England in, for example, the years 804, 1542(?), 1684 and 1748. The number of known locust years in Germany was 16 from 1301-1400; one from 1401–1500; 7 from 1501–1600; 9 from 1601–1700; 21 from 1701–1750; in all 54. Numbers are higher after 1700 because by then, records were much more accurate and included quite small outbreaks, whereas the earlier sources covered only major catastrophes or else have survived only as fragments. Records exist for 134 locust years in Europe, but the probable total is nearer 400. The major locust migrations in Germany were in 593, 873–875, 1337–1339, 1542–1543, 1693 and 1747–1749. Serious infestations of locusts are reported from Saxony in 875, 1338, 1475, 1501, 1541–1542, 1546, 1623, 1659, 1661, 1680, 1693–1695, 1728–1731, 1748 and 1875. The last swarm in Germany was observed in Brandenburg in 1883.

In Africa, there were 40 locust years between 1910 and 1970. Between 1949 and 1963 infestation continued without a break. In 1958, in Ethiopia alone, the major African species of migratory locust *Schistocera gregaria* destroyed enough grain to have fed a million people for an entire year.

The Mole Cricket *(Gryllotalpa gryllotalpa)*

The fore-tibiae of the mole cricket are modified into remarkably efficient digging shovels with which the creatures excavate their subterranean passages. Associated with this, the prothorax, containing the muscles that operate this tool, is very large (the cricket is sometimes known as the "ground crab", German *Erdkrebs*). Another peculiarity of the mole cricket is that the females are also capable of stridulation. In this, however, they are restricted to a short warning call, which the males also use when alarmed, especially when they are disturbed during courtship. The female ovipositor is vestigial. Mole crickets feed primarily on earthworms and insect larvae that they find while digging in the soil. But young roots and embryo plants are also eaten. Crop damage was reported as early as 1718, in the *Schlesische Heimatkunde* (Local History and Geography of Silesia), "caused by the *Werren* which are commonly found in Silesia this month. They are particularly injurious to fields of barley and flax. Their natural enemy is the hoopoe. They occur in particularly large numbers with early heat and drought." The dialect name *Werre* for mole cricket is widespread in that region, and probably explains the appearance of a mole cricket in the coat of arms of the Austrian family Wernberger. In his *Fauna Suecica*, Linnaeus observes: "Particularly in the gardens in Schonen, the mole cricket eats vegetables to such an extent that every year the gardeners suffer serious losses." Today, any damage is only local and insignificant and the species has become progressively rarer.

The Zurich physician Johann de Muralto (1718) provides us with a description, with illustrations, of the digestive tract and the gizzard. It was the age of anatomical dissection of insects and on account of its size, the mole cricket proved an ideal subject. "Within the abdomen, behind the oesophagus, we find a pear-shaped bladder containing a viscous, earthy, oily liquid. This bladder is none other than the stomach, which is surrounded by innumerable lacteal vessels. On account of the air contained therein, and following the recommendation of Pythagoras, we have subsequently had to consider the latter as tracheae. We observed a further folded and denticulate stomach as in ruminants. The end of the gut continues downwards in a straight run, abundantly furnished with tracheae."

Even today, in school biology lessons, the mole cricket and the mole are compared and interpreted as an example of convergent evolution. It is not surprising to find that the roots of this comparison are very old. They go back to the Italian physician Ferrante Imperato, who in 1599, in a paper entitled *An Insect Similar to the Mole*, writes: "The mole, from which the name of the insect is borrowed, is a black mammal of subterranean habit. The eyes are not discernable externally, but exist indistinctly beneath the skin. It has no voice. The legs are naked and as a consequence of living underground, are very suitable for digging in the soil. The insect illustrated here is very similar in the structure of the legs and in the subterranean mode of life . . . it is greatly hated by gardeners on account of the damage it causes by eating the roots of plants. If driven out of the soil, it burrows down into it again rapidly using its legs. It is particularly fond of rich and damp earth."

"We classify the Gryllotalpa as one of the crickets, because it has in common with these the habit of nocturnal stridulation, and call it mole because it burrows constantly. It cannot be numbered among the beetles since it has no elytra. It is four times the size of the largest Cantharide, particularly when it is adult . . . It spends the greater part of its life in marshy or damp ground, but at night comes to the surface of the soil. It is a very slow creature and its capacity for flight is as poor as that for jumping, for which reason nobody considers it to be a grasshopper . . . It amasses grains of wheat, barley and oats as food for the winter." These are the words of Thomas Moufet.

In fact, these large and ungainly-looking insects are able to fly, although their flight is restricted and scarcely elegant. The organs of flight are the hind wings which, when at rest, are rolled up lengthwise and partly covered by the short forewings. To the human ear, the mating song of the male is difficult to locate. The females follow the call and, under the soil, climb on to the male's back for mating. In *Gryllotalpa vinea*, a species of mole cricket living in France, the male constructs a smooth-walled funnel-shaped burrow with double openings which act as "loud-speakers" to amplify the sounds. The song is audible for up to 500 m.

In Caspar Schwenckfeld's *Theriotropheum Silesiae*, we read: "Werre, Twäre. The name comes from the high-pitched sound, audible from afar, which it emits in summer, especially during the night. It is an oviparous insect of the family of crickets, as long and thick-bodied as one's ring-finger. The fore-part resembles a river crayfish, the hind part a cricket. The pest is particularly common in barley and flax fields, which it burrows through and lays waste in the manner of moles. It is

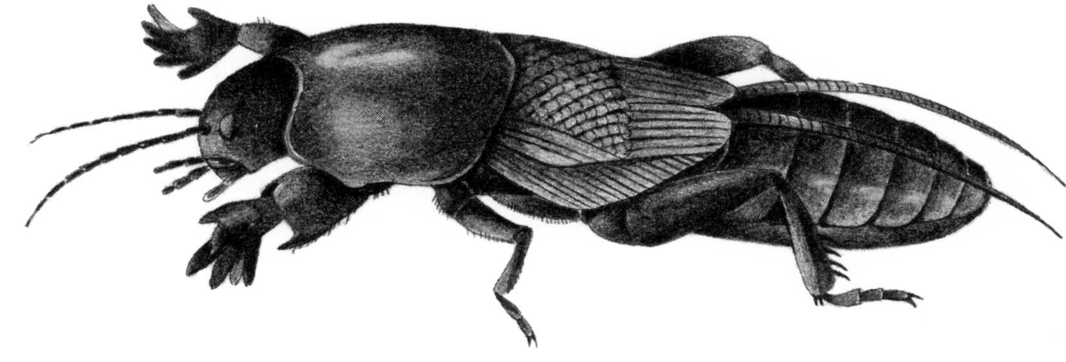

Female Mole Cricket *(Gryllotalpa gryllotalpa)*; the stout thorax, the forelegs modified for digging and other features show it to be well adapted to a subterranean life.

hated by farmers. The winged insect makes furrows when it crawls out of the soil. It consumes roots entirely, and likewise the outer layer of many plants . . . It builds its nest in the earth. The eggs are yellowish. It is vocal, particularly at night. In spring, the peasants listen out for its voice, for they rarely entrust the barley to the ground before its chirp is heard. Hoopoes eat them and feed them to their young. The head, worn round the neck, cures fever."

The phenological reference to the sowing date for barley is interesting. Observations of nature of this kind held a much greater significance in earlier times than they do today. In the *Erh Ya* of Pu Shang (born 507 B.C.), a pupil of Confucius, the sound of the mole cricket is used to determine the season.

Experiments which were cruel and pointless, but noteworthy as entirely typical of the period are described by Jean Goedart (1620–1668), a Dutch painter and keen entomologist, who bred and illustrated 140 species of insects, thereby contributing significantly to the sum of knowledge about insects at that time. "I called this insect a mole cricket because it has a share of the characters of both. It is very strong and tenacious and does not die easily. It seems as if one can rob it of life only by force. After its head had been torn off, it stayed alive for another 12 hours. I once kept one suspended on a thread in the sun for 6 days and 6 nights, and only on the seventh day did it die, blackened and scorched. Their diligence in building their nests is admirable. For this purpose, they choose a firm piece of soil in which they construct an opening as the entrance and exit. Inside, they excavate a cavity about the size of two nuts, and there they conceal up to 100, sometimes up to 150 eggs. When they have laid all their eggs, they close the opening. Round them they build galleries in which they walk and keep watch. They make various other holes in the earth in which they can hide if necessary. In addition, they are so diligent that, when the weather is fine, they will remove the outer soil above the nest to a depth of two fingers, so that the sun will help their eggs to hatch. People try to catch them with small pots which they sink into the soil, and out of which the insects cannot climb. They can also be removed by destroying the eggs in the nest."

The description of the egg cavity constructed by the female at a depth of 5 to 25 cm is an apt one. Each female prepares several nests with a total of some 500 eggs. Nest-building behaviour and egg-laying behaviour are clearly linked. If the nest is damaged before the eggs are laid, the female builds a new nest. If it is destroyed afterwards, it is not repaired.

The Field Cricket *(Gryllus campestris)*

Writing about a journey he made to North Africa, Thomas Shaw (1692–1751), a professor from Oxford, speaks of the "cicada", by which he means the Field Cricket *(Gryllus campestris)*. "In the hotter months of the summer, especially from mid-day to the middle of the afternoon, the cicada is perpetually stunning our ears with its most excessively shrill and ungrateful noise. It is in this respect the most troublesome and impertinent of insects, perching upon a twig, and squalling sometimes two or three hours without ceasing; thereby too often disturbing the studies or the short repose that is frequently indulged in these hot climates at those hours. The *tettix* of the Greeks must have had a quite different voice, more soft surely and melodious; otherwise the fine orators of Homer, who are compared to it, can be looked upon no better than so many loquacious scolds."

In Ancient China, the song of the cricket was particularly highly esteemed. The insects were often kept in bamboo cages which people wore suspended from their belt. Many of these cricket cages were richly ornamented, precious works of art made of sandalwood, jade or ivory, patterned with dragons and flowers. Special diets, sometimes in the form of pre-chewed food, were devised for the insects. An account written between A.D. 742 and 756 runs: "When autumn comes, the ladies of the palace collect crickets and put them into golden cages. They place the cages beside their pillows and listen to the voice of the insects during the night."

A popular sport in Ancient China was cricket fighting. The crickets that were to fight were fattened on special food and given a tonic before the fight. Large sums of money were wagered and passions ran high; it is said that successful crickets were as valuable as good horses. The crickets even had titles (Shu lip = victorious cricket). Reports tell of such crickets being given a ceremonial burial in a silver funeral casket. Cricket fights were especially fashionable at the time of the Sung Dynasty (960–1278), but even today, events of this kind are not unknown in Japan and also in Florence. It is said that grasshopper traders still existed in Hamburg even after the 17th century.

The insects, sold in small cages, will undoubtedly have been able to delight the customers with their song only for a very short time. The conditions in which the grasshoppers were kept and the approaching chill of autumn probably soon put an end to their brief life.

Each of the two forewings of crickets possesses both a stridulatory vein and a stridulatory "file". Usually the right forewing lies over the left (only 5 per cent are "left-winged"). If one places the insect's left forewing over the right, the male so treated continues to stridulate, but less successfully than before, and it attempts to re-establish the normal position—right forewing on top—as soon as possible. A male cricket stridulates approximately 40,000 times in four hours. It can be proved experimentally, using sound equipment, that the females perceive the male through their sense of hearing and not, for example, by the sense of smell. If the tympanal (auditory) organs of the female are experimentally destroyed, she remains indifferent to the stridulations of a male even in the immediate vicinity. If only one of the two organs of hearing is destroyed, she will approach the stridulating male, but this time no longer in a straight line, but by a roundabout route. When a female appears in response to the male's mating call, the male turns his hind end towards her and moves his forewings considerably more rapidly than hitherto, producing a much more gentle stridulation at a far higher pitch. Stimulated by this, the female mounts the male and the latter curves his abdomen upwards so that mating can take place. Again, the sperm is contained in a spermatophore. After mating, the male pursues the female to prevent her from consuming the spermatophore before the sperm has been discharged. She does so as soon as the male has moved away. Mating may be repeated several times. Before each copulation, a new highly elaborate spermatophore must be constructed. In *Gryllus campestris*, this takes only a few hours.

Crickets display a distinct diurnal rhythm in their song. They begin at mid-morning and there is an interval at noon-time. Towards evening, stridulation becomes progressively more regular and lasts until after midnight.

Thomas Moufet shows a distinctly critical attitude, particularly concerning the production of sound. "According to Pliny, sound is produced by the wings being rubbed together, and indeed, our apothecary Jacob Garett was able, in his meticulous way, to imitate the chirping by rubbing the wings together. Therefore I am surprised that Scaliger, an erudite scholar, should attribute it to a cavity or passage in the abdomen. Salinus attributes it to a clashing of the teeth, as Pliny had already claimed, wrongly, for grasshoppers. When their wings are pressed close to their body on account of the narrowness of their cave, a gentle noise is produced; but outside where they can move their wings easily, a very loud stridulation. Without moving their wings, they cannot stridulate at all. By cutting off or pulling off the wings, it is easy enough to convince oneself that all stridulation ceases. When the sun shines warmly, which they much enjoy, but also at night, they stridulate outside their holes. On meadows and pasture lands, they often do not like to be in shaded or densely overgrown places . . . The further away from us they are, the more loudly do they stridulate, while those sitting nearby remain silent and withdraw into their holes. According to Albertus, there is a cricket which remains alive for a long time and goes on chirping even when

On a cold and frosty day, a cricket visited her neighbour, the ant.
"Good neighbour," said she, "please lend me some food. I am hungry
and have nothing to eat."
"But did you not gather food for the winter?" asked the ant. "I had no time to do so" was
the answer. "No time, Mistress Cricket, what did you have to do in the summer?"
"I sang and made music," answered the cricket. "Very well then," pronounced the ant,
"since you made music all summer, you may dance all winter. Anyone who
does not work will not eat either."

Martin Luther (1483–1546)

it is dissected or its head crushed. If this is true, it probably originates from the abdominal cavity to which Scaliger attributes all stridulation. The boys catch them by introducing an ant tied to a hair into the hole, having first removed any dust so that the crickets cannot hide themselves, and they pull them out together with the ant which has seized them. A faster, less troublesome method of catching them is as follows: insert a long, thin stick or straw into the hole and draw them out with it; once outside, they begin to leap immediately. For this reason, we use the phrase 'more stupid than a cricket' for anyone who shows himself easily to his enemies or runs into every ambush. They feed on fresh millet, ripe grain and apples."

Twenty-eight muscles of the mesothorax are involved in stridulation, in a pattern of movement directed by the mesothoracic ganglion, so that in experiments, crickets can actually stridulate when they are headless. As children, we used to entice crickets from their holes with a blade of grass by a method that never failed. One only had to make sure in advance that there was a male sitting outside the hole.

The former rector of the Graues Kloster (Grey Monastery) in Berlin, Johann Leonhard Frisch (1666–1743), describes an interesting way of expelling House Crickets *(Acheta domesticus)*. "Field Crickets are very quarrelsome among themselves. This natural incompatibility among Field Crickets provides a means of driving out House Crickets. If one introduces one or several of these "wild" crickets into a room where House Crickets are proving troublesome, the wild ones drive out the others within a few days and afterwards, they themselves also disappear."

Male crickets are especially intolerant of one another. If they meet in the open, they produce a shrill "warning song". If the intrusive male refuses to retreat in face of the established resident of a burrow, fighting and "rivalry song" follow. Inside narrow containers, the insects will kill one another.

Crickets usually deposit their eggs singly in the ground. In *Gryllus campestris*, embryonic development lasts about 2 weeks. After this, the larvae hatch and go through 10 to 12 moults before reaching the imaginal stage. But they do not achieve this within a single year. In the penultimate nymphal instar or even the antepenultimate, the nymph prepares a subterranean burrow some 40 cm long in the soil, sloping fairly steeply to a depth of about 30 cm. At the bottom of this, it spends the period of hibernation in which its vital functions are reduced to some 10 per cent of normal. The final moult occurs in the following spring.

It is not surprising that such conspicuous insects should have been used as medicaments. However, any successes must have been based on purely psychological effects. In the 16th century Adam Lonicer writes: "Crickets, also known as House Crickets. Grillus is useful in cases of discharging ears, if it is dug up together with its soil and applied. For kidney stone and other bladder pains, the cricket should be washed in hot water and consumed."

Edward Wotton remarks: "According to Nigidius, the cricket has a particular magic power because it walks backwards, burrows into soil and sings at night . . . It is good for earache if it is dug out together with the soil and applied to the ear. They can also be used to alleviate pain in the tonsils by touching the tonsils with hands that have crushed crickets."

The House Cricket
(Acheta domesticus)

The House Cricket is of a more slender and delicate build than the Field Cricket. It also differs in that its colouring is lighter and its hind wings, when folded lengthwise in the resting position, protrude beyond the covering wings. In Central Europe, this heat-loving species lives almost exclusively in cellars, houses, bakeries and so on, although it is occasionally found in warm places outdoors, particularly on rubbish dumps. In southern Europe, it is commonly found in the open. The sequence of generations for outdoor species always requires a full year; in human habitations, it is not dependent upon seasons and in warm places such as bakeries, may be significantly shorter. Crickets are said to bring good luck to a house. It was probably the nocturnal song of the males that earned them this reputation, although many people find the noise disturbs their rest. This is the insect that inspired a poem by the German poet Friedrich Rückert (1788–1866) and a story "The Cricket on the Hearth" by Charles Dickens (1812–1870).

Albertus Magnus already distinguishes between Field and House Crickets. "The cicada, of which there are two species, one which chirps in the house and one which chirps on shrubs and herbs." Of the House Cricket, Caspar Schwenckfeld writes: "House Cricket: these are light yellow grasshoppers, similar to cicadas. Two delicate hair-like lashes protrude from under the eyes. Of the six legs, the hind pair is the longest . . . two long, pointed, bristly appendages project from the hind end . . . In winter, they sit on the walls of chimney mantels, hearths and stoves, and make themselves more than irksome by their nocturnal chirping. Yet there are those who find their song a pleasant soporific." On the two abdominal appendages (cerci) mentioned by Schwenckfeld, there are special auditory hairs in addition to tactile hairs and shank hairs that permit the perception of gravity.

"House Crickets with their chirping and calling are a troublesome thing in the house for a landlord, since they often fall into the food and drink of men and animals. They can be expelled as follows: Take some carrots, cook them and add Arsenicum; spread them in the crevices, cracks and holes in which the crickets are located, and so they will die. But take good care that no one else eats any of it. In winter, a bundle of pea-straw can also be placed in the room and they will all crawl eagerly into it. Afterwards, carry it out into the cold or the snow, and they will soon grow numb and die of cold, for they cannot tolerate the cold. That is why they always remain close to the stove." (Johann Colerus, *Household Book*, 1590)

A cricket, drawn by Adam Lonicer.

Stick Insects and Leaf Insects

(Phasmatodea)

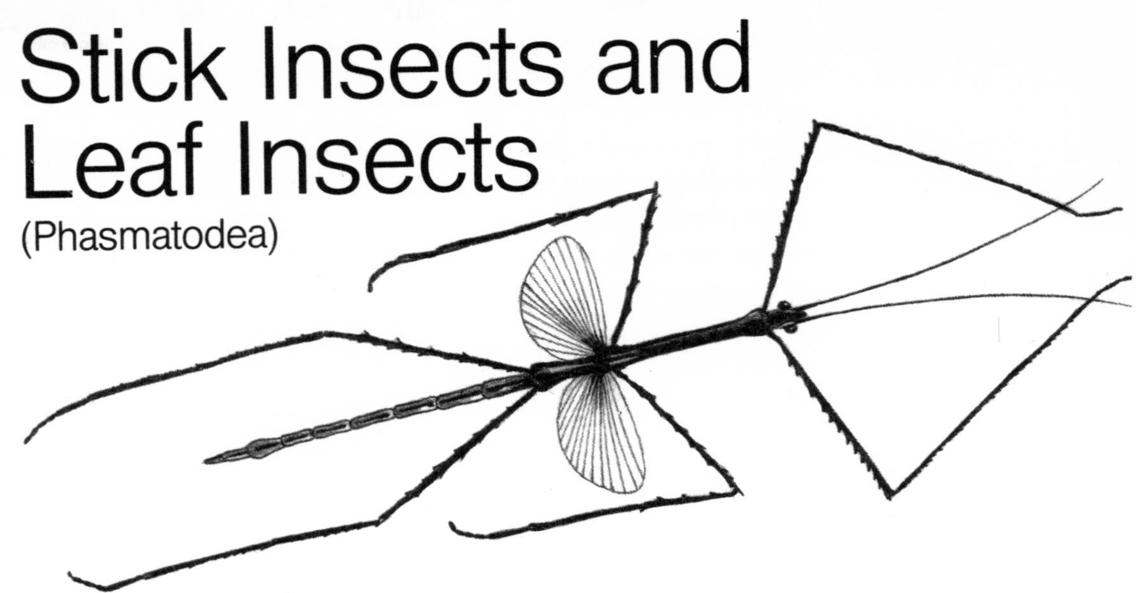

The Phasmatodea occur in three distinct forms: slender, rod-like (Stick Insects or Walking Sticks); broad, leaf-like (Leaf Insects) and short, stout creatures. The Phasmids are considered as large or very large insects. With a body length of 33–35 cm, certain Phasmids are the longest of all recent insect species.

The females of the Malayan Giant Stick Insect *(Heteropteryx dilatata)* show specific threatening behaviour. When they are alarmed, they hold the powerful hind legs, that are heavily furnished with thorn-like spines, extended towards the source of disturbance. If an enemy approaches, the "shin" of the leg snaps sharply against the "thigh", like a jack-knife, and the intruder may be nipped painfully. In addition, the wings are moved to produce a hissing sound. The male "threatens" by displaying its wine-red hind wings, thus achieving the effect of a sudden increase in body size.

The phenomenon of catalepsy is remarkable. It is a condition of immobility in which the muscles are fully relaxed. The state can readily be induced by allowing a Stick Insect to fall or by handling it roughly. During catalepsy, the limbs can be moved into any position and this will be maintained until the insect "wakes up".

Most of the Stick Insects described so far are natives of the tropics, while there are far fewer subtropical species. Two species, *Bacillus rossius* and *Bacillus gallicus*, live in southern Europe and North Africa. None occurs in Central Europe, although certain species are sometimes kept as pets or as laboratory animals, and many of these live for a long time. The Indian Stick Insect, *Carausius morosus*, which grows to a length of 7 to 8 cm, is the species most usually kept in Europe. The eggs are simply dropped to the ground, and 13 to 20 weeks elapse before the larvae hatch. A large number of different plants are suitable as food, those preferred being the leaves of dog-rose, lime, raspberry, blackberry, privet, dead nettle, ivy and spiderwort. After 4 to 5 months and 5 to 6 moults, the insects are sexually mature. The females live for 6 to 12 months. They lay some 200 to 450 hard-shelled eggs. Reproduction is almost exclusively parthenogenetic. Males occur rather rarely; they are smaller (5.5 cm), more slender and the hind legs project beyond the abdomen. The literature contains several reports of breeding from "fertilized" *Carausius* eggs, which, however, produced exclusively females. The species *Sipyloidea sipylus*, native to Assam, Java, Sumatra and the Molucca Islands, is larger (9 cm) than *Carausius morosus*. The adults are winged and are light in colour. The hind wings are a delicate rose pink, and permit the insect a short, fluttering

Above:

The Stick Insect *Pharnacia serratipes* is up to 33 cm in length.

flight. Only females occur in this species. The eggs are not dropped but attached to a suitable material such as pieces of bark or timber, twigs or cardboard. *Baculum extradentatus* from Indochina is a comparatively large Stick Insect in which males and females occur approximately in the ratio 1:1. The males are distinctly smaller (7.0–7.5 cm) and much thinner than the females (9.0–9.5 cm). As in *Carausius morosus*, the eggs are allowed to fall unheeded to the ground. A striking feature is the swaying gait, caused mainly by the very long legs. The forelegs are almost as long as the entire body.

One of the most impressive figures among the Phasmids is *Extatosoma tiaratum*, which is remarkable for its large size (female up to 15 cm, male up to 10 cm in length) and bizarre appearance. Unlike the females, the males are fully winged. *Extatosoma tiaratum* comes from New Zealand and Australia. Great heat and high humidity are essential for hatching the eggs, which are produced in large numbers (up to 400 eggs per female).

In contrast to the above-mentioned species, *Anisomorpha buprestoides* of Florida has a decidedly unassuming outward appearance. It is smaller than *Carausius morosus* (female 8 cm, male 5 cm in length), dark brown, but interesting and not altogether harmless, since the imagines can eject a poisonous secretion from glands on the front of the pronotum at a distance of 30 to 50 cm. If this comes into contact with the handler's eyes, it can cause a sharp, unpleasant burning sensation. The couple remain in the copulatory position until they die. The female's abdomen becomes markedly distended by the many eggs which are then laid in large numbers.

Sucking Lice

(Anoplura)

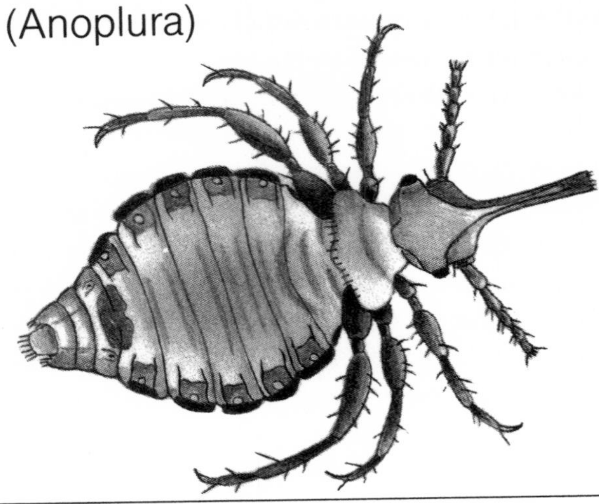

Greek writers tell how Homer died of anger because he was unable to solve a riddle. On the island of Jos, some fishermen met him, who, when questioned about their catch, replied: "What we caught, we left behind, what we failed to catch, we bring with us." Homer applied this riddle to the catching of fish, and was unable to puzzle out the meaning. The answer is: lice.

Lice are included among the plagues imposed upon the Egyptians by Moses and Aaron during the Exodus. "Stretch out thy rod, and smite the dust of the land, that it may become lice throughout all the land of Egypt. And they did so; . . . and it became lice in man, and in beast; all the dust of the land became lice throughout all the land of Egypt." (Exodus, Ch. 8, 16–17) These events have been represented pictorially several times; the copperplate engraving by Israhel van Meckenem (1440–1503) is particularly famous.

According to the Talmud, the louse is created out of sweat and not by the usual reproductive processes. Nits were seen as appertaining to lice, but not recognized as their eggs. Lice were also acknowledged to be carriers of disease (contagious leprosy), in itself a considerable discovery for that time. Head lice were combed out and killed directly on the comb. An instruction runs: "Kill the louse and let me hear the cracking of my enemy." Regular changing of clothing is recommended as a means of dealing with body lice.

Lice, especially body lice, transmit various diseases. A particularly dangerous, indeed often fatal one, is epidemic typhus, caused by the micro-organism *Rickettsia prowazeki*. Infection probably occurs primarily as a result of louse faeces and crushed lice being rubbed into the skin. During and after the First World War, this disease claimed several million lives. The discovery of DDT at the end of the Second World War prevented what might well have been a disastrous typhus epidemic. Later, the body louse virtually disappeared in Europe. In recent years, the head louse has made an appearance surprisingly frequently, although the reasons for this are still not clear. Another Rickettsia *(R. quintana)*, which causes trench fever (Wolhynia or quintan fever) is transmitted by lice in a similar way to typhus. In the case of relapsing or recurrent fever (vector: *Spirochaeta recurrentis*), transmission is the result of crushed lice being rubbed into small skin lesions. It is not surprising that very early sources state that the louse comes into being by spontaneous generation from dust or sweat. Clarification of its biology came much later. The eggs (nits) are attached by the female usually to clothing material, using a cement-like substance that ensures firm adhesion. They have a lid, the structure of which is characteristic of each species. The louse

Above:

Elephant Lice (sub-order Rhynchophthirina), of which there are only two species (genus *Haematomyzus*), are found on both species of elephant and on warthogs. The mouthparts are adapted to pierce the tough, rough-textured elephant hide.

The forelegs of the male Body Louse (right) are distinctly curved, enabling it to maintain a firm hold on the hind legs of the female during copulation and also to attach itself securely to hairs.

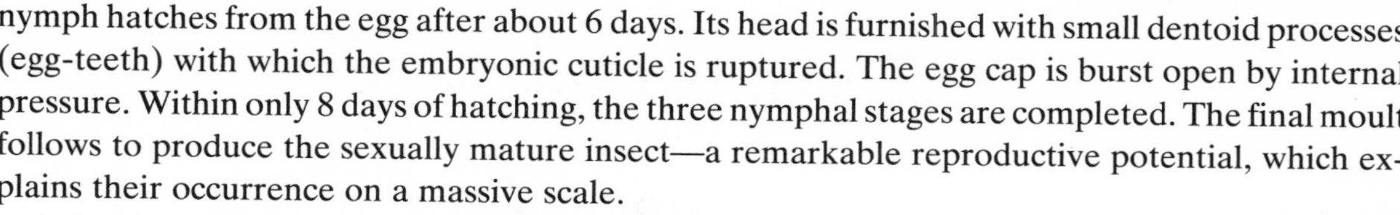

nymph hatches from the egg after about 6 days. Its head is furnished with small dentoid processes (egg-teeth) with which the embryonic cuticle is ruptured. The egg cap is burst open by internal pressure. Within only 8 days of hatching, the three nymphal stages are completed. The final moult follows to produce the sexually mature insect—a remarkable reproductive potential, which explains their occurrence on a massive scale.

Aristotle's acquaintance with the life-cycle of the louse was limited. He writes that nothing develops from the nits that are produced by copulation. In his view, lice are generated out of the flesh of animals. He writes: "When lice are coming there is a kind of small eruption visible, unaccompanied by any discharge of purulent matter; and, if you prick an animal when in this condition at the spot of eruption, the lice jump out." He considers lice to have been responsible for the death in Syria in the 6th century B.C. of the poets Alcman and Pherecydes. And he writes that those people who are frequently troubled by lice rarely suffer from headaches. Aristotle also speaks of lice on animals. "And lice are generated in other animals than man. For birds are infested with them; and pheasants, unless they clean themselves in the dust, are actually destroyed by them. All other winged animals that are furnished with feathers are similarly infested, and all hair-coated creatures also, with the single exception of the ass, which is infested neither with lice nor with ticks. Cattle suffer both from lice and from ticks. Sheep and goats breed ticks, but do not breed lice. Pigs breed lice large and hard. In dogs are found the flea peculiar to the animal, the *Cynoroestes*."

To this, one should note that sucking lice occur exclusively on mammals. What is said about "bird lice" refers to Mallophaga (biting lice). In general, lice show considerable host-specificity. Although some 300 species of lice have so far been described, not all groups of mammals are affected. Monotremes, marsupials, bats, whales, bears, martens, cats and hedgehogs have no sucking lice. They occur most frequently on ungulates and rodents. The louse *Haematopinus asini* is found on the donkey and the horse (Aristotle was mistaken here), *H. eurysternus* and *Linognathus vituli* on cattle, *H. suis* on pigs. The louse parasitic on dogs is *Linognathus setosus*. A second error: the goat (like the chamois) is host to the louse *L. stenopsis*.

Kamal al-Din al-Damiri had a good deal to say about lice. For example: "It is in the nature of the louse to be red when on red hair, black when on black, white on white, and when the hair changes colour, their colour also changes." This statement is incorrect, but it suggests that the head lice of different races show morphological differences. "It is a creature in which the females are larger than the males." In lice, as in most insects, the females are in fact the larger. "Lice occur on chickens and pigeons and infest monkeys." Monkeys are indeed host to lice.

But what follows is mere legend. "As for the monkey louse, it occurs in mountainous country. Its bite is fatal. It is the largest of the lice." "If anyone wants to know whether a woman with child is carrying a boy or a girl, let him take a louse and press a little of her milk over the louse in the hand. If the louse emerges from the milk, she is carrying a girl, but if it does not emerge, she is carrying a boy." They are also recommended for medicinal use. "For a patient suffering from urine retention, take a louse and introduce it into the urethra; he will then urinate at that time. If a woman washes the roots of her hair with beetroot water, it will keep lice away." Obviously lice were so common at that time that they even entered people's dreams, and such dreams were interpreted by Kamal al-Din al-Damiri as follows: "Lice in a dream found on a new shirt mean riches. Large numbers of lice signify illness and imprisonment. Anyone who dreams he is a louse is slandering someone. Who kills lice in a dream will defeat his enemies."

Here one might add that among certain tribes of South American Indians, the eating of lice is customary. The Indians eat their own lice as well as those of nearby members, collecting them reciprocally from each other's body. This is interpreted as absorbing part of the other's soul.

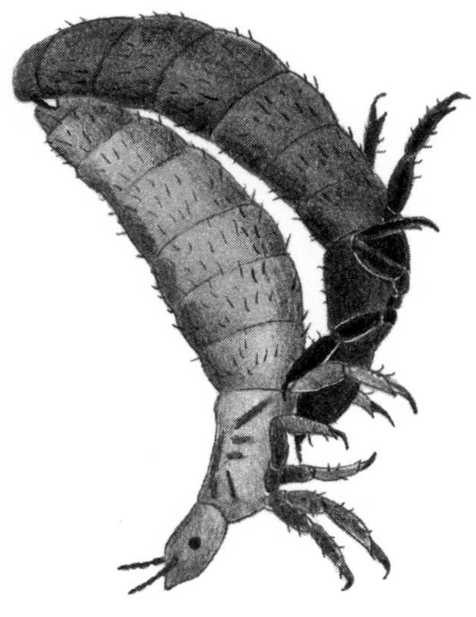

Mating position of the Body Louse *(Pediculus humanus)*.

Much of what Al-Qazwini writes is drawn from other books, but he appears to add something new when he writes that the louse generated from putrescent sweat "lays an egg from which lice develop in the usual way". But he also transmits fictions. Grey hair is infested by "partly black, partly white lice". And he provides an explanation for the above method of sex determination. "Milk for a boy-child is thick while that for a girl is thin, and so does not hinder the emergence of the louse."

Albertus Magnus illustrates the growth of knowledge in the Middle Ages. He writes: "Lice are generated in the dirty pores of humans and are very fond of warmth . . . They prefer people of voracious eating habits . . . The principal means of combatting them is quicksilver and lead." He fails to explain how the two metals are to be used.

In *Hortus sanitatis*, published in 1480, an illustration shows a mother removing lice by washing her son's head. Perhaps effective additives were already in use at that time.

Some progress is seen in Johann Sperling's *Zoologia physica*. In Chapter 10, entitled "On lice", he says: "They do not develop from dirt, not from excrement, neither from flesh nor from blood, but as a result of mating, with the nits or eggs as the intermediate stage." He also notes that lice desert a dying host. This is true of many ectoparasites living on warm-blooded animals (including, for instance, fleas). Sperling formulated the principle of sexual procreation in lice in advance of the great Francesco Redi (1626–1698) who is generally credited with overthrowing the theory of spontaneous generation and establishing Redi's Principle. Redi wrote: "Lice do not originate

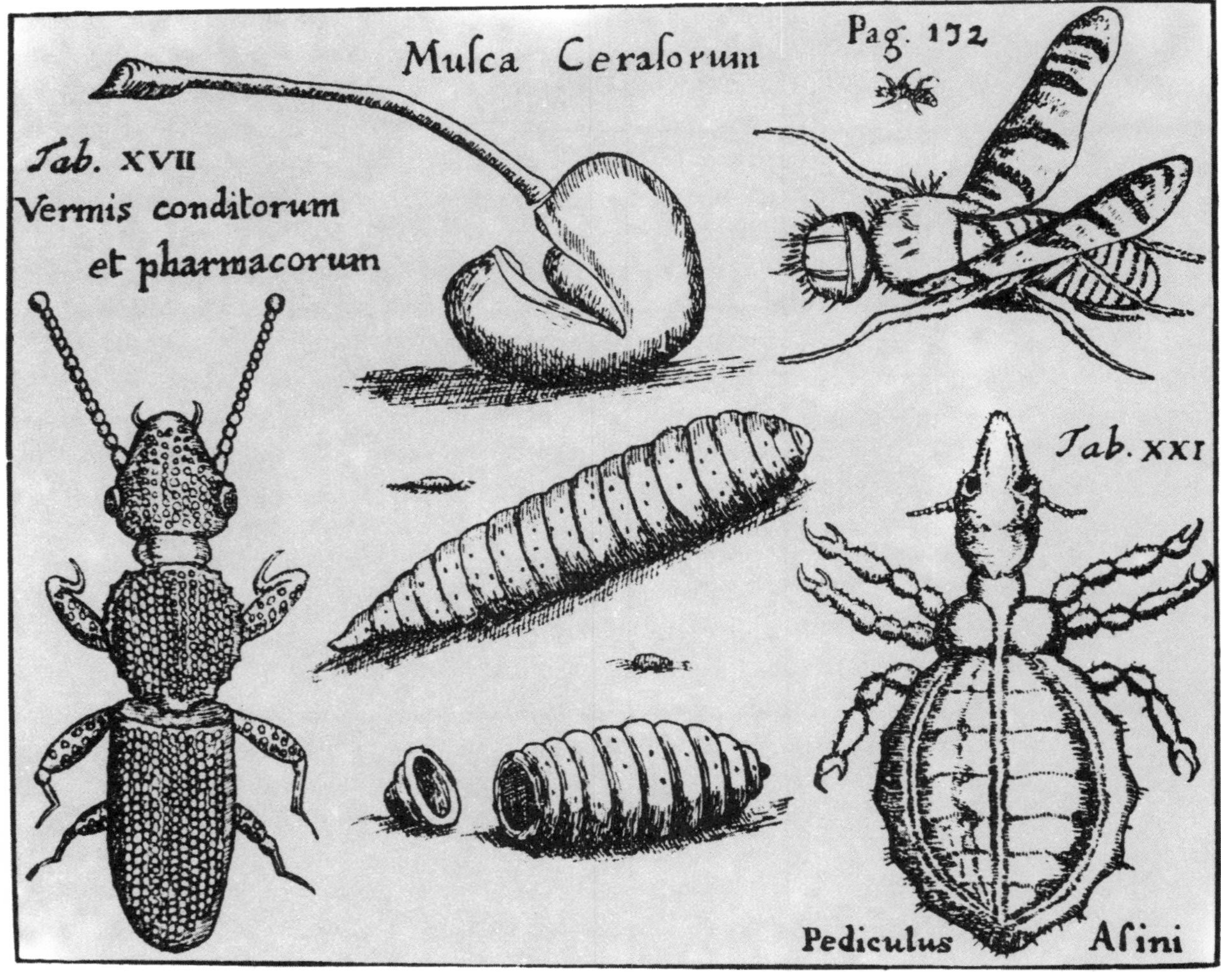

Francesco Redi was the first to depict the Cherry Fly *(Rhagoletis cerasi)* and the Saw-toothed Grain Beetle *(Oryzaephilus surinamensis)*. Below right, *Haematopinus asini*.

from the host animal, but always from eggs that are laid by impregnated females." He provides an illustration of a donkey-louse which clearly shows the leg ending in a single claw with the particular curvature of the claw and tarsus that follows closely that of the hair of the host. Lice have to be able to maintain a firm hold on the hairs and to withstand scratching and scraping. If they fall off, they are unlikely to survive.

There is a striking picture of a louse in Robert Hooke's (1635–1730) *Micrographia*, one of the earliest volumes of microscopic illustrations, published in 1665. In his chapter entitled "On lice", Hooke gives a very precise description, including many of his own observations, in particular of the sucking process and the clinging legs.

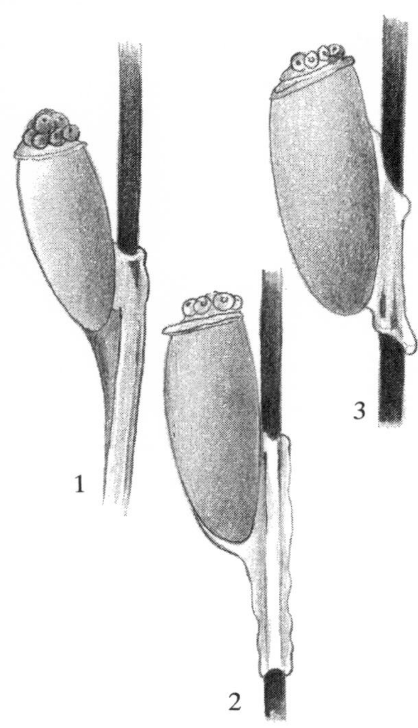

The eggs of lice (nits) are cemented to hairs. There are inter-specific differences in the structure of the egg-lid and the manner of attachment.
1 Grab Louse *(Pthirus pubis)*
2 Head Louse *(Pediculus capitis)*
3 Body Louse *(Pediculus humanis)*

The end of the head is cone-shaped and furnished with small teeth which abrade the skin of the host. Blood is sucked up through a channel formed by three stylets that are retractable into a pouch when not in use. The head louse and the body louse suck continuously for a period of 8 to 15 minutes at a time. The mouth parts of the crab louse penetrate the skin for a longer time, but sucking is not continuous. The blood is stored in the forepart of the mid-intestine; considerable elasticity extends its capacity. But only a small quantity is stored since lice remain close to their source of food. Together with the illustration of a louse and its egg, Jan Swammerdam shows the intestinal tract with its accessory glands, the nervous system and the male genitalia. His drawings are extremely informative and detailed, clearly based on excellently dissected specimens. It is even possible to distinguish those parts of the intestine containing the symbionts. It was not until well after Swammerdam's time that the symbiosis was discovered that exists between lice and bacteria-like organisms that live extra-cellularly and provide the lice with essential active substances. In many species, these symbionts are concentrated in special cells (mycetocytes) of the mid-intestine (genus *Haematopinus*), in others in special organs (mycetomes), for instance in *Pediculus*. It is vitally important for the lice that the symbionts are transmitted to the next generation. In the older female larva, the symbionts pass from the mycetome into the ovarian ampoules, and from there, later on, into the egg cells, into the embryo and finally into the mycetome of the freshly hatched larvae.

The mating position of lice is worthy of note. The male moves underneath the female and clasps the female's hind legs with its forelegs (double function of the male's gripping legs). Later the female takes up an upright position, so that the male is attached only to the hind end of the female. Copulation lasts about an hour.

True Bugs

(Heteroptera)

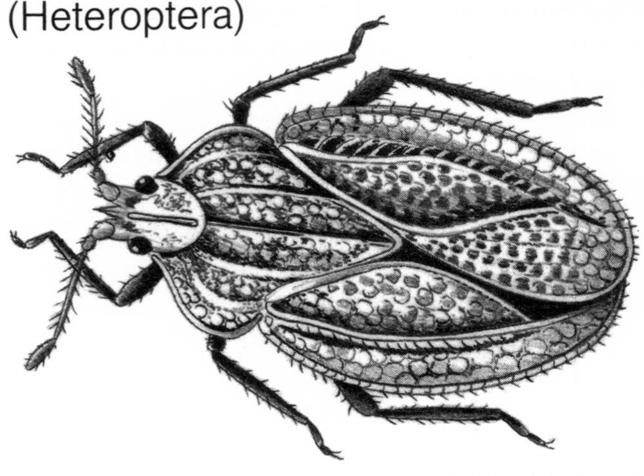

At the mention of the word "bug", most people think first of the notorious Bedbug *(Cimex lectularius)*. The situation is much the same in historical writings; the many other species receive scarcely a mention, but a good deal has been written concerning them. Heinrich Heine (1797–1856) even wrote a poem entitled "Der Wanzerich". The English author, John Southall, published a *Treatise on Buggs* (1730), containing basic observations on its biology and on means of combatting it:

"Buggs have been known to be in England above sixty Years, and every Season increasing so upon us, as to become terrible to almost every Inhabitant in and about this Metropolis . . .

"By often nightly watching and daily observing them with the best of Helps, having discover'd Males from Females, I determin'd and then did put up a Pair in a Glass, as believing that to keep them the Year round, would be the only and best way to find the Nature of their breeding, feeding, etc. and be a means to discover what had occasion'd the Difficulties I had met with in my Endeavours and Practice of destroying them . . .

"As I put up the Pair aforesaid, so did I another Pair that day Fortnight, and so every Fortnight for eighteen Months, did I put up others, with various Foods.

"The first, second, third, and fourth Pair lived, but did not presently breed, it not being then their Season of so doing: But in about ten Days after I put up the fifth Pair, they all spawn'd much about the time of each other; and in about three Weeks the Spawn came to life.

"The Eggs or Nits are white, and having when spawn'd a clammy glutinous Substance, they stick to any thing spawn'd upon . . . The Eggs are oval, and as small as the smallest Maw-seed . . .

"I found by my account of above forty Pair so put up with various Foods, not only their best-beloved Foods, but also their Method of Breeding . . .

"*Viz*. Their beloved Foods are Blood, dry'd Paste, Size, Deal, Beach, Osier, and some other Woods, the Sap of which they such; and on any one of these will they live the Year round.

"Oak, Walnut, Cedar and Mahogoney they will not feed upon; all Pairs I put up with those Woods for Food, having been soon starved to death.

"Wild Buggs are watchful and cunning, and tho' timorous of us, yet in fight one with another, are very fierce; I having often seen some (that I brought up from a day old, always inur'd to Light and Company) fight as eagerly as Dogs or Cocks, and sometimes one or both have died on the Spot. From those so brought up tame, I made the greatest Discoveries.

Above:

Lace Bug *(Tingis reticulata)* from Europe.

Bedbugs *(Cimex lectularius)* mating.

"They are hot in Nature, generate often . . . They generally spawn about fifty at a time, of which Spawn about forty odd in about three Weeks time usually come to life; the Residue proving addle . . .

"Thus they spawn four times in a Season; *viz.* in *March*, *May*, *July*, and *September*: by which 'tis apparent to a Demonstration, that from every Pair that lives out the Season, about two hundred Eggs or Nits are produc'd; and that out of them, one hundred and sixty, or one hundred and seventy, come to Life and Perfection . . .

"The second and most prevailing Error is, That Buggs bite some Persons, and not others: When in Reality, they bite every Human Body that comes in their way . . .

"The best Reason which can be given in support of this Error, is, That where two Persons lie in one Bed, one shall be apparently bit, the other not.

"Buggs indeed, where there are two Sorts, may feed most on that Blood which best pleases their Palate; but that they do taste the other also, to me is apparent: And whenever that Bedfellow who is most liked by Buggs shall lie from home, the other will so sensibly feel the effects to be as above, that they will no longer think themselves bite-free."

Within the order of Heteroptera, the family Cimicidae comprises some 40 species, exclusively parasitical on warm-blooded animals, two of which are obligatory parasites on man: *Cimex lectularius* (cosmopolitan) and *Cimex hemipterus* (tropical zone). There are other Cimicidae which may be facultative parasites on man; in Europe, for example, the principal one is the House Martin Bug *(Oeciacus hirundinis)*. Most of these facultative human parasites live primarily on bats and birds (swallows, pigeons, hens). It can be assumed that those species now obligatory parasites on man, originally lived on bats and birds (swallows, pigeons).

A Swedish writer, Peter Kahn (1713–1797), refers to this in a description of his travels. "In Canada, the bedbug is very common. The Indians appear to be completely free of it. It is uncertain whether they were introduced from Europe or are endemic, since bedbugs are often found deeply embedded under the wings of bats. So it is generally assumed that the bats have picked them up in a hollow tree and carried them from there into the houses."

In mating, the male intromittent organ or aedeagus (not a true "penis") is not introduced into the vagina (the latter exists, but is used only for depositing eggs) but into the separate organ of Ribaga that occurs as a narrow slit on the female's right side between the fourth and fifth abdominal sternite. Therefore during copulation, the male sits aslant the female with the head to the left. The organ of Ribaga serves not only for mating, but also for digesting the spermatozoa necessary

Colasiella matercula is a bug of deviant form with raptorial forelegs. The body resembles that of Stick Insects.

Assassin Bug (Reduviidae). Figure in fine steel by Hans Jähne (born 1926).

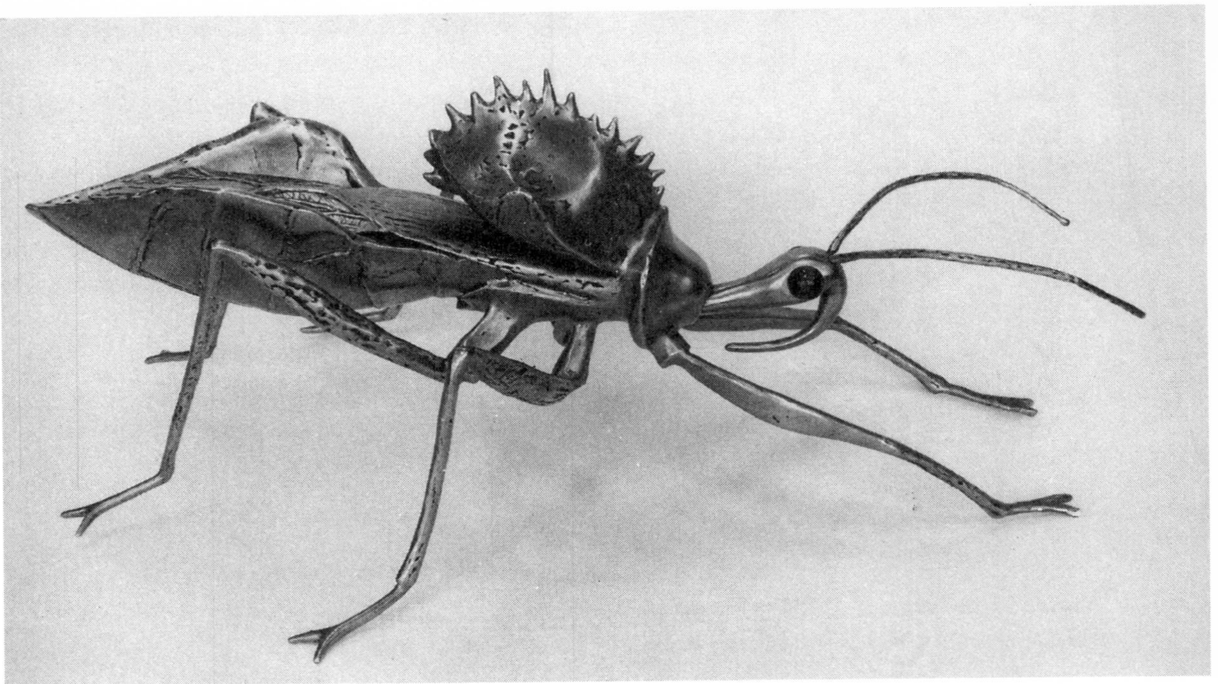

for fertilizing the eggs. It contains amoeboid cells (amoebocytes) which absorb the seminal secretions. Those spermatozoa not absorbed in the organ of Ribaga, pass through the body cavity into the receptaculum seminis, and on the way, more of them are digested by amoeboid cells.

The various remedies prescribed for dealing with bugs are rich in fantasy. J. J. Salberg, in the proceedings of the Swedish Academy of Sciences (1745), gives an example: "1 pound sal ammoniac, $1\frac{1}{2}$ pounds potash, $\frac{1}{2}$ pound quicklime, $\frac{1}{2}$ pound common verdigris. Pulverize each one separately, then mix them quickly in a large stone mortar and put into a small copper distilling flask; pour over a jug of good strong grain spirit, cover with the lid of the flask; enclose it in a wet still, etc., distill with cold water and collect the distillate in a bottle with crystalized verdigris until the liquid is a fine blue colour. Spray into cracks using a metal spray. The verdigris causes the small eggs or the still lifeless young to contract and shrivel up, as it were, so that they cannot mature and come to life."

Four hundred years earlier, Kamal al-Din al-Damiri wrote: "It is said to have its origin in warm blood, and has an extravagant fondness for humans. It has no means of protection, for it is instantly visible . . . In Egypt and such countries, it occurs in massive numbers. Al-Qazwini says that bugs never enter a house that has been fumigated with copper and coriander seeds. Burning pine-wood sawdust is also effective."

A good deal of early information exists on the medical use of bedbugs. Pedanius Dioscorides from Anazarbus in Cilicia Campestris writes: "Koreis. Bedbugs. Cimices of ye bed, (being taken) to the number of seven of them & put in meate with beanes, and swallowed downe before the fitt, doe help such as have ye quartaine ague. And being swallowed downe without beanes, (they help such as are) bitten by an Aspick. Being smellt vnto, they call back such againe as are fallen into a swonne by the strangulation of the Vulua. Being dranck with wine or vinegar, they expell horse leaches. Being beaten small & put into the Urinaria Fistula they cure the Dysuria." (The *Greek Herbal of Dioscorides*, Englished by John Goodyear; A.D. 1655.)

In his *Opus de re medicina*, Paulus Aegineta follows Dioscorides to some extent. "Bedbugs are very sharp. Taken in vinegar, they are said to cause leeches to fall off." In 1685, Matthaeus

Wagner's *The Travelling Samaritan or the Short Pharmacopoeia / of Good and Proven Medicinal Preparations / of which the Traveller can avail himself in Case of Need and in the Absence of a Medicus* recommends: "To promote obstructed or retained urine . . . the following is a well proven experiment / take a good portion of Bedbugs or Wall-lice / let them boil in Olive Oil / and then allow the male privy parts to depend therein / as hot as can be borne."

An early indication of the great diversity within the order of Bugs is found in Johann Sperling's *Zoologia physica*, which is also a typical example of the compendia of that day:

"Praeceptum: The bug is an insect with an unpleasant smell, which is detested for its biting.
Quaestiones: 1. Food: They feed on human blood, forest bugs on plant juices.
2. Reproduction: The body of the bug is almost wider than it is long. When it is gorged with blood, it can easily be crushed. But when this is done, the stink is disgusting.
3. Origin: They originate in beds and particularly in cracks."
Sperling lags behind Ulisse Aldrovandi, who names a large number of species of bug in his *De Animalibus insectis*, for example:
No. 4. The universally familiar Bedbug (*Cimex lectularius*)
No. 7. yellowish, with a human face on the wing covers (probably *Dolycoris baccarum*)
No. 11. a small, entirely grey forest bug (probably *Picromerus bidens*)
No. 13. red-brown with black longitudinal stripes (probably *Graphosoma lineatum*)
No. 16. spotted yellow, black and white (probably *Eurydema oleraceum*)"

Guilelmus Rondeletius is one of the first to mention Water Bugs (Backswimmers, *Notonecta*): "In summer we often see small flies floating on the surface of the water. They have eyes that are very large in relation to the size of the body, a rounded back and flat belly and 6 legs, of which the hind pair is the largest, to propel the body forward in water. When swimming, they extend their two wings. They can fly in the air as well as swim in the water. They swim with the belly upwards, and fly with the belly downwards, and so both alternately. The belly is striped black and green."

Many authors divide Bugs into two sub-orders: the Water Bugs (Cryptocerata), in which the antennae are very small and not visible when seen from above, and Land Bugs (Gymnocerata), in which the antennae are always clearly visible from above. Some species of Land Bugs live on the surface of wate. Included here is the genus *Halobates*. These species live on the open sea, often far from land, and complete their entire development there. They lay their eggs on drifting seaweed, sometimes on the shells of Sea Snails (Neritids) or even on seabirds' feathers. A typical feature is the strikingly small abdomen. *Halobates* is one of a small number of insects that has successfully colonized the ocean, an environment otherwise almost empty of insects.

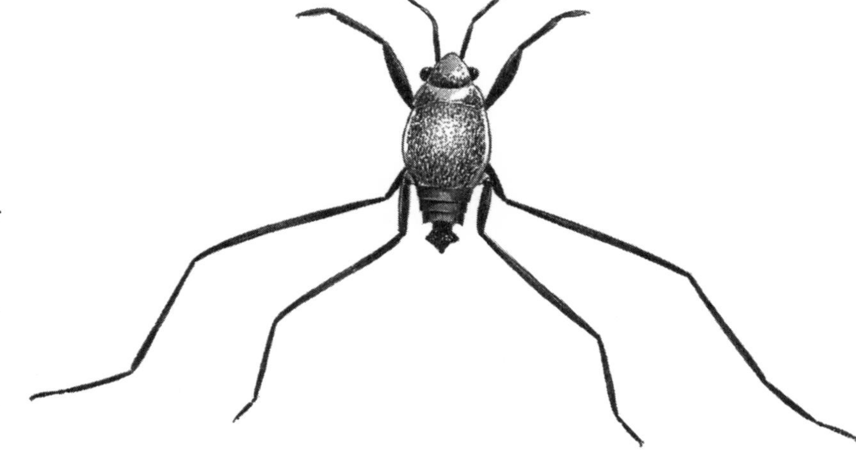

Bugs of the genus *Halobates* (Water Skippers, Water Striders, Ocean Bugs) are among the few insects to have conquered the ocean. They are wingless, live on the surface of the open sea many hundreds of kilometres from land, and deposit their eggs on drifting algae.

Homopterans
(Homoptera)

From the very large and heterogeneous order of Homoptera (membranous-winged bugs that subsist on vegetarian tissue), those that particularly drew the attention of man in early times were certain of the cicadas, lantern flies, aphids and, because of their commercially useful secretions, the scale insects. Whiteflies (Aleyrodina) and Jumping Plant Lice (Psyllina) attracted rather less interest.

Cicadas (Cicadina)

"Cicadas live happily
For they have silent wives."

Xenarchos of Rhodes

What we know today might cause us to modify our ideas on the happiness of the cicadas. Modern acoustic techniques show that even small species of cicadas produce sounds inaudible to us, and that the females are capable of song, even antiphonic song together with the males, as a means of locating a mate. The cicadas referred to by the Greeks are the Singing Cicadas (Cicadidae). Their "songs" are produced by a method almost unique among sound-producing insects. Cicadas possess a tymbal organ in the upper part of the abdomen. Contraction of the "song" muscles causes distortion of the tymbal, a chitinous membrane, which springs back sharply by its own elasticity when the muscle is released. As children, we often played with a tin box, pressing in the lid, then causing it to spring back into place again by squeezing the sides of the tin, producing a "clacking" sound as it did so. Although we did not realize it, this was approximately the principle of sound production in the kettledrum. The song muscle is contracted 170–180 times per second depending upon species, and the membrane vibrates 2,200 to 8,000 times per second. The tone can be altered by special tensor muscles and by the position of the abdomen, so that different songs can be produced by individual species (e.g. mating or pair-forming calls). Large tracheal air sacs in the abdomen function as resonators. The song of the cicada varies between species, each having its own rhythmically constructed calls. Both sexes are capable of hearing sound, although they perceive the rhythm more clearly than the frequency.

In classical Antiquity, the loud chirping of cicadas was considered to be thoroughly agreeable—an attitude incomprehensible to many people today. An Ancient Greek legend tells of a contest between two rival lute players. In the course of playing, the musician from Locris broke two strings. Defeat seemed inevitable, until a cicada landed on his instrument and sang so beautifully that victory was awarded to the Locrian. A monument was erected to celebrate the event, and during the Renaissance, the figure of a cicada on a lute came to symbolize music. The earliest representations of cicadas are found in the Near East (3rd century B.C.). Cicada fibulae (brooches)

Above:

Winged female of the Black Soil Plant Louse *(Aphis fabae)*.

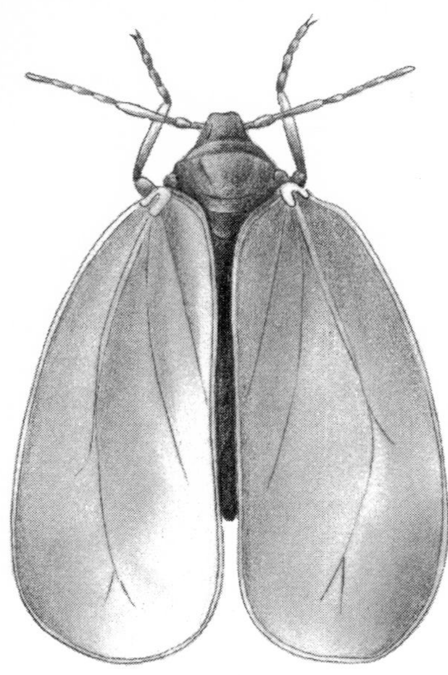

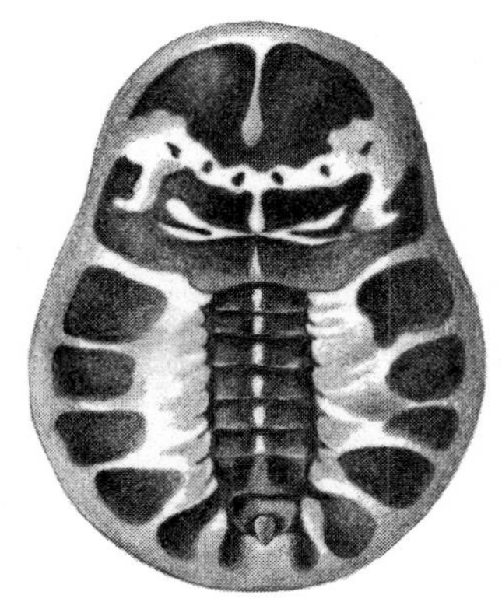

Aleyrodids (Aleyrodina), commonly known as Whiteflies, can be destructive in greenhouses. The adults are conspicuous on account of a fine white waxy powder covering the wings.
Above: *Aleurodea proletella*.
Below: The 4th larval instar of *Aleurochiton aceris* that has developed into a "winter pupa" with a thick covering of wax filaments, frequently to be found on maple.

are found in the art of Iran, Mesopotamia, Egypt, Babylonia, Mycenae, Scythia and the Germanic tribes, particularly at the time of the Great Migration. Certain Greek coins bore a design of cicadas, as did gems of the early Roman and Imperial period.

In Homer's *Iliad*, we read: "Like cicadas that in a forest sit upon a tree and utter their lily-like voice; even so sat the elders of the Trojans upon the tower."

Cicadas were especially revered in Ancient China. "In early Chinese bronzes, the cicada is the central element of masks—the glutton masks; it also occurs in the white ware of the Shang Period (about 1523–1027 B.C.), that is, at about the same time as the bronzes, and already in association with the monster mask. According to Ancient Chinese belief, the cicada has special powers; it can magically transform its body into a new form, it never grows weary or old. This probably explains its use as a burial offering. Cicadas, often made of jade or other semi-precious stones, were placed on or in the mouth of the dead, undoubtedly as a symbol of resurrection . . . The cicada also symbolizes happiness and eternal youth. Together with the butterfly, it remained the favourite animal motif for Chinese painters and poets. Cicadas were also widely used as ornamentation, especially as belt buckles. The frothy secretion of the Froghopper, known as Cuckoo Spit, is considered to be a symbol of fertility." (Schimitschek, 1968)

The *Pen ts'ao* recommends the use of cicada exuviae for smallpox, skin rashes and hoarseness. According to Dioscorides, fried cicadas are helpful in cases of bladder infection. We are indebted to the religious mystic, Saint Hildegard, for a compilation of the views and practices current in the popular medicine of her day. On the use of cicadas, she writes: "If a cicada died naturally, anyone who is troubled by running ulcers should grind it with flint and apply the dust frequently to the affected part. The latter will then dry out." In *Opus de re medicina* by Paulus Aegineta, raw, dried cicadas are prescribed for colic, 3.5 or 7 to them to be taken with an equal number of peppercorns. When fried, they are said to be good for stomach pains.

One of the earliest descriptions of the mouthparts of cicadas is given by Aristotle. Comparing them to other insects, he writes: "The tettix or cicada, alone of such creatures, is unprovided with a mouth, but it is provided with a tongue-like formation . . . and this formation in the cicada is long, continuous and devoid of any split; and by the aid of this the creature feeds on dew."

The cicadas absorb plant juices with mouth parts that are adapted for piercing and suction. The liquid food passes first into a filter chamber, which relieves the stomach of the burden of excess quantities of liquid, since water can be discharged directly through the adjacent epithelia into the hind gut. The enriched liquid food undergoes further processing in the mid-intestine. Intra-cellular micro-organisms are almost always active in supplementing the provision of essential materials. Sometimes several (up to six) species of symbionts are concentrated in mycetomes at different parts of the body (including the curious appendages of the Tree-hoppers). In the ovary, the symbionts migrate into the egg cell, and thus transmission to the offspring is ensured.

Aristotle had some curious ideas on copulation in insects. "The female pushes from underneath her sexual organ into the body of the male above, this being the reverse of the operation observed in other creatures . . . The intercourse of the sexes in their case is of long duration . . . in most cases of insect copulation this process is speedily followd up by parturition."

In fact, there exist certain beetles of the family Helodidae in which the female possesses a penis-like organ of copulation, with which it extracts the spermatophores from the male. But they are a rare exception and would certainly have been unknown to Aristotle.

On the subject of cicada, Aristotle gives more details: "Of the cicada there are two kinds; one, small in size, the first to come and the last to disappear; the other, large, the singing one, that comes last and first disappears . . . The cicada is not found where there are no trees; and this accounts for the fact that in the district surrounding the city of Cyrene it is not found at all in the

Apple Sucker *(Psylla mali)*, a representative of the sub-order Psyllina (Jumping Plant Lice) within the order Homoptera. The insects have a remarkable leaping capacity.

plain country, but is found in great numbers in the neighbourhood of the city, and especially where olive-trees are growing: for an olive grove is not thickly shaded. And the cicada is not found in cold places, and consequently is not found in any grove that keeps out the sunlight . . . They lay their eggs in fallow lands, boring a hole with the pointed organ they carry in the rear . . . and this fact may account for their numbers in the territory adjacent to the city of Cyrene. The cicadae also lay their eggs in the canes on which husbandmen prop vines, perforating the canes; and also in the stalks of the squill. This brood runs into the ground. And they are most numerous in rainy weather. The grub, on attaining full size in the ground, becomes a tettigometra (or nymph), and the creature is sweetest to the taste at this stage before the husk is broken. When the summer solstice comes, the creature issues from the husk at night-time, and in a moment, as the husk breaks, the larva becomes the perfect cicada. The creature, also, at once turns black in colour and harder and larger, and takes to singing. In both species, the larger and the smaller, it is the male that sings, and the female is unvocal. At first, the males are the sweeter eating; but after copulation, the females, as they are full then of white eggs . . . If you present your finger to a cicada and bend the tip of it and then extend it again, it will endure the presentation more quietly than if you were to keep your finger outstretched altogether; and it will set to climbing your finger: for the creature is so weak-sighted that it will take to climbing your finger as though that were a moving leaf."

This passage reveals the beginnings of an ecological approach, and an impressively detailed and exact description of the biology of singing cicadas.

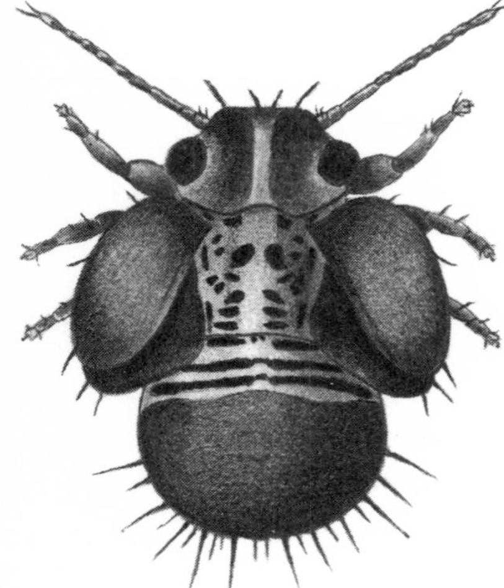

Nymph of the Pear Sucker *(Psylla piricola)* in the final instar.

Like almost all cicadas, Singing Cicadas (Cicadidae) lay their eggs above the ground in the tissue of plants, although the nymphs are subterranean, feeding on roots. When a nymph has hatched, it falls to the ground and burrows into it. It is able to do this and subsequently to live in the ground because its forelegs are specially adapted for grasping and cutting. They are not fossorial organs like those of mole crickets nor prehensile organs like those of Mantids and many bugs, but are scissor-like devices in which the enlarged and modified tibia and femur slide across one another in a cutting action, like scissors. The tarsus is not used. The period of nymphal development varies in cicadas. Fabre suggests four years for *Cicada plebeja*, the species common in southern Europe, and it is known that the nymphs of *Magicicada septendecim* in North America require 17 years (as

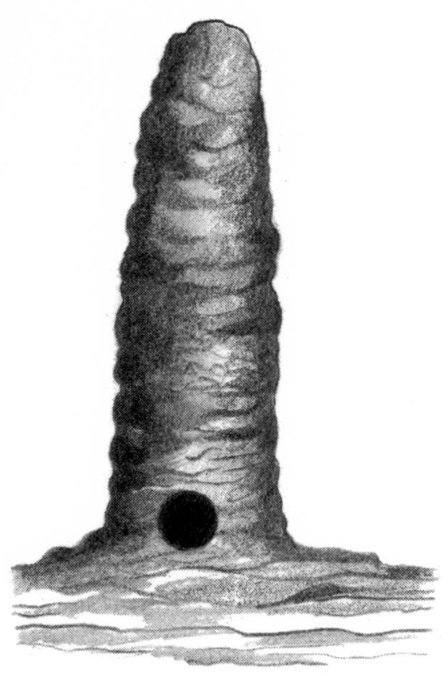

their name implies). The depth underground at which the nymphs live varies. In *Magicicada septendecim*, it is usually 1–60 cm, but nymphs have been found much deeper in the soil (up to about 3 m). Before the imago hatches, the nymphs leave the ground and climb up on to plants, and particularly trees; *Cicada plebeja* to a height of about 0.5 m, *Magicicada septendecim* usually 3–4 m. There they establish a firm hold, the skin of the back splits in a manner similar to that of the dragonfly naiad, and the imago hatches, hardens, takes on colour and within a few hours, is ready to fly. The final stage nymphs wait for good weather conditions before they leave the soil. So it sometimes happens that several hundred of them emerge under a tree in a single night. Before they leave the soil, the nymphs of most Singing Cicadas prepare a smooth-sided passage leading upwards to just beneath the soil surface. Certain ones construct earthen cones or chimneys that are about 25–30 cm high (exceptionally up to 50 cm), also with a smooth inner surface, and closed at the upper extremity. The significance of these towers is uncertain. It may be that they are a kind of "weather station". If they are damaged, the nymphs repair them. If one falls over, a new tower is built, but only a small one. When the time comes to leave the tower, the nymph breaks a hole through it at the top, or at the bottom close to the ground.

Authors of earlier centuries also took an interest in tropical cicadas. In the 17th century, Christian Mentzel, a physician of Potsdam, prepared sketches of various cicadas from India (viewed from above and below) as well as nymphs in their final instar. The physician Hermann Nicolai Grimm describes an occasion on which manna was produced by cicadas in Ceylon (Sri Lanka), and also talks of glowing cicadas. "In Ceylon, I witnessed the creation of manna, a delicate, easily-soluble material, pleasant to the taste, that was produced on certain trees by creatures the size of a small bee. Head and chest are covered by a shield-shaped integument. They have long legs on which they leap away if touched. At the time of this activity, they are wingless, nor do they move from the branch upon which they are sitting, and they are covered by a white substance like flour. It seems that these creatures suck the sap of plants and from it, using certain components of the air, create manna. So they can simply remain in one place without needing to search for sustenance on herbs and plants as bees do. For they suck the juices of the tree on which they are sitting. Their work is greatly hindered by rain."

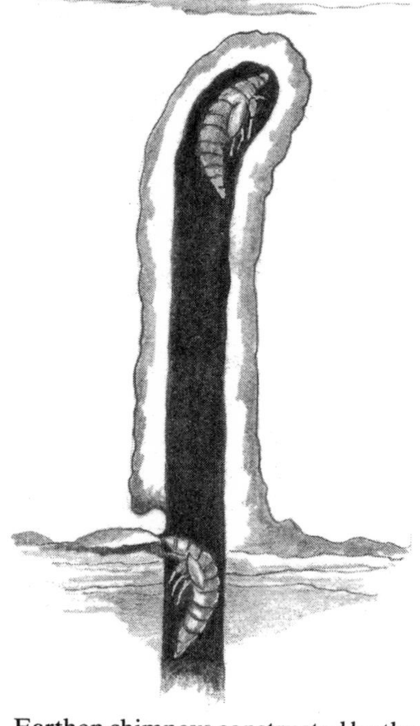

Earthen chimneys constructed by the Seventeen-year Cicada *(Magicicada septendecim)*.
Above: External aspect with emergence hole.
Below: Section (description in text).

The plant juices they ingest contain relatively little protein and much sugar. In order to obtain sufficient protein, sap-sucking bugs take in excess quantities of sugar, which they then excrete with the faeces. The amount of sugar in the faeces varies greatly between species of cicada. Froghoppers or Cuckoo-spit Insects (Cercopidae), the nymphs of which use the fluid they excrete to

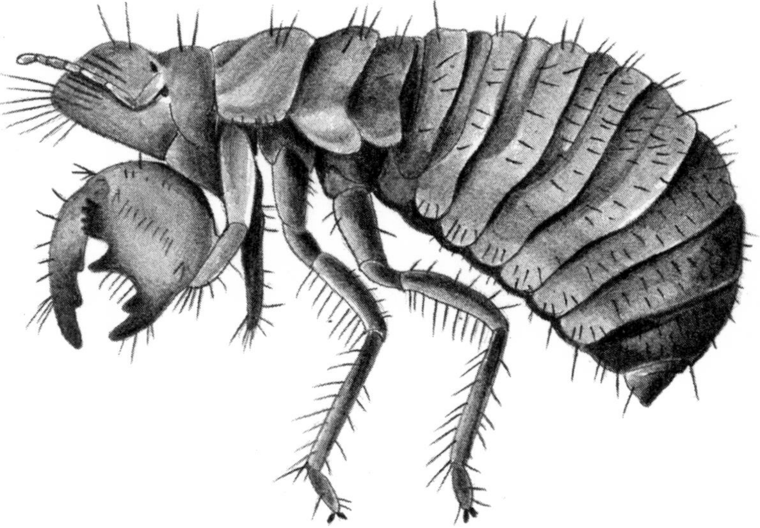

Larva, in the 4th instar, of the Periodic or Seventeen-year Cicada *(Magicicada septendecim)*, a native of North America. The powerful femur and tibia of the forelegs are an adaptation to the subterranean mode of life.

Hunch-backed Cicada (*Heteronotus* spec.). Figure in fine steel by Hans Jähne.

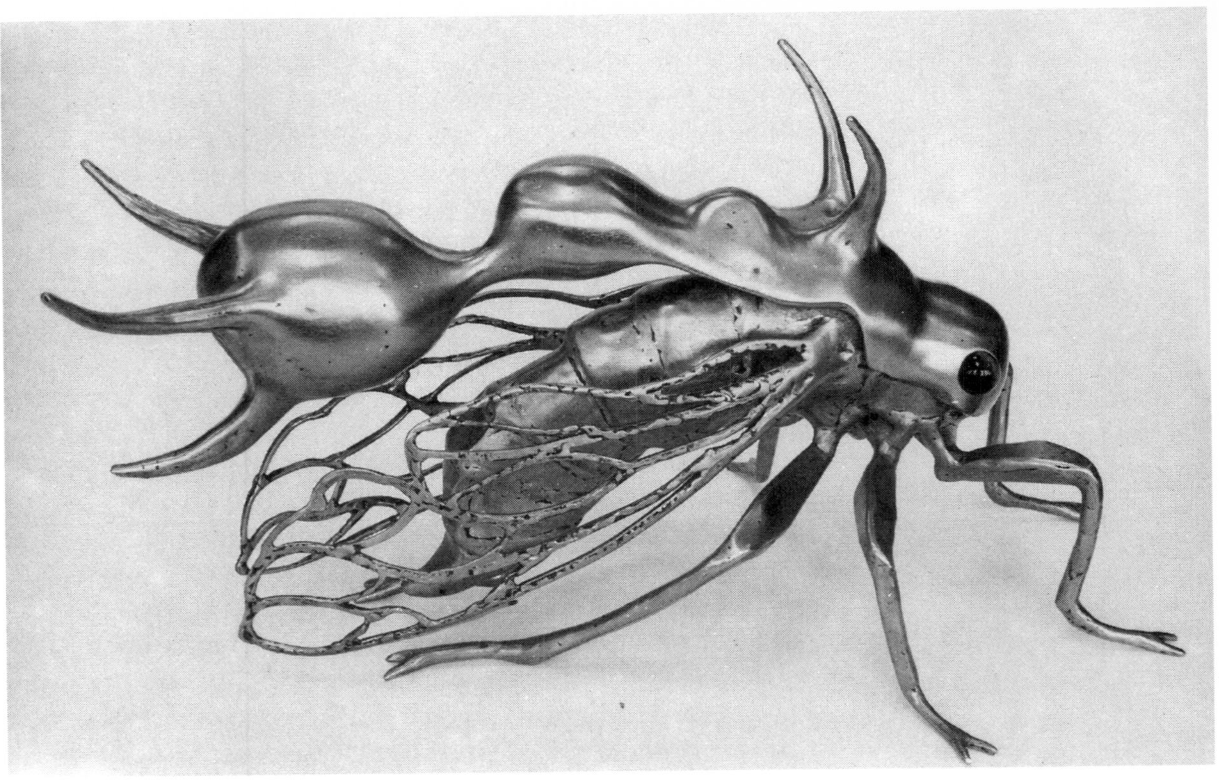

"Nobody, hearing them chirp, was aware that they were soon to die."

Matsuo Basho (1643–1694)

produce protective froth with which they surround themselves, secrete no sugar; apparently they have solved the problem in another way. In the Singing Cicadas, the liquid faeces are stored in a bladder-like extension of the hind gut and ejected periodically. When one cicada begins, all those round about follow suit. This is probably the origin of the "rain trees", and explains the production of "manna" (the solidified juice, rich in sugar, of various trees). ". . . And when the dew that lay was gone up, behold, upon the face of the wilderness there lay a small round thing, as small as the hoar frost on the ground . . . And it was like coriander seed, white, and the taste of it was like wafers made with honey." (Exodus 16) The manna mentioned in the Bible, and which Aaron, at Moses's command, kept in the ark of the covenant, is generally considered to have been produced by insects of the *Coccus* genus on a species of tamarisk, but two species of cicada also played a part. The Biblical story of the manna in the wilderness has inspired various works of art, such as the altar of Nicolas of Verdun at Klosterneuburg (1181). It portrays Aaron placing the golden pot containing the manna into the ark of the covenant. The "Israelites gathering Manna" is the subject of a painting by Maerten de Vos (1532–1603). In his *Principles of Pharmacology* (*c.* 970), Abu Mansur Muwaffaq mentions the use of manna as a medicinal preparation: "It relieves the breast, is effective for coughs and remedies colicky pains." Dean Braitenbach of Mainz, in an account of his pilgrimage to Mount Sinai, writes in 1483: "And it is sweet like honey, and remains clinging to your teeth when you eat it." For centuries, larch manna has been a familiar substance; it was listed in the 1542 Customs Tariff for Paris, and as *manna laricina*, is a recognized purgative.

According to the epic, the *Edda*, a sweet dew, upon which the bees fed, fell from the mighty ash tree Yggdrasil, that supports the universe.

Lantern Flies (Fulgoriformes)

Europeans generally have little opportunity to appreciate the brilliance of colouring displayed by lantern flies, of which a wide variety of species occurs, mainly in the tropics, many of them of considerable size. A striking feature is often the bizarre bulbous, snout-like extensions of the front of the head, which are patterned with additional markings. There is one species which, viewed in profile and with imagination, is not unlike a small crocodile. Maria Sibylla Merian (1647–1717) first drew attention to the lantern fly, and to many other insects, with her precise, accurately observed hand-coloured copperplate engravings, worked in a style entirely her own. She described these insects as luminous, and the popular name for them today reflects this idea. However, it is a mistaken one, for lantern flies emit no light. It may be that Merian's specimens were affected by luminous bacteria, and it was these that misled the meticulous observer.

At fifty-two years of age, with admirable spirit, she travelled by sailing ship to the then Dutch colony of Surinam, there to study the unknown world of tropical insects. She had already recorded her observations of many European species, furnishing illustrations which were remarkably true to nature, and brief descriptions.

It is instructive to read her own account of her motivation for the work, since today one may well wonder about the sources of her capacity and her interest in natural sciences. "Ever since my youth, I have studied insects. I began with silk worms in my native town of Frankfurt am Main. Then later I observed that all the beautiful butterflies and moths grow from caterpillars. So I collected all the caterpillars I could find, in order to study their metamorphosis. To be able to pursue investigations with greater precision, I withdrew from society entirely and occupied myself wholly with drawing, so that I should be able to depict insects with realism. I collected all the insects I found near Frankfurt and Nuremberg and painted them on parchment . . . Then I went to Friesland and Holland, where I continued to study insects, particularly in Friesland, for in Holland, I had opportunity to carry out my investigations only on bushes and in plateau country. However, at this time, interested people also brought me caterpillars so that I could study their metamorphosis, and I compiled a series of observations which one day I shall be able to add to my two earlier volumes. But in Holland I saw nothing more interesting than the various insects that had been brought back from the two Indies, particularly since I obtained permission to examine the curiosity cabinet owned by Mr. Nicolas Witsen, the renowned Mayor of Amsterdam and Director of the East India Company, and that of Mr. Jonas Witsen, Secretary of that city . . . Here I found innumerable insects, about whose origin, procreation and metamorphosis nothing was known. This made me determined to undertake the long journey to Surinam in America. The gentlemen mentioned had obtained the greater part of their insects from this hot and humid country. My departure took place in June 1699 and I remained in Surinam until June 1701, in order to complete my observations in peace, and then travelled back to Holland, where I arrived on September 13. I painted the creatures that appear on these seventy-two plates carefully on parchment in their natural size and environment, and they can be examined at my house along with the insect specimens. However, I did not find in that country the conditions of comfort and convenience that I would have wished for studying the insects. For the climate was so excessively hot that my constitution could not tolerate it any longer, and I was obliged to return earlier than I had originally resolved . . . I do not wish to make any profit from this publication and would like merely to cover my own costs.

As for plates and paper, I have spared nothing in order to satisfy in every respect the exacting demands of insect and plant lovers. I shall be satisfied if I have achieved that . . . I could easily have made the descriptions more detailed, but since today great care is required in that respect, and the scholars are completely at variance among themselves, I have restricted myself simply to reporting my observations and so offering some new material to the investigations."

Aphids (Aphidina)

In summer, aphids flying about in masses attract the attention even of those people who have no garden of their own in which, in the spring, they might already have observed, with some alarm, dense colonies of the creatures. The damage that aphids cause by sucking at plants or by transmitting plant viruses is considerable. They have a certain practical value as producers of honey-dew, which is an important food for bees.

Aphids have somewhat complicated life-cycles, of which we shall consider two examples here. In the Rose Aphid *(Macrosiphum rosae)*, as in most aphids, fertilized eggs laid in the autumn remain as eggs over the winter. The larvae hatch in the spring. They suck at plants and moult up to five times, then they produce fully-formed young parthenogenetically, all of which are female. After only two weeks, these are already sexually mature and produce live female larvae. Some ten generations can succeed one another in favourable years. The stem-mother or fundatrice, the female that emerges from an overwintered egg and founds such a colony, usually gives birth to about 20 young. As generation succeeds generation, fertility decreases. Towards autumn, winged aphids also occur in the colonies and these are able to colonize new plants (the alternation of host is usually from a woody winter host to a herbaceous summer host). These winged forms are also parthenogenetic and viviparous, but they produce apterous males and females, and are therefore called *sexuparae*. The males and females to which they give birth are the *sexuales*. These mate and the females lay fertilized eggs that then overwinter.

In addition to this straightforward reproductive cycle that is typical of many aphid species, there are some that are more complex, such as that of Pine Blight Aphids (Adelgidae). In the Eastern Spruce Gall Aphid *(Sacchiphantes abietis)* and the Red Spruce Gall Aphid *(Adelges laricis)*, the fundatrice overwinters in the base of a spruce leaf bud under a covering of waxy down that it prepares for itself in the autumn. When the bud begins to sprout in the spring, the aphid wakens from its winter sleep and begins to feed by sucking. Affected by their saliva, the leaf germs do not develop into typical needles, but into broad, scale-like structures. Now the fundatrice lays some 150 to 200 eggs, from which the larvae very quickly hatch and set about sucking the plant juices. This further increases the proliferation of plant tissue, so that finally a uniform, closed structure is formed, known as the pineapple gall. Although closed externally, there are hollow spaces internally among the formative leaf tissues in which the larvae develop into adult winged insects. These aphids are the migrants which fly to the larches. Here each lays some 40 unfertilized eggs out of which the third generation hatches as larvae which overwinter on branches, and in the following spring suck juices from the larch needles and lay eggs, which produce the fourth generation, the alate sexuparae; these fly back to the spruce where they lay their eggs. From these eggs, the fifth generation hatches, the wingless sexuales which now mate. Each female lays an egg out of which the new fundatrice develops in September, and proceeds to overwinter, as described above. This holocycle (complete life-cycle) is made up of five generations that make use of two host plants, that on which the fundatrice lives being known as the primary host and the other as the secondary host. But both *Sacchiphantes abietis* and *Adelges laricis* are able to dispense with the secondary host by developing a parallel series in the spruce. In that case, insects of the second generation do not migrate to a larch, but lay their eggs on the primary host, where they develop into pseudo-fundatrices. It may be that as the result of the "short-circuiting" process, cyclical parthenogenesis becomes constant parthenogenesis. In *Adelges laricis*, a short-circuit of this kind can occur on the larch. In that case, the progeny of the third generation are only partly winged sexuparae, the rest are again apterous aphids that remain on the larch.

Today it is easy enough to read the details of such life-cycles, and to forget the difficulties that faced researchers in elucidating them. One of the many discoveries made by Van Leeuwenhoek was that of parthenogenetic reproduction in aphids. Using his microscope (he built some 200),

On right:

50 A Shield Bug *(Carpocoris purpureipennis)* from Bulgaria.

51 Left: The Red Assassin Bug, *Rhinocoris iracundus*, from Central Europe, sucking up a caterpillar which hangs on its trunk.

52 Right: Water Scorpions *(Nepa rubra)* from Central Europe are predacious water bugs that capture their prey with the forelegs. They usually lie in shallow water with the respiratory tube piercing the water surface, and can remain thus submerged for an unlimited period.

53 Above: The Creeping Water Bug *(Aphelocheirus aestivalis)*, a rare European species, can live permanently under water by means of physical gaseous exchange (plastron respiration). A mantle of air is held in a dense pile of fine hairs (approximately 2,000,000 per mm^2). The bug is predacious, living at the bottom of streams and lakes.

54 Below: Water Boatmen, here *Corixa punctata* (Central Europe), usually live in small groups.

On left:

55 Above: Singing Cicada *(Huechys incarnata)* from Java.

56 Below: Among the Cicadidae, the Mountain Cicada *(Cicadetta montana)* is the species in Europe that extends the farthest distance north.

57 Above: Fifth larval instar of *Palomena viridissima*, a European species of Plant Bugs (Pentatomidae). The larvae can be recognized by the absence of wings. Almost invariably, there are five larval instars, with a progressive increase in the relative size of the wing rudiments. The wings are fully developed only in the last ecdysis from the final instar to the imago.

58 Below: The Striped Bug *(Graphosoma lineatum)* from Bulgaria on an umbellate flower.

59 Above left: *Mustha serrata* from Central Greece.

60 Above right: *Phloea corticata* from Brazil.

61 Below: *Pachyles gigas* from Mexico (left) and *Petacelis remipes* from Africa (right).

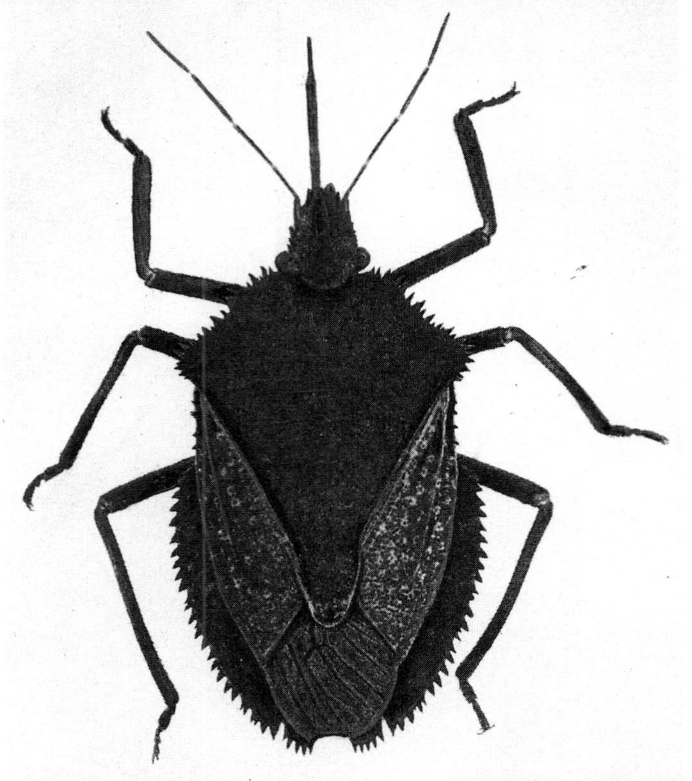

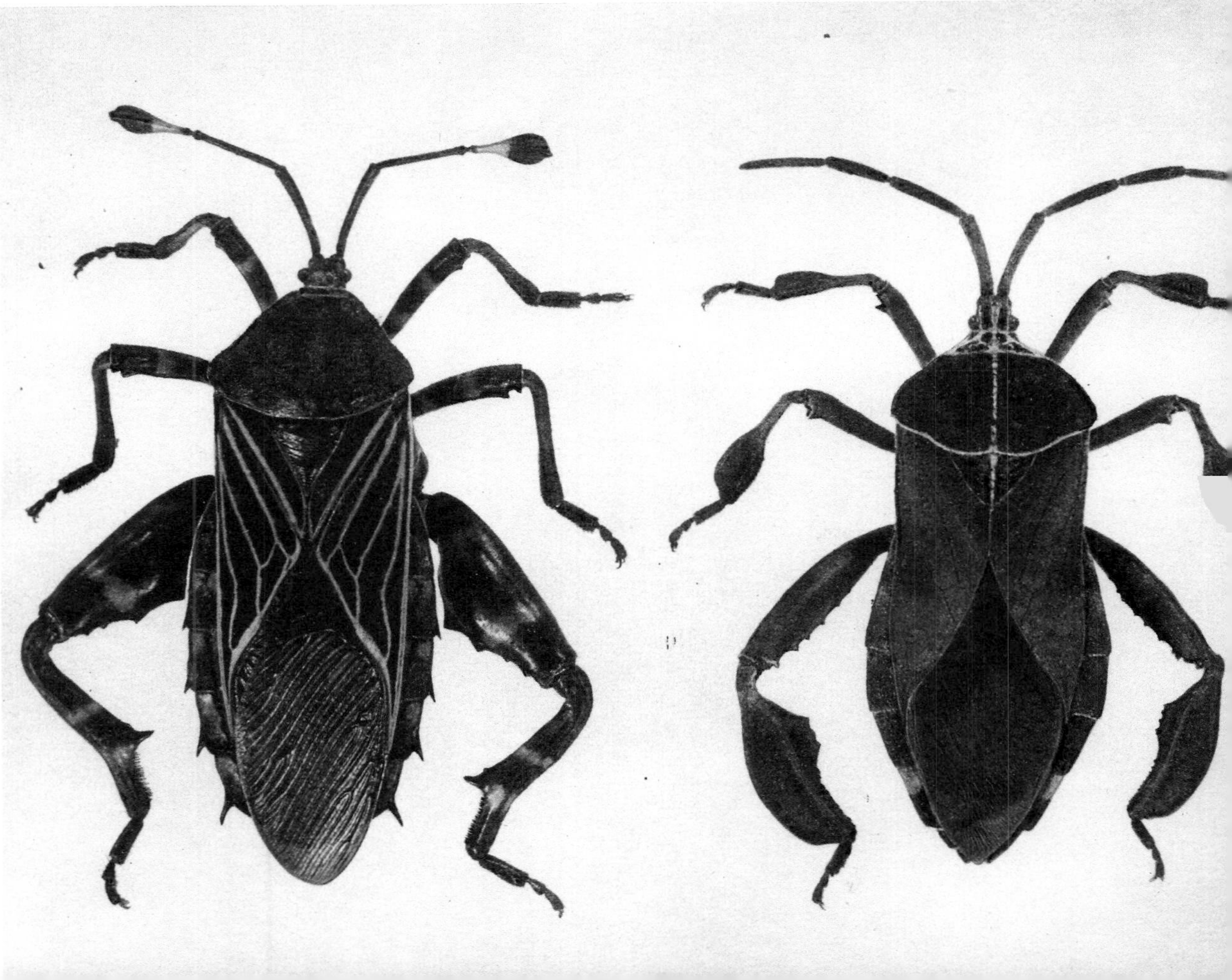

On right:

62 Above left: *Meropanchys nigricans* from Brazil.
Centre: *Menenotus lunatus* from Brazil.
Right: *Edessa cervus* from Brazil.

63 Below left: *Mictis pectoralis* from Central Africa.
Right: *Metopodus compressipes* from America.

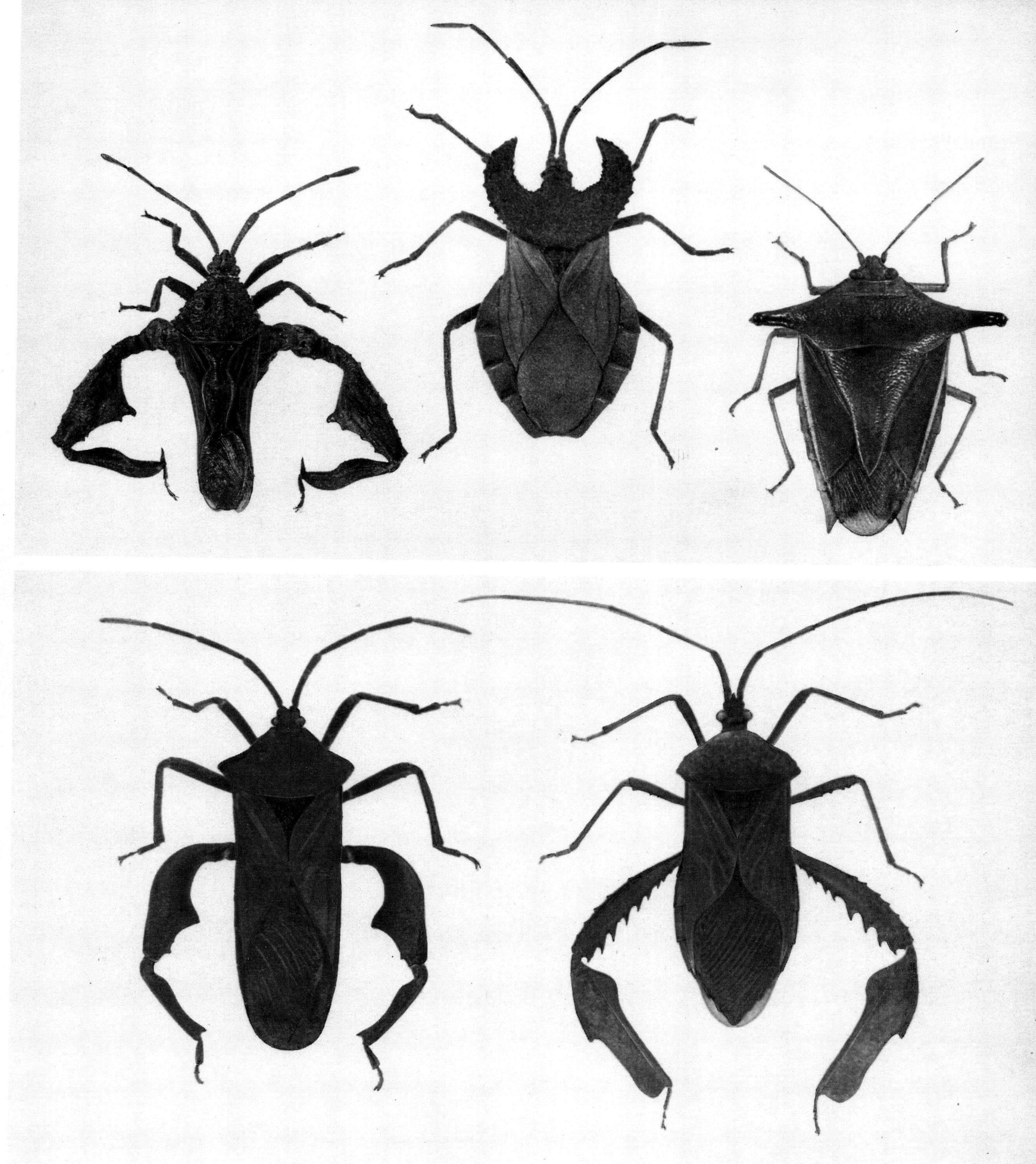

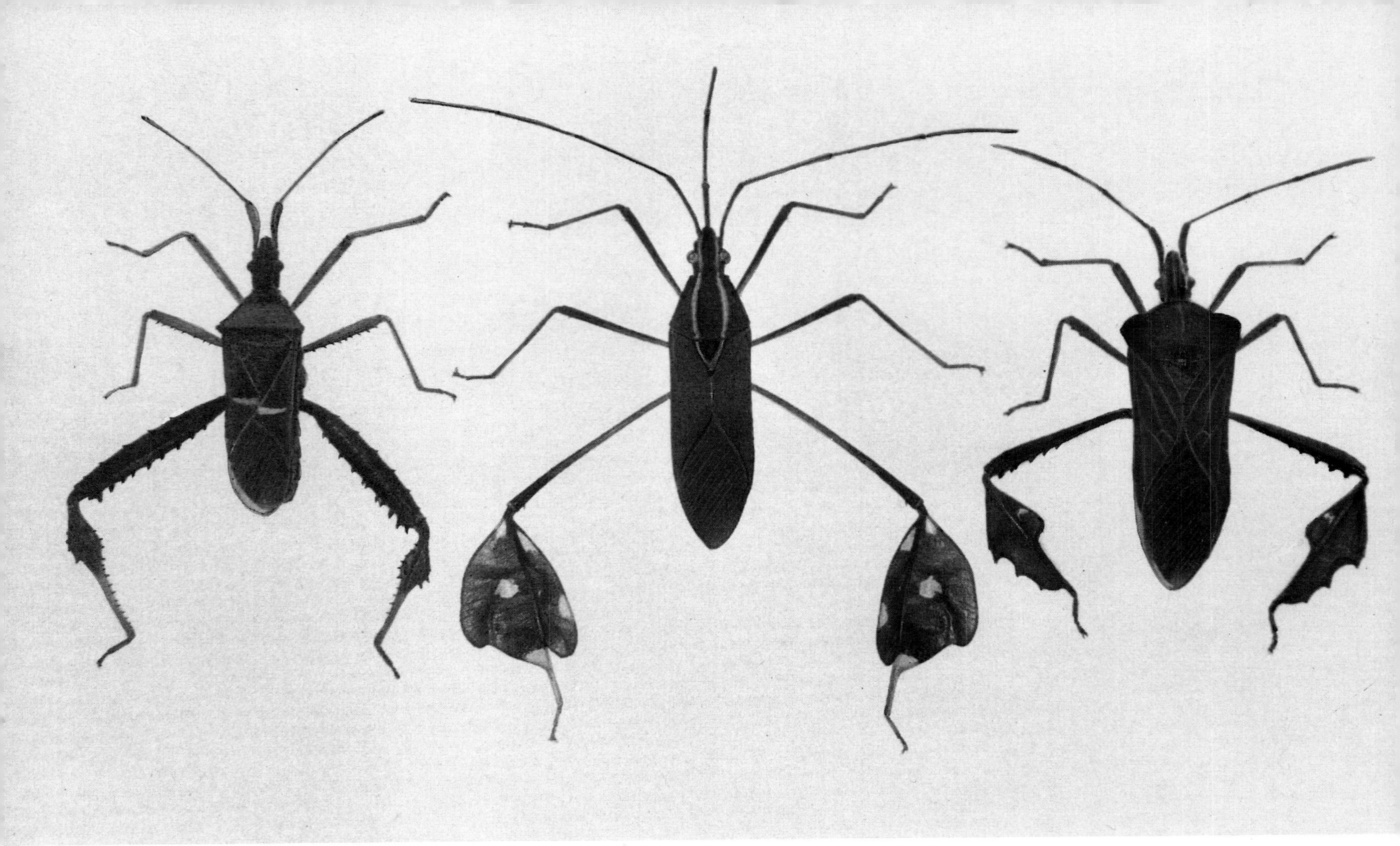

64 The hind legs of these tropical bugs are furnished with leaf-like excrescences.
Abowe left: *Anisoscelis cicta* from Brazil.
Centre: *Diactor bilineatus* from Brazil.
Right: *Anisoscelis serratulus* from Mexico.

65 Below left: *Pachycoris* spec. from the Philippines.
Right: *Coptosoma affine* from Natal.
Side-view, to show the large scutellum covering almost the entire abdomen.

On right, left column:

66 Above: *Umbonia orozimbo* from Mexico.

67 Centre: *Membracis sanguineophaga* from Brazil.

68 Below: *Bocydium rufiglobum* from Peru.

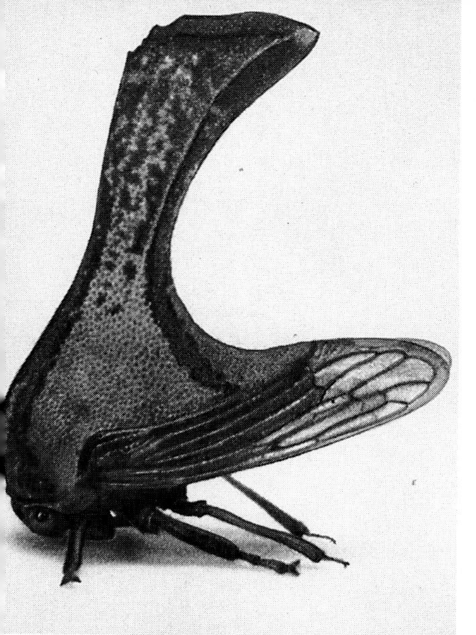

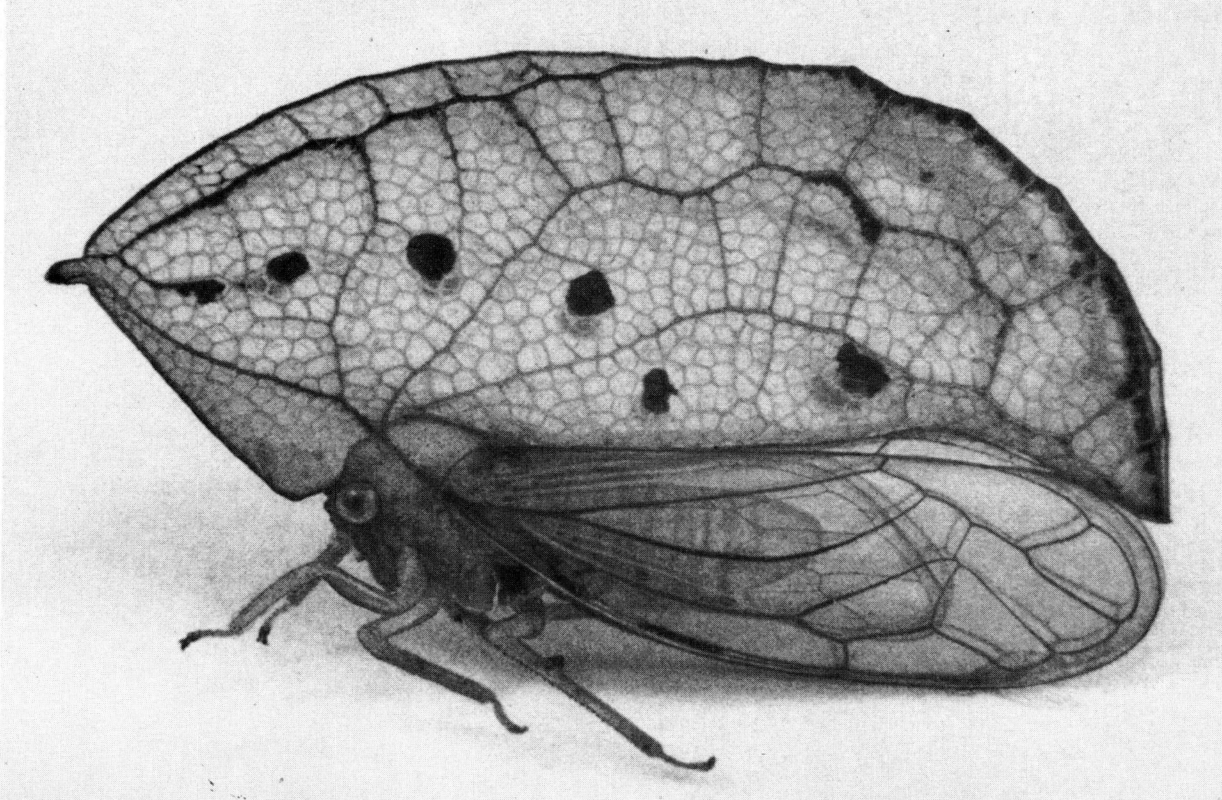

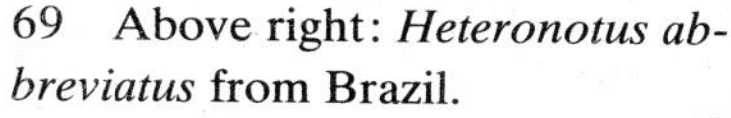

69 Above right: *Heteronotus abbreviatus* from Brazil.

70 Below right: *Oeda inflata* from Brazil.

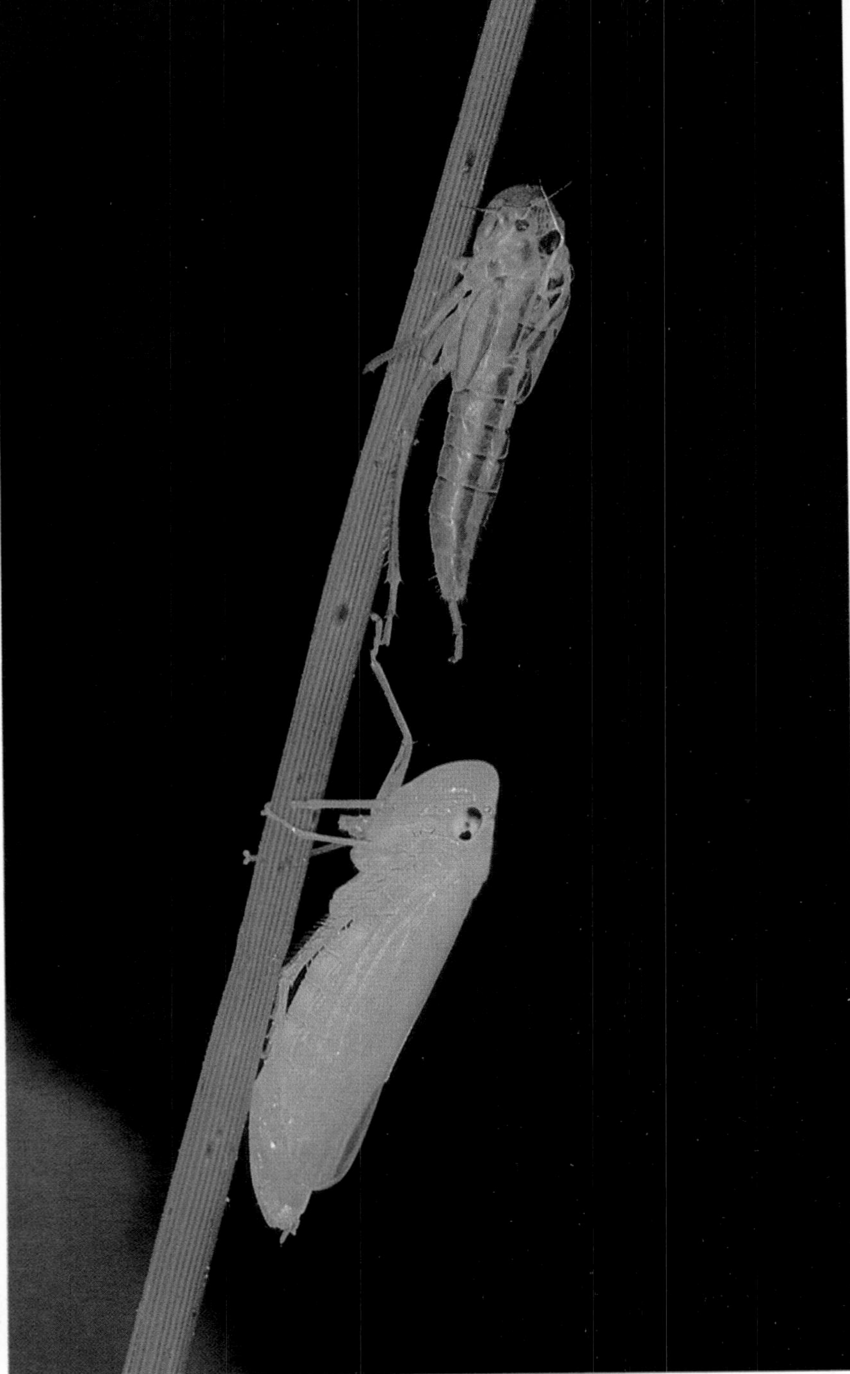

71 Left: The nymphs of Cuckoo-spit Insects or Froghoppers (Cercopidae) live enclosed in a frothy liquid that they themselves secrete. Here, the Meadow Froghopper *(Philaenus spumarius)* on the plant bedstraw.

72 Right: Newly-hatched European Leafhopper *(Ciccadella viridis)*. Above, the final larval skin (exuvia) can be seen.

On right:

73 The Froghopper *(Cercopis vulnerata)* from Central Europe in the process of mating. The nymphs, enclosed in a covering of froth, feed on the roots of herbaceous plants.

74 Left: The Woolly Apple Aphis *(Eriosoma lanigerum)* sometimes causes damage to apple trees. A particular characteristic of this plant louse is the secretion of a flocculent white waxy substance. The species, introduced from America, has become very widespread in Europe.

75 Right: A European Aphid colony *(Thelaxis dryophila)* on a bud of an oak-tree, with many visiting ants. Below left, the egg of a Hover-fly (Syrphidae).

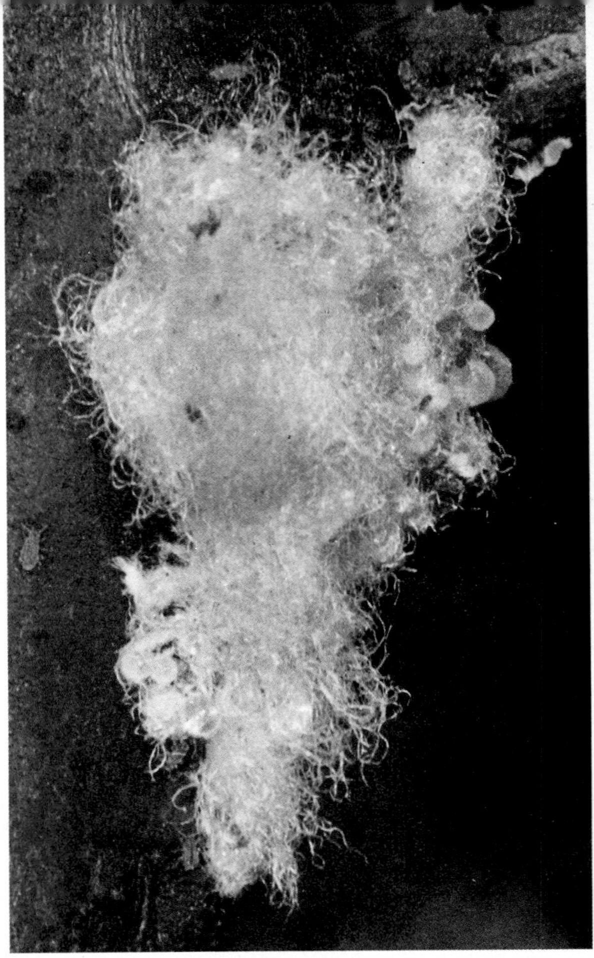

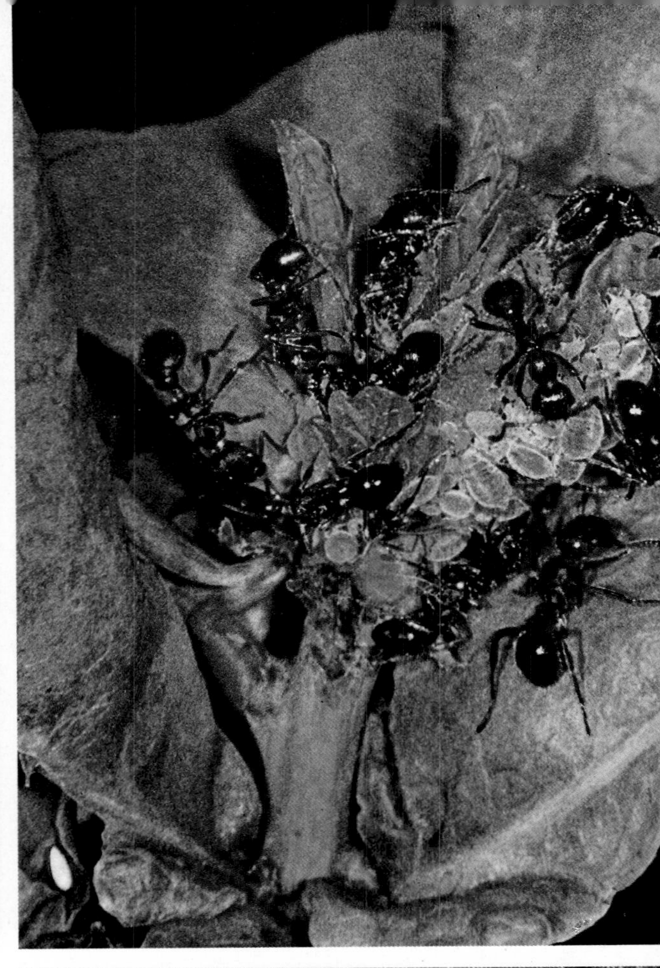

76 Left: Armoured Scale Lice (Diaspididae) of the species *Parthenolecanium rufulum* on an oak tree branch (Central Europe). Some of the Scales show a small hole out of which a parasitic wasp (Encyrtidae) has hatched.

77 Right: The Elder Aphid *(Aphis sambuci)* forms especially dense colonies (Central Europe).

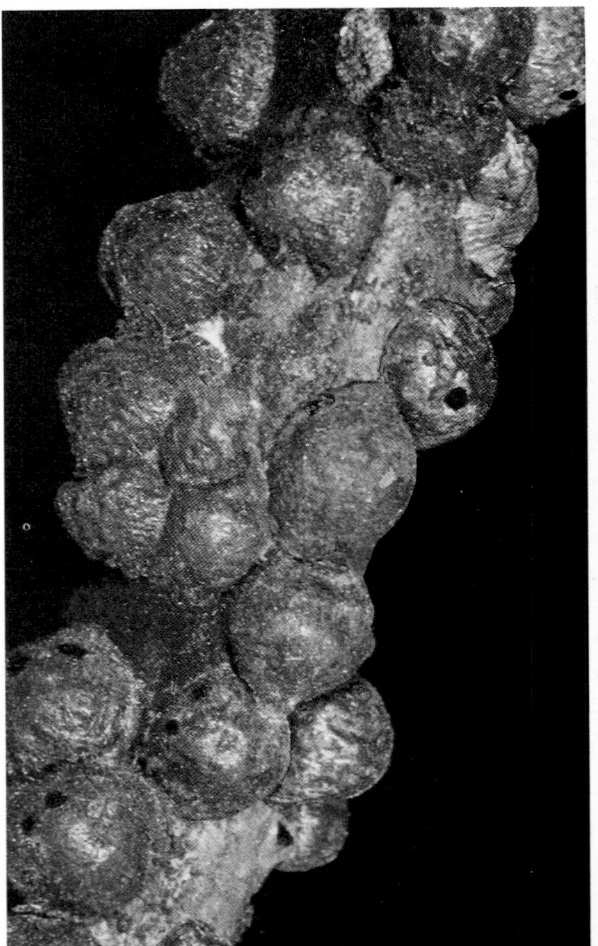

78 Cicadas that produce remarkable waxy secretions.
Left: *Poeciloptera phalaenoides* from Brazil.
Right: *Lystra pulverulenta* from Brazil.
Below: *Phenax variegata* from Brazil.

79 Above: The curiously-shaped head of the Lantern Fly *Phriotus diadema* from Brazil.

80 Below: Lantern Flies
Left: *Phriotus diadema* from Brazil; the head of this species carries a serrated prolongation.
Right: *Hotinus candelaria* from China, with the head extended to form a long curved horn.
Below: *Fulgora laternaria* from Brazil.

81 The Elm Louse *Schizoneura lanuginosa* (Central Europe) causes the development of large bladder-shaped galls on elms.

82 Colonies of a red species of aphid *(Dactynotus tanaceti)* (Europe) infest the leaves of the Parsley Fern *(Tanacetum vulgare)*. They attack the underside of the lower leaves which subsequently turn yellow.

Development cycle of the Black Bean Aphid *(Aphis fabae)*.

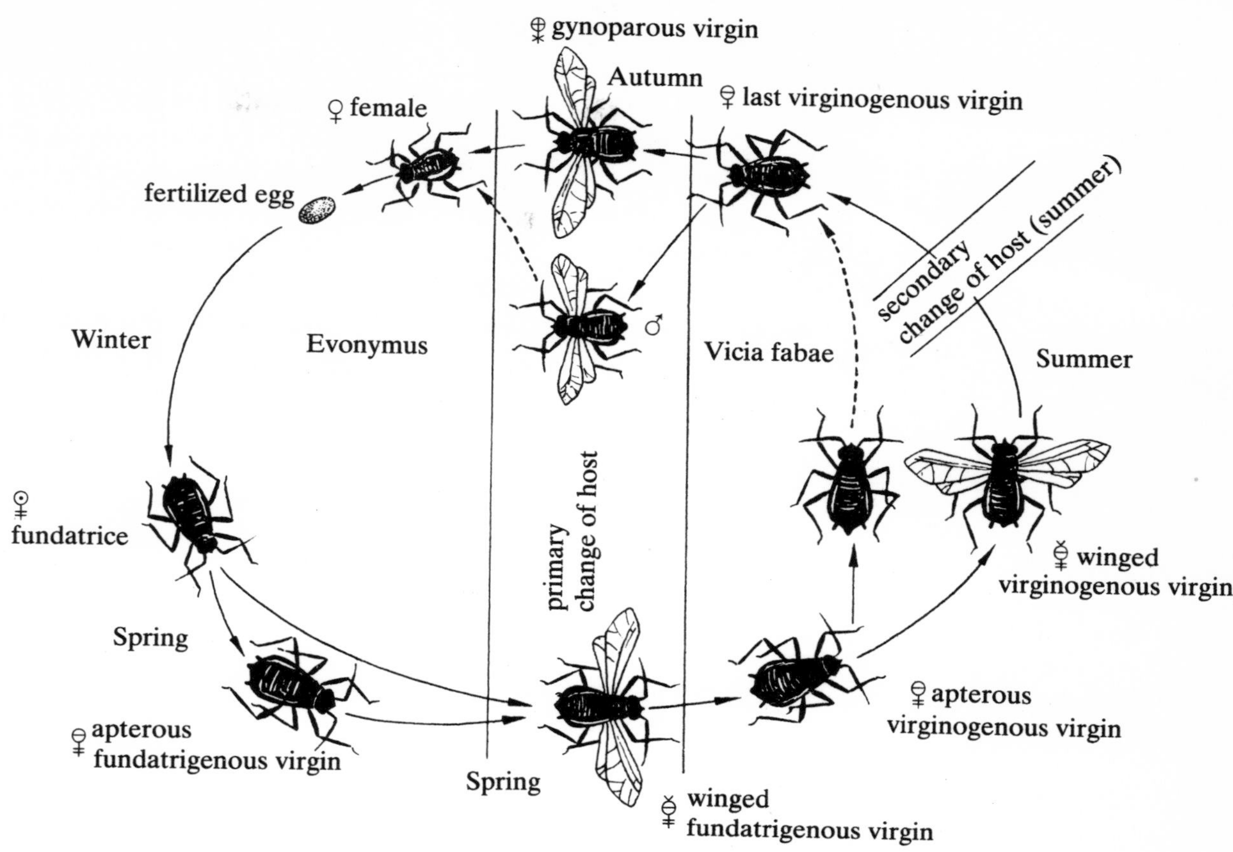

he examined many dissections; never was he able to find aphid eggs inside the adult body, but always young insects exactly like the mother in everything but size. Out of various specimens, he obtained 20, 28, 32 and 33 such nymphs.

The accounts given by Charles Bonnet (1720–1793) in Geneva show the accuracy of observation and description typical of the time. Bonnet's experiments substantiated Van Leeuwenhoek's discovery and earned him ample praise from the great master Réaumur. In 1744, Bonnet's collected works were published under the title *Insectologie*. By now, his eyesight had deteriorated to such an extent that, sadly, scarcely any further entomological discoveries were to follow. Here is his account of observation made of aphids isolated immediately after birth, an experiment suggested by Réaumur as a means of confirming parthenogenesis: "It was on 20th May, towards 5 o'clock in the evening, when my aphid, as soon as it was born, was placed in complete seclusion, as I have already described. From that time on, I took care to keep an exact journal of her life. I noted down every detail of even her smallest movements. No step she took seemed unimportant to me. Not only did I observe her every day, hour by hour, usually starting at 4 or 5 o'clock in the morning and not stopping until perhaps 9 or 10 o'clock in the evening; but several times every hour and constantly I carried out my examination with a magnifying glass, in order to observe more accurately and to inform myself of the most private actions of my small hermit. Although this constant diligence proved somewhat strenuous and burdensome, I have reason to congratulate myself on having become accustomed to it. Besides, the aim that I had set myself seemed to me too important to be pursued with no more than the ordinary degree of attention . . . My aphid moulted four times: on the 23rd towards evening, on the 26th at about 2 o'clock in the afternoon, on the 29th at about 7 o'clock in the morning, and on the 31st in the evening towards 7 o'clock . . . Perhaps I may be forgiven for a certain childishness on my part when I describe the anxiety caused

83 Pineapple-shaped gall produced by the Red Spruce Gall Aphid *(Adelges laricis)* from Europe.

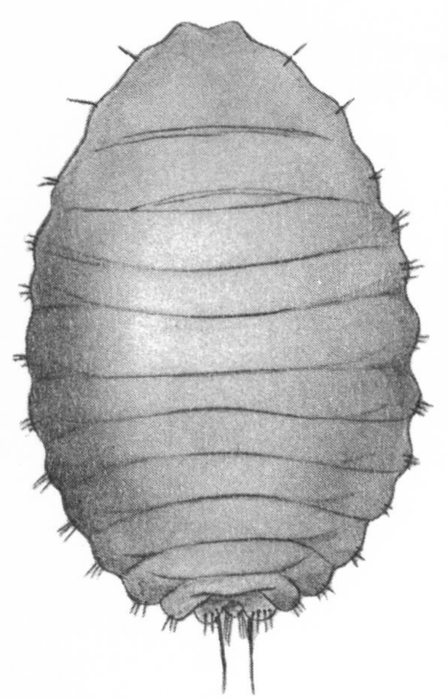

Female of the Citrus Mealy Bug *(Pseudococcus citri)*. Female Scale Insects are always wingless and usually sedentary.

me by my aphid in her final metamorphosis. Although the conditions in which she was kept precluded all possibility of intrusion by another insect into her hermitage, I nevertheless found her so distended and gleaming that she seemed to me to have the appearance of an aphid with an internal worm. That she seemed not to make the slightest movement increased my fear and anxiety. Unfortunately I was able to observe her only by the light of a wax candle. Finally I grew calmer when I observed that she was shedding her skin. But I was not entirely free of concern. She lay on her side and soon after that, turned onto her back, so that her entire underside was visible. I noted that she was still making movements with her feet, which until then had been drawn up in the manner of a pupa and placed against the breast. She moved herself backwards and forwards in an irregular way as if wanting to alter her position. But because the feet were still very weak at that time, having just emerged from the folds of the old skin, they did not yet seem skilful enough to perform their work. In this position, on an almost upright leaf, the aphid was held only by the old skin, hanging from it by the extreme tip of her body. She was in danger of having a nasty fall as soon as she disengaged herself completely from the skin. This precarious situation made me uneasy and I was not satisfied until she had gradually reached a safe position . . . But it is time to come to the most important point in the life of my hermit . . . She had now become a fully mature aphid. On the 1st June in the evening at about 7 o'clock, I observed with the greatest satisfaction that she had given birth, and from that time on, would have to be called an aphid mother. From that day onward until the 21st, she brought 95 young into the world, all fully alive, most of them before my very eyes."

Bonnet's final summary, although made almost two hundred and fifty years ago, is basically correct. "In the fair season of the year, the female aphids give birth to live young; thus they are viviparous. Towards mid-autumn, they lay true eggs; then they cease being viviparous and become oviparous. I made this discovery in autumn 1740, and it was subsequently confirmed by renowned observers. I showed in my book that the females are able to alter their entire behaviour when they want either to bring live young into the world or to lay eggs."

Scale insects (Coccina)

Scale insects belong to an animal group of superlatives, although for a long time their life history remained something of a mystery. Little was known of their complex cycle of development, nor was it realized that in addition to the invariably wingless females, there are winged males, the hind wings of which are completely atrophied or reduced to stirrup-like structures, and nobody had foreseen the immense difficulties involved in controlling those species of scale insects that damage growing plants.

Even Linnaeus was relatively unfamiliar with scale insects; in his *Journey to Gotland* (1745), he described a *Coccus aquaticus*, that lives under stones in streams. Later it turned out that Linnaeus was referring to leeches' eggs.

Pela wax

Scale insects first drew man's interest by the value of their products. Like beeswax, pela, the waxy exudate of one species of scale insect, *Ceroplastes ceriferus*, was found to be useful. In China, egg-bearing female scale insects were placed on the branches of young ash-trees in the spring. In August the branches were harvested and the wax recovered in boiling water. In comparison with beeswax, pela wax has a high melting point (81–83 °C) and is almost odourless. It is used today to harden wax mixtures, to impregnate silk and paper and in the manufacture of wool dyes (Schimitschek, 1968). Its virtues are acknowledged in the *Pen ts'ao*. "The white wax in question here is not the same wax as that produced by bees. It is formed by a small insect. These insects feed on the juice of the tree tung-ch'ing and transform it gradually into a white fatty secretion which they attach to the branches of this tree. Some say that this is the excreta of the worms, but they are mis-

Male of the Orange Scale Insect *(Icerya purchasi)*. In the male, the hind wings are reduced to hook-like rudiments.

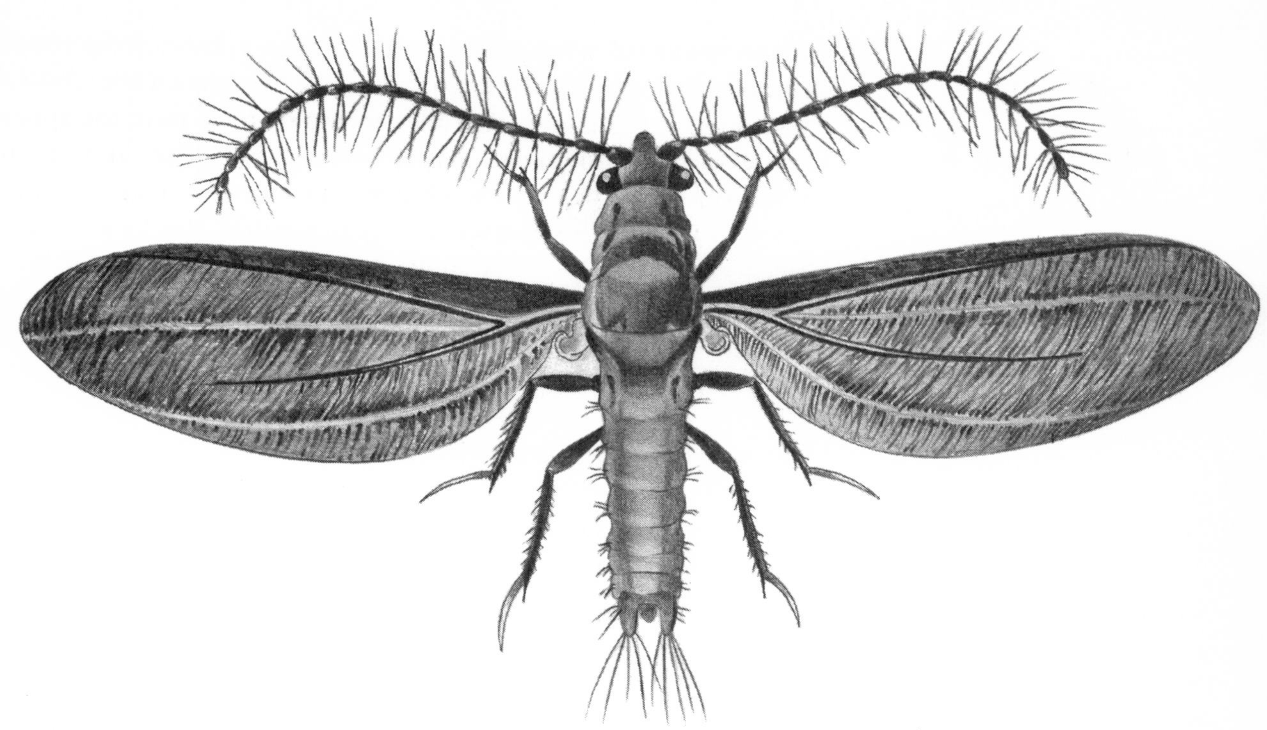

taken. This fat is gathered up in autumn. It is melted at the fire and then put into cold water in a container in which it solidifies. If a piece is broken apart, it is found to have veins like a white stone. It is smooth and gleaming. People mix it with oil and obtain light from it. It is much superior to beeswax . . . When the sun enters the 15th degree of the sign of Gemini, everything swarms with these insects. They draw sap from the branches. From their mouths they exude a particular mucous secretion which settles on the branches of the tree and gradually becomes a white wax. When the sun enters the 15th degree of the sign of Virgo, harvesting begins, the wax being stripped from the trees . . . They sit so thickly in such great numbers like grapes on the tree, that they could be taken for its fruit . . . Each of their nests contains several hundred small eggs. When the sun stands centrally within the sign of Taurus, the eggs are collected, laid upon leaves of the jo tree and hung upon this tree as soon as the sun leaves the sign of Gemini. The sun draws the nests apart, opens the eggs within them and the worms that emerge immediately begin their work on the tree. But they must be protected from ants which like to eat these worms. In its nature, the wax is neither cooling nor warming and has no harmful properties. It is beneficial to the flesh of the body, assuages rushing blood and all kinds of pains. It increases strength and unites the nerves and joints. Made into powders and pills, it kills the worms that cause consumption. It is particularly indispensable in surgery; it has various uses in various salves."

Shellac

The extraction of shellac is an ancient trade in India. The Lac Insect *(Tachardia lacca)* is placed on branches of the Lacquer tree *(Butea frondosa)*, where the larvae and females enclose themselves in a red protective covering; this is scraped off, decolorized, purified and processed to make shellac. Shellac is unrivalled as a coating for wooden and metal objects and was used in the manufacture of gramophone records. The first reports of this material were brought to Europe in 1710 by Father Tachard. He believed it to be produced by ants. Geoffroy jun. is not at all sure which insect is responsible. In 1714, in the reports of the French Academy, he writes: "On closer examination, the lac seemed to me to be a kind of beehive, such as bees and other insects build. When it is broken open, cells of symmetrical construction are found inside, which indicates that it is not of vegetable origin. The cells are elongate-oval and sometimes round. Usually they are inflated at the middle, with the pointed extremity at the end facing the branch and the rounded extremity at the other end; here there is a small hole of the same kind as that found, on closer observation, across the whole surface of the lac.

These cells certainly accommodate something, and not merely excrement, as certain people think. Here there are small, more or less inflated bodies which the first observers took for wings or other parts of the Lac Ant. These small bodies are of a beautiful red colour, sometimes in a lighter and sometimes in a darker shade, and when they are scraped off, they disintegrate into dust, which in beauty of colour is no whit inferior to cochineal."

In 1781, in his paper *Natural History of the Insect which produces the Gum Lacca*, J. Kerr was the first to identify the Lac Insect as a coccid.

Dyes

Scale insects also provided certain dyes that have today been replaced by chemical dyes, but which were once of considerable economic importance. Carmine and scarlet were the colours produced mainly by three species: *Kermes ilicis* in the Mediterranean area, *Porphyrophora polonica* in East and Central Europe and *Coccus cacti* in Mexico.

The kermes insect (or scarlet grain) was already well-known in ancient civilizations, particularly in Phoenicia. Solomon, King of Israel (reigned from about 970–930 B.C.) wrote to Hiram, King of Tyre (reigned 1000–970 B.C.): "Send me a man who is able to work in gold, silver ore, iron, carmine and scarlet dye." The list illustrates the value attached to the coccid dyestuffs. Pedanius Dioscorides also mentions the kermes insect: "Kokkos baphike. Coccum tinctile is a little shrub, full of sprigs to which cling the grains as Lentils, which being taken out are laid up in store. But ye best is that of Galatia, & that of Armenia, then that in Asia, & that of Cilicia, & last of all, that in Spain. It hath a binding faculty, being good for wounds & hurts of ye Sinews, being beaten small & laid on with Acetum. But that in Cilicia grows upon oaks, in fashion like to a little snail, which ye women there, gathering with ye mouth, doe call Coccum." *(The Greek Herbal of Dioscorides*, Book IV, p. 48)

In Pliny's time, the North African and Spanish Provinces of the Roman Empire paid a large proportion of their tribute in the form of these coccids which were used to dye the uniforms of the senior officers. The garments of the priests were also dyed in this way. In Venice, Genoa and Marseilles in the Middle Ages, dyers' guilds flourished, and statues still exist today as reminders of the time when kermes enjoyed considerable commercial importance.

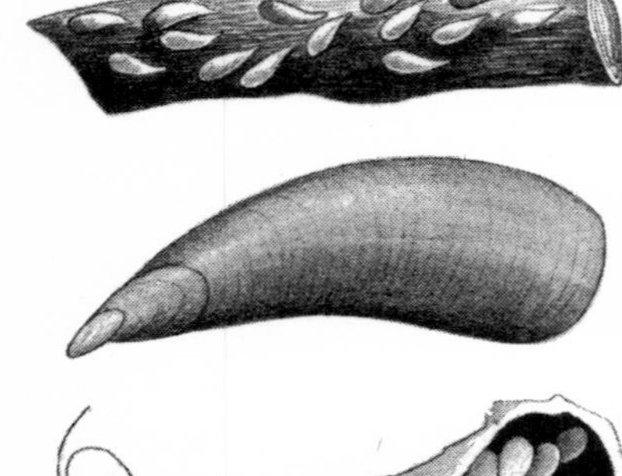

The Oyster Scale *(Lepidosaphes ulmi)* occurs widely on fruit trees. Below, a Scale that has been detached and turned over. The female and eggs are visible.

The Arabian scholar Ibn al-Baithar (1197–1248), writes in his *Encyclopaedia of Arabian Botany and Pharmacology*: "The creature is lentiform, quite small at first, then growing slowly to the size of a chick-pea. Internally it contains a blood-coloured mass, and numerous small creatures sit at the upper side of the kermes. When the grain is ripe, it opens and allows the creatures to escape, and they disperse across the tree and into the grains . . . Then they grow until May. This is the time when the grain opens. The Qirmiz traders crush them and mix the watery parts, the blood-red and other parts together well. In the month of Pentecost, the small creatures emerge from the undamaged grains. The creature is red and resembles a lentil. It moves close to the grain and dies here. Until June, its weight decreases, but it retains its form even when it ages. It is then more suitable for dyeing."

Use of an insect for pharmaceutical purposes has usually accompanied the other forms of utilization. Mattiolo's *New Kräuterbuch* (New herbal; 1563) contains the note: "Also produces small reddish pellets; if they are crushed and applied with vinegar, they heal fresh wounds and bloody eyes extremely well."

Female and two larvae of the Nettle Scale *(Orthezia urticae)*. Notable are the shield-like or tubular white waxy secretions.

The efficacy ascribed to this insect as a cardiac stimulant is particularly important. In *Antidotarium Bononiense* (1770) one can still read: "This medicine holds the leading place among cardiac remedies."

Curiously enough, uncertainty about the nature of the insects that produce kermes persisted until recent times, and the statements contained in early literature, which were in part correct, were never followed up. In 1714, in a *Botanical Treatise on the Origin and Nature of Kermes*, Nissoli, a thorough and careful scientific researcher, writes: "There are almost as many opinions on the origin of kermes as there are writers who have dealt with the subject. Some consider them to be true galls, others to be solidified plant secretions, and others again believe that they originate from small larvae. The last view, which Strobelberger in his treatise on the medicinal preparation of alkermes ascribes to Brassavola, seems to me best to conform to the facts.

At the beginning of May, small white spots the 24th part of an inch in diameter can be seen on the stem, twigs and leaves of the coccus oak. Their surface is rough and villose and, when crushed, they give off a red liquid similar to blood. They grow slowly inside their white woolly covering. When adult, they contain innumerable small red eggs . . . Each egg contains a small, red, six-legged creature with two antennae and a double, crescent-shaped tail . . . As soon as the creatures have hatched, they leave the shell of the parent kermes in search of food and a suitable place for their young. The idea expressed by almost all writers that these insects develop wings corresponds less well with reality. The midges or flies frequently seen flying round the kermes probably originate from some oak gall. As soon as the kermes matures, it is collected and prepared in a variety of ways, depending upon whether it is to be used for the well-known kermes prescription or for the purpose of dyeing. In medicine, it is one of the best cardiac tonics known, useful in cases of abortus and much else. In the dye trade, it has been partly superseded today by cochineals."

Encyclopaedias are always a little behind their time, as was the *Natur-, Kunst- und Handlungslexicon* (Encyclopaedia of Nature, Art and Commerce) by J. Hübner (1731). "Cocculae baccae, coccid seeds are berries the size of a large pea, round, ash-grey and curved somewhat inwards at the bottom where they are attached to the stalk . . . They are brought to us from Alexandria hanging on the stem like grapes. The nature of the plants that make up this cargo is still uncertain."

Porphyrophora polonica provided the material known as Polish cochineal which came to Germany in the Middle Ages as tribute from the East. In the 12th and 13th centuries it was part of the compulsory contributions exacted from the peasants and serfs, and was used for dyeing linen and silk cloth. A contemporary account written in 1672 by Martin Bernhard von Bernitz describes the role of this pigment bearer. "This coccus, commonly known in Germany as the blood of Saint John, because it is found only round about the time of St. John's Day, is gathered by superstitious people on that day at midday to the accompaniment of certain ceremonials . . . I have found this coccus very often in sandy areas near Warsaw; it is particularly common in the place at which Polish kings were elected. Some people also assert that the coccus is found on the Pimpinella, the Hernaria and the roots of oak trees. But although I have searched diligently for it, I have not observed such a thing . . . The Turks and Armenians who buy this coccus from the Jews, dye their wool, silk and the tackle of their horses with it. Turkish women use this coccus dissolved in wine or in the juice of lemons or pomegranates every day to colour the nails of their hands and toes. In earlier days, our merchants used to sell the coccus to the Dutch at a high price, and I remember having seen it once when I visited His Magnificence Peter Heinrich, who told me that the Dutch scarlet-dyers would mix this coccid with equal quantities of the Indian one, to obtain a more intense and beautiful colour . . . Smallholders and others who collect it pay close attention at the time of the summer equinox or a little later, when these grains are ripe and bursting with red juice. They are gathered with a small hand spatula. With one hand the plant is drawn up high, while the spatula held in the other, tears up the roots. The berries are collected from it and the plant replaced into the same hole from which it was snatched. The speed with which all this is completed is a never-ending source of amazement. Then a sieve is used to separate the coccus from the soil clinging to it."

In North Germany, the Polish cochineal was known as "the blood of the beheaded John the Baptist". It was gathered on June 23.

The coccids were used as an embrocation to be applied to the region of the heart, and as the "blood of St. John", were believed to cure many diseases.

The Aztecs, in the early civilizations, already extracted scarlet dyestuff from the True Cochineal Insect *(Coccus cacti)*; old drawings and writings show that they received them as tribute, from, for example, the city of Nocheztlán. These coccids are native to Mexico, where they live on various species of Opuntia, the prickly pear genus of the cactus family, and in the Aztec language are known as *nocheznopalli* (= the prickly pear that produces blood-coloured fruits). This new source of dye soon attracted the attention of the Spaniards (López de Gomera). Later, vast quantities of the material were brought to Europe for the manufacture of carmine dye. *Coccus cacti* together with its host plants, the Opuntias, was introduced to various Mediterranean countries and to the eastern region. One hectare yielded some 400 kg cochineal. In 1587, the Spanish fleet is said to have brought 65,000 kg cochineal to Europe, and between 1758 and 1782, merchants in Amsterdam imported 423,000 kg every year. Although cochineal was supplanted by chemical dyes after 1880, it now appears to be regaining some of its importance in the food and cosmetic industries as a natural colouring matter.

Beetles

(Coleoptera)

In the first edition of his *Fauna Suecica*, Linnaeus lists 294 species of beetles, in the famous 10th edition of *Systema Naturae* 654. By the end of the 19th century, almost 100,000 species of beetles were known, and at the present time some 350,000 species have been described. Beetles comprise by far the largest number of species of any order of insects, indeed of any group in the animal kingdom. As a comparison, there are only 8,600 species of birds and 5,000 species of mammals. Weevils (Curculionidae) alone, as the largest family of beetles, number 50,000 species.

Beetles also achieve records for size. With a body length of up to 16 cm, two species of Longhorn Beetles are not only the largest beetles but at the same time the largest insects in the world. They are *Titanus giganteus* from the Amazon region and *Xixuthrus heros* from the Fiji Islands. Similarly the smallest known beetle in the world is also one of the smallest of all insects. It is a Fringed Ant Beetle (*Nanosella fungi*, family Ptiliidae), which occurs in North America. As an adult it is only 0.25 mm in length. Single-celled Slipper Animalcules (*Paramecium caudatum*) reach a length of 0.12 to 0.33 mm. So the smallest beetle is smaller than a large protozoon.

Beetles were and still are useful to man, but also harmful. On the one hand, many species are scavengers consuming noxious plant and animal waste, or as predators destroying insect pests; on the other hand, many species damage growing crops, such as the Colorado beetles, while others infest stored foods. A number of species of beetles used to have some importance as food. One might mention the famous cockchafer bouillon which was still being served in leading French restaurants in the second half of the 19th century. Many species of beetle have been used for pharmaceutical purposes. One of the most notable examples is that of Oil Beetles (Meloidae) which were used as a poison and also as a medicine and aphrodisiac. The active principle of these beetles is cantharidine.

The cult of the sacred *Scarabaeus* is well known and existed not only among the Egyptians but also in other civilizations. In addition to Scarabs, many other species played an important part in ethnic cultic practices, in particular the Ladybird. Poets and writers have frequently used beetles, particularly glowworms, as motifs in lyric and prose.

Beetles were also introduced into craftwork, coin manufacture, glyptography, even heraldry. Representations of beetles abound in drawing, painting and sculpture. The earliest known sculpture depicting an insect is of a beetle (probably a specimen of *Necrophorus*) and was made of coal in the Magdalenian period, 25,000 to 30,000 years ago.

Above:

Trichaptus mutillarius from Brazil looks like a furry toy. It is matt black with eight large creamy-white spots and two bright orange ones.

Lacewings

(Planipennia)

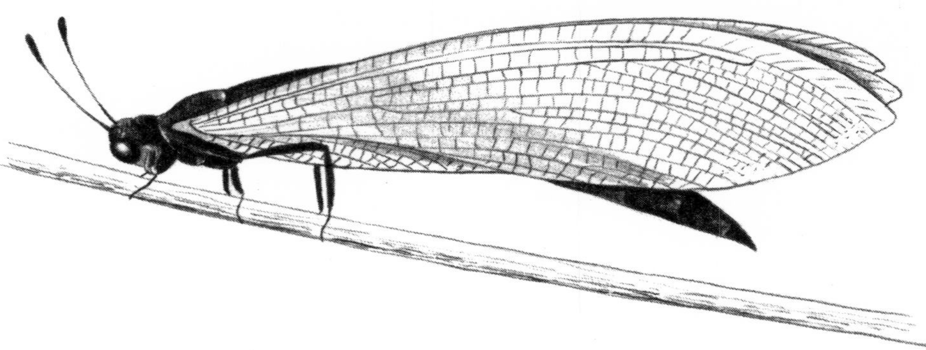

Out of the very diverse order of Lacewings (Planipennia) which includes the Coniopterygidae (Dusty Wings), Sisyridae (Spongilla Flies), Osmylidae (Osmylids), Mantispidae (Mantis Flies), Hemerobiidae (Aphis Lions), Ascalaphidae (Ascalaphid Flies), Chrysopidae (Green Lacewings), Myrmeleonidae (Ant Lion Flies) and others, we shall look in some detail here only at the Green Lacewings and the Ant Lions.

Green Lacewings (Chrysopidae)

Several European species overwinter in imaginal form in concealed sites in the open, and often in human habitations. When aphid time begins in the spring, the females deposit their eggs in a strikingly individual manner. They press the tip of the abdomen on a leaf, then lift it slowly. Then a small quantity of viscous fluid is secreted from accessory glands on the genitalia, which rapidly hardens. Thus they produce a stalk-like thread which, in the European species, can be 5 to 10 mm long, and the egg is placed on the top of this pedicle. The action is repeated so that clusters of varying numbers of eggs (10–30) are formed. One female will produce several such batches; the total number of eggs may be several hundred. In 1700 Gustav Gahrliep described these eggs as "small, curious growths". They were thought to be fungi and were given the name of *Ascophora ovalis* (egg-shaped tube-bearers). Réaumur, in 1737, was the first to recognize their true nature. After a good many days—the number depends primarily upon temperature and humidity—the larvae break through the egg membrane with the help of an egg-tooth. At first they feed on young aphids. The larval period, interrupted by two moults, lasts 10 to 30 days. Within this time, some 120 to 140 aphids are consumed. A feature unusual in insects living above ground is the absence of an anal orifice. The faeces are stored in the hind gut to be discharged by the imago. In the larvae of many species, bristle-like hairs arising from tubercles on the sides of the segments bear hooks at the end; on these, the larvae, by bending their head well back, hang the dead bodies of their victims from which they have drained the juices.

Not only empty aphid skins are collected but also other debris such as fragments of bark, and in captivity, scraps of paper, threads etc. Before they pupate, the Chrysopidae larvae spin a cocoon from which, after about three weeks, there emerges not the expected imago, but a pupa, which has cut its way out using its mandibles. This pupa moves about in a somewhat ungainly way for about half an hour, then attaches itself to the underside of a leaf. The skin on the forepart of the back ruptures and the imago emerges.

Above:

Ant Lion Fly *(Myrmeleon formicarius)* at rest.

Ant Lion Flies (Myrmeleonidae)

The Ant Lions, as the larvae of this family of Lacewings are known, first made their appearance in literature hundreds of years ago. The *Physiologus*, for example, presents a somewhat fantastical description of them, accompanied by Faustian philosophizing. "It has the face of a lion and the hindquarters of an ant. Its father is a carnivore, but its mother eats vegetable food. When they engender the Ant Lion, they bring it forth with two characteristics. It cannot eat meat because of the nature of its mother, nor plant food because of the nature of its father. So it perishes, because it has no sustenance. In just such a way, every man has a double soul, inconstant in all his ways."

With rather more accuracy, Rabanus Maurus writes: "The Ant Lion is a small creature, extremely hostile to ants. It conceals itself in dust and kills ants that carry provisions. It is justly called formicaleon: towards ants it behaves like a lion, although towards other creatures only like an ant."

Thomas of Cantimpré, a Dominican friar and later Predicant-General of the Order for Germany, was one of the leading representatives of anti-scientific darkness, although he studied for four years under Albertus Magnus in Cologne. But at the same time, he was a nature-lover. On the subject of Ant Lions, he writes: "This worm is of the family of Ants, but considerably larger. As long as the Ant Lion is small, it is peaceable and keeps its fury to itself. But when it becomes powerful and strong, it scorns its erstwhile associates and turns to greater ones. Once it has grown to full size and power, it lurks concealed close to the track made by ants, and lies in wait like a true brigand. When the ants go to work and return carrying some object, the Ant Lion takes it from them, strangles the ants and consumes them. In winter, it steals the food stocks that the ants have gathered in the summer, because it has procured and collected nothing for itself. Not unlike this worm are those idle persons who take from the workers what they have earned by the sweat of their brow."

Albertus Magnus is somewhat more precise than his pupil. "It is not an ant as some maintain. For I have frequently observed and often pointed out to friends that this creature is similar in form to a tick. It conceals itself in sand, digging a hemispherical cavity, one pole of which is its mouth. When ants pass by gathering food, it catches and devours them. I have observed this repeatedly. In winter, they are said to plunder the food stocks of ants, because in summer, they themselves do not lay in stores of food."

Five hundred years later, Hasselquist (1722–1752), a Swede on a study tour commissioned by Linnaeus, wrote in his diary: "At the pyramids. What pleased me most here was the Ant Lion which has its own kingdom in this place. They leapt about in the sand in hundreds, just like ants. They all held pebbles, sand, rough fragments of wood or some other thing between their neat pincers, with which they hurried to the homes they had built for themselves in the sand. Round about, I found many habitations made by this worm. They were thrown up in the sand like small mole-hills, about as large as two fists, and rather depressed on the top. In the centre of this area was a small hole, the size of a reed-stalk, through which they went in and out. I assailed them in their entrenchments, destroying a few of the latter in order to examine their internal structure and organization. But I deceived myself, for I did no more than destroy their outer defences, and they had prepared a secret path so skilfully that it was useless to seek out the inner part of the structure."

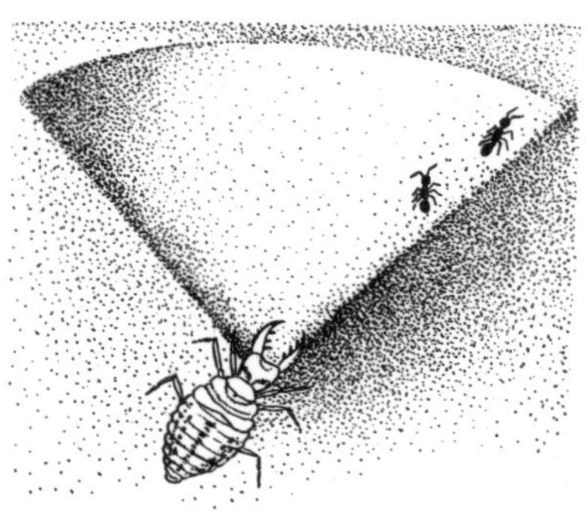

Section of a sand pit constructed by an Ant Lion (Myrmeleonidae) to catch its prey. The larva waits at the bottom of the pit ready to pounce.

Among the writers, one of the most accurate observers was August Johann Roesel von Rosenhof, who in a paper entitled *The cunning and skilful Ant-Robber which transforms itself into a Terrestrial and Nocturnal Dragonfly or into a Terrestrial and Nocturnal Nymph and its Truly Amazing Characteristics,* wrote: "As I have already indicated, the Ant Robber frequently lies hidden during the day at the side of the base of the pit; at night it is usually to be found in the middle, lying in wait with pincer-jaws at the ready, like a hunter waiting for game with his gun cocked.

Does it perhaps know that insects are more likely to fall into the pit at night than during the day, or are they better able to avoid the trap set for them during the day? Both, it may be supposed, particularly since the Ant Robber usually constructs a new pit in the evening. Accordingly, I often watched very closely when it was having a meal, employing for this purpose a good magnifying glass; but I could at no time perceive any other instrument except its pincers alone, with which it seemed to suck dry its prey, holding it up out of the sand with their two extreme tips: if there had been anything else there, I could not have failed to perceive it, for these two tips protrude a long way from the head. There is then nothing apart from the two parts of the pincers themselves, which presumably must be hollow . . . Since there is no doubt that our insect draws in its food through its prehensile pincers, the question arises—for as I said above, no rectal passage exists—as to the means by which the waste part of the food is removed from the body. All insects so far described by me have a rectum, which you can quite easily see if you squeeze the abdomen slightly, when it will protrude from the hind segment. I sought it for a long time, but was unable to find it; yet neither could I imagine that the insect predators did not have to excrete waste matter, particularly since I know that spiders, for example, which also suck only the juices from their prey, are nevertheless obliged to excrete the waste portion of their food. Could it be that everything our insect ingests is used up to its benefit and growth, or is a remnant of it lost by evaporation, as Herr Réaumur believes? This certainly appears to be the case, for even that great biologist was unable to discover that Ant Lions discharge any excrement. To this end, he fed them copiously with large quantities of midges, and when they had eaten their fill and seemed replete, and indeed looked thoroughly satiated, he placed them on a clean porcelain dish, but found no indication whatever that they gave off waste matter."

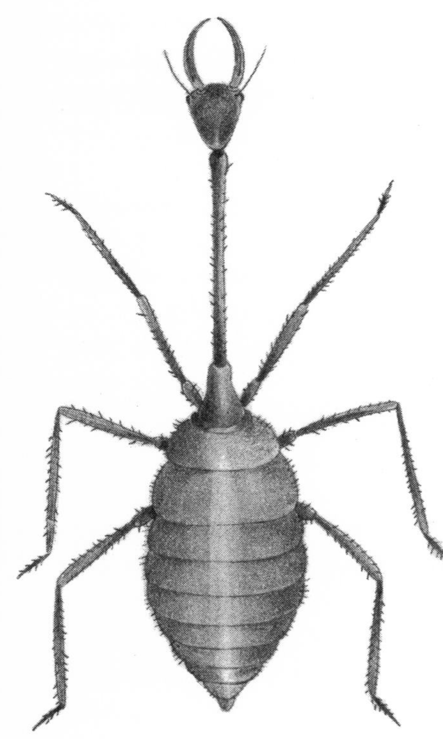

Larva of *Pterocroce storeyi* (family Neuropteridae) from North Africa. Note the unusually long neck.

The sites on which Ant Lions occur in large numbers usually have plenty of fine sand or sandy soil, little rain and plenty of sunshine. If a larva is dug up and placed on dry sand, it can be seen to perform twitching movements with the abdomen, shuffling its way backwards, abdomen first, down into the sand, more or less rapidly, depending upon the type of sand. The forward-directed bristle-like hairs covering its body thickly help in this process by preventing movement in the opposite direction. When the Ant Lion is so far into the sand that grains of sand fall in upon its head and prothorax, it flicks them off with energetic movements of the foreparts of the body. Constant repetition of this process produces the conical pit. The Ant Lion performs the same movements when a small insect, perhaps an ant, has fallen into the pit, and in trying to climb its wall, sets the sand in motion. This, of course, is a reflex action and not a carefully thought-out and cunning ploy to catch prey. Once the victim has slid to the floor of the pit, it is seized by the suctorial jaws and its juices extracted. In fact, the larva has no rectum, the waste matter is stored and excreted by the imago. Excrements are also used for the cocoon.

The earliest pupation occurs in June. The larva moves deeper into the sand, extends its heavy abdomen lengthwise and from it, extrudes white silken threads which form a hollow sphere held in place by the surrounding sand. Inside this hollow sphere, it undergoes metamorphosis into an exarate pupa, which after about 4 weeks, produces the imago. It emerges in the evening. During the day, the insects rest with wings disposed in a roof-like manner. Unless they are disturbed, they do not fly until evening. Their flight is ponderous.

Hymenopterans

(Hymenoptera)

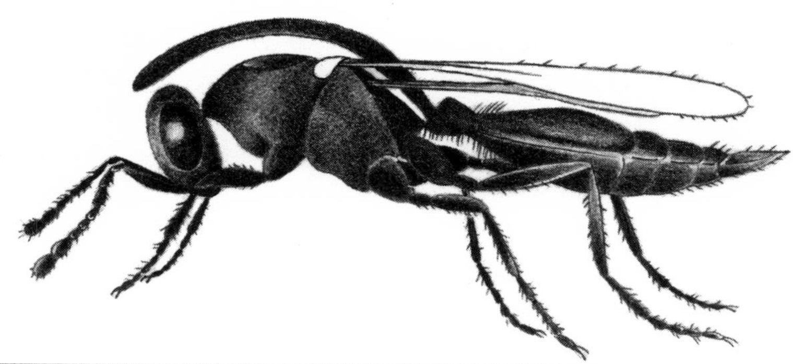

The best known member of the Hymenoptera is undoubtedly the honey bee, which is at the same time the insect with which man established the earliest and closest links. This species has not been included here, since it already has a very extensive literature of its own. We shall look in particular at some of the other Hymenoptera that have also drawn the attention of man over the centuries, such as bumble bees, hornets, wasps, Ichneumon "flies" and ants.

Bumble Bees
(Bombus)

It is not surprising that the conspicuous appearance of the bumble bee caused it to be noticed early, and it was already depicted by artists in Ancient Egypt. Largely forgotten today is the use of this insect in popular medicine, which is referred to by Saint Hildegard: "Let anyone who has inflamed eyes take the large bladder that is between the head and body of the bumble bee, and when he lies down to sleep, let him spray the liquid it contains into his eyes. Immediately afterwards, he should coat his eyelids and eyelashes with olive oil. If he does this once or twice a month, he will regain clear vision. Anyone who has ugly nails should apply to them the same fluid from the bumble bee until they are improved. Anyone suffering from serious scabies of the head can heal the condition by rubbing in this fluid."

Today we know that such treatments have no direct curative effect. But undoubtedly people believed that these large and beautiful insects possessed special powers. They inspired the Russian composer Nikolai Andreyevich Rimsky-Korsakov (1844–1908) to compose his "Flight of the Bumble Bee".

Thomas Moufet was one of the first to describe the life cycle of the bumble bee. "Bombylius, the largest species among those which come into being out of honeycombs, received their name from the murmuring sound they make, for in Greek, *bombyliazein* means to murmur, and the German name *Hummel* and the English names humble and bumble bee were given in imitation of the humming sound they make . . . They are of only very limited usefulness to man. For this reason, the Greeks call a lazy and useless person *anthropos bombylion*, because it is a completely useless bee. They nest among rocks on the ground and here they build nests with two or, more rarely, three entrances. Inside the nests, they make some attempt to produce wild honey but this only in small quantities, as Albertus recalls and Pennius observed. The latter once found as much honey as could scarcely be removed in three handfuls. Some of the English bumble bees have a sting which is very painful. Their honey is watery and sweetish. They attach wax to the hind

Above:

Parasitic Proctotrupoid Wasp (*Inostemma* spec.). When at rest, the insect holds the long ovipositor retracted inside a horny process arising from the first abdominal segment and curving forward over the head. This species develops in the larvae of Gall Midges.

legs, as bees do. They copulate with bodies turned away, sitting on plants or trees, and they remain a long time in this position. From time to time they beat their wings and produce a humming sound, in the nature of a nuptial song."

In European species of bumble bees, the females hibernate after fertilization, and in spring, each founds a new family. On warm spring days, the large, heavy females seek out a suitable place for the future nest. Once such a site is found, the female constructs a waxen receptacle, but not out of pure wax such as is used by species of the genus *Apis*. The wax of the bumble bees is produced in epidermal glands of the abdomen and secreted between the segments on the underside and back. They eke out this valuable substance by mixing it with tree resin, pollen and chewed plant material. The first eggs are deposited into the bowl they have thus fashioned, on a base of pollen and nectar, known as "bee-bread", and the whole protected by a wax covering. Adjacent to this egg cell, the bee constructs a cell to hold honey (a store for the queen in inclement weather) and similar ones for a supply of pollen. The larvae developing from the eggs are fed. Soon they are ready to pupate, and each larva spins itself an upright cocoon. The queen removes the surrounding wax, which is now superfluous, and makes use of it elsewhere. The young bees emerging from the cocoons are females. The empty cocoons are then converted into containers to hold nectar and pollen. The newly-emerged young are small and their sexual organs undeveloped. They are known as workers or auxiliary females, and help the queen in her work, collect pollen and feed both their younger siblings that are still developing as larvae and the queen herself, so that she can remain in the nest and restrict her activity to egg-laying. In the course of the summer, progressively larger females are produced, because the queen has less work to do and is better fed, and finally at the end of the season, males are also produced from unfertilized eggs. They leave the nest and live outside it on nectar and pollen. Meanwhile very large females with fully developed sexual organs have developed within the nest. Mating occurs principally outside the nest, but probably also not infrequently inside it. The males die and the fertilized females return to the nest. In autumn,

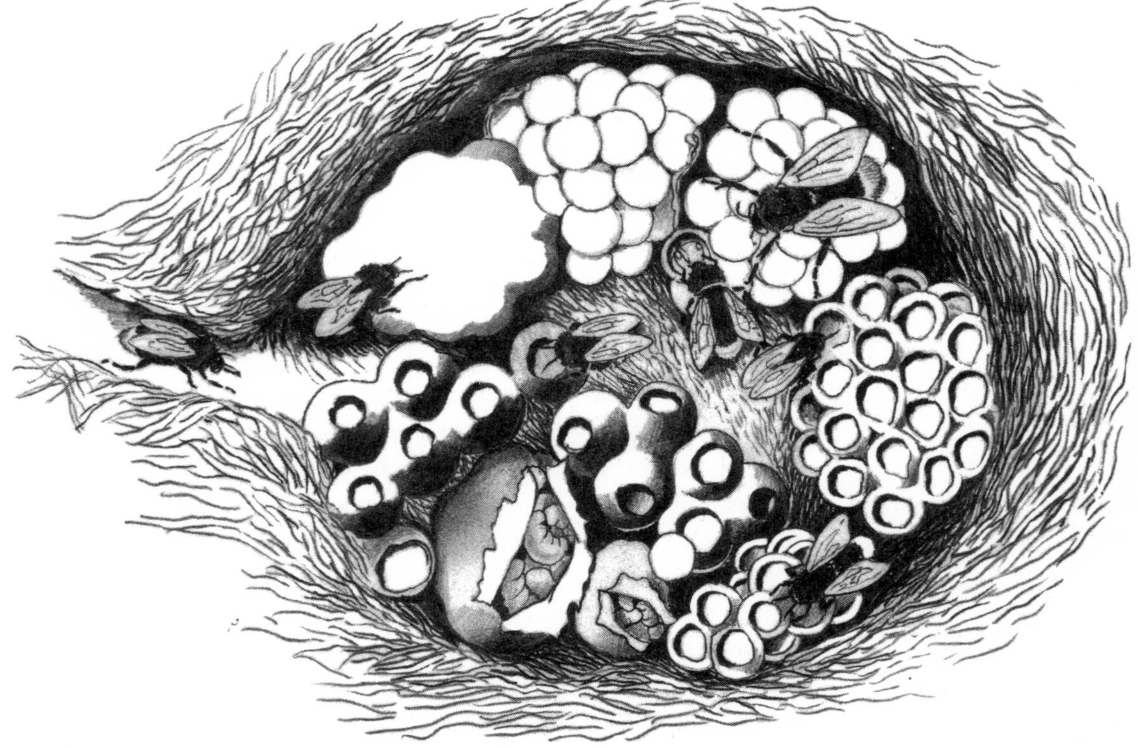

Nest of the Red-tailed Bumble Bee *(Bombus lapidarius)*.
The cells are arranged in groups and stand upright.
Above: A batch of eggs capped over with wax; a bumble bee is hatching.
Below and left: Larvae, one of which is being fed.
Right: Cells containing food stores.

the old queen dies, as do the remaining workers. The fertilized females hibernate either in a secluded corner of their own or communally in the old nest. But in spring, each female founds her own new family. Bumble bee families are not particularly large, consisting usually of between 50 and 100 individuals, although as many as 300 to 500 have been found in a single nest.

Particularly interesting are Cuckoo Bees of the genus *Psithyrus* which are social parasites of bumble bees. The best-known species in Europe are *P. vestalis* and *P. rupestris*. *P. vestalis* lays its "cuckoo's eggs" in the nests of the Ground Bumble Bee *(Bombus terrestris)* and *P. rupestris* in that of the Black Bumble Bee *(B. lapidarius)*. The *Psithyrus* larvae are reared by the workers of the host species. Not infrequently, the inquiline will kill the *Bombus* queen. There are even species of *Bombus* that will kill or drive out the resident in this way, and as a result, the phase of nest founding can be omitted, undoubtedly a step on the way to brood-parasitism.

Differentiation of the two genera must date back a long way. Apart from the fact that the *Psithyrus* female lacks any indication of polliniferous apparatus on the hind legs, the following finding is noteworthy: the corpora pedunculata, the mushroom-shaped bodies in the brain, are developed only slightly in the males of both genera, but in the females they vary: in *Psithyrus* they are just as small as in the males, but in *Bombus* much larger, since it is here that the instincts of brood-care, nest construction and food gathering are located. *Psithyrus*, of course, produces no equivalent of the *Bombus* workers.

Hornets *(Vespa crabro)*

In Europe, hornets (*Vespa crabro* and *V. orientalis*) as the largest species of wasps have always attracted attention and caused considerable alarm. One illustration of a hornet dates back to Ancient Egypt. In many countries today there is, unfortunately, a discernible decline in the numbers of these splendid and distinctive creatures, for reasons not altogether clear. Hornets often build their nests, which can be very large, in hollow trees (and it is well known that tree numbers are decreasing), or make use of cavities in the wooden parts of buildings and even birds' nesting boxes. The material used for nest construction in usually decayed wood which has previously been masticated, giving it a yellowish to reddish-brown colour. Hornets are largely predacious in habit, feeding upon various insects.

It was primarily the sting of the hornet that interested man. The Bible tells how hornets drive off enemies and punish evildoers; for example, in Joshua: "And I sent the hornet before you, which drove them out from before you, even the two Kings of the Amorites." Bodenheimer (1928) also speaks of how the hornet is presented in the Talmud. "A nine year old child is said to have been killed by a sting, and in particularly unfortunate circumstances, also adults. The book of the Sanhedrin describes as the cruellest of atrocities the action in which the inhabitants of Sodom spread honey on the skin of an all too charitable girl and subjected her to the stinging of hornets. Simple hornet stings were cured by the application of squashed flies or by one thirty-second part of the urine of a 40-day old child."

It is not clear how the legend arose that hornets originate from horses. It persisted for many centuries. Isidore of Seville writes: "Hornets are so called because they come into being out of horses." Galenus and the zoologists of the Arabian period also claim that hornets develop from worms that emerge from horses. Possibly the observation of hornets visiting carrion provided the basis for this mistaken belief.

A quotation from Ulisse Aldrovandi's first book, on the subject of comb-constructing Hymenoptera, illustrates his meticulous observation of natural phenomena. "They construct subterranean nests, removing the soil in a manner similar to that of ants. But when they have lost their king, they gather on any convenient tree and build their nest there. Several years ago, on my estate, I myself observed such a nest in a hollow oak. Hornets of a fearful size are said to live in India.

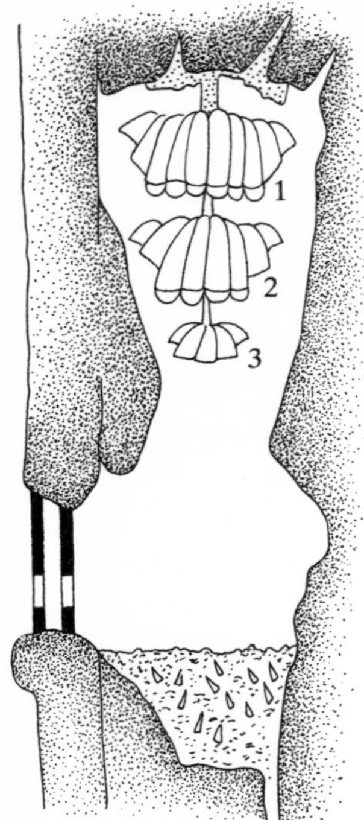

Diagram of the hornets' nest of *Vespa crabro* situated in a high tree. It has only a single central support and there is no envelope. Where necessary, the opening into the trec hollow is partially closed off. The numbers on the combs indicate the sequence of construction.

"Hornets do not gather winter stocks as bees do. They feed on flesh, dung and insects, but are also partial to sweet apples. Although some people are of the opinion that hornets come into existence from the dead bodies of horses or bullocks, in reality they reproduce by coitus, as has frequently been observed. Their larvae develop in cells, and one can find imagines on the point of emerging, pupae and small larvae all together at one time. In the cells, there is always a small quantity of honey. They grow particularly at the time of the full moon in the autumn, not in the spring.

"The hornets' nest consists of an area of hexagonal cells, similar to those of bees and wasps, only much greater, which are constructed from a cork-like and parchment-like mass. It can easily be distinguished from wasps' nests by the greater size of the cells. Five to 6 tiers of cells lie one above the other, usually 6, as was the case in the nest found by my bailiff on my estate in the upper part of a cavity in an oak tree. Its substance was very similar to birch bark and it is said to be made up of dust-like fragments of decayed poplar and willow mixed with the insect's mucid saliva. The mass is not solid, but consists of numerous lamellae, superimposed one on another. Between the individual layers, duct-like passages have been left free, by means of which the insects can make their way from the top to the bottom. The external covering of the nest has the entrance at the bottom. There is adequate access to the individual cells. We also observed a nest that had been placed with especial skill at the top of a tree. The openings of the individual cells were directed downwards so that they might be protected from rain, wind and tempest. We have also observed much larger hornets' nests, with 7 tiers, for example. I found such a one on a roof beam in my country house, with circular layers of comb and filled cells. The distance between the layers was the width of two fingers and the height of the cell, the breadth of one finger, and between there were vertical supporting pillars. The holes in the upper half of the nest were larger, for the parents, the lower ones smaller and intended for the children . . . The hornets feel very much at home among wild plants. Like bees, they have a king, which is larger in comparison, and there is only the one, whereas bees have several. If a number of hornets lose their way, they join together in a swarm and select a king. A full-grown king assembles a swarm and with this, founds a new community. They are a very harmonious, close-knit society and do not drive out their progeny as bees do, in order to look for food, but keep them with them and extend their nest.

"Hornets are friends of scorpions and woodpeckers, enemies of owls. It is probably competition for food that makes them fight with bees and flies.

"Boiled and distilled hornet water causes the skin to swell considerably but painlessly on contact. It is a component of theriac. The sting of the hornet is much more painful and dangerous than that of the wasp. Most dangerous are those stings delivered during the dog days. Three times nine stings are believed to kill a man."

The subterranean nests are probably exceptional; a female is the central figure of a hornet society, not a male (nor is it with bees), and the "king" cannot be elected. "She" holds that position by virtue of her ovaries.

Social Wasps (Vespidae)

There can be very few people who, perhaps as children, have not come into personal and possibly painful contact with wasps. So it is not surprising that the early literature contains many references to these insects. Below, we preface a few typical examples of these, presented in chronological order, with some notes on the biology of wasps.

Both the species living socially in quite large colonies (True Wasps, Vespinae) and those living in smaller families (the sub-family of Polistes—Polistinae) practise brood care, in that they feed their larvae with insects, especially flies, that they have killed, chewed up and regurgitated (and also nectar). The nests of True Wasps have an external covering and consist of several combs,

Wenn dich die Lästerzunge sticht,
so laß dir dies zum Troste sagen:
Die schlechtesten Früchte sind es nicht,
woran die Wespen nagen.

G. A. Bürger (1747–1794)

When vicious tongues defame you.
Let this thought comfort you,
The poorest fruits are not the ones
At which the wasps will chew.

sometimes as many as 12, linked together by small suspensory pillars. Individual species prefer different sites for their nests. *Dolichovespula media* almost always suspends its nest from branches. Other species build their nests in the ground, or under the floorboards of garden sheds. And finally, we know of two European species that build no nest at all, but like cuckoos, lay their eggs in the nests of others of their kind: *Sulcopolistes* in the nests of *Polistes* and *Vespula austriaca* in the nests of *Paravespula rufa*.

Wasp venom

In the Ebers Papyrus, a medical compendium written in about 1550 B.C., the cure recommended for wasp stings is the application of the fat of the genu-bird (that is, the Common Roller). From the most ancient sources until the present day, prescriptions to cure the effect of stings have lacked neither variety nor imagination. Pedanius Dioscorides recommends a poultice of mallow: "And being anointed on it is available for ye stingings of bees and waspes, and if a man beforehand be anointed therewith raw, beaten small with oyle, hee remaines vnstrikable." *(The Greek Herbal of Dioscorides)*

Homer, in the *Iliad*, uses the courage and valour of wasps as a simile: "And straightway they poured forth like wasps that have their dwelling by the wayside, and that boys are ever wont to vex, always tormenting them in their nests beside the way in childish sport, and a common evil they make for many. And they, if ever some wayfaring man passing by stir unwittingly, fly forth every one of them, with a heart of valour, and each defends his children."

In densely populated nests holding several thousand individuals, mass defensive action can be very unpleasant. In the common species *Paravespula germanica* and *P. vulgaris*, living in the ground, a special substance is produced in the venom gland which, when venom is sprayed towards an attacker, serves as an alarm signal to summon other members of the community to action. It is rare for anyone deliberately to encourage a wasp's sting. But certain South American Indians believe they can increase their success in fishing and hunting by enduring stings in the arm.

Aristotle makes a comparative examination of insect stings, and speaking of wasps, says: "Those that have the sting in the rear, use it, being courageous, as a weapon. But some bear the sting inside, because they are winged, like the bees and wasps; for delicate as it is, it would be easily damaged if it were an external organ."

The wasp sting has a special feature: the barbs of the sting can, as a result of their cutting action, be withdrawn from the skin, in contrast to the sting of the honey bee which remains in the skin.

Life cycle

An unknown author, possibly a pupil of Aristotle, provided considerable information on the subject of wasps. His text is included in Aristotle's *Historia animalium*. "The mode of reproduction of wasps is as follows. At the approach of summer, when the leaders have found a sheltered spot, they take to moulding their combs, and construct the so-called sphecons—little nests containing four cells or thereabouts, and in these are produced working-wasps but not mothers. When these are grown up, then they construct other larger combs upon the first, and then again in like manner others; so that by the close of autumn there are numerous large combs, in which the leader, the so-called mother, engenders no longer working-wasps but mothers. These develop high up in the

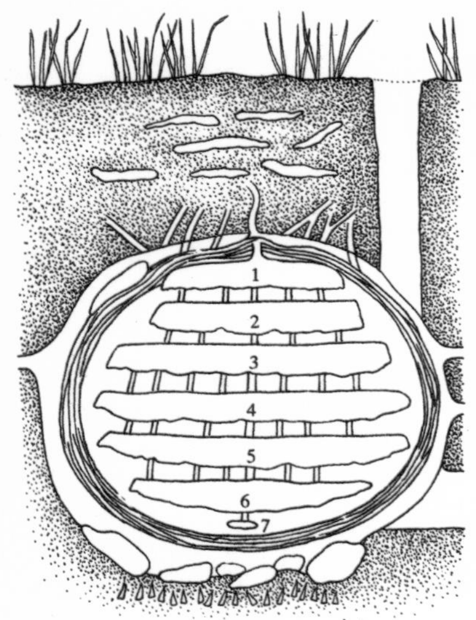

Diagram showing the nest of the German Wasp *(Paravespula germanica)* in the ground. The combs always hang with the openings downwards. The wasps' nest is invested with an external envelope, the individual combs are separated by suspensory pillars. The numbers on the combs indicate the sequence of construction.

nest as large grubs, in cells that occur in groups of four or rather more, pretty much in the same way as we have seen the grubs of the king-bees to be produced in their cells. After the birth of the working-grubs in the cells, the leaders do nothing and the workers have to supply them with nourishment; and this is inferred from the fact that the leaders (of the working-wasps) no longer fly out at this time, but rest quietly indoors."

The observations are accurate; the only points not clearly understood at that time concern the existence of males, which are not produced until towards the end of the summer from unfertilized eggs, and the frequent occurrence of copulation within the nest. The following quotation confirms this. "Of the ordinary wasps some are destitute of stings, like the drone-bees, and some are provided with them. Those unprovided therewith are smaller and less spirited and never fight, while the others are big and courageous; and these latter, by some, are called males, and the stingless, females . . . Some of the tame wasps have been observed when sexually united, but it was not determined whether both, or neither, had stings, or whether one had a sting and the other had not; wild wasps have been seen under similar circumstances, when one was seen to have a sting but the case of the other was left undetermined."

The opposite, of course, is true. The males have no sting, the females (queen, workers) can sting. It is clear that wasps proved something of a problem on fruit even in very early times; in the *Book of Agriculture* by Abu Zakaryya Jahya Ibn al-Awwam (2nd half of 12th century), we find the following instructions: "Take a common reed together with its root, crush well with an equal quantity of soil taken from the graveyard, and knead with some camel hairs. From the mass thus obtained, make figures of birds with outstretched wings and let them dry in the sun. These figures should be attached to sticks in the form of a cross, and set up everywhere in fields and gardens, and also hung on trees and vines. They drive off birds and wasps that try to eat the fruit."

Of wasps, Albertus Magnus writes: "There are many species of wasp, all of which gather up honey that is inedible, build their nests on walls or in the ground and feed on excreta or the flesh of dead animals. Their sting is more powerful than a bee's sting and sometimes very dangerous, particularly that of a large species with a black head." The latter may refer to hornets. Otherwise his information is somewhat meagre. The mention of feeding on the flesh of dead animals (which can certainly be observed sometimes) is reminiscent of ancient views (cf. Isidore of Seville) which held that wasps originate from asses.

Derham (1724) provides an interesting observation: "At the beginning of July 1723, I saw large numbers of wasps flying about the wooden boards of the lead roof of the collegiate chapel at Windsor Castle. They were larger than common wasps, and I thought they had come here to rasp off fragments of wood from which to build their nests. But when I noticed a queen among them, which otherwise never take part in work, I began to be more attentive, and on July 6th, I noticed a cluster of 3 wasps, one of which was a queen and two smaller ones. Soon after that I saw 8 to 10 wasps in a cluster, and other similar aggregations. Each time I found a queen in their midst and always but a single one.

The other wasps were different both from the queen and from common wasps, which made me suspect that they were males and females. On looking more closely, I actually found a queen and one of the other wasps closely linked in copula, tail to tail, and it was some considerable time before they separated. Upon that I caught all the wasps I was able to take from the roof of the chapel, yet could discover none of the common worker wasps among them, but always several males with a queen, usually in copula."

This is certainly a rare and remarkable observation. He also provides clarification concerning the males. "In all the nests that I examined, I always found males, and their number varied according to the size of the nest and the population of wasps. The males are bred in the two upper

On right:

84 *Purpuricenus kaehleri* from Yugoslavia together with a Brushed Flower Beetle *(Trichius)* and a specimen of *Meligethes*, below left, on an umbellate flower. Flowers like this provide various kinds of food for the beetles, but in addition, they are an important meeting place of the sexes —insect "discotheques", as it were.

On left:

The males of some of the larger beetles

85 Above left: Goliath Beetle *(Goliathus cacicus)* from Africa, up to 12 cm long.

86 Above right: Elephant Beetle *(Megasoma elephas)* from Central America, up to 13 cm long and with the greatest body volume.

87 Below: Hercules Beetle *(Dynastes hercules)* from Central America, up to 18 cm long.

88 Three Rhinoceros Beetles (genus *Golofa*) with vertical frontal horn and a horny process on the prothorax.
From left to right: *Golofa aegon* from Ecuador, *G. claviger* from Chiriquí, *G. laevicornis* from Mexico.

89 Above left: This European *Stenocorus meridianus* is about to fly off. The light-coloured surface of the abdomen is a distinctive feature.

90 Above right: Male Cockchafer or May Bug *(Melolontha melolontha)*. A reminder that although this insect is relatively rare in Europe today, until a few years ago it was a serious pest in agriculture and forestry.

91 Below: A Ground Beetle, *Anthia mannerheimi*, from Central Asia in the process of devouring a cricket.

On right:

92 Summer Chafers *(Amphimallon solstitiale)* from Central Europe, in an unusual grouping. At the very bottom is a female, above are five males.

On left:

93 South American Pill-rolling Beetles.
Above left: *Phanaeus lanifer* from Cayenne.
Centre: *Phanaeus bonnariensis* from South America.
Right: *Phanaeus faunus* from Brazil.

94 Below: Brood balls of a Pill-rolling Beetle.

1/2

3/4

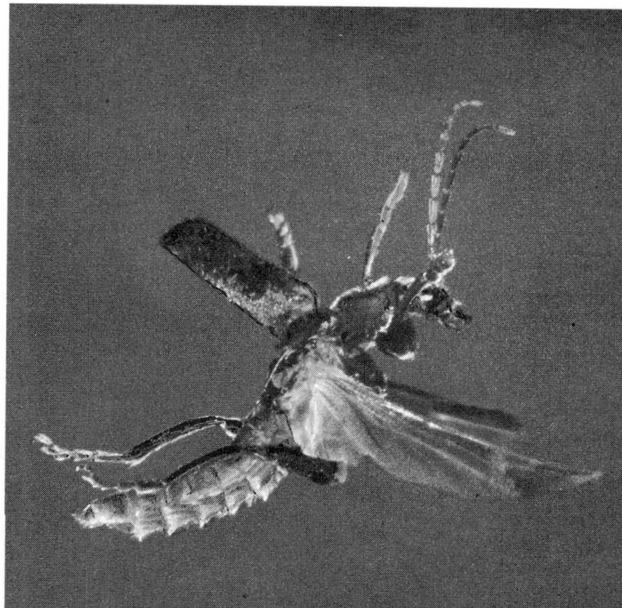

5/6

95 Flight action of a European Soldier Beetle *(Cantharis fusca)*

1 the hind wings are suitably adjusted before flight;
2 the forewings are spread;
3 the hind wings are unfolded;
4 launching phase;
5 take-off;
6 free flight.

96 Blister Beetle *(Mylabris variabilis)* from Bulgaria. Because they contain an active substance, cantharidin, these beetles have been used in pharmaceutical practice since early times.

On right:

97 Tropical Tortoise Beetles (Cassidinae).
Above left: *Pseudomesomphalia saundersi* from South America.

98 Above right: *Pseudomesomphalia pascoei* from Central America.

99 Below left: *Pseudomesomphalia perimunda* from northwestern Mexico.

100 Below right: *Glima mirabilis* from Brazil.

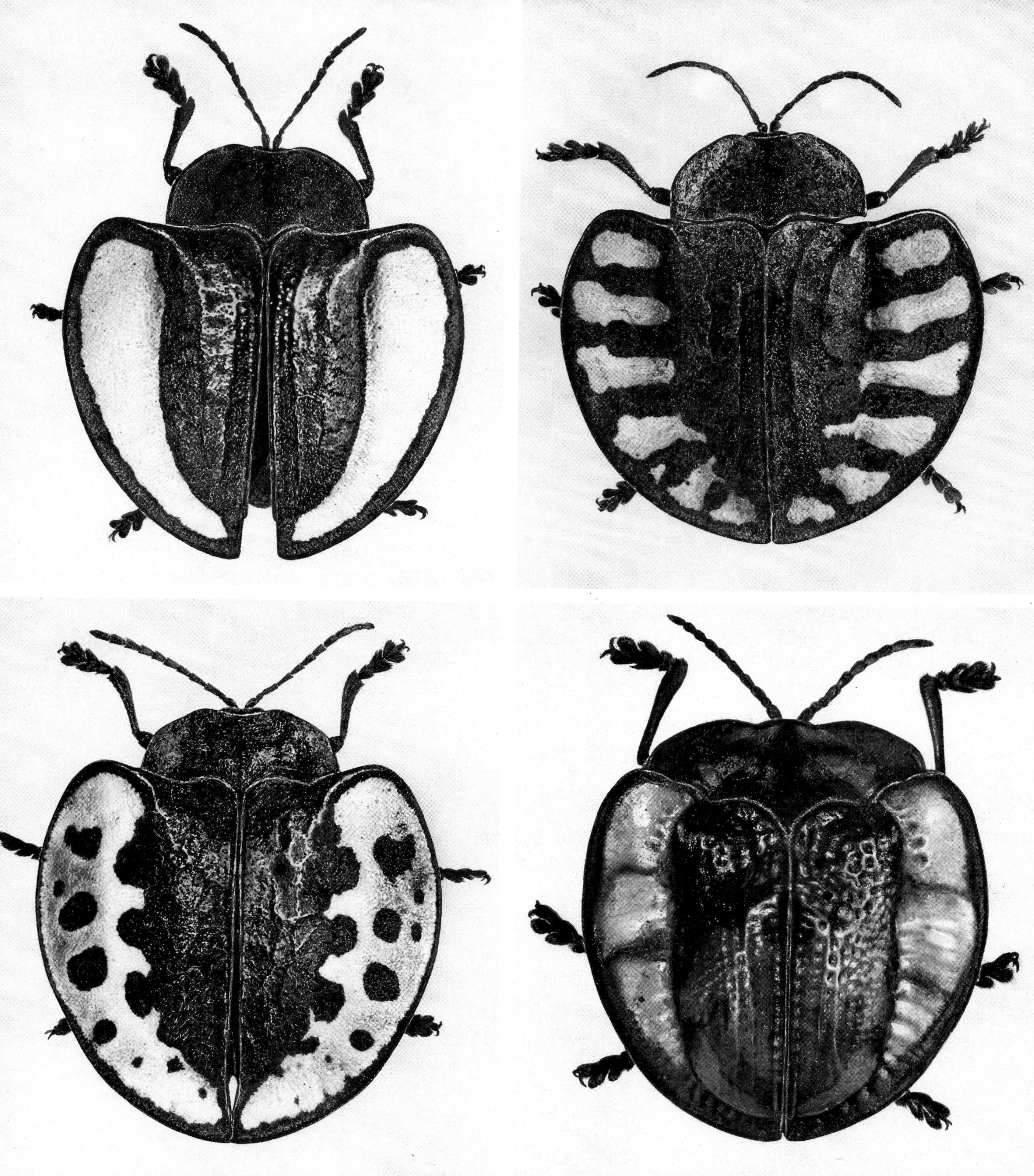

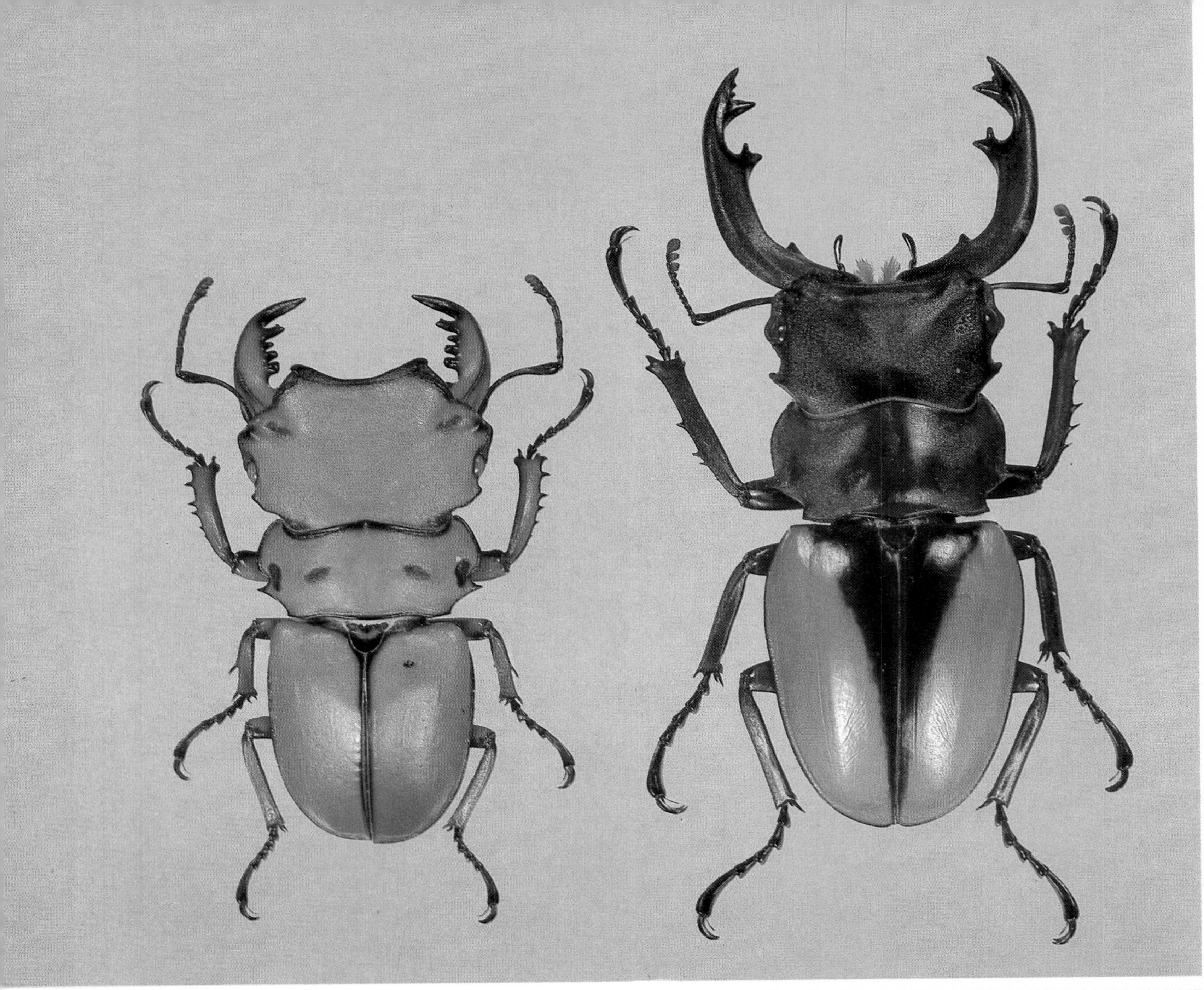

101 Male Stag Beetles
Above left: *Homoderus mellyi* from Cameroon. This beetle is light ochre in colour with sparse black markings.
Above right: *Odontolabis cuvera* from northern India, a black species with ochre-coloured elytra.

102 Below: *Psalidognathus atys* from Ecuador is a Longicorn Beetle somewhat similar in the shape of its body to the Stag Beetle.

103 Above left: The Metallic Beetle *Julodis klugi* var. *viridipennis* from South Africa is thickly covered with tufts of coloured bristles.

104 Below left: A hornet-like Lamellicorn Beetle *(Ancistrostoma vittigerum)* from Peru. Note the large abdominal "barb".

105 Above right: *Steraspis squamosa* from Central Africa belongs to the brilliantly coloured family of Metallic Beetles (Buprestidae).

106 Below right: The Weevil *Entimus splendidus* from Brazil is one of the particularly brightly-coloured representatives of this large family of beetles.

On left:

107/108 Above: A Diving Beetle *(Colymbetes fuscus)* from Central Europe in various phases of flight. Diving Beetles usually fly well; colonization of new habitats and dispersion of the species take place almost entirely by air.

109/110 Below: In many species of True Water Beetles (Dytiscidae), the forelegs of the male are greatly broadened and furnished with adhesive sucking pads which permit a firm hold on the female during copulation. Here, the European species *Graphoderus cinereus*. Left: enlarged x 80; right: detail enlarged x 250.
Photos: H. Schneider, Leipzig.

111 Above: Larva of the Water Scavenger Beetle *(Cybister laterali-marginalis)* from Central Europe with the larva of a Smooth Newt it has seized as prey.

112 Below: The females of some species of Water Beetle (here, *Helochares obscurus*) carry their egg pouches with them until the larvae hatch.

113 Above left: *Rhodope* spec. from Armenia, a Lacewing Fly (Planipennia) with unusually elongate hind wings.
Centre: A representative of the Butterfly Lions (Ascalaphidae) from the Caucasus. A striking feature of this Neuropteran family is the yellow and black wing colouring.
Right: *Corydalis batesi* from Venezuela, an Alder Fly (Megaloptera) with elongated mandibles.

114 Green Lacewings (Chrysopidae) deposit their eggs on top of a rapidly-hardening secretory thread produced by accessory glands of the reproductive system (Central Europe).

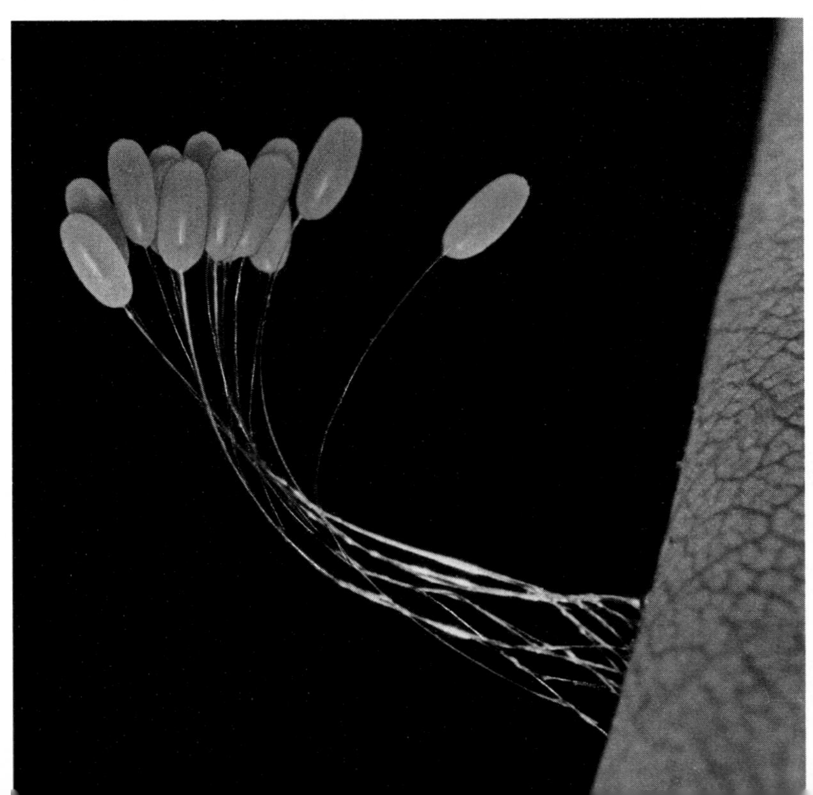

115 Above: Lacewings (Chrysopidae) are also known as Golden Eyes because of the metallic lustre of the eyes. Here, *Chrysopa perla* from Central Europe. The larvae feed principally on aphids.

116 Below: The Giant Lacewing *(Osmylus fulvicephalus)* lives along the borders of streams in Central Europe. The soil along the river bank is also the home of its larvae, which feed mainly on the larvae of midges.

117 Digger Wasps (Sphecidae) paralyze their prey by stinging, then carry them into breeding chambers and deposit an egg upon them. The larva feeds upon this supply of live stored food. The breeding burrows constructed by *Crossocerus* spec., here in rotting oak wood, are stuffed full of midges (Central Europe).

118 Above, a female, below, a male of the Dagger Wasp, Scolia *flavifrons*, from southern Europe. The largest of the European Hymenopterans, it parasitizes the larvae of Stag Beetles and Rhinoceros Beetles.

119 Large Horntail or Wood Wasp *(Urocerus gigas)* (Central Europe) depositing eggs. *Urocerus* species lay their eggs in the wood of conifers (pine, spruce, fir, larch). When an egg is laid, the ovipositor is placed vertically on the substrate. The horny sheath, clearly visible in the photograph, is not involved in the laying process. The two drilling bristles bore alternately into the wood. Several eggs are passed along the groove formed by the stylets. The whole process of egg laying takes up to two hours. Repeating the process many times, a female may deposit several hundred eggs.

120 Sawfly larvae (Tenthredinidae), unlike caterpillars, lack abdominal feet only on the first abdominal segment. Illustrated here, the two-coloured larva of *Pteronidea salicis* on willow (Central Europe).

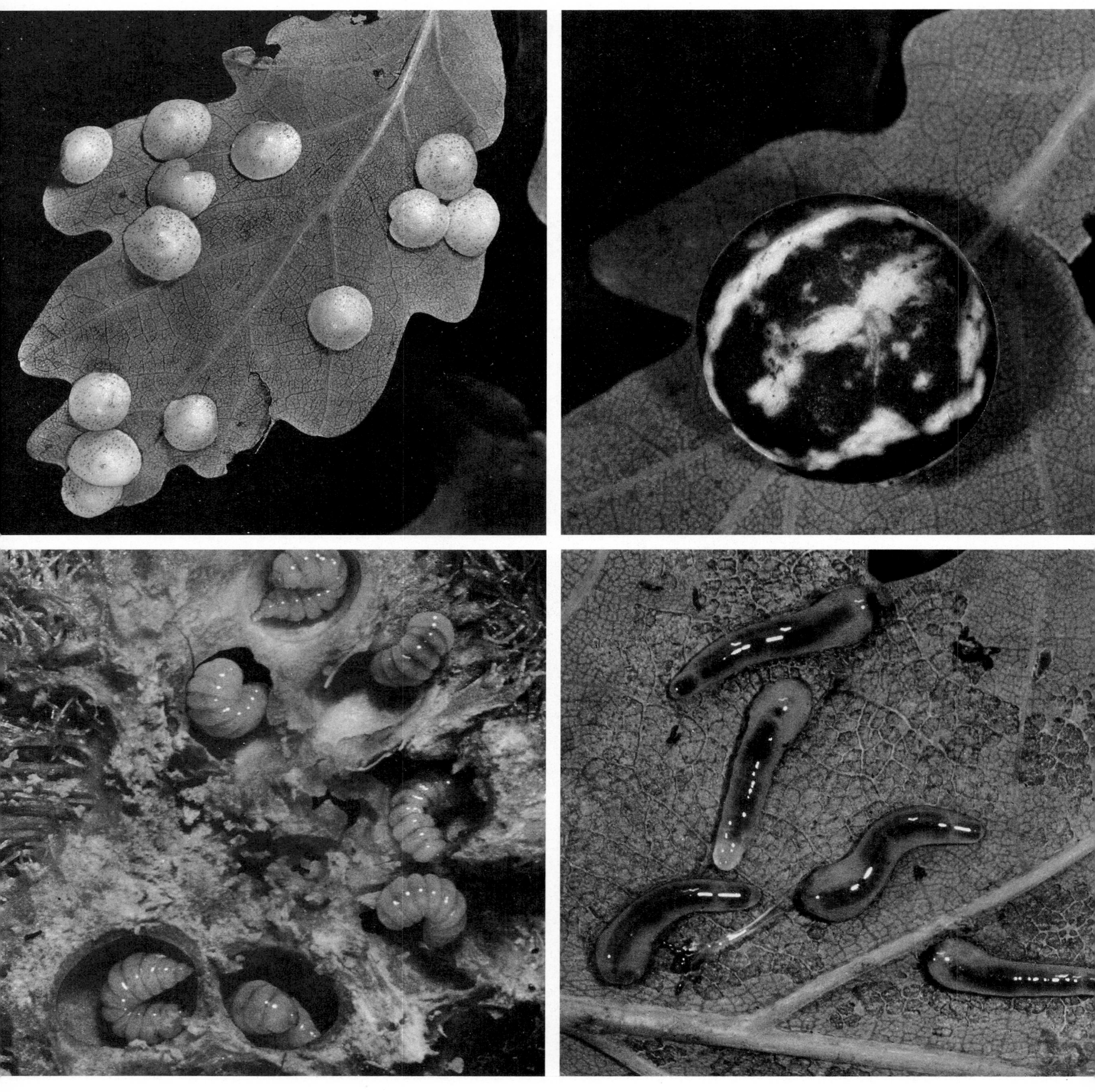

On left:

121 Above left: Lenticular galls produced by the Gall Wasp *Neuroterus quercusbaccarum* on an oak leaf (Central Europe).

122 Above right: The spherical gall of *Cynips longiventris* on oak leaves has a pattern of white stripes on a red ground colour (Central Europe).

123 Below left: The Mossy Rose Gall Wasp *(Diplolepis rosae)* gives rise to bedeguar or pin-cushion galls up to 5 cm in diameter, covered with filamentous outgrowths (Central Europe). For centuries, these "sleep apples" were believed to promote sound sleep if laid under one's pillow at night. Here, a gall viewed in section, showing the Gall Wasp larvae inside the larval cells.

124 Below right: Sawfly larvae (genus *Caliroa*) from Central Europe, which often live gregariously on leaves (here, oak). The larvae are covered with slime and have a slug-like appearance.

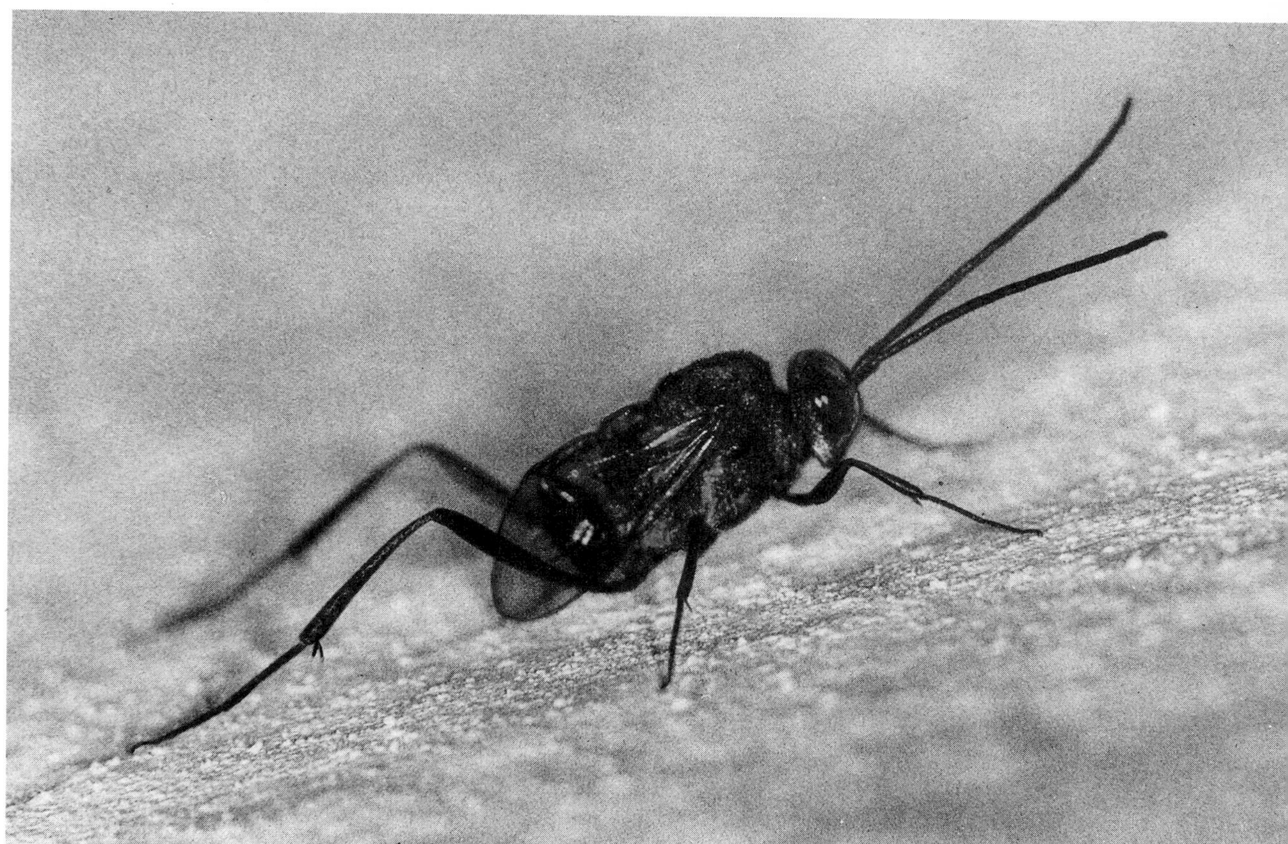

125 Above: In their larval stage, Ensign Wasps (Evaniidae) are parasites of the oothecae of cockroaches (Central Europe).

126 Below: Pupae of the European family of Eulophidae which belong to the super-family of Chalcid Flies (Chalcidoidea). The larvae of many genera develop as external parasites of caterpillars and Sawfly larvae. After the death of the host larva, which usually coincides with the end of their own larval development, many species pupate immediately beside the remains of the host, and so these groups are known as "gravestone pupae".

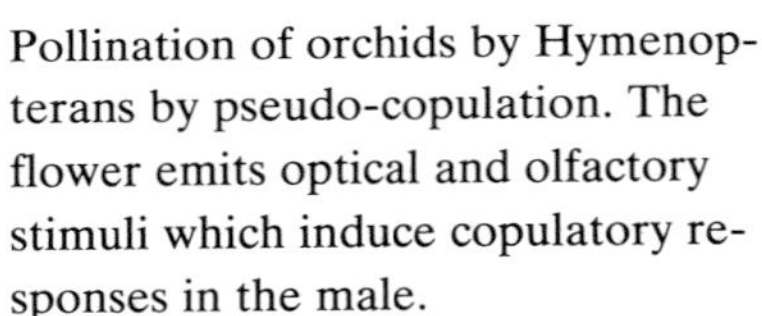

Pollination of orchids by Hymenopterans by pseudo-copulation. The flower emits optical and olfactory stimuli which induce copulatory responses in the male.

Left column:

127 Flower of *Ophrys speculum*.

128 Male *Campsoscolia ciliata* flies to the flower.

129 Above right: The insect reaches the flower, the pollen grains adhere to the forepart of the body.

130 Below: Flower of *Ophrys speculum* and female *Campsoscolia ciliata* juxtaposed to show the visual similarity.

131 Above: Two males of *Andrena flavipes* on *Ophrys fusca*. The insects are "mating" in reverse position, in contrast to *Campsoscolia ciliata*.

132 Below: Pollin grains are carried off on the end of the abdomen of *Andrena flavipes*.
Photos on these two pages:
H. F. Paulus, Freiburg/Breisgau.

133/134 Above: Honey Bee *(Apis mellifera)* collecting pollen from Meadow Foxtail. The pollen of grasses can be collected by bees only in the early hours of the morning while it is still moist. Its use as food is a rare exception.

135 Below: Buff-tailed Bumble Bee *(Bombus terrestris)* frequenting blossom (Central Europe).

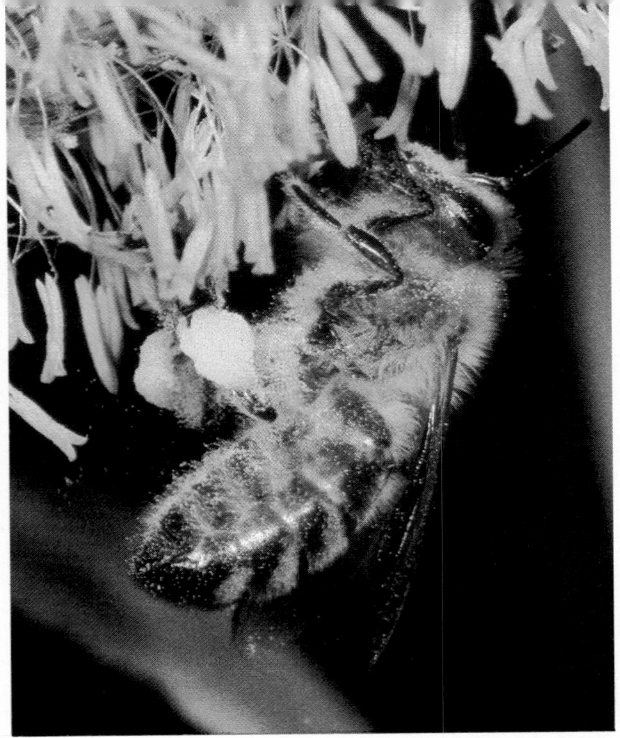

On right:

136 Common Carder Bee *(Bombus agrorum)* from Central Europe.

137 The nest of the Field Wasp (genus *Polistes*) from Bulgaria consists of a single tier of cells with no outer covering, attached by a pedicle to the supporting surface. Basically, the eggs are laid by a single female, which could be called the queen. However, the other females (the progeny of the female founder of the nest) participate in egg-laying, nest construction, care of the eggs, larvae and pupae, and the collection of food.

138 Ants of the sub-family Myrmicinae (species *Myrmica laevinodis*) in their nest together with larvae (Central Europe).

rows of cells, or else they spend most of their time there. The antennae of the males are longer than those of the females and workers . . . The main difference lies in the genitalia. Here I will attempt to describe those of the male, as well as possible without illustrations, in so far as they can be made visible externally by pressure."

From *Spectacle de la Nature*

In the 18th century, popular scientific literature began to deal with the subject of insects. A book that was widely read and translated into all the major languages, was that by Abbé Noel Antoine Pluche (1688–1761) entitled *Spectacle de la Nature or Nature Display'd (being Discourses on such Particulars of Natural History as were thought most proper to Excite the Curiosity and Form the Minds of Youth)*. Presented in the form of a dialogue, it includes a passage on wasps. The following is a sample:

Ancient Egyptian depiction of a wasp.

"The Prior: At first, a small egg can be found at the very back of each cell, glued there to prevent it from falling out. The mother crawls into the cell quite often, without doubt in order to impart some gentle warmth to the egg and thus to encourage the emergence of the young. Out of the egg appears a small worm which is fed diligently and within a short time, turns into a large, thick, fat worm which fills the entire chamber. The common wasps bring food home, the mother takes it from them, breaks it into small pieces and puts a portion into the mouth of each worm. They are served one after another, and each one receives as much as the other, except that the large worms, from which the males and females develop, are fed more frequently than the small ones. Just turn the wasps' nest over and examine the entrance to the cells. What do you find there?

The Chevalier: I see the fat worms of which you have just spoken. One of them is opening its mouth because it takes my finger for its mother.

The Prior: It has had nothing to eat since yesterday, so it will by hungry . . .

The Prior: Some insects remain in the pupal stage for years at a time. But the wasp for no longer than 12 to 14 days at most. After that, when it finds itself in its full armour, it rends the tissue of its cell; first it extends one palp, then the second one. This is followed by a foot, slowly the head appears, gradually the whole body makes the opening large enough to crawl through, and finally the wasp stands there with all its requisite limbs, dries its damp wings by wiping them several times with its hind legs, and then flies off into open country, where it helps the others to plunder, for right from the very first day, it is their equal in skill and malice.

The Chevalier: How can that be, suddenly, without any instruction?

The Prior: Without the least instruction. As soon as the small wasps crawl from their cell, they fly off after prey; as soon as the male emerges from its cell, it plays seriously for some time, then visits the most beautiful female wasp in the area. As soon as the female appears, it is busy about its household tasks."

Everything described by Pluche is correct. Today we have discovered certain additional facts, for instance, that the larvae produce a labial secretion that is taken up by the imagines, and transmitted by the workers to others, including larvae; apparently it is of considerable importance to the colony as a social bonding mechanism. The phenomenon, known as trophallaxis, occurs among many colony-forming insects.

Ichneumon Flies (Ichneumonidae)

True Ichneumons make up an insect group with very many species, of which about 4,000 are known in Europe, out of a world total of some 60,000 species, into which much research still remains to be done. Surprisingly enough, these insects were already mentioned in very early entomological writings, although with their parasitical habits, their natural tendency is to remain somewhat in the background. It is, of course, not always easy to determine which species or groups are the subject of these early descriptions, and many of the observations undoubtedly refer to other parasitic Hymenoptera—such as Braconids (Braconidae), Chalcid Flies (Chalcidoidea), Proctotrupid Flies (Proctotrupoidea), Digger Wasps (Sphecidae).

There are some Ancient Egyptian drawings of Ichneumons still in existence. Aristotle observed them in some detail: "The wasps that are nicknamed 'the ichneumons' (or hunters), less in size than the ordinary wasp, kill spiders and carry off the dead bodies to a wall or some such place with a hole in it; this hole they smear over with mud and lay their grubs inside it, and from the grubs come the hunter wasps." Clearly he is speaking not of Ichneumons but of the genus *Sceliphron* (family of Digger Wasps—Sphecidae), the handsome females of which are a striking phenomenon in Greece. The spiders they hunt down are placed in clay cells. Once a cell is filled with "provisions", the female lays an egg, closes the cell and starts on the next one.

Thomas Moufet illustrates various of the Ichneumonidae, Jan Swammerdam recognized their parasitic way of life, which previously had been little understood, and it was Martin Lister who first explained that Ichneumons derive from maternal eggs laid in the caterpillar. René Antoine Ferchault, Seigneur de Réaumur (1683–1756), known to his contemporaries as the 18th-century Pliny, was undoubtedly one of the most important of entomologists. He was a universal scholar, although today many people are familiar only with his thermometric scale. Between 1734 and 1742, Réaumur published the six volumes of his *Mémoires pour servir à l'histoire des insectes*. The whole work is on an unusually large scale and combines a wealth of information on the morphology, biology, ecology and physiology of the arthropods (Réaumur equated them with the insects). Below, we quote a brief extract on Ichneumons from this work, but not without first pointing out that we are indebted to him for the earliest and exceptionally good illustrations of *Apanteles* larvae (*Apanteles glomeratus*, family Braconidae) in the caterpillars of Cabbage Whites. He writes: "As we have already seen in dealing with the enemies of caterpillars, many other insects simply use them as a nest for their young. The name Ichneumon denotes rather this characteristic feature, for the groups so designated comprise very different genera. All insects with complete metamorphosis appear to some extent destined to serve as a means of reproduction for Ichneumons. In general, the Ichneumons make use of three methods of achieving their ends, all three of which are equally reliable. Some lay their eggs, often up to 20 or 30, but sometimes only 2 or 3, or even a single egg, in the young host larva, implanting it inside the body of the host by means of the ovipositor. Just how minute these creatures are can be appreciated from the fact that they often lay their eggs in those of other insects and hatch from them. Valisnieri believed that the young wasp larva penetrates the eggs, but I believe that the wasp itself lays its eggs inside those of the host species . . . From grasshoppers' eggs that had been parasitized by a small Ichneumon, large numbers of these wasps hatched after 3 weeks. The second group is content merely to attach its eggs to the body of the host larva. Those of the third group are constantly on watch for nests of other insects. No matter how well concealed these may be or with what care they are closed up, the Ichneumons still manage in spite of that to deposit their eggs there. Other species are able to penetrate dense layers of wood, sand or mortar by means of an especially long ovipositor . . .

"But let us now examine the true purpose of the female's long tail. I could not conceive of its function until I was able to observe such a wasp in the process of using it, undisturbed by my presence. It was an Ichneumon that was busily engaged upon a nest of a Sphegidae species which was full of green caterpillars put there as food for lavae The tail, which in reality is made up of three filaments, had the appearance of a single slender thread. The female began to raise and lower it and to bend it at will. Finally the tail, brought forward under the abdomen, jutted out far beyond the head and no longer projected backwards at all. Undoubtedly her purpose was to drill through the hard covering of the nest. The sing, or the central thread, bears at its extremity saw-like teeth that can drill holes. Unfortunately I could not follow the process exactly. I saw only the alternat-

Left: An Aphid Ichneumon (Aphidiidae) deposits an egg in an aphid. The abdomen is brought forward between the legs.
Right: As a parasite of Horntails (Siricidae), the Horntail Ichneumon *(Rhyssa persuasoria)* has an appropriately long thread-like ovipositor with which it is able to penetrate wood and reach the Horntail larva.

ing movements of the sting. The length of time taken to open up the hole by this sawing action was a good quarter of an hour, and I also confirmed this later in observing other Ichneumons."

Obviously Réaumur applies the name Ichneumon to all parasitic Hymenoptera, and does not use the term in the narrower sense usual today.

Johann Leonhard Frisch, in connection with an infestation of Gipsy Moths *(Lymantria dispar)* on lime trees in Berlin also speaks of Ichneumons. "And because few gardeners and country people know about the skin-casting process in caterpillars, and even less that after moulting, the caterpillars always look different from hitherto; or that some of these caterpillars do not complete all four moults, but their bodies are occupied internally by the small wasps with maggots, so that they die while still small and are unable to grow: so many people think that these black caterpillars will not grow and the creatures that creep three or four times out of their old skin are quite different. These maggots feed on the body juices of the caterpillar, and when they are large enough, they crawl out from the centre of the body: in the case of small caterpillars often a single one, which is found nearby enclosed in a white egg, in the case of large ones often whole masses, from which eggs, a few weeks later, just such small wasps emerge."

All the Ichneumonidae live as parasites, almost all choose insects as their host, some species live on spiders' eggs (Gelinae). Many species are hyperparasites or second-degree parasites, that parasitize another parasite. There are both endo- and ectoparasites. The males die shortly after copulation, a process that has rarely been observed, the females soon after oviposition. In those species that lay only a single egg in each of their victims, it often happens that a female does not complete the process of oviposition within a single year. In this case, it overwinters and the following year, seeks out new hosts. The majority of Ichneumons use butterfly caterpillars as their hosts. Some species are restricted to a single host, but most have several and some many. The imagines live on nectar and honeydew, in contrast to the parasitic larvae.

In some species, the ovipositor of the female is exceedingly long, in accordance with the task it has to perform. The Ichneumon's terebra is furnished with rows of barbs that prevent it slipping out of the host prematurely. In *Rhyssa persuasoria*, which parasitizes wood-feeding larvae, the ovipositor carries a small saw at the front end only, the rest of it being smooth so that it can move freely up and down within the wood. The parasitism of *Rhyssa* is a truly remarkable phenomenon in many respects. How does the Ichneumon Fly know that Horntail larvae are inside the wood? Its perception of vibration (its sense of hearing or smell?) must be extraordinarily sensitive. It uses its antennae to explore the surface of the wood by touch. Then it drills, or rather saws deep into the wood with its ovipositor which is longer than its own body, often spending several hours on the work (but usually some 30 minutes), sometimes moving round in a circle as it does so, constantly moving its terebra back and forth in the groove until it reaches the larva. An egg is deposited along the channel formed by the groove and the ridges, which in passing through the long, slender ovipositor is greatly deformed to a length of 20 mm. After the egg is laid, the ovipositor is withdrawn from the wood and the search for the next Horntail larva begins. The number of eggs can be small because of the excellent brood care.

The ecological importance of Ichneumons is considerable. They can be used as biological controls, limiting the multiplication of plant-eating insects. The indiscriminate use of broad-spectrum insecticides also has the effect of destroying parasitic Hymenoptera which play an important part in maintaining the ecological balance. Where long-term crops are cultivated (trees, shrubs) and the potential exists for building up self-regulating feeding networks, very restricted use should be made of indiscriminate chemical measures of control.

Ants (Formicidae)

Early knowledge concerning ants

From the earliest times, ants have captured the attention of men. In particular their social behaviour has aroused admiration and caused many analogies to be drawn with man-made society, which we today, sobered by the results of scientific research and aware of the laws governing the development of human society, recognize as historical testimony to the state of entomological knowledge at that time. But occasionally there are early signs of experimental observation, as the following passage from the Talmud shows. "Ants like shade more than sunshine. One day a cloak was deliberately spread across the entrance to an ants' nest so that the latter lay in the shade. An ant emerged and returned to the nest after it had been marked by the observer. Immediately the ants came forth in a mass. The person in question now removed the cover and the ants killed the supposed traitor. Thus the word of Solomon is correct which says that ants have no ruler, for otherwise they would not have killed this ant without permission."

The *Physiologus*, the zoological chapbook of the Middle Ages, presents a mixture of correct observations and a variety of moralizing conclusions. The ants are ascribed three characteristics. "Their first characteristic: when they walk along in procession, each one carries its grain of food in its mouth, and those that have nothing or are without a grain, do not say to those that are laden: 'Give us of your grain', nor do they rob them of it by force, but they go on and gather for themselves. This recalls the Wise and Foolish Virgins. The second characteristic: when the ant stores up food in the ground, it bites the grains into two pieces, so that the grains will not germinate during the winter, causing her to go hungry. And furthermore, the ant is clever enough to know whether it is hot or when the skies are about to drench her. If you notice an ant carrying into its hole grains of wheat it has found outside, you may know that rainy weather is coming, but when she carries food out from inside and spreads it abroad, then know that the weather is fine. The third characteristic: the ant often goes into the field, climbs an ear of corn and carries the grain down: but before she climbs up, she sniffs at the lower part of the stalks and from the scent, recognizes wheat or barley. If it is barley, she moves away from it to the wheat and collects that ear of corn."

The forecasting of weather has always been a matter of importance. In the centuries before sensitive measuring equipment, international weather stations and exchange of information, even satellite photographs, people used to try to make prognostications by observing natural phe-

"Go to the ant, thou sluggard; consider her ways, and be wise:
Which having no guide, overseer, or ruler,
Provideth her meat in the summer, and gathereth her food in the harvest."

The Proverbs of Solomon (992–965 B.C.)

nomena. The *Household Book* written by a preacher Johann Colerus (died 1639) and published in about 1590, notes: "When ants scatter in all directions, carry their eggs out of the heap and hastily drag them back in again, rain will soon moisten the ground. If the ants are lazy and sluggish in their work or even come to a standstill, contrary to their otherwise industrious habit, and if they carry their eggs out of their dwellings, this signifies wind and blustery weather. When ants gather small sand-pebbles with their legs and feet in order to increase their own weight, they fear an approaching storm."

Albertus Magnus writes in his major zoological work *De animalibus*: "Formica, the ant, is a small insect which still at an advanced age increases in body size and in intelligence. It is very provident, and although it builds combs for itself as bees do, it yet gathers up dry grain. They always keep to their pathways, and as a result, good order reigns. They dry damp grains of corn lest they rot. They know the weather in advance, for before storms, they always assemble at home. They abhor sulphur and origano, so much so that they immediately quit their abodes if a powder of these substances is scattered over them. When they bite, they eject a poisonous liquid that causes blisters. In old age, some of them begin to fly. They suck their food from fruits and the bodies of animals that they find. They first produce eggs which then turn into white worms that are enveloped in small membranes. These are carried to the surface into the sun, and from them the ants develop."

Arabian scholars of the 13th century also devoted special attention to ants. Kamal al-Din al-Damiri reports: "Naml, the ant. It is also known as the Father of the Flesh, and the ant is the mother of the action of gathering in. It is called the ant or emmet on account of its industry, that is, its ceaseless activity in spite of the small size of its feet. The ant does not mate nor marry, but it lays some small object in the ground. This develops until the ants eggs have formed, from which they emerge . . . And the ant deploys great energy in seeking out food. When it has found something, it informs the others so that they may come to join it. People also say that only their leaders act thus. It is in their nature to gather provisions in the summer for the winter . . . One of the reasons for their dying is the growth of wings. When the ants have developed thus far, they make the sparrows fat. For the latter prey upon them when they reach the stage of flying. Abu-al-Atahiya referred to this in the lines of a poem: And when the wings of the ant are such/That it can fly/its end is near . . .

"Proverbs: People say: 'It is possible that the man who is not concerned about a threat may be killed by the bite of an ant.' And "more miserly than an ant", and "weaker, more numerous, more persistent than ants".

"Interpretations of dreams: For weak people, ants in a dream signify avarice. – For anyone who dreams he sees ants carrying heavy loads into his house, all good things will enter his house with them. – If someone sees them on his bed, it means many children for him. – If ants are seen emerging from the house, it betokens a change in the number of members of the family. – If anyone sees ants flying in front of a place where there is a sick person, that person will die, or travellers leaving the place will have bad luck. – The ant is an indication of fertility and food, because they are found only in places where they have a secure livelihood . . . People also say that he who sees an ant emerge from any place will be overcome by grief."

Al-Qazwini's *Curiosities of Creation and Created Beings* includes certain other aspects. "The ant is a creature extremely greedy for food; so it drags things along with it that are heavier than itself. In pulling, one ant helps the other. It gathers sufficient food to last it for two years, if it lived as long. But its life is not longer than a year . . . Among many wonderful things about them is the construction of a village under the ground. In it, there are dwellings, corridors, galleries, curved storeys which they fill with grain and supplies for the winter . . . Among the wondrous features of the ant is that in spite of its delicate form and slight weight, it has a better sense of smell than other animals. If something falls from a man's hand on to a place where no ant is to be seen, the ants immediately come to this object like an extended black thread . . . If an ant finds something that it cannot carry, it takes a portion of it that it can carry in order to let the others know about it . . . so it reports to all the others. Then they all assemble and draw it along with diligence and care. If they know that one of them is being negligent and lazy at its work, they kill it. If there is moisture in the grains of cereal that they have gathered into their cave, they fear that it will sprout and be spoiled. Therefore they separate each grain into two pieces, so that the capacity for growth within it is destroyed. They peel grains of barley and shell peas and beans, but do not break them, since their growth is already diminished by peeling . . . Then at certain times the ant takes the pieces and spreads them out in the sun, where they are exposed to the effects of the air and the heat of the sun, so that they are not damaged by the dampness of their abode. It notices if clouds arrive, and so brings the grains back into its house, for fear of rain; if something gets damp, the ant spreads it out in the sun on a brighter day."

Swammerdam's artificial nest

It would be well at this point to include something of what we know about ants today, thereby also throwing some light upon the state of knowledge of the early researchers. Since their day, much information has been gained by keeping ants in artificial nests—a technique invented by Jan Swammerdam, of whom we have already heard several times. "This is how I contrived it: I took a large, concave earthenware dish. I attached a rim of wax some five fingers broad round its margin, which I filled with water so that the ants would not escape from their own clearly-defined area. After this I filled the dish with soil and placed the community of ants in it. Within a few days, they laid their eggs there. The worms emerged which I have already described, and which are commonly but incorrectly called ants' eggs. No pen can describe the love, care and solicitude of the common worker ants with which they treat the young, bring them to the surface, bear them from one place to another. They do this with great tenderness. They grip the young between their teeth. They neglect nothing that is necessary to feed them and bring them up.

"If the ground they inhabited became dry, they carried their young lower down. But if I poured water on it, one would see to one's surprise how, with great solicitude and impelled by their love, they again carried off their young and took them to a dry place. If I added still more water, they all carried their young to the outermost and highest points. If I moistened dry earth only slightly, they afterwards brought their young to it, they moved it very slightly and sucked up the moisture mingled with the fine particles of soil.

"Many times I planned to bring the young ants without the worker ants to the surface, but I was never able to succeed."

Food

The mouthparts of ants are adapted for biting, but they take in only liquid and very soft food. The oesophagus extends first into the crop, which can be described as the "social stomach". Its contents can be regurgitated through the mouth at any time and fed to nest companions, larvae or ant-guests (myrmecophiles). The crop is succeeded by the proventriculus, the fore-stomach. Its function is to pump some of the food stored in the crop into the glandular stomach, which is not lined with chitin but has very soft walls containing many glandular cells. In contrast to the crop, this is the ant's "private" stomach.

When an ant, out foraging, finds something useful—food or building material—it attempts first of all to take it back to the nest alone. Sometimes it performs prodigious feats. If the object is too heavy, nest companions are alerted, and working together, they try to effect the transfer. If this does not succeed, an object such as the dead body of a large insect or other prey is dismembered and carried off in parts. In gathering foodstuffs, many species employ the relay principle. For example, in the *Messor* species which gather seeds of grain, some of the insects carry them from the site at which they were found as far as an intermediate station between that place and the nest, and here the seeds are collected in turn by other workers. The process is similar with liquid food. Sometimes female *Lasius* workers can be observed with greatly distended abdomens indicating a full crop. If such an ant meets another, the second can take over the liquid into its own crop to feed the inhabitants of the nest, unless it happens to encounter a sister-ant on the way to which it can transfer the food for further transportation. The American species *Myrmecocystus* have developed the habit of storing honeydew in living honey-containers. These honey-pot ants are highly valued as an item of food in Central America, South Africa and Australia, eaten either without any preparation or processed into alcoholic drinks. The Aztecs and Incas are said to have held this species of ant in high regard. The creatures live largely on the juices secreted sporadically by certain galls on a scrub oak. Worker ants collect this liquid in their crops and use it to fill the crops of newly-hatched individuals whose intersegmental membranes are still very extensible. After this, these distended repletes hang from the rough roof of an underground chamber, ready at any time to provide food for other ants from their store.

Ants are omnivorous. They obtain the protein they require mainly from insects they have attacked or found dead. In times of need, they will consume the young in their own nest. Species of the genus *Messor* gather in grains of seed with which they are clearly able to fulfil their protein requirement. Other ants also do this, but to a lesser extent than the *Messor* species, for which this activity has earned the name of Harvester Ants. Quite often the ants leave seeds lying along their route, particularly when the relay system of transportation is being used, so that they contribute to the distribution of those plants. Many plants are specially adapted to this process in that they have oil-bearing appendages on their seeds (elaiosomes) which are exceedingly palatable to ants. Such plants are known as myrmecophilous. Greater Celandine *(Chelidonium majus)*, Hazelwort *(Asarum europaeum)* and Heart's-ease *(Viola tricolor)* are well-known examples in the European flora. In spring in particular, ants can often be seen visiting flowers. In this case they are interested in the sugar-rich nectar.

The ants' need for sugar is also the basis of the remarkable relationship existing with aphids and scale insects which live exclusively on plant juices containing little protein but large quantities of

In various species of ants, especially those of the genus *Myrmecocystus*, liquid food is stored in certain workers, causing them to become greatly distended, until finally they are "living honey pots"; these repletes are considered a delicacy by local people, especially one Australian species is preferred by the Aborigines. Here, *Prendepis imparis*.
Left: Worker in normal condition.
Right: Replete.

sugar. In order to obtain sufficient protein, the aphids must ingest a superfluity of sugar, which they then discharge with their excretions. For ants, these excretions are a welcome source of food. Ants can be observed tapping the aphids with their antennae, causing the latter to discharge drops of liquid. It used to be thought that this liquid was secreted through the two small cornicles or tubes that are situated on the hind end of the abdomen. In fact, it comes from the anus, and the two small tubes are used to liberate waxy glandular secretions as a defence against attack. Aphids show a graduated sequence of stages in their adaptation to ants. Species that are never visited by ants eject a spray of excrement well away from their body; species that are accustomed to ants do so only when no ants are present; and the species that are extremely myrmecophilous have lost entirely the capacity to spray their excreta any considerable distance. In certain European *Lasius* species, adaptation has progressed even further. *Lasius flavus*, the Yellow Meadow Ant, for example, rears root lice. In autumn, the ants collect the eggs of this aphid, keep them in their nests during the winter, and in spring they place the newly-hatched aphids onto plant roots. If danger threatens, they carry the aphid eggs down into the lower chambers of the nest as they do their own eggs, larvae and pupae.

Reproduction and establishment of the nest

In the majority of species of ants, nest building is preceded by a nuptial flight during which mating takes place. Such flights were frequently observed in earlier times. In the publications of the *Academia natura curiosorum*, we read: "1694. On July 18, 1679, Carolus Rayger, a physician from Posen, observed a great swarm of flying ants which descended to the earth after two hours and shed their wings."

Johann Günther, a German physician of Striegau, wrote in 1720 in the journal *Sammlung von Natur- und Medicin- wie auch hierzu gehörigen Kunst- und Literatur-Geschichten so sich in Schlesien and anderen Ländern begeben* (Collection of Natural and Medical Histories together with the associated Art and Literary Histories, as they occur in Silesia and other Countries): "From Upper Hungary, on September 5, an indescribable swarm of flying ants was observed which had settled on the roofs. They were washed off by a shower of rain, so that next morning the townspeople had to walk on nothing but heaps of ants."

Swarming is important as a means of dispersion, making full use of the area available and restricting inbreeding. Over a more or less extensive neighbourhood, the nuptial swarms of several and often many colonies take place synchronously and the individuals intermingle in the air. Together, they all make for high-lying positions, hill-tops, look-out towers and so on. Weather conditions that are warm and not too dry trigger off the swarming instinct. The number of individuals involved can be immense. In the formicary of a South American *Atta*, some 3,500 females and 35,000 males were counted shortly before swarming time.

William Gould's *Account of English Ants* (1747) is a classic work of formicology. "Of their Government, a Description of the several Queens, the Respect shown them by the Common Ants, Extent of their Power, etc." we read: "A colony of Ants, from the latter End of August, to the beginning of June, is usually composed of a large Female and various Companies of Workers. We may stile the former, the Queen. Besides these, there are in the latter End of June, all July and Part of August, a Number of winged Ants . . . The Government of Ants has been universally taken for a Republic or Common-Wealth, and accordingly they have been treated as a Body consisting of Males and Females . . . The common Ants which usually present themselves to our View are like the common Bees, of neither sex . . . Every perfect Colony of Ants, has at least one Queen, who, in the Space of Seven or Eight Months, gives Birth to a Family, at a moderate Computation amounting to Four or Five Thousand . . . She is easily distinguished by her superior Largeness, different Colour, and the particular Respect shown her by the rest . . . If you place a

"Hör Narr richt nach der Ameise dich!
In guter Zeit versorgt sie sich,
dass du nicht müssest Mangel leiden,
wenn andere haben ihre Freuden."

Hear, Fool, be guided by the Ant
Who in good times, stores up supplies for herself,
So that you do not have to suffer shortage
When others have their pleasures.

Sebastian Brant (1485–1521),
from: Das Narrenschiff *(The Ship of Fools)*

Queen Ant with her Retinue under a Glass, you will in a few Moments be convinced of the Honour they pay, and Esteem they entertain for her . . . As soon as she has deposited a Parcel of Eggs, she leaves them to the Care of the Workers . . . In October, the Ants with their Queens begin to retire downwards, and in the Depth of Winter are to be found in some of the remotest Apartments encircled with a large Cluster of Attendants, and as it were benumbed. From January to the beginning of May they lay Eggs at Intervals and sparingly. From thence to September they come nearer the Surface. The latter End of June, and particularly in July, their Bodies are surprisingly distended with Egg. All which by September, they commonly deposit."

In those species that build independent nests, the nuptial flight is followed by the foundation of a new colony. The male dies very soon after copulation, and a period of hard work begins for the female. She sheds her wings and searches for a suitable nest site. Arboreal species bore their way into wood, subterranean nest-dwellers burrow into soil, other species find a suitable recess beneath a stone. In every case, a sealed chamber is prepared. Here the first eggs are laid and the mother remains with her brood. In tropical species it can be about 4 weeks and in European species more than 9 months before the female obtains any food. Three factors help her to survive this period of fasting: 1. considerable fat reserves are stored in the abdomen; 2. degeneration of the flight muscles, now no longer used, provides nutrient material; 3. instinct causes the ant to act in a manner expedient to that particular situation: she consumes some 80 to 90 percent of the eggs. Larvae hatch from the remaining 10 to 20 percent. One of them is probably given preferential feeding (they are fed with secretions of the mother's salivary glands and possibly regurgitated chewed eggs); this larva receives most food and is the first to pupate. Preferential treatment then passes to another one.

Once the first imagines have hatched, the situation is saved. The young leave the chamber and forage for food for the mother, which meanwhile continues her activity of egg-laying, and cares for the younger siblings still in the larval stage. These first workers are very small; clearly their development has been affected by the deficiency of their diet.

Fungus gardens

The South American *Atta* or Parasol Ants are successful fungus farmers. A number of individuals from a colony of *Atta* or *Acromyrmex*, in which the total population may number millions, leave the nest in long lines and make their way behind a scout ant, often by a circuitous route, to the tree discovered by the scout. It is soon climbed. Now each ant cuts a fragment of leaf with its sharp mandibles and, moving in close formation with the other worker ants, carries it, held in its mandibles, back to the nest. As in the case of the *Messor* ants, the material is comminuted and insalivated in a communal chewing process. This mulch, well fertilized with excrement, serves as the substratum for the fungus culture. To discover the source of the fungus, it is necessary to go back to the foundation of the nest. With Leaf-cutting Ants, this is again an independent process, that is, a fertilized female, working alone, without help, founds a new family which then develops into a colony. Before the nuptial flight, the female deposits a fragment of fungus from the fungus garden in its original home into a spheroidal pocket opening into its mouth cavity (the infrabucal sac). After it has found a suitable nest site and constructed a brood chamber there, its first concern is to establish a fungus garden. It expels the pellet of fungoid mycelium, tears it up into small pieces and dresses each portion with manure by holding it in its mandibles close to the tip of its abdomen and allowing a drop of excrement to fall upon it. In this way, it begins to cultivate the first fungus garden of the new nest.

Penicillium and other moulds are inhibited by the salivary secretions of the ants, so the fungus beds do not need "weeding". The only work required by the fungi cultures is the repeated application of freshly chewed material and a special biting action causing the mycelium to form the fruiting bodies of the fungus that serve the ants as food.

The earliest report of Leaf-cutting Ants goes back to Ambrosius Peres (1555), who, writing from Baja Salvatoris, told of immense numbers of huge ants, their mouths furnished with great pincer-like appendages for cutting fruits. "Everything they have bitten into dries up. Therefore the native people feed them carefully, so that they are sated and in this year at least spare the fruit fields."

Maria Sibylla Merian also depicts the Leaf-cutting Ants in word and picture. "In America, there are some extraordinarily large ants which, in a single night, can so defoliate trees that you would think they were broomshanks rather than trees. They have curved teeth which engage together like knives and with which they cut down the foliage. The tree then looks like a tree in a European winter landscape. Thousands of such ants cut the leaves from the trees and then drag them from the ground into their nests as prey. They are used as food, not for themselves but for their young, which are small worms . . . They build caves in the ground some 8 feet deep, and construct them in a manner that could not be improved upon by men. When they want to reach a point to which there is no ready access, they form a bridge by maintaining a firm hold on one another's body, until the wind assists the last ant of the free-hanging chain to seize hold of a point of support on the opposite side. Immediately a thousand other ants stream across this bridge. These ants are constantly at war with spiders and all terrestrial insects. Once a year they leave their caverns in countless swarms, make their way into houses, hurry through the rooms and kill

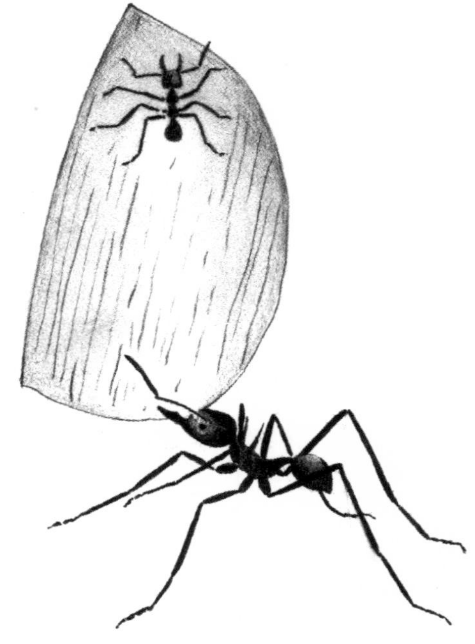

The Leaf-cutting Ant *(Atta cephalotes)* is accompanied as it works by a small worker ant. The task of the latter is to protect the larger ant from a Hunch-backed Fly *(Apocephalus)* that seeks to lay an egg on the back of the ant's head. The fly larvae develop in the head of the ant and finally kill it.
The Leaf-cutting Ant is removing a fragment of leaf (left); it will then carry it to the nest (right).

all the insects, great and small, that they meet by sucking them dry. In a moment, they devour large spiders, throwing themselves upon them in such numbers that there is no possibility of defence. Even humans are forced to take refuge. When they have cleared a house of insects, room by room, they go on into the next and so on, until they return to their holes."

Red Forest Ants

A model of peaceable behaviour towards members of the same species is the little Red Forest Ant *Formica polyctena*.

Here the nuptial flight is largely abandoned and copulation occurs usually on the nest, often in the nest. The colonies are highly polygynous. Five thousand queens have been counted in a single compound nest. Often sections of such a colony found new nests. After this, the link between the individual nests may be broken, and as a result, off-shoots of the colony develop. A large number of females in a nest can also result when initially several fertilized females join together in its establishment. Close-packed ranks of thousands of *Formica polyctena* can sometimes be observed moving through a district. They look like a white ribbon several centimetres in width, for many of the workers carry pupae in their mandibles. Strangely enough, some of the nest companions are also carried. Presumably these are members which so far have worked exclusively inside the nest and have never left it. The queens are carried in the same way. The ability to establish a nest independently has been completely lost by *Formica polyctena*, and right from the start, the queens rely on the help of the workers. A migration such as that described above, usually covers a distance of some 50 m to a tree trunk, over which a new dome-shaped mound-nest is constructed. In the course of time, large colonies may develop in this way.

Thief Ants

Thief Ants are interesting in several respects. They show considerable difference in size. In *Solenopsis fugax*, for example, the workers are about 1.5 to 2 mm long, while the sexually developed females are 10 mm long. Probably the difference in size has developed as a result of the way of life, that is, the workers of a species that was originally larger became smaller, while the sexually active ants retained their size. Thief Ants build their nests in close proximity to larger species, whose food supplies and even eggs and young larvae they steal. In addition they live on the excrement of root lice (Aphids). Their nest galleries are so narrow that their large neighbours are unable to follow them there. The sexually developed Thief Ants do not go out stealing food but are fed by the workers. In one South African Thief Ant *(Carebara vidua)* that steals its food from the termite *Termes natalensis*, the size difference is even more striking.

When the Amazon Ant *(Polyergus rufescens)* sets about establishing a nest, a fertilized female enters the nest of *Formica fusca*, rather more rarely of *F. rufibarbis* and exceptionally that of other species of *Formica*, kills the queen and seeks adoption in her place. The *Polyergus* nests are always monogynous, for no *Polyergus* female is accepted in a nest of that species. The number of auxiliary worker ants is constantly replenished and increased. Pillaging forays are almost always directed against nests of the species to which the slaves already selected belong, and they often take part in the raids.

Weaver Ants

Weaver Ants inhabit the tropical regions of the Old World. Their nests, constructed of leaves fastened together by threads of silk and lined inside with a delicate silken tissue, are suspended in the tops of trees. The silk used by the ants is produced by their larvae. The threads consist of protein substances that solidify rapidly on contact with the air. They are produced from the labial glands which are particularly highly developed in the larvae of Weaver Ants *(Oecophylla)*. The ants hold the larvae and are using them as both distaff and shuttle, that is, as a kind of tools to build the nest.

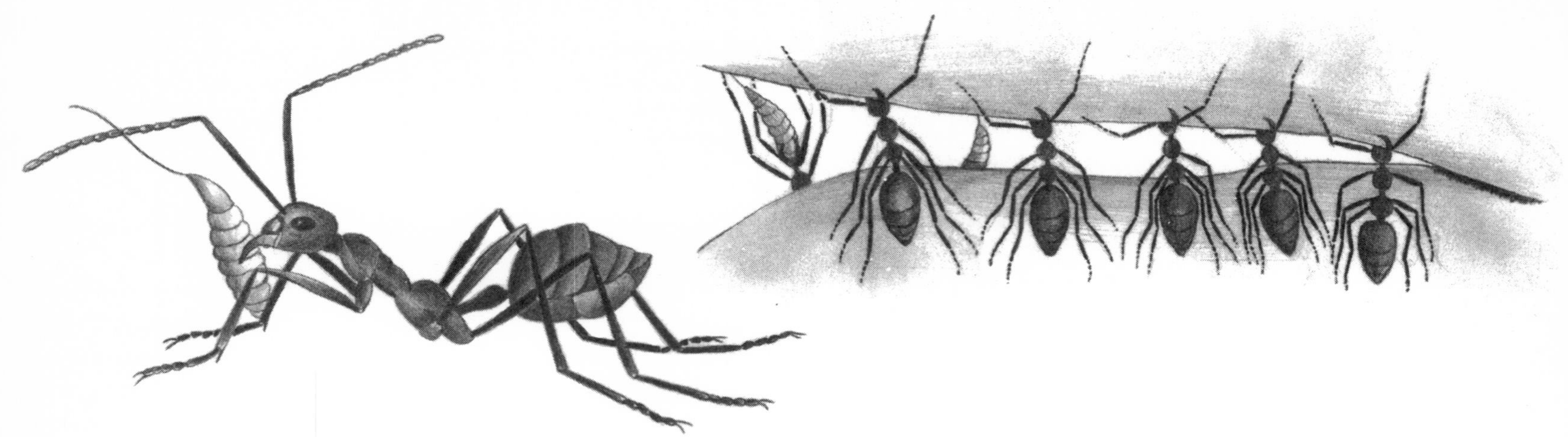

The Ant *Oecophylla smaragdina* makes use of the larva's ability to spin silk in order to fasten together the edges of leaves. On the left, a worker secreting a thread of silk from its powerfully developed salivary gland. On the right, a row of worker ants holding together the edges of two leaves. On the other side, the larvae are carried back and forth, spinning together the leaf margins.

Because of the ferocity of Weaver Ants, it is impossible for other insects to live on the trees on which they have placed their nests. Astute Chinese traders made use of this fact in earlier centuries. They wrapped the nests in gauze, cut them from the tree and sold them to the owners of gardens who then suspended them in their trees, primarily citrus trees, to protect them from insect pests. In some places, the trade in *Oecophylla* nests reached considerable proportions.

Another example of biological control by ants is probably even older. The Talmud says: "Bring ants from a distance of at least one parasang [approximately 5,000 to 6,000 m; the Author], and cast them on to the offending ants nest." (The ants in question are Harvester Ants of the genus *Messor*; the Author.) "Fierce fighting breaks out between the two colonies in which they annihilate one another. But if you bring ants from any shorter distance, they recognize each other and do not fight."

Plants inhabited by ants

Acacias which are indigenous to Africa and tropical America are an example of plants that are used by ants. As in many tree-like leguminous plants, the secondary leaves are modified into hollow thorns. Ants gnaw holes into these and use them as their abode. *Acacia sphaerocephala*, a native of Mexico, also provides food for ants in the form of edible corpuscles at the tips of the pinnules (Belt's corpuscles). East Africa is the home of the acacia *Acacia fistula*. Its thorns grow into gall-like structures, the size of chestnuts, which at first are filled with a loose tissue that later becomes detached from the wall and dries out. Ants, in this case *Cremastogaster tricolor*, gnaw holes into this structure. When the wind blows through these holes, sounds are produced similar to the notes of a flute.

Early methods of control

Many preparations have been recommended for controlling ants, some rather fantastical, and quite often they also affected those species that are beneficial. Lucius Junius Columella (A.D. 1–68) suggests the following: "If ants are causing damage in the garden, they must be driven out, if they live there, by the heart of an owl, but if they come in from outside, surround the entire garden with a line of ash or white chalk. They can be driven from trees by a mixture of red ochre and vinegar or red ochre, butter and tar applied around the trunk. Others believe the koracinus fish to be an excellent remedy, if it is hung on the tree." Kamal al-Din al-Damiri suggests other measures. "If you block up the ants' nest with cow dung, they do not open it, but flee from this place, and it is just the same with chicken dung. If you block the ants' galleries with a stone upon which many insects are sitting, the ants die. If you crush caraway seeds and place them in the galleries, it prevents the ants from emerging, and cumin seeds are just as effective . . . If you allow a little tar to drip into an ants' nest, they die, and if you pound sulphur and scatter it into the nest,

"The little Ant argued with the Fly as to which of the two
Could do the more. The Fly spoke first:
'Do you presume to measure your qualities against ours?
As soon as a sacrifice is made, I partake of the sacrificial feast,
I tarry among the altars, fly in the temples,
I alight on the king's head as often as I will,
I even kiss the matron's chaste cheek.
I do no work, yet feast on the finest foods.
What of the kind is granted to you, peasant woman?'
'O, it is splendid to associate with the gods,
But only for those who are invited, not for unbidden guests.
You boast of knowing the king and fine ladies?
When I am diligently gathering food for the winter,
I see you sitting in the dung round crumbling walls.
You may go to the altar but soon are chased from there;
You do no work, so you have nothing when most in need.
You pride yourself on things at which we blush.
In summer, you scorn me, yet when cold days come you are silent,
When benumbed by frost you stiffen to a corpse,
My well-stocked home receives me, safe from harm.
Now have I indeed brought down your vaunting pride.'
This fable shows us different characters.
Those that delight in deceptive splendour,
And alongside them, those that seek true glory."

After Aesop (c. *550* B.C.)

the ants are destroyed. If the cloak of a woman in her menses is suspended before any object, the ants will not approach it."

Petrus de Crescentii gives the following advice to prevent ants from climbing up trees and plants: "Take the material as instructed by Palladius, mix it with half the quantity of vinegar or wine lees and spread this round the trunk of the tree, or some liquid pitch, but carefully so that the tree itself is not harmed by the medicament. Or take, which in my opinion is even better, a woollen or linen rag, or hay or straw, and tie it firmly at the highest point of the trunk, but in such a way that the lower edge looks irregular like a ridge. Or take a wide round earthenware vessel with a large hole in the middle, through which the plant can be pushed in such a way that the vessel can still hold water. Then the ants cannot get at the plant. Or else spread bird-lime around the stem. By all these methods it is possible forcibly to keep the vast hordes of ants away from the trees. Some people believe that a silk cord soaked in oil and tied round the tree affords sufficient protection."

One final remedy is taken from the *Théâtre d'Agriculture* (1600) by Olivier de Serres. "If ants are troublesome on trees, shake them down from the tree. They can be prevented from climbing it again by the application of a layer of olive or nut oil round the trunk at a height of 4 feet over which coal dust is sprinkled so that it adheres to the oil. This prevents the ants from climbing the trees, and those below this ring are able to damage neither the tender shoots nor the fruits. But if you want to exterminate the ants completely, break up the soil somewhat around the trees and scatter soot, ashes, charcoal and the sap that has oozed from oak trees, either together or separately, at the foot of the trees. These substances kill the ants or drive them a good distance away, particularly when the first rain falls upon them. In the absence of rain, watering will suffice." The diversity of methods is a sure indication that none of them was really effective.

Ants as beneficial to man

Today ants are considered beneficial mainly in their role as predators on other insect pests. In earlier times, other aspects predominated, such as the practice, mentioned in the Talmud, of using the heads of large species *(Camponotus, Messor)* to suture wounds. After aligning the lips of the wound, the ants were made to bite into it and the bodies were snipped off. The heads functioned as surgical clips.

Kamal al-Din al-Damiri writes: "Take ants' eggs, crush them and apply them to a part of the body and the growth of hair there is prevented . . . If you take seven long ants and place them in a bottle that is filled with mixed fat, close the neck of the bottle and bury the bottle in dung for a day and a night, take it out again, remove the fat and spread it on the glans penis and the area above it, the power of memory will be stimulated and activity increased."

After that, one might well recommend a good Scandinavian gin which still today is said to include ant extract among its ingredients. And should this not be to hand, one can read in Linnaeus about "Formica media rubra, the Piss Ant. So-named is the ant that builds its large mounds in thickets of corn and grain, and is at all times ready to revenge itself by stinging, although its sting is not its worst line of defence, since at the same time it discharges a liquid behind it, so that it is commonly believed it is pissing at its enemies . . . From the abode of these ants emanates a most excellently tart and refreshing odour if you prod the nest and hold your hand above it. They have a most pleasant, slightly sour taste when chewed, and for this reason alone, are used in pharmacy."

In Brazil, the Leaf-cutting Ant *Atta sexdens* is eaten either raw or fried in oil, and is said to be effective for swollen tonsils. In the USA, ants fried in oil and coated with chocolate can be bought in tins.

Ants in fable

The ant also plays a role in poetry and fiction, as for instance, in a classic folktale which, in earlier times, was taken for gospel truth, and which dates back to Herodotus (484–425 B.C.), sometimes called the Father of History. "There are other Indians settled northward . . . whose mode of life resembles that of the Bactrians. They are the most warlike of the Indians, and these are they who are sent to procure the gold; for near this part is a desert by reason of the sand. In this desert then, and in the sand, there are ants in size somewhat less indeed than dogs, but larger than foxes. Some of them are in the possession of the king of the Persians, which were taken there. These ants, forming their habitations under ground, heap up the sand, as the ants in Greece do, and in the same manner; and they are very like them in shape. The sand that is heaped up is mixed with gold. The Indians therefore go to the desert to get this sand, each man having three camels, on either side a male one harnessed to draw by the side, and a female in the middle, this last the man mounts himself, having taken care to yoke one that has been separated from her young as recently born as possible . . . The Indians then set out for the gold, having before calculated the time, so as to be engaged in their plunder during the hottest part of the day, for during the heat the ants hide themselves under ground . . . When the Indians arrive at the spot, having sacks with them, they fill these with the sand, and return with all possible expedition. For the ants, as the Persians say, immediately discovering them by the smell, pursue them, and they are equalled in swiftness by no other animal, so that if the Indians did not get the start of them while the ants were assembling, not a man of them could be saved . . . Thus the Indians, as the Persians say, obtain the greatest part of their gold."

In the writings of Rabanus Maurus, we find the following interesting observation: "There are said to be ants in Ethiopia that have the stature of dogs and which scratch up gold dust with their feet, but guard it carefully lest anyone should steal it; those who take any of it, they hunt to the death." It is very rare for belief in a popular traditional tale to have persisted for well over a thousand years.

Butterflies

(Lepidoptera)

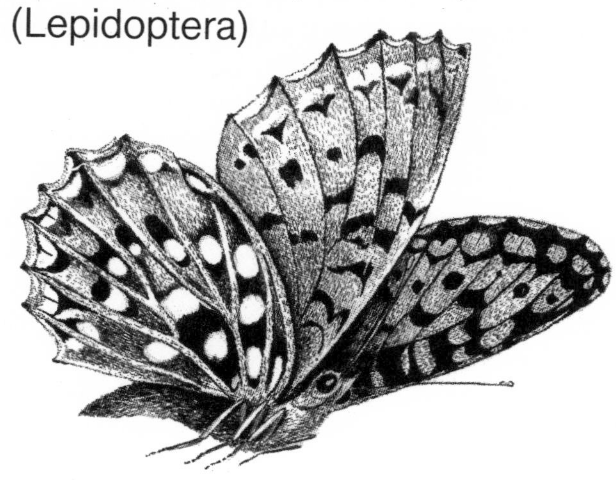

The Austrian lyric poet Nikolaus Lenau (1802–1850) wrote a poem entitled "The Butterfly", Carl Spitteler (1845–1924) composed a collection of poems "Butterflies". A well-known painting is the strange "Butterfly Catcher" by Carl Spitzweg (1808–1885) or Dante Gabriel Rosetti's (1828–1882) "Venus verticordia". In addition to its role as an artistic motif, the butterfly was the object of cultic veneration and, of course, achieved notoriety for the damage it caused.

When we think of butterflies, it is initially of their attractive form and the often extraordinarily beautiful wing colouring, particularly in tropical species. But our links with these insects are not based exclusively on their favourable attributes. As caterpillars, they have often caused widespread devastation in agriculture and forestry. On the other hand, certain species were among the earliest animals to be domesticated and bred for their economic importance. By examining a number of examples (Moths, Swallowtails, Case Moths, Cabbage Whites, caterpillars) we shall seek to illustrate certain aspects of the diverse links that exist between man and this group of animals. The Silk Moth *(Bombyx mori)*, which has extremely high economic value, is not included here, because an extensive specialized literature on this insect already exists.

Clothes Moths (Tineidae)

Clothes moths are among those Lepidoptera that attracted man's notice at a very early stage, this time as destructive pests. Still today, they persist to some extent in their destructive role, and new means of controlling them are still being developed. In the 13th century, writing in a compendium on the subject of moths, and still basing his views on the theory of spontaneous generation, Bartholomaeus Anglicus states: "The moth is a clothes worm that comes into being from the decomposition of clothing if it is left for too long in a close atmosphere without being exposed to the wind, or folded up in the fresh air. It is a sensitive creature and hides within the clothes, so that it is rarely seen. Bay leaves, the needles of cedars and cypresses and the like, laid among clothes, protect them as they also protect books from damage by moths." The creatures are, of course, caterpillars and not worms, but the word "worm" was often used, as it still is today, in an unadmissably broad sense.

We can read more about the control of moths in the writings of Ferrante Imperato (1599): "If by simmering, you reduce to about half the lees and skimmings from oil, and spread this substance on the base and into the corners of a chest or cupboard, the clothes placed therein will never be attacked by moths. Only the chest must be good and dry before you place the clothes in it."

Above:

Mesoacidalia charlotta

"What purpose can that grizzled ancient have,
Leafing back and forth through antique books
Until far into the night?
As if there were anything to be found there!
But see, he is not at home,
Today, I shall spy out his secret."
Chirping thus, a little sparrow flies into the room;
Books large and small lie everywhere.
With deliberation, he selects the largest,
And in his turn sets about leafing through it.
'Yellowed paper, badly flecked with age.
What value can it possibly have.
Yet wait!' His bright eye flashes
Quickly he is ready with his little beak.
'Two moths! how big and plump!'
Eagerly he gobbles them up
and chirps 'Who would ever have imagined
that he also hunts for moths!'"

Julius Sturm (1816–1896)

Ulisse Aldrovandi comments at greater length: "Having dealt with the worms that occur on animals and plants, it is appropriate to talk about the worms that destroy the clothing materials fabricated by man. Moths spare the clothes neither of the rich nor of the poor, and they also are guilty of destroying manuscripts from the hand of Aristotle and Theophrastus. Pliny considers that dust and aridity are the generators of moths. This dust engenders the moths in wool and clothing, particularly when they are threadbare and stored together with spiders . . . On the other hand I do not believe what the Philosopher [Aristotle; the Author] writes, namely that the wool from sheep slain by the wolf is safe from moths. According to certain passages from Aristotle and Pliny quoted by Bartholomaeus Anglicus, such wool is attacked both by lice and moths. But no moths come into being from linen or linen paper nor are the latter harmed by them . . . When woollen clothes are kept for a long time in a close and oppressive atmosphere, they are especially susceptible to infestation by moths. To control them, Marcus Cato recommends that they be dipped into a decoction of the juice pressed from olives. Pliny recommends placing wormwood between the clothes. The strongly-scented iris is also much used. Equally effective is aniseed, particularly ground, and also chrysanthemum which has a good scent. The strong smell of lemons or of cypress pollen when these are distributed among the clothes, is said to be effective. A decoction of Asa foetida drives fleas and moths from clothes. More recent authors commend the effect of powdered rosemary. If the clothes are already infested, Fallopius advises that they be washed in water in which underclothing worn by a woman in her menses has been washed. Pliny also says that clothes from a dead body remain untouched by moths."

Caspar Schwenckfeld refers to other species of moths, although he did not yet distinguish between them. "Very small, whitish worms which feed upon clothes, paper, books etc. They originate from dirt, dew or the excrement of butterflies. They are especially common in linen clothes, in the fleece of sheep bitten by a wolf, and in those of dead people. Moths also occur in apples, pears, roots, certain brassicas, bedeguars, galls and beehives. Moths are kept away by substances that are bitter and strong-smelling, for example, by bay and cypress leaves, absinthe, lavender flowers."

In Central Europe alone, there are some 53 known species in the family of Moths (Tineidae), and they are much more diverse in their biology than might be expected from an acquaintance with the Clothes Moth *(Tineola bisselliella)* alone. Some of them are pests in stored goods, such as the Case-bearing Moth *(Tinea pellionella)* in furs, the Corn Moth *(Nemapogon granellus)*, *Nemapogon cloacellus* and the Tapestry Moth *(Trichophaga tapezella)* in carpets. Other species live in tree fungi, rotting wood, animal fleeces, even in the pellets of raptorial birds.

Réaumur also found moths to be a source of considerable interest, as the following passage shows: "In the previous essay, we admired the skill with which the caterpillars of moths spin their cocoons. Now we must consider how we can protect ourselves from their voracity. The wide-

Orneodes pygmaea (family Orneodidae), a moth from Sri Lanka with wings deeply divided into plumes.

spread habit of giving carpets and other textiles a thorough beating and brushing once a year is an excellent preventative measure, if it is carried out at the right time. This is the middle of August or at the latest, the beginning of September, when the majority of the young grubs have hatched and most of the adults have disappeared. At any other time, beating and brushing is quite ineffective, because it does no damage to the older caterpillars in their stoutly spun cases. But freshly hatched grubs fall off immediately. Whenever I lifted out carefully those pieces of material on which I was hatching them, a good many fell off straight away, and all of them if I pulled briskly. A breath of wind is enough at this stage to blow them away. They attack fabrics of all colours, but the quality of the cloth is very important. They are especially fond of loose weaves, and the loosest threads are always the ones they bite at first. But the more tightly-twisted the threads and the firmer the weave, the less is the cloth attacked. I have seen very well preserved old tapestries and textiles that displayed both these merits, and new ones that had neither of these two virtues and were completely destroyed. Thus those tapestries worked in the Auvergne generally suffer more than those from Flanders. Certain cloths, beautiful in themselves, had to be ruled out entirely for such purposes.

"However, if driven by need, the moth caterpillars will eat every kind of cloth, but in good quality materials, the damage only becomes obvious later . . . From my many experiments, I single out the following. I placed a large number of caterpillars of moths in powder glasses, putting in each case 20 caterpillars onto a piece of blue or green serge. It is very laborious to collect caterpillars, but caterpillars that are bred, usually reproduce in a ratio of at least 20 : 1, and even females enclosed in glass jars lay eggs willingly. In this way, I raised a sufficient number of caterpillars for my experiments. My first consideration was the following: in nature or in storage, no animal skin suffers from moths before it has been treated. Untreated rabbit skins among my specimens remained unharmed, while treated ones were chewed greedily, and soon looked as if they had been shaved. When we process and treat skins and linen for our own use, we make them into agreeable food for moth caterpillars at the same time. The principal distinction between treated and untreated goods of both types is that the latter are very greasy. White materials do not require grease to be removed from them, but simply the impurities adhering to them; however, materials that are to be dyed required de-greasing. But if, after dyeing, these are oiled again slightly, they ought to remain free of moths. My first experiments were related to this. Caterpillars placed upon linen cloth thus prepared or those placed upon serge that had been rubbed against it, ate scarcely at all for a few weeks, and then began to do so only slowly and eventually completed their development, but much later than control grubs on de-greased linen.

"In experiments in which grey and blue serge were kept together in a jar, with sometimes one and sometimes the other being rubbed against oily linen, it was always the serge not so treated that was eaten, as could easily be seen from the colour of the cases and of the excrement. As for other oils and fats, it seems that only olive oil is equally effective as the natural animal fat found in the hair of animals. These experiments suggest a method of moth control. Upholstery fabrics and the like should be treated with fleece-wool or with lanolin fat that the apothecary obtains from it, softened in hot water: rub it off in the first case, brush it off in the second.

"Oiled materials were not the only ones I experimented with, but others that I immersed in vinegar, a decoction of wormwood, tobacco liquor, sea-salt, soda solution etc. In addition, I experimented with strong-smelling plants such as rosemary, wormwood, myrtle, lemon rind etc. that have been recommended as reliable means of protection, as well as stock gilly-flowers, orange oil etc. None of these substances actually protects the fabric from moths, while certain of them, such as orris root, actually prove attractive to them. Hanging up cantharides, as recommended by Maris, is equally ineffective against moths. If need be, the grubs will feed on quite unpleasant materials. As a reserve, they first fall back upon their cases, then cover up the holes with their excrement; cases of this kind indicate that they find the materials available unpalatable, as for example, with rags treated with tobacco liquor, pepper, soda solution, olive oil. But there are even better remedies.

"Countrywomen often place pine-cones in cupboards where they keep clothes. We would be wrong to reject such remedies out of hand. The protection afforded by the pine-cones can only come from the resinous smell. So I chose quite strong smells of the same category, and dipped one rag in turpentine, while I rubbed one side of another cloth again with turpentine and put each into a jar with caterpillars. The result was unexpected, even to me. Next morning, all the caterpillars had died after convulsive twitching. The majority had abandoned their cases, which they otherwise never do, and lay naked and rigid on the ground."

Clothes Moths lay their eggs unattached on suitable material. The grubs live in spun tubes open at both ends. In groups, they take in a greater quantity of food per head than when alone. The male grubs require less food than the females. The female, whose capacity for flight is restricted, secretes pheromones from glandular cells in the abdomen which attract the flying male.

The *Household Book* of Johann Colerus contains various remedies for moths. "If wormwood or aniseed or goat's liver, 2 to 3 cedar twigs, the rind of a lemon or citrus fruit or pieces of fern are placed in cupboards with clothes or between clothes, they will drive out moths and cockroaches. To ensure that moths or mice will not damage a hand-written book, simply pour some wormwood water into the ink. Or make a candle of pure tallow from a ram, wrap it in a thin cloth and place it into the cupboard and it will also prevent moths from getting at the clothes."

Paracelsus recommends a universal remedy. "If gum mastic, camphor, amber, moss and especially civet are placed among clothes, not only will the garments be protected from moths, but any moths, fleas, lice, bugs or other worms contained therein will be driven out."

Every age has sought an effective method of protection; today the wide availability of chemical products has at last provided it.

"It is the festive, the nuptial form, creative and at the same time death-acceptive, that previously was a dormant pupa, and before the pupa, a voracious caterpillar. The butterfly does not live to feed and to become old, it lives only to love and to procreate, and for this purpose, it is attired in fabulously splendid garb, with wings many times larger than its body, and which in cut and colour, in scales and bloom, express the secret of its existence in a language extremely diverse and ingenious, that it may live with the utmost intensity, in order, by added enchantment and seduction, to entice the opposite sex to celebrate the more radiantly the festival of procreation."

Hermann Hesse (1877–1962)

Swallowtail Butterfly *(Papilio machaon)*

The first detailed description and illustration of the Swallowtail butterfly appears in the volume on the Lepidoptera in Ulisse Aldrovandi's *De Animalibus insectis*; apparently the beauty of this butterfly had failed to catch the attention of earlier authors. "The last butterfly on this Plate, depicted from above and from below, is one that I obtained in July 1592. In 26 days it had developed from a small, hairy caterpillar with red, white and black markings. I had found the latter towards midday on a tamarisk shrub. During the following night, it transformed itself into a green pupa that hung suspended on a thread. For 15 days, it retained the same colour, then became partly yellowish and partly black. From this I concluded that it was already undergoing metamorphosis into the butterfly whose colours were gleaming through the pupal skin. And indeed the emergent butterfly displayed just such a colouring. The black and yellow colouring is more intensive on the forewings than on the hind wings. The latter, which are usually the smaller, are in this case the more beautiful. They are prolonged and terminate in a kind of tail. The body above is black as far as the sides and yellow below, and in relation to the size of the wings is slender. The large eyes are jet black, as are the antennae which are squared off at the tip. At the outer edges of the hind wings there are spots, red to pink in colour, which seen from above, appear circular, from below semicircular. All in all, it is an elegant butterfly. It can be seen everywhere in fields and gardens."

Maria Sibylla Merian also took an interest in this butterfly. On one plate, she illustrates it on Fennel *(Foeniculum vulgare)* as caterpillar, pupa and imago, and writes: "I came across this attractive and prettily striped caterpillar in August on fennel (which is depicted here with the caterpillar visible on the underside), upon which it was feeding. Such caterpillars are a beautiful green in colour and have stripes of a velvety blackness with golden-yellow spots upon the stripes; if they are touched roughly, they immediately extend two yellow hornlike processes at the front of the head like a snail. At the front and below, on either side, they also have three small pointed feet or claws, then two vacant segments where there are no feet; and then again four segments and below, on either side, four round little feet; there follow again two vacant segments and right at the hind end, two more round little feet with which they take a very firm hold. Where there is no fennel, they eat carrots. Gardeners call it the 'fruit caterpillar' because they believe it does great harm to fruit, but as I said above, I have never found it on anything but fennel and carrots. However, it has a curious odour that is like fruit when a lot of different kinds are stored together. When they have grown to full size, they discard their skin or integument completely and it remains hanging nearby above them, as I have shown in my drawing; they suspend themselves on a wall, head-downwards and attach the caudal extremity as firmly as if it were glued fast. At the midpoint of the body they spin a white silken thread so that suspension is further secured. Within half a day

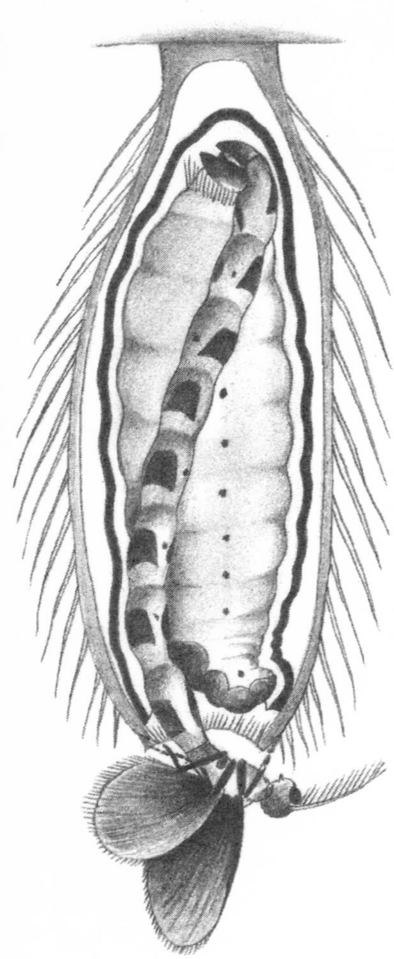

Bagworm Moth (Psychidae) mating. The abdomen of the male is extremely protrusible, the female is devoid of wings and legs, and remains within the larval case.

they have turned into date kernels with the appearance of a child in swaddling clothes; one can even make out a human face there, as in the one I show hanging on the fennel. These date kernels are grey and partly green in colour. They remain suspended in this form until April or May. I had a number of them emerge as early as December, but I blame that on my having kept them in a warm room. The 'bird of summer' then, that can be seen to have emerged here, has 4 wings, the two upper wings being beautifully yellow and black, as are the lower two, except that they are a fine blue colour in the dotted parts or areas, and the undermost, egg-shaped field is the same but also includes red colouring. The body remains black and yellow, has 6 black feet and at the front of the head, a long rostrum which it twines right round; if you place some sugar before it, it lays the long beak on the sugar as if to eat it. I have frequently observed it using this organ to draw sweetness from the flowers."

It may have been the great beauty of butterflies that made them the subject of a wide variety of cultic, symbolic and mystical beliefs. For the Toltecs, butterflies symbolized fire, the image associated with their fluttering movements in flight. In the Ancient Greek and Mycenaean cultures, there are representations of butterflies in which the abdomen is strongly emphasized and which can perhaps be interpreted as originally being fertility symbols. These butterflies sometimes have the form of a phallus with butterfly wings. Very often, Aphrodite, Venus and the Cupids are depicted with the wings of butterflies. From this, the concept of Psyche subsequently developed. Psyche was at first a bird of death, later the personification of the soul. The phenomenon of insect metamorphosis, already familiar in early times, probably accorded well with ideas then current concerning resurrection and the transmigration of souls. Butterflies retained this significance into the Christian era. In the painting "Ullrich von Hutten's Tomb" by the Romantic artist Caspar David Friedrich (1774–1840), a butterfly emerges from the black mouth of a tomb, symbolizing the immortal soul. In folklore, butterflies are sometimes held responsible, as witches, for the theft of milk, cream and butter. Butterflies are also looked upon as demons of disease, capable of causing fever and other afflictions. In Ancient China, the benevolent nature of the butterfly tends to predominate. There, it was the symbol of joy, summer and the union of lovers, a role which butterflies play even in present-day lyrical poetry.

Friedrich Schnack (1888–1979) concludes the legend of Homer's butterflies with the following sentence: "But in the narrow space between lip and lip hovered, fragile as a spirit, a white butterfly with ink-black flecks on its hind wings and blood-red eye-spots, dark-ringed, before the mouth of the dying Homer, the Apollo Butterfly."

Bagworm Moths or Basketworm Moths (Psychidae)

The example of the Bagworm Moths (Psychidae) shows that even certain moths living a secluded life were noticed in early times. Aristotle writes: "There is a grub entitled the 'faggot-bearer', as strange a creature as is known. Its head projects outside its shell, mottled in colour, and its feet are near the end or apex, as is the case with grubs in general; but the rest of its body is cased in a tunic as it were of spider's web, and there are little dry twigs about it, that look as though they had stuck by accident to the creature as it went walking about. But these twig-like formations are naturally connected with the tunic, for just as the shell is with the body of the snail so is the whole superstructure with our grub; and they do not drop off, but can only be torn off, as though they were all of a piece with him, and the removal of the tunic is as fatal to this grub as the removal of the shell would be to the snail. In course of time this grub becomes a chrysalis, as is the case with the silkworm, and lives in a motionless condition. But as yet it is not known into what winged condition it is transformed." Ulisse Aldrovandi was probably the first to observe the metamorphosis of the Bagworm caterpillars into a moth. The starting point was a larval case from a pine tree. He illustrates both case and moth. It probably belonged to the genus *Psyche (Xylophthorus)*.

In his *Metamorphosis naturalis*, Jean Goedart illustrated the life cycles of a considerable number of insects. Left: Peacock Butterfly *(Inachis io)*, right: Magpie Moth *(Abraxas grossulariata)*.

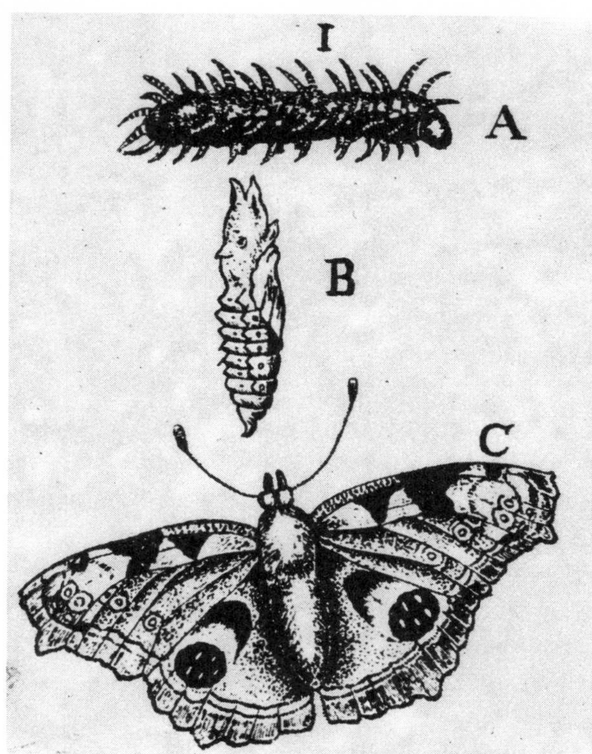

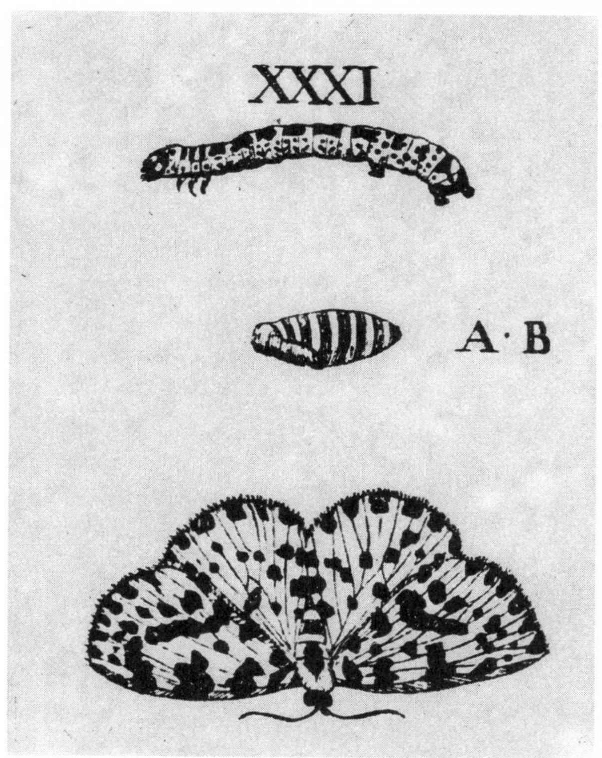

Caterpillars

Even today, it is not easy in every instance to assign a given caterpillar to the correct Lepidoptera species. In early writings, those caterpillars that attracted attention by colour or form, or because of the damage they caused, were treated as entirely independent creatures. This is not surprising since the relationship between caterpillar and butterfly was not recognized until relatively late.

Dangerous caterpillars

The caterpillars of many of the Lepidoptera are more or less densely clothed with hairs, and as a result, some of them can occasionally be troublesome or even dangerous to man. In the *Erh Ya*, there is an early mention of a hairy caterpillar that secretes a poison when touched. There is a whole series of families in the order of Lepidoptera that come into this category. The Lymantriidae (Tussock Moths, e.g. *Euproctis chrysorrhoea*, the European Gold Tail), the Lasiocampidae (e.g. *Macrothylacia rubi*, the Fox Moth), the Saturniidae (e.g. *Eudia pavonia*, the Emperor Moth) and predominantly in Central Europe, the family of Processionary Moths (Thaumetopoeidae) represented by only two species. Among the families named, these last are the most troublesome in this respect. Whether the irritation they cause is due to mechanical action alone or to chemical secretions or to a combination of the two has not yet been satisfactorily established. In the case of the Megalopygidae, a family related to the Burnets and Foresters (Zygaenidae) and which comprises some 200 species, most of them neo-tropical, poison-filled glandular hairs are certainly present. The first two larval instars of the European Processionary Moth *(Thaumetopoea processionea)* possess no urticating hairs; there follow three instars with poisonous setae. The larval skins that are shed during growth decompose and the fractured, dust-fine setae pass into the air. Anyone walking through a wood infested by Processionary caterpillars risks serious inflammation of the skin on any part of the body coming into contact with the setae. The irritation they cause to the conjunctiva of the eye can be extremely painful. If the hairs are inhaled, they can induce bronchitis and asthmatic attacks. Certain Indian tribes roast hairy caterpillars and apply them to the noses of their hunting dogs to intensify the animal's sense of smell.

Wer kann der Raupe, die am Zweige kriecht,
von ihrem künft'gen Futter sprechen?
Und wer der Puppe, die am Boden liegt,
die zarte Schale helfen durchzubrechen?
Es kommt die Zeit, sie drängt sich selber los
und eilt auf Fittichen der Rose in den Schoss.

Johann Wolfgang von Goethe (1749–1832),
from: "Ilmenau" (poem)

Who can tell the grub that crawls upon the branch
Of feasting yet to come?
Who help the pupa on the ground
To split asunder its delicate shell?
The time is ripe, it thrusts its own way out
And hastens on wings to the heart of the rose.

Early knowledge about caterpillars

There are frequent descriptions of the destruction of plants by caterpillars, as for example, that by Rabanus Maurus. "Eruca [Latin: caterpillar; the Author] is a broad-leaf worm that develops in leaves and shoots. It does not progress like the locust, passing rapidly from one place to another, leaving half-eaten plants behind, but remains on the same shrubs which undergo complete destruction, it devours them slowly and lazily, but completely. Plautus: malefica involuta!"

Kamal al-Din al-Damiri was obviously familiar with the phenomenon of metamorphosis, although this knowledge was temporarily lost again later on. "Certain red worms on wild plants which turn into butterflies when they shed their skin . . . Other people think they are white worms with a red head that live in the sand and look like ladies' fingers . . . As 'crawling creatures', their consumption is forbidden. Characteristics: when ground and applied to torn tendons and muscles, these worms have an immediate and highly beneficial effect."

Albertus Magnus remarks: "The caterpillar is a long worm of various colours with many short legs."

The caterpillars of most of the larger Lepidoptera carry a pair of abdominal legs or "prolegs" on segments 3 to 6, and on the terminal abdominal segment the so-called "claspers" or grasping prolegs. In the larvae of the primitive moths, the Micropterygidae, the number of abdominal limbs is increased, in those of many Noctuid Moths (Noctuidae) and particularly of all Geometers (Geometridae, also known as Loopers, Inchworms, Span-worms) it is reduced. In the larvae of the Microlepidopterans and of the Swift Moths (Hepialidae), the apex of the leg, the "planta", is provided with a series of hooks or crochets disposed in a complete multi-serial circle. The caterpillars of the remaining Lepidoptera possess semi-coronate prolegs with only the outer rim of the planta bearing crochets.

Measures to control caterpillars

The very interesting and relatively independent work *Opus ruralium commodorum libri XII* by the Italian writer Petrus de Crescentii includes the following note on the subject of caterpillars: "To prevent damage by caterpillars, always immerse seed before it is sown in the juice of the houseleek or in the blood of caterpillars. If they become troublesome, set children on to collect and kill them. Follow the instructions of Palladius and plant peas among bitter vetch, then no pests will develop. For this reason, in many places, a row of plants, especially cabbage, is planted among fenugreek."

In gardens, mixed cultivation of plants is once more recommended today, although few people are aware that the idea is some seven hundred years old.

In his book *Hortus sanitatis*, published in about 1480, Johannes Wonnecke von Caub shows a tree stripped of its leaves by caterpillars, and writes: "Eruca is a leaf-worm found in cabbage or vine leaves; it is so named from its chewing habit. Plautus mentions it. I would curse the creature that wraps itself in the foliage of vines and eats leaf and blossom. This misfortune occurs when there is a long spell of damp weather. Preventive measures: Palladius: To deal with caterpillars, moisten the seed that is to be sown with the sap of the house-leek or the blood of the caterpillars.

Some strew the ash of fig wood or sow sea onions in their gardens. Others ask a menstruating woman to walk round the garden."

An authority in his own time was Pietro Andrea Matthioli (born 1501). He published a commentary on Dioscorides (1548) which went into many editions and enjoyed wide distribution. In it he says: "When I was quite small, there was a terrible caterpillar year throughout the whole of Tuscany. At the time, these pupae were found in vast quantities hanging hind end upwards from trees, plants, walls and houses. Their colour was so luminously gold and silvery that one would certainly have believed them to be of solid gold or silver, had one not seen them moving [undoubtedly the Painted Lady, *Vanessa cardui*, the Author]. They look just like babes in swaddling clothes, with a human face and a twin-peaked mitre on the head . . . As a means of combatting caterpillars, Pliny recommends hanging up the skull of a horse or a river crayfish in the middle of the garden, or else touching the cabbage and other plants with a beaker filled with blood. Columella suggests picking them off by hand and shaking them from the plant in the early morning. This must be done especially in damp places where they come into being after rain. If upon shaking, they fall torpid to the ground, they will not climb again on to the plant. Careful gardeners moisten seeds before sowing with the sap of the houseleek. In this way, they prevent the caterpillars from approaching them. Democritus maintains that if a woman who is in her menses runs three times round the garden, with dishevelled hair, all the caterpillars fall to the ground dead. But in my opinion, all that is mere experimentation for the superstitious masses and is not for the enlightened." One cannot but agree with Matthioli's opinion; the only suggestion that might still be relevant for the small garden of today is that of Columella.

As might be expected, Johann Colerus provides a chapter on caterpillars in his *Household Book*. "Caterpillars also cause great damage to trees for they devour the leaves and often lie thickly one on top of another, like a heap of young snakes; see that they are picked off and dropped into water or burned; or cast them from the trees, pour soil on them and tread them firmly with the feet, or set light to a handful of straw and singe them with it—they will soon die in this way. Or take equal parts of the urine of oxen and lees of oil, boil them together and when the liquid is cold, sprinkle the trees with it, but in doing so, take care lest any of this decoction splashes the face or hands, for it is poisonous. Or fumigate the trees with bitumen and sulphur, or use the following fumigant: galbanum, the horny coverings of goat's hooves, staghorn and the like, station it against the wind, so that the smoke and the stench can move towards the caterpillars. Also soak the ashes of ravens in water for three days, stirring frequently, and sprinkle the trees with it . . . To prevent caterpillars eating cabbage, take horse dung and wormwood, boil together in a cauldron, allow to cool and stir in a small quantity of human excrement, sprinkle it on the plants . . . They have other enemies such as the sparrow, cuckoo and other birds, although a landlord should not rely upon them, but must remove the caterpillars as he can; and because this vermin is said to have its origin in the droppings of papilionids, butterflies and moths, these should also be removed, in accordance with the proverb: Principiis obsta."

In his *Natural History* (1599), Ferrante Imperato suggests the following method: "To destroy caterpillars, smear the lower part of the tree all round with tar, then collect a species of large ant in a cloth, which you hang on the tree. Because of the tar, the ants cannot leave the tree, and must seek their food on it, and so they destroy all the caterpillars without touching any of the fruit. A very trustworthy gentleman told me about this."

Ecclesiastical courts even brought law suits against caterpillars, as, for example, in Troyes in 1516 and in Valence in 1585. In 1600 Olivier de Serres gives some thoroughly practical instructions in his *Théâtre d'Agriculture*. "The most reliable method of protecting garden trees from damage by caterpillars is carefully to gather and destroy their progeny in the winter. At this time,

"Eruca, as Liber Rerum says
Is an insect that habitually eats
Cabbage and the foliage of trees.
You may say that its colouring is ugly
Its name in our language is caterpillar.
It is well known that long ago
Egypt was plagued by these insects.
Half-way through August—it is said—
Perhaps when it rains or there is heavy dew
It changes its skin
And flies into the air.
They are very damaging to fruit.
Then and later, when their end is near,
They deposit their seed
In foliage and afterwards die,
So that they are seen no more,
Until the warm weather begins again
And after that they eat the leaves once more.
So with the sunshine and the dew,
They live free of any trouble."

Albertus Magnus, from: Liber de natura rerum

it is very easily done. The eggs alone are collected and crushed. They can be found on the branches of trees in large numbers inside leaves that they have spun together. The decision to deal with them is guaranteed success if an attentive man applies himself to this task during the entire winter, until the spring. Should this man not have worked diligently, the fact will be revealed later on, when to his shame, large numbers of caterpillars hatch out from the eggs he has overlooked and attack the trees. In this case, these harmful caterpillars must again be picked off, and that immediately they have hatched. For at this time, they still remain together and are easy to destroy. Later on, all one's efforts are in vain."

The diversity of caterpillars

Ulisse Aldrovandi describes many different caterpillars and illustrates them in his volume on butterflies, including, for example, *Acherontia atropos* (Death's Head Hawk Moth), *Papilio machaon* (Swallowtail), *Thyria jacobaeae* and *Cerura vinula* (Puss Moth). Of the latter species, he writes: "In a retracted position, the black head looks like the head of a mouse or cat. Above the black, rounded part there is a white band into which, on either side, a black point projects, like an ear. Two other black spots at the centre simulate a nose, and under it, there are three more small spots. The body is green, the colour especially intense at the boundaries of the segments. A longitudinal median line extends from head to tail. The two little tails can be raised and are covered with black spots."

An example of the kind of description that was typical of its time is found in a work which was written in 1598 by Johann Bauhin, and which was based on his own observations. "Eruca hirsuta. On September 10, near Eichelberg, I caught a large, densely haired caterpillar. On January 15, it was still very lively, although I had confined it without food. I also observed it on October 16, 1596. It is red-brown in colour, in certain parts reddish. Eruca hirsuta alia. A different hairy caterpillar, which was coloured entirely brown. It was sketched some time after it had been in captivity. It was caught in Eichelberg on September 15, and now, in October, is still alive." Eruca hirsuta is a literal translation of "hairy caterpillar". Today, these designations read almost like binary nomenclature.

The occurrence of Noctuids in vast numbers gave rise to the following passage in Gabriel Rzaczynski's *Curiosities in the Natural History of the Kingdom of Poland* (1721). "In 1683, after heavy rainstorms, innumerable worms appeared in the fields of Podolia, which consumed all the growing corn together with its roots. The pest appeared everywhere in orderly columns. This insect was green, the length of an earthworm and occurs normally among bushes or on cabbage plants. But where any part of the field remained unaffected, it produced a greater harvest than previously the entire field. Even land that had before been completely infertile for eight years produced high yields."

On right:

139 Small Tortoiseshell *(Aglais urticae)*, a butterfly still common in Central Europe, the caterpillar of which feeds on Stinging Nettles.

140 Butterflies with transparent wings.
Above: *Callitaera aurora* from South America.
Centre: *Hetaera piera* from South America.
Below: *Cresseda cressida* from Australia.

On right:

141 Above: *Panogena jasmini*, a Hawk Moth from Madagascar.
Below: Oleander Hawk Moth *(Daphnis nerii)* from southern Europe.

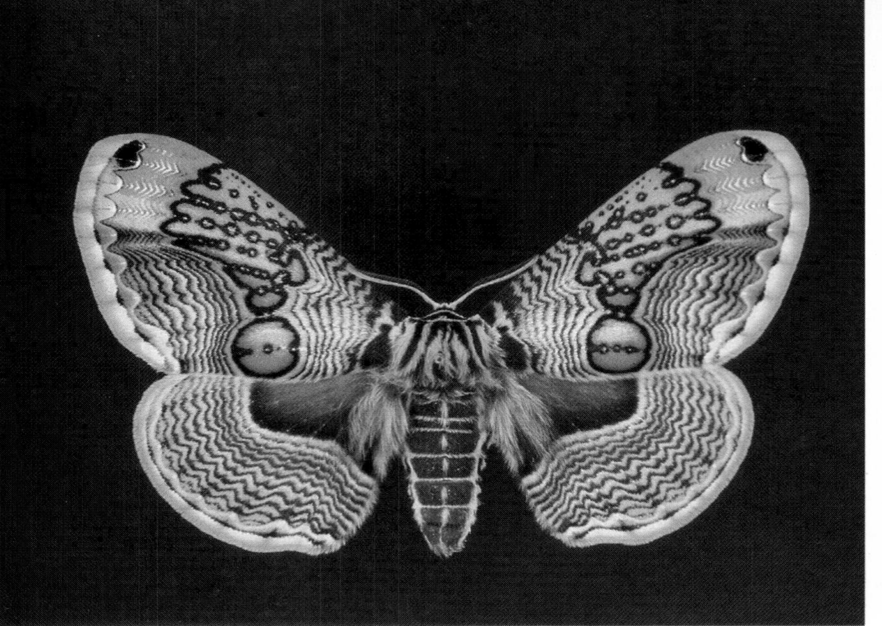

142 Above left: *Brahmea japonica* from Japan. The wing marking of parallel wavy lines is typical of the family of Brahmaeidae. Markings on the right and the left forewings are not entirely identical.

143 Above right: *Gynania maja* (Saturniidae) from South Africa.

144 Below: Female *Argema mittrei* from Madagascar.

145 *Automeris io* (Saturniidae) from the USA. The caterpillar can cause damage to cotton plants and fruit trees.

146 *Graellsia isabellae*, the Giant Silkworm Moth (Syssphingidae) from Spain. The only European member of the group of Eye-spotted Moths in which the hind wings of the male terminate in a markedly elongated point. The caterpillars live on pines.

On left:

147 Above: *Papilio blumei* from the Island of Sulawesi.

148 Below left: *Chrysiridia madagascariensis* from Madagascar.

149 Below right: *Teinopalpum imperialis* from India.

150 *Troides paradisea* from New Guinea.

151 Above: Female *Zygaena carniolica*, the Six-spot Burnet from Central Europe.

152 Below: Common Blues *(Polyommatus icarus)* mating.

On right:

153 The Large Copper *(Thersamonia dispar rutilus)* is found in Central Europe mainly on marshy meadows. Here, a male.

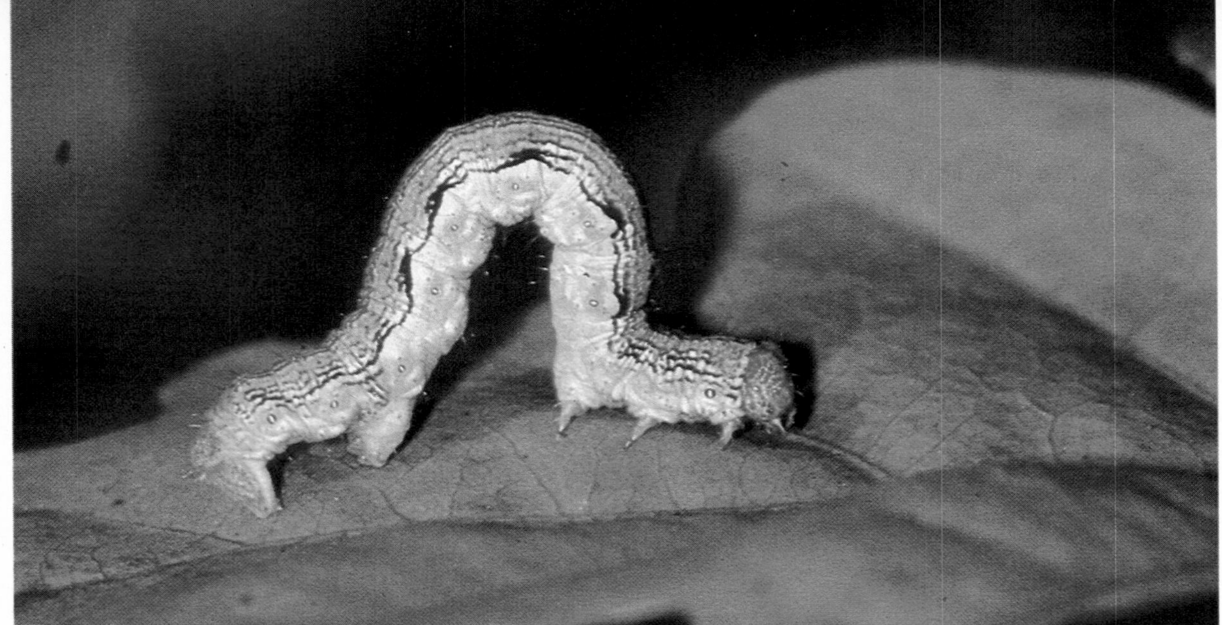

154 Above left: Caterpillar of the Pale Tussock Moth *(Dasychira pudibunda)* from Central Europe.

155 Above right: Typical features of Loopers or Inchworms, the caterpillars of Geometrids (Geometridae), are their characteristic mode of locomotion (illustrated in the phase before extension) and the reduction of most of the pairs of prolegs.

156 Below: The caterpillar of the Garden Tiger Moth *(Arctia caja)* is particularly striking with its dense clothing of long hairs.

157 Above: The caterpillar of a Bagworm Moth *(Psyche casta)* from Central Europe has built a tubular dwelling for itself out of fragments of grass.

158 Below: Caterpillars of the Small Elephant Hawk Moth *(Deilephila porcellus)* from Europe feed on bedstraw *(Galium)*. They occur in various colourings.

159 Egg of the Turnip Dart *(Agrotis segetum)* with a highly-textured pattern of lengthwise and crosswise ribs. A stellate arrangement of ribs surrounds the micropylar rosette.

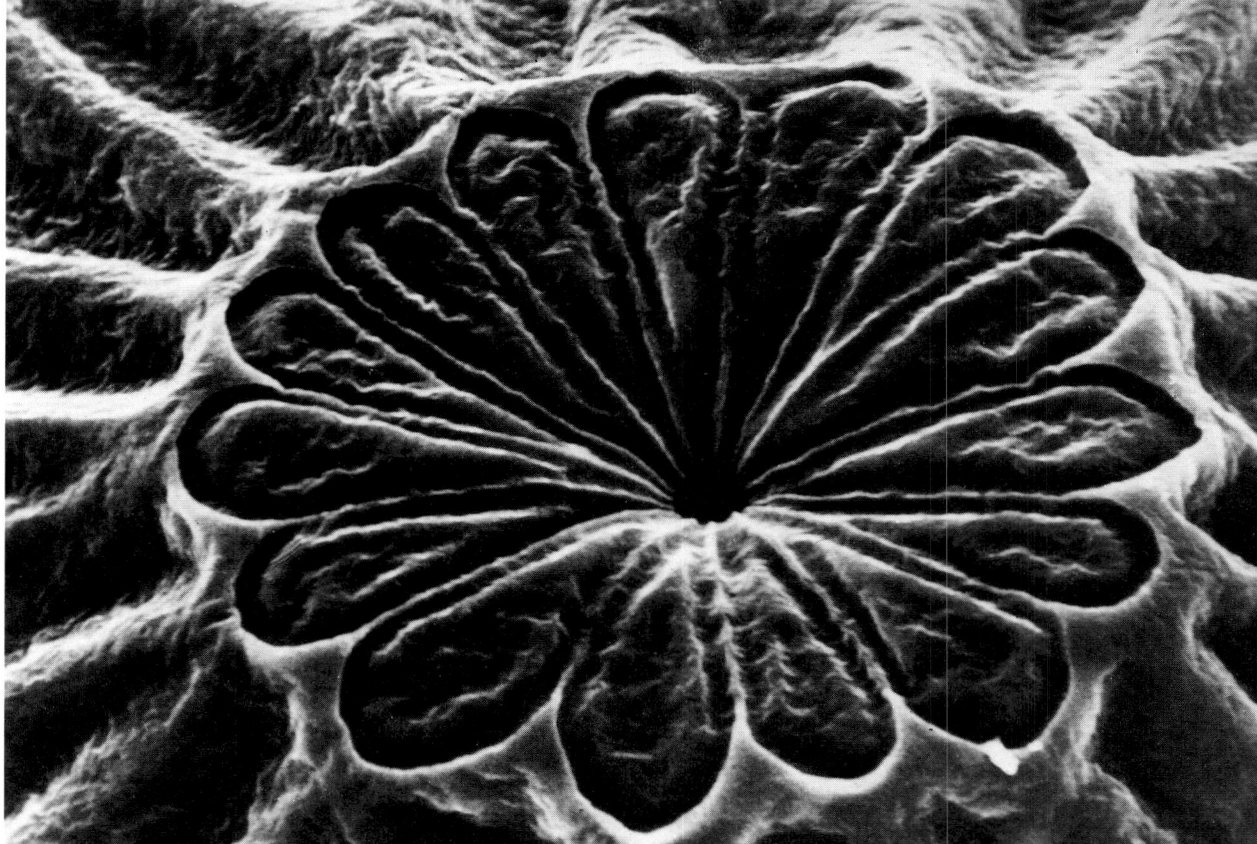

160 The micropylar rosette, surrounded by the star of ribs, consists of 15 segments, each enclosed by a ridge.
Photos: C. D. Edlich, Potsdam.

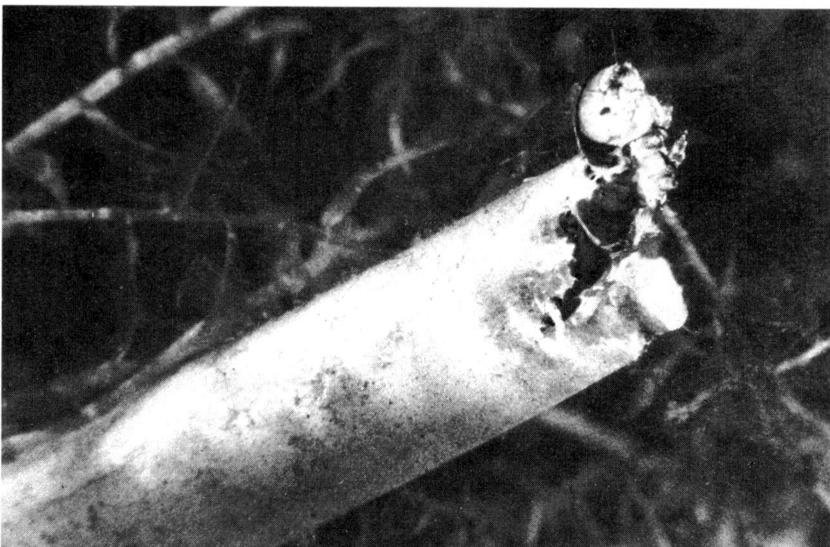

161 Above: Plume Moths *(Pterophorus pentadactylus)* from Central Europe are characterized by the deep division of the wings into plumes. The larvae feed on clover and bindweed.

162/163 Below: The caterpillars of some species of butterflies live under water, as, for example, those of *Cataclysta lemnata* from Central Europe. They construct a cocoon of duckweed (left) or make use of a rush blade (right).

164 Above: Flower-bud gall caused by the Gall Midge *Bayeria capitigena* on cypress spurge in Europe.

165 Below: The conspicuous galls of the Gall Midge *Rhopalomyia tanaceticola* (Europe) are found on the flower-heads of parsley fern *(Tanacetum vulgare)*.

On right:

166 Above: Hover-fly *(Syrphus ribesii)* from Central Europe.

167 Below left: Larva of the Hover-fly, *Syrphus ribesii*. These larvae feed on aphids. To complete their larval development, they require several hundred aphids.

168 Below right: *Volucella pellucens*, a large European species of Hover-fly, the larvae of which live in the nests of social wasps.

169 Above: Syrphid larvae (*Mylesia* spec.) live on decaying organic material.

170 Below left: Syrphidae *(Xanthogramma ornatum)*.

171 Below right: Syrphidae *(Merodon clavipes)*, the larvae of which are phytophagous.

On right:

172 The larva of *Volucella inanis* (Syrphidae) lives parasitically in the nests of wasps.

On left:

173 Above: The Robber Fly (Asilidae, genus *Laphria*) from Central Europe. Note the powerful proboscis, adapted for piercing and sucking, with which these predacious flies perforate their prey in flight after seizing them with their forelegs.

174 Below: Black Flies or Buffalo Gnats (Melusinidae) depositing eggs on float-grass (Central Europe).

175 Stinkhorn, densely covered with flies—an example of the strong attraction this fungus has for certain species of insects.

176 Above: A Flesh Fly of the European family Sarcophagidae. The larvae of some species are parasites of earthworms, others are carrion- or dungfeeders.

177 Below: Greenbottle Flies of the European genus *Lucilia* frequently visit blossoms. Although many species live upon dead organic matter, some are parasitic on other animals, for example, on frogs.

On right:

178 Above left: The larvae of Caterpillar Flies (Tachinidae) live as internal parasites in caterpillars and other insects such as beetles, sawflies and grasshoppers. Many of the species contribute substantially to maintaining a balance in ecological systems. Illustrated here, a female *Echinomyia fera*, sometimes known as the Hedgehog Fly on account of its dense covering of bristly hairs; it attaches its eggs to caterpillars.

179 Above right: Male Crane-flies (Tipulidae) can be recognized by the pectinate or serrate antennae (Central Europe). Depicted is *Ctenophora pectinicornis*.

180 Below: A female Crane-fly (Tipulidae) of the species *Ctenophora pectinicornis*.

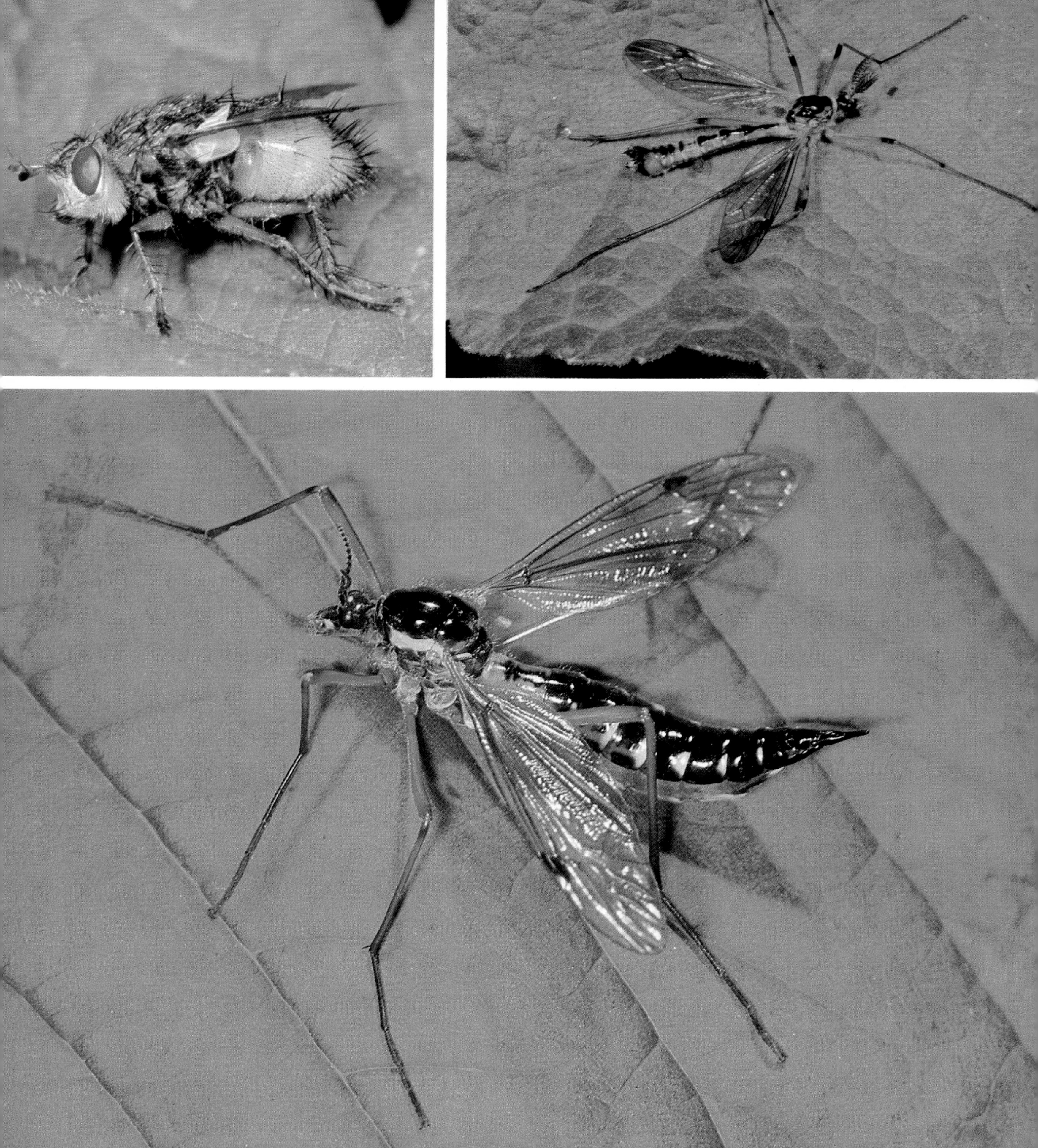

181 Above Mosquito larvae (*Aedes* spec.).

182 Below left: A mosquito (*Aedes* spec.).

183 Below: On the right, the mosquito in a state of repletion (Europe).

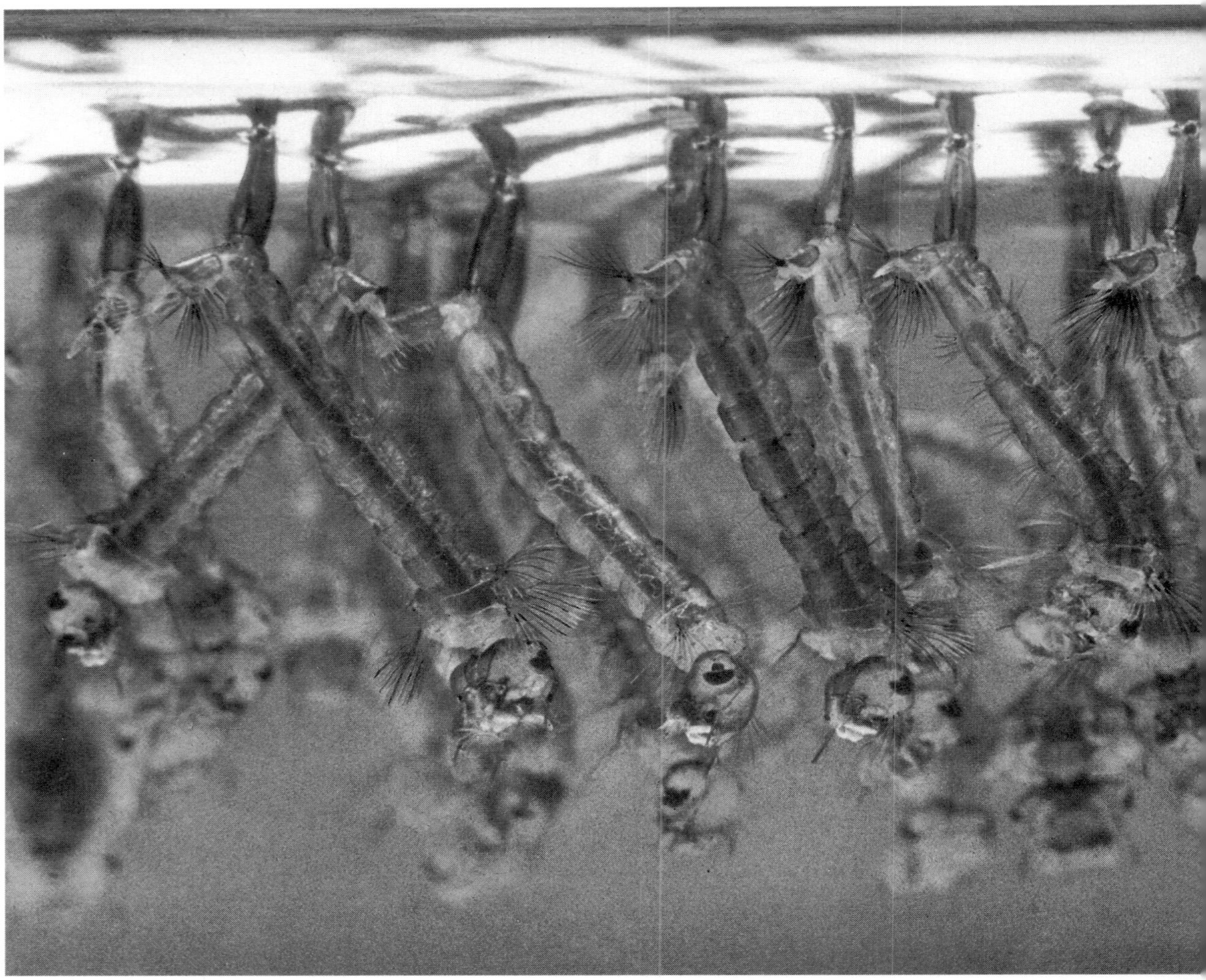

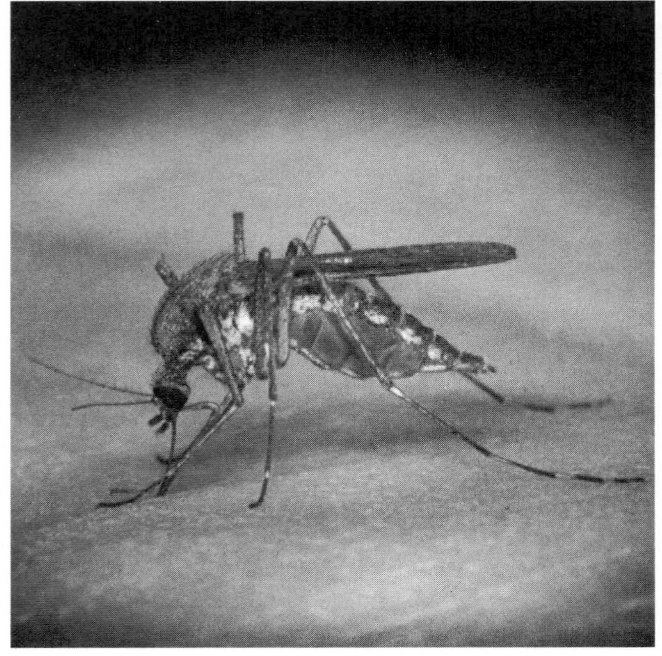

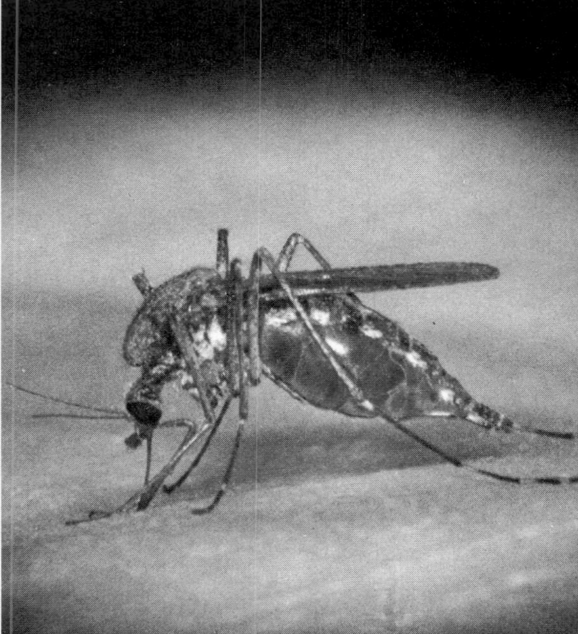

On right:

184 Above: The glass-like, transparent larvae of the Lake Fly or Phantom Mosquito *(Chaoborus crystallinus)* has two pairs of tracheal air-sacs inside the body which enable the larvae to maintain a horizontal position in water.

185 Below left: Many-branched antennae are a feature of male Lake Flies *(Chaoborus crystallinus)*.

186 Below right: Female Lake Fly *(Chaoborus crystallinus)*.

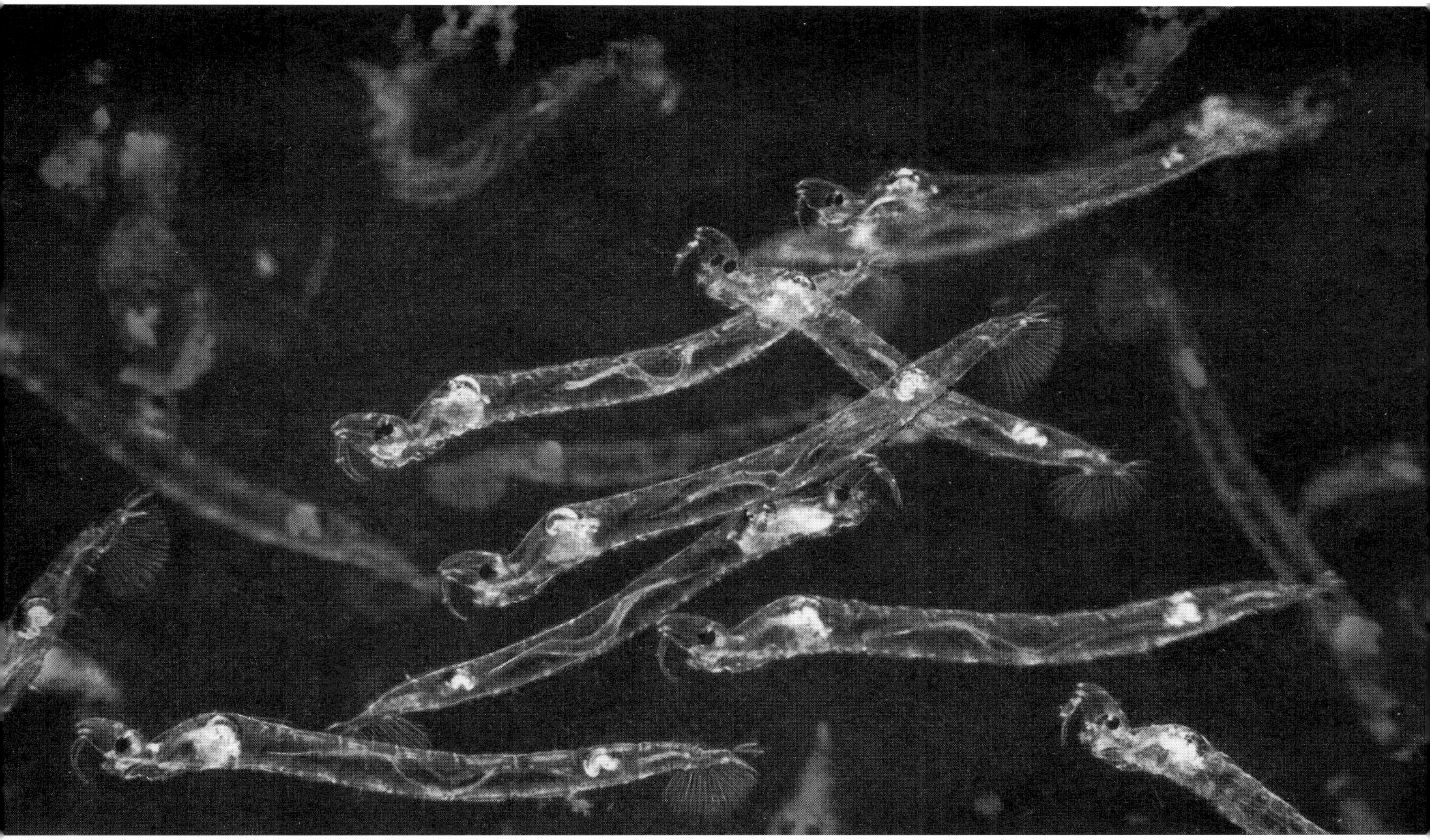

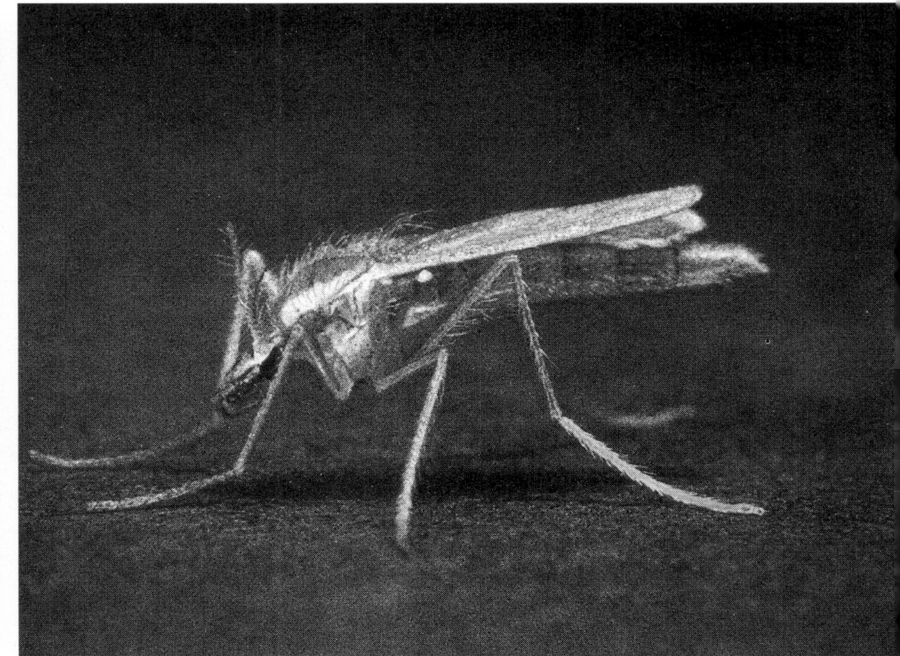

The majority of caterpillars feed on plants. It was therefore a matter for some surprise when, in 1972, Montgomery discovered the caterpillars of a Pug Moth (genus *Eupithecia*) on Hawaii which caught and consumed small live insects. The victims are insects that move across the caterpillar's back. In response to contact with special sensory hairs, the caterpillar twists round with great rapidity and seizes the prey in the trap formed by its sharp-clawed legs.

Loopers (also known as Inchworms, the caterpillars of Geometrid Moths) can be recognized in the following passage written by Marco Aurelio Severino (1580–1656): "Locomotion in worms occurs in a diversity of manners. Some prop themselves up on the forelegs alone, after having first raised the body up high, supporting themselves with only the tail. As soon as the toothed tail has found a secure hold, they push the rest of the body forwards and gain a firm anchorage with the feet. Then they draw the hind part of the body along again." By "worms", Severino of course refers to caterpillars.

Our ancestors also had their difficulties with *Agrotis* caterpillars (Cut-worms). In the *Collection of Natural and Medical Histories together with Relevant Histories of Art and Literature as they occur in Silesia and other Countries* of 1719, we read: "Of the many worms or ground caterpillars, such as have until this November eaten away the roots of vegetables. This autumn, from October to November, there were large numbers of cut-worms in our cabbage gardens; most of them were grey, in part also brown and some were black, 2–3 segments in length and as thick as the stem of a tobacco pipe at its thickest part, with a short mouth, horned, that opens laterally and can bite powerfully. It has also completely devoured tender roots of lettuce, carrots and spinach. Many plants in the fields of endive salad were also found lying on the ground because the roots had been eaten away and the plant denied support and food. The insects were unable to bite through large and strong roots in this way. This pest was so common that various smallholders said they had never before seen them in such abundance . . . These worms were found not only in the rich soil round Breslau, but also in great quantities in the rest of Silesia, where they devoured entirely the roots of the corn; these latter worms are said to be smaller than our local ones, undoubtedly as a result of differences in soil and diet."

Schimitschek (1968) tells of a strange use to which the caterpillars were put: "A somewhat curious trend in painting is represented by the Tirolean cobweb and larval web paintings, which can be seen as characteristic of the spirit of Rococo. Paint was applied directly to the silken galleries or webs spun by larvae and to spiders' webs. The first artist to carry out such paintings was Elias Prunner of Dietenheim near Bruneck. In 1765 he offered his paintings on larval webs to the Empress Maria Theresa when the Court visited Tirol. Most of the cobweb paintings from the second half of the 18th century were the work of Johann Burgmann of Bruneck. Similar work was carried out by Johann Ruep of Taufers, Johann Heinrich Störklin and in the 18th century, by various Salzburg artists. Between 1830 and 1870, the technique was continued in the Puster Valley. Here the work concentrated mainly on painting on larval webs, and those principally used were those spun by *Yponomeuta padellus* and *Y. evonymellus*."

The feeding process

Réaumur devoted a good deal of attention to caterpillars, and the following passage is an example of the thoroughness of his observations. "By alternately opening and closing the jaws, the caterpillars tear small fragments from the leaves of the plants upon which they feed. Some species, when young or throughout their entire development, eat only the parenchyma of the leaves, and avoid the veins, but most of them devour the entire leaf. It is entertaining for ten or twenty minutes at a time to watch them feeding voraciously, and to see the skill they develop in this pursuit. Some caterpillars feed only at night or in the evening, others day and night; others again feed for an hour at a time, between quite long intervals. A caterpillar beginning to feed at the edge of a leaf, stations itself in such a way that at least one part of the edge of the leaf lies between its thoracic feet and one part between its abdominal feet, maintaining a firm hold on that part of the leaf at which it wants to eat. For the first bite, the caterpillar extends itself full length and holds its head as far as possible away from the leaf. As it claps its jaws shut, the part of the leaf lying between is cut through. The bites follow one another in rapid succession and each time, the tiny portion of leaf is

187 This specimen of Ascalaphidae belongs to the few Lacewings with brilliantly coloured wings.

swallowed immediately. With each bite, the head gets closer to the legs, and as the bites progress, it describes a curve and so produces a semi-circular hole in the leaf. When the head gets too close to the thoracic legs, the caterpillar draws in its abdomen and extends its body by stretching forwards, grasping the next higher part of the leaf with its thoracic legs. A notch in the centre of the caterpillar's upper lip proves useful to it in feeding. It serves as one point of support during grazing—the others being the legs, and so the leaf always lies medially along the line of the caterpillar's back, symmetrically aligned to both jaws. As the body is pushed forward, this notch moves forward along the edge of the leaf; this would scarcely be possible in a backward movement, since the head would have to be removed from the leaf in the second phase of movement . . ."

The Cabbage White
(Pieris brassicae)

The Cabbage White (or perhaps better, the Large Garden White) has caused damage to cruciferous crops ever since they began to be cultivated in fields and gardens. As a result, they are mentioned fairly frequently in early literature. Aristotle writes: "The butterfly is generated from caterpillars which grow on green leaves, chiefly leaves of the raphanus, which some call crambe or cabbage. At first it is less than a grain of millet; it then grows into a small grub; and in three days it is a tiny caterpillar. After this it grows on and on, and becomes quiescent and changes its shape, and is now called a chrysalis. The outer shell is hard, and the chrysalis moves if you touch it. It attaches itself by cobweb-like filaments, and is unfurnished with mouth or any other apparent organ. After a little while, the outer covering bursts asunder, and out flies the winged creature that we call the psyche or butterfly. At first, when it is a caterpillar, it feeds and ejects excrement; but when it turns into a chrysalis it neither feeds nor ejects excrement."

Pedanius Dioscorides claims that the caterpillars of Cabbage Whites can be put to medical use. "The Erucae, which breed vpon pot-herbes, being anointed with oyle about anyone, are sayd to save him harmlesse from the biting of poisnous beasts." *(The Greek Herbal of Dioscorides)*

And Claudius Aelianus tells us: "Caterpillars feed upon vegetables and in a short while destroy them. But they in turn are destroyed if a woman with her monthly courses upon her walks through the vegetables."

The views of Albertus Magnus on the biology of Cabbage Whites are typical of his time. "The caterpillars on cruciferous plants, for example, come into existence without fertilization. The worm-like stage is followed by an egg-like pupal stage with a hard skin and without movement. During this transitional stage, preparation takes place for the development of the eggs before the egg-laying period. Then the perfect winged imago hatches, and in autumn makes a nest of spun tissue for its eggs. Caterpillars again develop from these eggs, and from them pupae and so on."

Even Ulisse Aldrovandi mentions "caterpillar eggs", which in fact are the pupae of Braconids (*Apanteles glomeratus*) (p.162). Nor was Caspar Schwenckfeld altogether conversant with the biology of the Cabbage White. "This universally familiar worm is long and soft and has many feet . . . it is many-coloured. The caterpillars develop either from the exudations of plants, at times of high humidity and from lukewarm decaying matter, or from the eggs of butterflies. They hatch from the pupae, usually in August, and lay on cabbage plants their long, whitish to yellow eggs that are like millet seed . . . There are almost as many caterpillars as there are species of plants." The last observation is probably a realistic one, indeed there may even be more.

Francesco Redi finally put an end to the myth concerning spontaneous generation in Cabbage Whites. He states emphatically in his book *Essays on the Genesis of Insects* that *Pieris* caterpillars come into being from the eggs that are deposited in large numbers on cabbage leaves but never from the cabbage leaves themselves.

Dipterans

(Diptera)

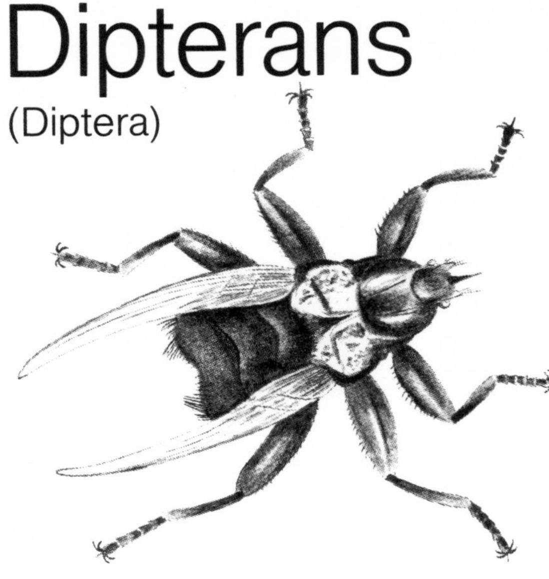

Even today, dipterology is one of the most difficult branches of entomology. In the majority of cases, a distinction can be drawn between individual species only after close and detailed examination by a specialist. In early entomological writings, only a small number of types are differentiated according to their behaviour, initially the fly and the mosquito.

Flies (Muscidae)

The Ancient Egyptian Order of Valour was in the form of a fly. Of it, Schimitschek (1977) writes: "In Egypt, pendants of this kind exist that date back to the Negada period, that is, about 3,500 B.C. The Ancient Egyptian Order of Flies may well derive from them. In Egypt, the "Order of the Golden Fly" was awarded for special bravery. It was worn on a chain hung round the neck. Nubians who had distinguished themselves in the Egyptian army were also honoured with this award. Such Nubians wearing the Order of the Golden Fly are depicted in the tomb of Rekh-mi Re in Shech Abd el Qirna near Thebes. There is a jasper amulet from the New Kingdom showing a fly with the head of a human. For a long time, the fly remained a symbol of good fortune." In Ancient Egypt, fly-brushes were in common use. In illustrations they can easily be distinguished from the larger fans used to provide a current of cool air. Pharaohs are usually depicted together with a high court official whose function it was to carry the fly whisk. In a document that was part of the burial offerings of an ancient mummy (the Giseh Papyrus) it says: "May the maggots not turn into flies within you."

Homer's *Iliad* contains a wealth of similes drawn from nature and especially from the animal kingdom. The presence of large numbers of flies in the Mediterranean area, and particularly in the vicinity of dairies, occasioned the following image: "Even as the many tribes of thick flies that hover about a herdsman's steading in the spring season, when milk drencheth the pails, even in like number stood the flowing-haired Achaians upon the plain in the face of the Trojans . . ." and "as when in a farmstead flies buzz about the full milk pails". The behaviour of horseflies or gadflies is to be taken as a model: "And in his breast she set the daring of the fly, that though it be driven away never so often from the skin of a man, ever persisteth in biting, and sweet to it is the blood of man." Homer also knew about metamorphosis in flies, as the following lines impressively show: ". . . but I have grievous fear lest meantime on the gashed wounds of Menoitois' valiant son flies light and breed worms therein, and defile his corpse—for the life is slain out of him—and so all his flesh shall rot."

Above:

The Louse Fly or Ked *(Crataerhina pallida)* from Europe. The larvae of Louse Flies develop within a uterus-like structure in the abdomen of the female and are fed by special nutritive glands known as "milk glands". Pupation occurs immediately after birth of the larva, so that these flies have also been called the Pupipara. They are external parasites on birds and mammals, from which they suck blood. As with most other ectoparasites of warm-blooded animals, the wings are often reduced or absent.

Aristotle on flies

Aristotle makes very early mention of the principal character of the order of insects known as Diptera, namely, the possession of two wings: "Of the winged creatures themselves, there are those that lead an unsettled life and must fly about in search of food, they are furnished with four wings and display an airy distension of the body, such as the bees and creatures related to them; they have two wings on either side of the body; the small ones among them, in contrast, are double-winged, such as the family of flies."

Aristotle also comments on reproduction in flies: "With regard to insects, the male is less than the female . . . Those animals cover and are covered in which there is a duality of sex, and the modes of covering are not in all cases similar . . . Insects copulate at the hinder end, and the smaller individual is the male . . . The female pushes from underneath her sexual organ into the body of the male above, this being the reverse of the operation observed in other creatures; and this organ in the case of some insects appears to be disproportionately large when compared to the size of the body, and that too in very minute creatures; in some insects the disproportion is not so striking. This phenomenon may be witnessed if any one will pull asunder flies that are copulating; and, by the way, these creatures are, under the circumstances, averse to separation; for the intercourse of the sexes in their case is of long duration, as may be observed with common everyday insects, such as the fly and the cantharis."

Today it is difficult to understand how, in view of the high level of observation of nature that existed in Antiquity, and which is demonstrated in this quotation, the dogma of spontaneous generation became so widespread and was able to persist so tenaciously that it is still found quite frequently in medieval writings. It may be that some passages of Aristotle have been misinterpreted, as might easily be possible in the case of the following: "Flies grow from grubs in the dung that farmers have gathered . . . The grub is exceedingly minute to begin with; first it assumes a reddish colour, and then from a quiescent state it takes on the power of motion; . . . it then becomes a small motionless grub; it then moves again, and again relapses into immobility; it then comes out a perfect fly, and moves away under the influence of the sun's heat or of a puff of air."

Early Arabian knowledge of flies and their pharmaceutical use

Kamal al-Din al-Damiri, whose words have already been quoted several times, also wrote variously on the subject of flies. "It has its name from its habit of constant fluttering movement; although according to others, it is because as often as it is driven off, it returns again. The fly is the most ignorant of all creatures, since it even hastens to its doom . . . On its very small black eyes, the fly possesses no eyelids. One of the functions of eyelids is to keep the surface of the eye clean and bright. In place of eyelids, God has given the fly two hands with which to keep clean the eye surface. This is why flies are seen repeatedly to wipe their eyes with their hands. There are various kinds of flies, but all are engendered out of putrefying matter . . . The house-fly multiplies by fertilization, but sometimes comes into being out of the human body. Characteristics: according to Al-Gahiz, milk mixed with al-qundus and sprinkled in a house will protect it from flies . . . Pulverized flies are useful as a hair restorer . . . A small quantity of rust scraped from iron and sprinkled on a dead fly will immediately restore it to life . . . A bundle of a particular grass hung on the door of a house will prevent any fly from entering there as long as it remains hanging on the door . . . I have observed flies carefully and found that they always defend themselves with the left wing, which is said to carry an agent of disease, just as the right wing is said to contain a remedy for that disease." The preening behaviour of flies and their constant mobility are accurately observed.

As we have seen above, interest in flies in the Arabian epoch was partly pharmaceutical, and this is reflected in the work *Principles of Pharmacology*, written in about 970 by the Persian author Abu Mansur Muwaffaq. "Nufal states that flies prevent the loss of the eyelashes; if flies are burned and applied to a site affected by alopecia, they encourage the growth of hair. If they are

The Bee Louse *(Braula coeca)*, a wingless fly, is only 1–1.5 mm in length. It lives on honey bees, feeding on the liquid food of the bees. Bee Lice are found especially on the queen. The larvae live on honey and pollen in tunnels they have mined in the walls and caps of honey cells.

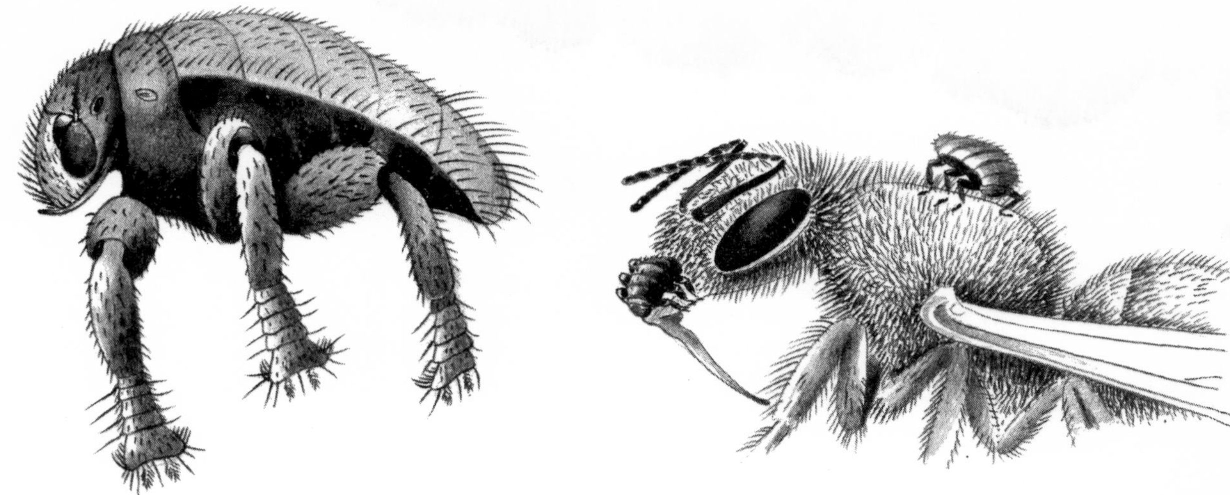

pounded and applied to the eyebrows, having first annointed the same with olive oil, or if the fat of burned flies is used in this way, the eyebrows will be attractively coloured. They are also useful as a treatment for affliction of the eyes. Dog-flies are more suitable for this purpose. The blood of the latter removes superfluous eyelashes." Ibn al-Baithar (1197–1248) suggests other purposes for their use. "If the head is cut from a large fly, the body crushed and applied to wasp stings and sores, the latter heal immediately." Such statements are to be seen as documents typical of their times; it is well to appreciate that at that early period hardly any effective medicaments were in existence.

Al-Qazwini sees them, wrongly, as related to bedbugs, but he was one of the first to stress the diversity of flies. "The flies have numerous species, originating from rotting materials. They are said to develop from the excrements of domestic animals . . . The fly hunts the bug and that is why you never see a bug during daytime but only in the night when the fly sleeps.

Damage caused by flies

The attitude to flies exemplified in Johann Sperling's *Zoologia physica*, published in 1661, is typical of its time. "Praeceptum: The fly is a loathsome, pestilential, impudent, tiresome and restless insect.

Quaestiones: 1. How do they feed? Flies sample almost everything and lick everything, but are particularly greedy for blood. It is the companion of our banquets and bedrooms. It will find out any table set with food, in the hovels of the poor as in the palaces of princes. They season the dishes before we taste them. They are very troublesome to man with their stings, and the more one tries to drive them off, the more fiercely they persist . . . 3. How are they engendered? They mate and do so often during flight. The generative material is the seed from which a worm develops first, later the fly.

Axiomata: 1. If placed in oil or water, apparently dead flies will return to life. 2. Worms develop out of the excreta of large flies. The fly is an unclean creature which befouls tables, pictures, clothes, books and so on with its excrement. And not infrequently, worms develop from this excrement, especially that of large flies, and the worms infest meat in particular. Scaliger saw how a fly deposited on to his hand the material from which a worm came into being. Flies consume everything, and excrete the worm material together with remnants of food from the hind body."

At that time, flies were obviously a much more serious annoyance than we can imagine today. Sperling has advanced beyond the idea of spontaneous generation, but uncertainty still exists about the process of egg laying.

The Death of the Fly

With eagerness he drinks the treach'rous potion,
Nor stops to rest, by the first taste misled;
Sweet is the draught, but soon all pow'r of motion
He finds has from his tender members fled;
No longer has he strength to plume his wing,
No longer strength to raise his head, poor thing!
E'en in enjoyment's hour his life he loses,
His little foot to bear his weight refuses;
So on he sips, and ere his draught is o' er,
Death veils his thousand eyes for evermore.

Johann Wolfgang von Goethe, translated by Edgar Alfred Bowring, London, 1853.

Early methods of controlling flies

Adam Lonicer studied numerous herbs and a number of insects, including flies; arsenic, which he mentions, is one of the first really effective pesticides, which continued in use until the present century. "Arsenicum kills flies if a little of it is put in the milk which midges drink. Smoke, incense and the boiling of black dwarf-elder also kill flies. Flies are good for eye afflictions and for the eyebrows. Burned and applied to the bald areas with honey, they rapidly promote hair growth. Flies are killed if a place is sprinkled with elderberry-water." Ferrante Imperato described in 1599 a "permanent" means of controlling flies: "If you want to rid a place permanently of flies, scratch the likeness of a fly in the stone of a ring, or draw the image of a fly, a spider or a snake on a copper plate during the second half of the constellation of Pisces. As you do so, say 'this is an image which will drive off all flies for ever'. Then bury it in the centre of your house, or hang it there. This must be done in the first half of the constellation of Taurus."

In the Middle Ages, the appearance of large numbers of insects was looked upon as a punishment from God. But it seems inexplicable to us today that legal proceedings should be instituted against insects. According to Schenkling, even flies were the object of such actions. "In 1121, Saint Bernhard placed a penalty of excommunication on flies that troubled his congregation, while at about the same time, a ban of excommunication was issued against flies in the Electorate of Mainz."

In his *Household Book* (1590), Johann Colerus describes methods of dealing with flies, among which the use of the mushroom fly agaric is important, since this fungus actually contains a substance toxic to flies. "Flies emerge round about St. Vitus's Day. Flies are repellant and troublesome insects if they occur in large numbers in rooms and houses. But they are at their most numerous where there are many cattle, or when there is fruit in a room. Then, many of them fall into food, drink, milk and so on. To combat them, God has made red fly agaric grow in the woods. If it is chopped finely and put into an earthenware dish with milk, they eat of it and soon perish. But the dish should be placed where no dog or cat can reach it, for it is fatal to them as well. Or make a hole in the bottom of a pot and spread some honey in it. When they fly on to the honey, cover the pot with a cloth and shake it. They will fall down into a bag. Then twist the bag so that they cannot get out of the pot again. When they are all in the bag, trample them to death or shake them into water or into the fire. Or take some hellebore, grind it to powder, mix it with milk and put it out for them. As soon as they drink of it, they die. But take care to keep your own food and drink covered, lest the poisoned flies fall into it."

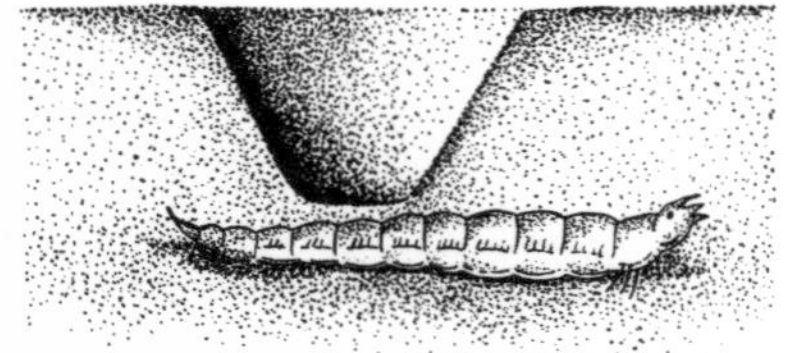

A species of Snipe-fly known as the "Worm Lion" *(Vermileo comstockii)* behaves in much the same way as the Ant Lion. The larva constructs pits in fine sand into which prey, particularly ants, fall and are overpowered.

The Stalk-eyed Fly *(Diopsis tenuipes)* is found in tropical Africa. The antennae are situated immediately beside the eyes on extremely long processes arising from the head capsule.

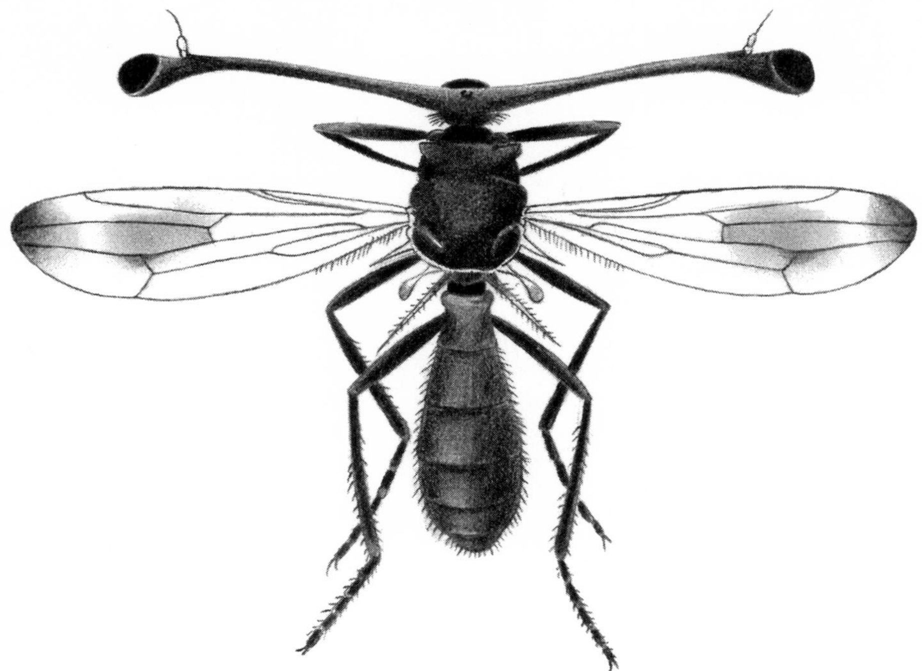

The diversity of flies

Ulisse Aldrovandi writes in considerable detail on the diversity of flies in his third volume on Diptera. Sixty-nine species are illustrated (three of them are Hymenopterans). He writes: "There are innumerable kinds of flies and most of them are not provided with names. The principal difference is their size; there are large, medium-sized and small ones . . . Apart from this, there are those with a small head and those with a large, those with a stout or slender abdomen, and those with a long or short one. Some are hairy, others not; some possess antennae, most do not. Usually they are black, but there are also those of a single colour and those speckled grey, blue, green etc. According to habitat, we can distinguish between those that live in houses, in fields and in woods, and those that live close to water. Most suck blood, but many from only one species of animal." Aldrovandi is mistaken about the antennae, however much we may otherwise approve of his text, which is undoubtedly considerably advanced for its time. Flies, like all insects, possess a pair of antennae, although in many species, they may be extremely short.

The observations made by Caspar Schwenckfeld are more detailed, and he names and distinguishes between several species. "Musca, fly. A two-winged insect, that is only too familiar, it flies on to food and can be driven off only with difficulty. The fly has a protruding, tubular proboscis with which it tastes food and sucks it up. It has six legs and hard, weak eyes. Flies copulate like other insects, but do not produce flies but worms. Or else they come into existence from damp or decaying matter . . . The various flies can differ in size, shape and colour. Musca infectoria, Blowfly or Bluebottle. It is larger than the House-fly, dark blue and hums and buzzes mightily. It brings its extended ovipositor into contact with meat and deposits small worms that are generally called maggots. Musca viridis. A green fly. It is similar to the House-fly in size and shape, but emerald-green in colour."

Giovanni Alphonso Borelli (1608–1679) published a very interesting book, *De motu animalium*, an introductory textbook on physiology, which in addition to locomotion, also considers circulation, respiration, feeding, digestion and reproduction. Borelli was unable to explain how flies and other insects, although their body possesses a certain weight, are yet able to maintain a hold on the smooth ceilings of rooms. He was at that time unaware of the efficient adhesive apparatus (claws, arolium, pulvilli) with which the terminal joint of the tarsus is armed.

The Inspector finds it very good
To rest awhile after his food
A fly comes up with buzzing sound
And close by, bumbles round and round.
From his doze he wakes with startled cry
With anger sees the buzzing fly.
That wicked fly now contemplate
Settled upon his balding pate!
"You shameless creature, wait awhile
And I will deal with you in style."
He creeps and takes a cup with care,
Soon he'll have the fly in there.
With skill he brings it down as planned,
And now he has her in his hand.
He peers inside with gloating eye
To see just where he has the fly.
But with a buzz she rushes free—
"A leg! that's little loss to me."
The fly swat now he brings to play
Soon he will get her in this way.
To make quite sure his aim is fair
He climbs upon an easy chair.
Crash! the chair and he are down,
The fly still flutters round and round.
With all his force he swipes away,
At last the fly has had its day.
What joy he felt when there he found
The insect lifeless on the ground.
A midday rest is most relaxing
But sometimes it can be quite taxing.

After Wilhelm Busch

Reproduction

Antony van Leeuwenhoek liked to present the results of his observations in statistical form, as in the following example. He "received from a surgeon a number of maggots from the flesh of an elderly woman, which he fed on owl-meat; soon they pupated, turned into flies and laid eggs". Based on his findings, he drew up the following reproductive table (quoted from Bodenheimer, 1928):

144	flies in the first month
72	females
133	eggs from each female
10,368	flies in the second month
5,184	females
144	eggs from each female
746,496	flies in the third month.

Calculations of this kind are still often made today to illustrate the reproductive capacity of many species of insect. For the House-fly, a potential total of offspring from a single female over a period of twelve months is given as 250 thousand billion (a figure lower than that obtained by the extrapolation of Van Leeuwenhoek's figures). Such vast numbers do not, of course, occur in nature, since they are affected by various limiting factors (climate, food supply, disease etc.).

In 1688, Sir Hans Sloane travelled to America. There he collected plants as well as 3,824 insects, and noted down many observations. "I have seen in Jamaica frequently a large grey Flesh-fly, lay tapering small Worms alive, which I believe produc'd Flies like the Mother after Nourishment in a short Time." There are also several European species that lay living young (viviparity), while others lay eggs that hatch immediately (ovoviviparity; cf. Sperling and Schwenckfeld). The change to the process by which the ova ripens within the body of the mother has important biological advantages. The larval food supply exists for only a few days in a suitable state (e.g. carrion) and it can serve immediately as food for the small larvae without there being a waiting period for the development of the egg.

Brückmann's fly traps

Franz Ernst Brückmann, known as the inventor of the first flea trap, also constructed various fly traps, which he describes in a booklet entitled *Die neuerfundene und curieuse Fliegenfalle* (The Newly-invented and Curious Fly Trap) (1735). "The fly trap is a wooden machine or oblong, rectangular box constructed out of thin boards, at least an ell in length . . . As soon as this box is placed in a room where impetuous flies are swarming, they will immediately become aware of the sweet scent of honey or syrup, for they are endowed with a sense of smell, and will hasten towards the box, where they are allowed to enter, to delight in the sweet substance and, uti in proverbio est, to eat their last meal. When a goodly crowd has assembled there, a slight pressure of the finger on the bar at once releases the chorda, the small board or lid springs from its catch and momento citius closes the box, and the entire horde of flies is enclosed and held prisoner. If such a box is now held to the ear, it is impossible for any pen to describe what a lamentable concert is to be heard, composed of all kinds of humming, buzzing, singing, sounding voices, with a complete lack of harmony, enough to afflict the ear, for one voice sings alto, another basso, as the father of the alto, another sings soprano while yet another pipes the tenor as the mother of the soprano; one intones in B minor, another in G major, parallel fifths, yet another in C sharp fiendish sounds, mi contra fa, diabolus in musica and the devil in the music. Anyone wanting to play the tragedy to the end and cause a veritable bloodbath, need only apply firm pressure several times to the extended rod which drives home the attached square of wood, thus squashing and killing all the flies within the box inside the space marked f. k. h.

The mating of Dance Flies *(Empis opaca)*. Before mating, whole groups of Dance Flies swarm in the air; the males catch prey which they present to the female as a "wedding gift"; certain species wrap the prey first in a web. Here, the female is feeding upon a fly it has received from the male.

If one repeats this process several times in a house or room which is alive with flies and midges, the house will soon be clear of them . . . The house would be kept clean and the white walls would not be sullied with droppings, the wall coverings, tables, chairs, kitchen utensils would remain unsoiled and unspotted, the maids would not need to do so much washing, one would not have to eat such filth in food or swallow the ovula of these insects, nor would the children suffer so much from worms . . . In the inns and taverns in the villages where the rooms, furniture and kitchen utensils are often thoroughly incrusted with fly droppings and in which travellers, seeking accommodation, have to spend their nights without sleep, even though they have paid good money, on account of the unpleasant music, humming, buzzing, twittering and stinging, this machine is quite indispensable, and it would be a good thing if the landlords were obliged by a firm statutory regulation to acquire such a fly trap; moreover, the royal edicts, which in taverns are generally affixed to the wall, would remain clean and would be legible to all, whereas now, since flies sully everything, showing no respect even for a signature from a noble hand or for the great seal, they usually become so blackened and illegible that no man can decipher such documents and patents, nor infer from them our lord and master's will concerning what he should or should not do."

Horse-flies (Tabanidae)

An early mention of Horse-flies occurs in the *Erh Ya*, an Ancient Chinese illustrated encyclopaedia, probably written by Pu Shang, a pupil of Confucius. In the classic work of Chinese pharmacy, the *Pen ts'ao,* published in 1108 in thirty volumes, the pharmaceutical use of Horse-flies is suggested. The manner in which they are to be caught varies depending upon the purpose for which they are intended. "The flies should be allowed to suck their fill of blood, then caught and dried . . . They should not be taken when gorged with blood but caught without blood. If they are full of blood, they are of no use for illnesses . . . If the creature sucks only the blood of cows and horses, the congealed blood should be collected from such wounds for curing diseases."

The rapid and painful bite of the Horse-fly is made possible by the modification of the mandibles into blade-like piercing organs. The laciniae, the hypopharynx and the labium are the mouthparts that work in conjunction with the mandibles to inflict the sting. The wound is comparatively large and often bleeds because substances that inhibit the coagulation of blood are secreted into

"Wenn Rosse auf den Weiden
Rosswespen beissen sehr,
Und wenn die Küh' vor beiden
Nicht können bleiben mehr,
Vor Bremsen und Stechmücken—
Ist Regen nicht mehr weit."

When horses on the pastures
By Horse-flies sore are tried,
And when the cows can scarce endure
The biting at their hide
By clegs and by mosquitoes—
Rain is not far away.

Hans Sachs (1494–1576),
from: Auguries of Rainy Weather

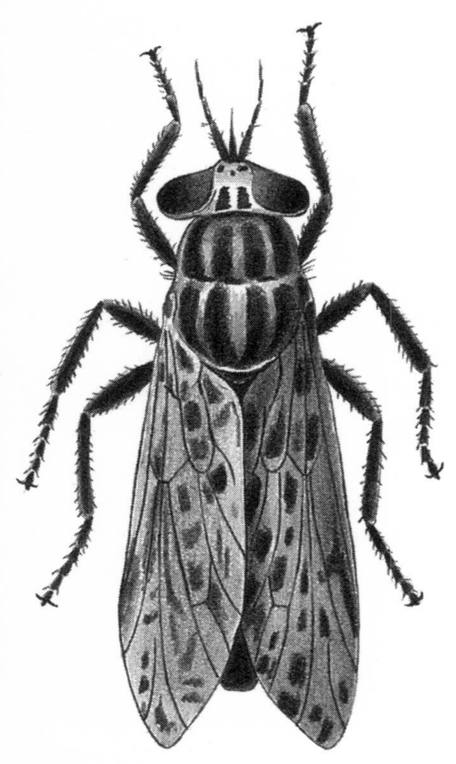

The Cleg (one of the Horse-flies) *(Chrysozona pluvialis)* is recognized by its dull, grey wings.

the wound by the Horse-fly. The blood produced by such a bite, which was used in China as a medicinal preparation, serves as food for various non-stinging flies. Homer, in his *Odyssey*, uses a simile drawn from the behaviour of the Horse-fly to describe the suitors who fearfully await the fatal shot from Odysseus's hand. "And down the hall like a herd of oxen they rushed that the hovering gadfly maddens and drives o'er the plain." Only the females have the blood-sucking habit and initially they seek out their victim by visual means. They are particularly attracted to a silhouette of dark or reddish colour with a convex curve. At closer range, they probably recognize the prey by the emission of heat. Depending upon species, Horse-flies tend to attack different regions of the body. *Chrysozona pluvialis* (the Cleg) usually bites the limbs, while *Chrysops* prefers the area of the head.

Aristotle was already aware of the link between Horse-flies and water, and assumes that they develop in water. The female usually deposits the eggs in stratified clusters close to water, either on plants or in the ground. The larvae live in the water or in damp soil. They feed on a variety of small creatures and on decaying organic matter. They kill their prey by means of poison which is injected through a channel within the powerful mandibles. In some cases, they also secrete digestive juices. The larvae pupate in the soil. In many species, the pupa is enclosed in a cocoon-like structure. Aristotle points out that a Horse-fly can be seen to be dead by an alteration in its eyes: "The myops dies from dropsy in the eyes." The eyes of a Horse-fly during life are exceptionally beautiful. They are of a brilliant iridescent golden-green, and many species exhibit patterns of coloured bands, the significance of which is not clear. Soon after death, the colour markings of the eye fade.

In his book *Quaestiones physicae* (1579), Johann Thomas Freigius of Basle refers to the proverbial saying "faster than a Horse-fly". No doubt it arose from observation of the rapid and agile flight of the common "Cleg" which is able to approach its prey in silent flight.

In 1721 in a book on the *Natural History of the Kingdom of Poland*, Gabriel Rzaczynski writes: "Throughout the whole of Poland, vast numbers of Tabani or Horse-flies have killed many cattle. Cattlemen even cover their animals with thick blankets to protect them from the insect's bites."

Horse-flies can cause considerable harm to grazing cattle and to deer, mainly by harassing them, but also by taking blood and by transmitting diseases (bacteria, trypanosomes, threadworms). Male Horse-flies feed upon the nectar of flowers. In the early morning, they fly to small clearings. Often they hover in one place, head-on to the wind, or pursue one another in flight. Somewhat later, the females appear (it is not clear whether they are attracted by visual or by auditory signals). Soon the first female is pursued by several males, one of which gains a hold on her back and both fall to the ground. Copulation follows, lasting about five minutes. Sometimes the female will hang freely suspended from the male, while the latter maintains a hold on a plant or similar object.

The Cheese Fly
(Piophila casei)

The Cheese Fly *(Piophila casei)* is a well-known pest in food stores; the female, undoubtedly attracted by the pronounced smell, deposits her eggs in clusters on the breeding substrate. (It infests other foods as well as cheese.) The larvae can be up to 10 mm in length and they burrow into the food. Larvae in their later stage are capable of jumping a considerable distance by bending the body into a tight curve, then suddenly releasing and extending it. Pupation occurs outside the cheese. Not every maggot found in a cheese is a Cheese Skipper, since other species also inhabit this substrate. So it cannot be assumed with certainty that the following early report refers to *Piophila casei*. In Caspar Schwenckfeld's day, flies in the cheese seem already to have aroused a certain amount of feeling; in 1603 he writes: "There are white worms that come into existence in soft cheese. The peasants eat them together with the cheese and suffer no harm. But they are difficult to digest and cause costiveness and thickening of the blood." Nowadays an early entomological work of this kind is interesting as an example of the current dogma of spontaneous generation and of the medical views that prevailed at that time.

Francesco Redi also used Cheese Flies in experiments he carried out to disprove the theory of spontaneous generation; he writes: "The same situation exists in the case of worms that develop in cheese as with flesh-worms. I observed worm-infested cheese. These maggots were also tapered at the front like the others, but were much more active and drew my attention especially by their ability to jump. From them, there developed rather small flies known as Cheese Flies. But if I separated the wormy parts of the cheese from the unaffected parts and isolated the two, worms and flies developed only from those pieces that were previously infested by worms. So in this case again, maggots developed only when the flies had access to the cheese, and never out of the cheese itself."

Johann Franziskus Griendel also discusses the larvae of Cheese Flies in his *Micrographia nova* (1687). "Worms 3 feet long and the breadth of six thumbs (measured under the microscope) also develop in soft cheese, which viewed through the microscope look gleaming white and hairless. On the head, they have two horns. Their mouth is extraordinary: when it is thrust forward, it is reddish in colour, when it is spread, long, blood-red threads extend from it. Sometimes the worm advances this proboscis, sometimes it retracts it. The worm lifts its body high and crawls forward. Also wonderful to behold is the way in which the entire central section of the body is raised and

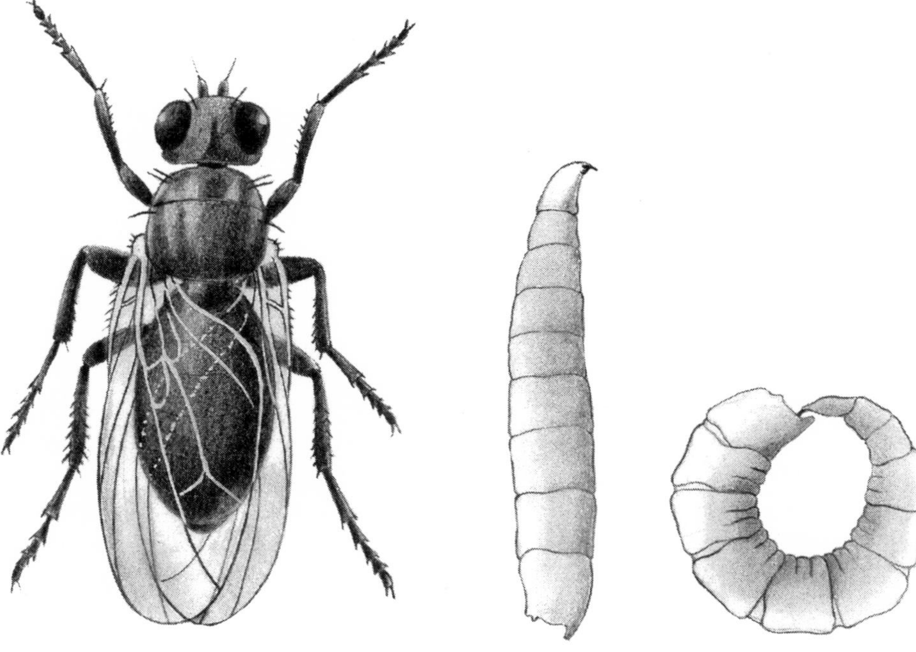

The Cheese Fly *(Piophila casei)* and its larva. The larvae can jump by curling the body tightly and then extending it.

the head brought into contact with the end of the body. Like the string of a bow, the worm extends itself suddenly and springs forward a hand's span from its original position."

Theophrastus Bombastus von Hohenheim, Paracelsus, recommends a method of protecting cheese from maggots. "Place some of the herb hypericum or Saint-John's-wort with the cheese. It possesses the strange power of protecting the cheese from all worms. It need only be placed near or on the cheese and no worm will grow therein. But if any are already within it, they will die and fall out."

Mosquitoes (Culicidae)

Some notes on mosquitoes

The early literature abounds in references to gnats and midges, and although these names are used loosely, the insect in question is usually one of the Culicidae. This family exhibits distinct sexual dimorphism in the antennae and proboscis. Only the females possess piercing, suctorial mouthparts. The mandibles and maxillae are modified into needle-like stylets, the hypopharynx conveys saliva and the labrum is the suctorial tube. In the males, the mouthparts are atrophied; usually they do not feed. In all species, copulation is initiated during flight. First the male seizes the female from above and the genital organs are brought into contact. The male allows itself to fall backwards and is carried along in flight by the female. At this stage, in most species, the bodies of the pair are united in a straight line, but in some species, the male has been observed to curve his body forwards below the female, so that the pair are locked together by their long legs, and the bodies ventrally aligned. But even in this position, the male performs no flight movements.

Some 200 species of mosquito have so far been described, 40 of which occur in Europe. The latter belong to several genera which differ considerably in their biology (ecology, succession of generations, way of life). There is a widespread but mistaken belief that only *Culex pipiens* is a serious nuisance here. But almost always, representatives of the genus *Aedes* with 23 European species are also involved, and sometimes also *Mansonia*.

Anopheline mosquitoes *(Anopheles)* deposit their eggs singly on water; *Theobaldia*, *Mansonia* and *Culex* in a compact mass or "egg raft"; *Aedes* and *Culicella* seek out dry sites in which to lay their eggs, in flood plains (riverside woodlands or meadows) which will be inundated when the next flooding occurs. Culicines usually overwinter as imagos, but *Aedes* and *Culicella* do so as eggs, which are able to develop only with the arrival of the spring floods. Others, such as *A. maculatus* and *A. annulipes*, produce a second generation, usually in the middle of the summer, which is able to develop because a rainy period generally occurs at some time during the summer. Any of these eggs not covered by water have to "wait" for the spring floods.

Domestic species of mosquito that overwinter as imagos in cellars are *Culex pipiens* and *Theobaldia annulata* (*Anopheles maculipennis* also occasionally overwinters in cellars, but more often in barns, stables, attics etc.). *Culex* and *Theobaldia* have a preference for polluted water. Likely breeding sites include not only rain barrels, watering cans and so on, but also accumulations of waste water, ditches in villages, even cess pools. In these species, overwintering depends upon environmental conditions. Where these are favourable, the generations succeed one another without interruption.

The larvae feed on microplankton which is conveyed to the oral orifice by means of currents set up by the wafting action of tufts of hair on the head. In addition, they use their well-developed mandibles to graze on dead leaves or other vegetation on the bottom of the body of water in which they live. With a single exception, they all come to the surface to breathe. If they are undisturbed, they will remain hanging at the surface of the water for a considerable time, *Aedes* and others by means of the respiratory siphon situated on the dorsal surface of a rear segment, while *Anopheles*, which lacks a siphon, floats horizontally with the entire length of the back in contact with the surface. The rear abdominal segment has two respiratory spiracles with valve closure. The pupae are

"How hath Nature bestowed all the five senses in a Gnat? and yet some there be, lesse creatures than they. But where hath she made the seat of her eies to see before it? where hath she set and disposed the tast? where hath she placed and inserted the instrument and organ of smelling? and above all, where hath she disposed that dreadful and terrible noise that it maketh, that wonderfull great sound in proportion of so little a body? can there be devised a thing more finely and cunningly wrought than the wings set to her body? Marke what long-shanked legs above ordinary she hath given unto them. See how she hath set that hungry hollow concavitie in stead of a belly: and hath made the same so thirstie and greedy after bloud, and mans especially.

Come to the weapon that it hath to pricke, pierce, and enter through the skinne, how artificially hath she pointed and sharpened it? and being so little as it is (as hardly the finenesse thereof cannot be seen) yet as if it were of bignesse and capacity answerable, framed it she hath most cunningly for a two-fold use: to wit, most sharpe pointed, to prick and enter; and withall, hollow like a pipe for to sucke in and convey the bloud through it."

Pliny the Younger: From the introduction of The Naturall Historie, *translated by Philemon Holland, London, 1634.*

active and possess a pair of respiratory horns by means of which they float at the surface of the water. The exception is *Mansonia richiardii*, in which the larval spiracle is furnished with saw-teeth and thus modified into drilling apparatus which pierces the lower shoots of plants growing at the bottom of the water. The two respiratory horns of the pupa are also used in this way.

Mosquitoes as carriers of disease

Anopheline mosquitoes are the primary hosts in which parasitic agents of disease (species of *Plasmodium*) go through the sexual cycle of reproduction. Human beings are the intermediate hosts in which asexual reproduction (schizogony) occurs. There are various species of the genus *Plasmodium* which have developmental cycles of varying lengths and which also differ in other characteristics. As a result, they produce a diversity of symptoms in the human beings they affect, and individual forms of malaria ranging from mild to highly dangerous.

In the 19th century, before the First World War, the only place in Europe in which malaria occurred was in an area of East Friesland. Afterwards, however, cases were again reported sporadically. Many ex-servicemen were *Plasmodium* carriers. The *Anopheles* mosquitoes remained, in spite of widespread measures of control, but the malaria disappeared. Again following the Second World War, the incidence of malaria increased, both as a recurrence of the disease among war veterans and as new, locally occurring cases among the remaining population. But again the cases became rarer and then disappeared entirely. In Europe, the temperature is not sufficiently high for the developmental cycle of the Anophelines to become established permanently.

It is different in the tropics. In India there were 40,000 cases of malaria in 1966, 1.4 million in 1972 and 6 million in 1976. In spite of widespread measures of control, the numbers continue to increase. The important contribution that entomological knowledge can make to the successful control of disease is shown by the history of yellow fever, a tropical virus disease. In 1881, *Aedes aegypti* was recognized as the carrier. By studying the biology of this mosquito, it was possible to introduce effective measures of control. "Without a means of combatting aegypti, there would be no Panama Canal. The many casualties in the early stages of building (more than 20,000 died) were victims of the yellow fever mosquito, although this was not recognized at the time." (Peus, 1950)

Fortuna lächelt, doch sie mag
Nur ungern voll beglücken;
Schenkt sie uns einen Sommertag,
So schenkt sie uns auch Mücken."

Wilhelm Busch

Dame Fortune smiles, yet to bestow
Unbounded bliss is rare;
Though she may grant a summer's day
Yet still the gnats are there.

Early knowledge about mosquitoes

A very early mention of methods of protection against mosquitoes is found in Herodotus. "From the large numbers of mosquitoes, they protect themselves in the following way: those who live above the marshlands are aided by the towers up which they climb when they want to sleep. For the mosquitoes cannot fly high on account of the winds. But those who dwell in the marshes have discovered another method in place of the towers. Each man has a net with which he fishes by day; but in the night he draws the net round the bed in which he lies, and sleeps beneath it. If anyone sleeps in his clothes or beneath a linen cover, the mosquitoes sting through this covering; but they do not even attempt to do so through the net."

Pythagoras is said to have cleared a Sicilian town of malaria by drainage. In about A.D. 170, in his *Description of Greece*, Pausanius tells how the land round the small town of Myus in Asia Minor was turned into a brackish area of swamp by the silting up of the river mouth, and how finally the inhabitants were forced to leave the town to escape from the mosquitoes. Apparently the earlier knowledge had been lost completely. Aristotle provides some information on the biology of midges or gnats, and probably refers to chironomid gnats (Chironomidae), a non-biting family. "Gnats grow from ascarids; and ascarids are engendered in the slime of wells, or in places where there is a deposit left by the draining off of water. This slime decays, and first turns white, then black, and finally blood-red; and at this stage there originate in it, as it were, little tiny bits of red weed, which at first wriggle about all clinging together, and finally break loose and swim in the water, and are hereupon known as ascarids. After a few days they stand straight up on the water motionless and hard, and by and by the husk breaks off and the gnats are seen sitting upon it, until the sun's heat or a puff of wind sets them in motion, when they fly away."

Die Mücken

Dich freut die warme Sonne
Du lebst im Monat Mai.
In deiner Regentonne
Da rührt sich allerlei.
Viel kleine Tierlein steigen
Bald auf- bald niederwärts.
Und, was besonders eigen,
Sie atmen mit dem Sterz.
Noch sind sie ohne Tücken,
Rein kindlich ist ihr Sinn.
Bald aber sind es Mücken
Und fliegen frei dahin.
Sie fliegen auf und nieder
Im Abendsonnenglanz
Und singen feine Lieder
Bei ihrem Hochzeitstanz.
Du gehst zu Bett um Zehne,
Du hast zu schlafen vor,
Dann hörst du jene Töne
Ganz dicht an deinem Ohr.
Drückst du auch in die Kissen
Dein wertes Angesicht,
Dich wird zu finden wissen
Der Rüssel, welcher sticht.
Merkst du, dass er dich impfe,
So reib mit Salmiak
Und dreh dich um und schimpfe
Auf dieses Mückenpack.

Wilhelm Busch

In his short epic poem *Culex*, the Roman poet Vergil (70 B.C. – A.D. 19) tells of a herdsman who is wakened by a mosquito and in this way saved from the imminent bite of a snake. He kills the snake, but also the insect that has saved him, and the latter, appearing to him in a dream, tells of its unhappy fate and gives him no rest until he builds a splendid sepulchre in its memory. According to Schimitschek, this is an allusion to the mausoleum of the Emperor Augustus.

Kamal al-Din al-Damiri compares mosquitoes to elephants, and is particularly impressed by the functioning of the suctorial proboscis. "They are similar to ticks, but have narrower legs and the liquid they suck up is clearly visible. In appearance they resemble the elephant, but in addition to the four legs, the trunk and the tail of the latter, they have two more legs and four wings. The elephant's trunk is solid, but that of the mosquito is hollow, and is linked with the mosquito's internal organs. When they sting, they can suck themselves full of human blood which enters directly into the stomach. So the mosquito's proboscis is at once pharynx and oesophagus."

Al-Qazwini expresses some quite different and equally interesting views concerning mosquitoes, which are very much in keeping with the spirit of the age. "If a mosquito lands upon an object, it cannot be seen because of the small size of its body. And what a small fraction of its body is its head, and what a small part of its head its brain. Yet God created within its brain the five inner powers. It possesses a sense of community, for it goes towards an animal and not towards the wall; it possesses imagination, for if it is driven off from a limb, it returns to it, since it knows that it is suitable as food; in addition instinct, for if it feels the movement of a hand, it flies away, since it knows that an enemy is pursuing it. It also has the faculty of memory, for when the hand is at rest,

Mosquitoes mating on the wing *(Aedes aegypti)*.

it returns to it, knowing that the enemy has departed. Further it possesses practical common sense, for once it has implanted its proboscis and sucked up the blood, it flies off immediately, knowing that the action causes pain and that the victim will soon be in pursuit. So it flies off with the utmost dispatch."

Albertus Magnus summarizes medieval knowledge concerning these insects:

"Cinifes are mosquitoes, flying worms with long legs. With a small rostrum, they penetrate the human skin. They come into existence from moisture and are numerous near bodies of water. In particular, they seek out humans and animals that sweat, and for this reason are so often found in the evening near those who sleep. In damp regions, it is necessary for beds to be covered with special nets as a protection against their stings." There is a remarkable illustration in *Hortus sanitatis*, 1536, showing a naked man being tormented by mosquitoes. The insects are almost as long as his forearm! Ferrante Imperato has remedies for most things including mosquitoes. "If anyone who wants to sleep, places a bunch of damp hemp stalks close by, no mosquito will disturb him or come near."

Olaus Magnus described the Scandinavian animal kingdom. Mosquitoes are of considerable prominence in those countries, and so find their due place in the literature. "In the countries lying farthest to the north, there are very large mosquitoes which cause great harm to people on water and on land with their biting and singing, particularly since there is constant daylight. But the people use wormwood as a protection against them; they sprinkle it with vinegar, dry it and make smoke from it, then the mosquitoes fly from the acrid smell. They also take flight if they are sprinkled with water in which wormwood, ruewort or coriander has been simmered, or if shoemaker's blacking is poured over them or they are subjected to smoke of juniper bushes. Anyone wanting to sleep must cover himself with a linen cloth or bark from a tree, so that he is safe from their piercing and singing."

Two passages by Caspar Schwenckfeld deserve mention here: "Culex. A family of small flies. The body is very small, the abdomen almost empty. The legs are very long, the tongue is tubular and modified for sucking and piercing; they are especially fond of human blood. Using the pro-

Mosquitoes

You love the warmth of sunshine,
Life in the month of May
At home in a great rain barrel
Where countless creatures play.
Now upwards and now downwards
These little insects sail,
And this is very curious,
To breathe, they use their tail.
Completely without malice,
Childlike still are they,
But soon they are mosquitoes
Get free and fly away.
Up and down they flutter
In the gleam of the evening sun,
The finest songs they utter
'Til the nuptial dance is done.
You go to bed at ten and hope
That peaceful sleep is near,
But suddenly that dreaded tone
No distance from your ear!
And though among the pillows
You try to hide your face,
Yet with unerring cunning
That sting will find its place.
And should you now be smitten,
Try Sal ammoniac
And turn and aim your curses
At that mosquito pack.

boscis, they insert a delicate and soft stylet through the skin which pierces to the bone, and suck up the blood . . . Scinifes Nocturnal Mosquitoes. Very small flies that irritate by biting. They harass cattle and sleeping humans greatly with their bites. For this reason, genteel and sensitive people hang nets round their beds so that, protected from the insects, they can sleep peacefully."

Crane-flies (Tipulidae)

Crane-flies are conspicuous insects principally on account of their size. Many people believe them capable of stinging, but mistakenly, since they possess no sting. They are mosquito-like in shape and are very large, with especially long legs. *Tipula maxima* can have a wing span of more than 4 cm. The larvae of most species are saprophytic, but some (known as leather-jackets) are occasional pests in meadows, gardens and nurseries. The larvae of the Marsh Crane-fly *(Tipula paludosa)* feed on roots during the day and at night eat parts of plants growing above the ground. *Tipula oleracea* (the Common Crane-fly) which in Europe sometimes produces two generations within a year, has a similar behaviour pattern to *Tipula paludosa*.

One of the earliest descriptions of a Crane-fly is given by Ulisse Aldrovandi, and it contains probably the first mention of the reduced hind wings (halteres). "The elongate, pointed head supports two rather curved antennae at the front. The convex thorax bears two wings. The abdomen is long, narrow and distinctly segmented. It consists of 7 or 8 segments. The end is curved slightly upwards, although the artist has not shown this clearly. The legs are so long that they seem as long as a man's little finger. Under the wings there are two appendages with special minute knobs at the end, which in a curious way resemble the antennae of an insect. But it is not clear why Nature has given them these appendages, nor have I found them in any other insect. The body is grey, the legs sometimes darker. The legs are divided into three parts, and at rest, are extended in the manner of spiders. Therefore when I first saw one, I took it for a winged spider, but on closer examination, I noticed the abdomen was long and the legs six in number, whereas spiders possess eight."

Further information was added by Thomas Moufet, together with an illustration of a Crane-fly and a sketch showing copulation. "Another fly is the Tipula, also known as the Longlegs or Cranes on account of its long legs. In England, it is called Crane-fly. We know four different species of this genus. The first species in which the tibia is extremely long, is like a forest spider in appearance. Its body, almost oval in shape, is whitish-grey, its wings silver. The jet-black eyes are distinctly protuberant. Both antennae are very short. The tail terminates in a point. Like the ostrich, its flight is almost a walk. Sometimes it also flies in the air, but not for long nor for any great distance. It loves the light so much that—as a result of this fondness—it is often burned. In autumn, it is common on meadows and pastures. So much for the male. The female is similar in appearance, but somewhat blacker and the end of the tail has a truncated appearance. In England, they are called Shepherds, because they generally appear where there are sheep. The above-mentioned tipulids copulate with the tails turned away, and fly in this position, sometimes bending towards one another as in an embrace."

Antony van Leeuwenhoek is less well-known for his literary talent than for his skill as a microscopist. He mentions the hemelt, which refers to the Leather-jacket, the species concerned is *Tipula paludosa*. "The hemelt. Early in May, I visited a meadow in the company of an experienced farmer. We collected a number of Leather-jackets in boxes, and they soon dried out and died. I placed others in an earthenware vessel, covered them with lawn and watered them daily in my laboratory museum. As soon as the lawn dried out, I fetched new, and at the same time made sure that those living free were still alive, and brought new worms as well. Until the end of July, I noticed no change. Meanwhile I was told that Leather-jackets turn into Crane-flies. But I wanted to see this for myself . . . Two days after pupation, I went into the meadow where I had earlier collected my specimens, and there I saw a large number of Crane-flies or Longlegs flying about.

I took some of these insects with me in a box, so that I could examine their eggs and the male's sperm. But all those that I dissected were of similar structure. It was just the same in the next three or four groups I caught. What I took to be the ovarium was to be found in all the specimens I dissected. Then it occurred to me that if I were to find in nature a male and female in copula, I would be able to distinguish between them. But three times I went out searching in vain. Then I found one creature in my house and one in my garden, which resembled the Crane-fly closely. But the abdomen was larger and ended in a point, whereas otherwise, it is thicker at the end. Upon dissection, I found numerous longish black eggs in the body of these insects; in one case I counted more than 200. Since I now always found eggs in these insects which were to be seen occasionally on the wing, the thought occurred to me as to whether they could not be different sexes of the same species . . . It became clear to me that these were indeed the females of the males I had previously caught; the larger abdomen serves as a container for the eggs, and the pointed extremity they insert into the soil in order to deposit their eggs into damp ground, which, I believe, would otherwise remain infertile. At home, I noted that of the insects I had brought back, 6 were female and 10–12 male. 3 females were engaged in copulation with the same number of males, so now I was certain that they belonged together . . . As already mentioned, there are more than 200 eggs in each female. So if all Crane-flies reproduced successfully, there would be so many of them within 2–3 years that they would destroy the roots of all grasses and plants. But as a result of dryness in the ground, rain, storms and extreme cold, so many of the worms and imagines are destroyed that only a fraction survives and damage remains moderate."

The painter Jean Goedart was a distinguished observer of nature. His *Metamorphosis naturalis* contains an interesting passage on Crane-flies (again *Tipula paludosa*). "Just as a man dislikes seeing at his table greedy guests who devour everything, so do country people dislike seeing in their fields this gluttonous worm that eats everything and is difficult to eradicate. For as a result of its particular natural disposition, it never crawls completely out of the soil, but shows only its head, which it instantly retracts when it hears a noise. It can be caught only with a hoe or spade. It seems to know how much it is hated by men, and so fears them as it does death. I placed this worm in a jar with soil, exposed it to the sun in a position neither too warm nor too cold, and gave it food and drink for some considerable time. In this jar, it changed into the creature illustrated at the centre of the Plate. Metamorphosis took place on May 29, and on June 25, a small two-winged insect with six legs hatched out, known to children as a Daddy-longlegs. These Daddy-longlegs have a hot and lustful temperament, and there are ten times as many males among them as females, which gives one no little cause for wonder. I have also observed with my own eyes that even as the male mates with the female, some 5 or 6 other males are flying round about, of which each one only awaits his own opportunity to copulate and to forestall his companions. Then the male remains for two days with the female in copula, to die soon after separation, whereas the female still feels herself quite strong. When the seed that the female has received begins to die and is ready to be deposited, she burrows into the soil with the end of her body and lays her seed there. It is from this seed that the dangerous creature originates, but only after three years have elapsed. One must consider as a miracle of Providence the way in which the reproduction of this worm is hereby held in check, so that the worm needs three years for its procreation, and that it produces so many more males than females."

Fleas

(Siphonaptera)

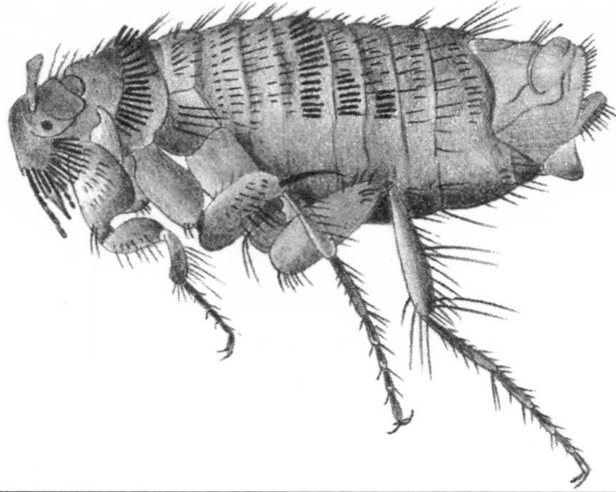

Fleas have obviously engaged man's attention since the earliest times. The well-known Papyrus Ebers, that was written down as a medical compendium in about 1550 B.C.; contains an early remedy for fleas. It recommends that date flour and water should be boiled and then drunk; the papyrus stipulates that the drink should afterwards be regurgitated and promises that the fleas will disappear.

The great master Aristotle was no doubt familiar with fleas from personal experience. On the subject of their development, he writes (it was to be almost two thousand years before the doctrine of spontaneous generation was dealt its final blow): "The flea is generated out of the slightest amount of putrefying matter; for wherever there is any dry excrement, a flea is sure to be found."

The larvae of fleas develop in the substrate of the nest, feeding on organic waste products of the host, and in many species, on dropped particles of blood sucked from the host by adult fleas and on the excrement of the imagines. And so human fleas live in "human nests", namely house, stable, larder—anywhere regularly frequented by the host; he is necessary as the blood donor, although he may not be the only one, since domestic animals of both the welcome and unwelcome variety also serve as a source of food for certain species of human fleas.

Dog fleas and cat fleas sometimes transfer to humans, and the same is true of poultry fleas (laboratory tests have shown that more than 40 species of flea will feed on human hosts). It is not surprising then that the writings of the Roman, Lucius Junius Columella, contains the following instructions: "If a dog is infested with fleas, rub into its coat a mixture of pulverized cumin and hellebore which have been added to water or the juice of the snake gourd, or if these are not available, the liquid discharged when olives are pressed."

Any dog owner today who found his pet infested with fleas would probably reject the formidable tinctures of the Romans; fortunately he possesses effective insecticides; these are also widely available to the poultry farmer. But some of the advice that Columella gives is sound: "The hen's nest must be cleaned frequently and lined with fresh straw, lest the fleas increase unduly there."

Fleas have probably never affected man more significantly than they did in the Middle Ages. As carriers of bubonic plague, they were responsible for the death of millions and for the depopulation of large tracts of land. Yet very little was known about these insects. A quotation from Isidore of Seville (died A.D. 636) illustrates this: "Pulices vero vocati sunt, quod e pulvere magis nu-

Above:

Mole Flea *(Hystrichopsylla talpae)*.

triuntur." (Fleas are so called because they feed almost exclusively on dust.) The author was a renowned scholar of his day and his *Origines sive Etymologiae* a standard work. Generations accepted its authority. So what basis could there be for recognizing a link such as that between rat flea, rat and man?

The scholastic and encyclopaedist, Thomas of Cantimpré, also took an interest in fleas, and writes: "It comes into being out of warmed dust and decaying damp matter." As a remedy, he recommends "rubbing the juice of wormwood on the body every evening". Albertus Magnus summarizes what was known at the time about various animals including the flea. "Fleas originate from damp, warm dust when it suddenly comes into contact with the warm body of an animal. They are black, round creatures that suck with their proboscis, so that swellings arise at these sites. It has long legs for jumping, and six feet for walking. Since it is very small, it leaps very quickly. It sucks so much blood that it constantly excretes it in a black, dry form. Its eggs are lenticular. A small male and large female are always found together. The fleas that come into existence in March and April, die in May. During this month, there are no fleas or only very few. Later, they live on until the winter, but they are especially bad in the winter."

A book that had wide distribution at that time, both in transcription and in translation, was *Liber de natura rerum*. In it, fleas are discussed in some detail. "These insects that come from dust and refuse / grow in abundance in hot weather." And as a means of combatting them: "When a man goes to sleep, let him rub his skin thoroughly with absinthium. As everyone knows, this is the herb called wormwood."

Other writers of that period also mention wormwood as a flea repellent. For example, Bartholomaeus Anglicus says that the plant vermouth and leaves of the wild fig-tree are poisonous to fleas, as is colocynth crushed and leached in water. He also notes: "The flea comes into existence white, but then immediately becomes black." He may have observed a flea freshly hatched from the pupa, for at this stage, it has still not developed its full colour.

Some of the medieval beliefs were in fact correct. There is a germ of truth even in the "site of generation". With very few exceptions, fleas lay their relatively large eggs (up to 0.5 mm) in the nest of the host (usually 8–10 eggs at one time, with a total of 400 eggs for the human flea). The eye-less, vermiform larvae develop here, and having passed through three larval instars, are ready to pupate. Pupation takes place in a cocoon spun by the larva from a secretion of the salivary glands, and concealed by an external covering of debris particles, so that it is well camouflaged. Inside it, the flea hatches, sometimes to emerge at once, but it may also remain inside the cocoon for some months, even overwintering there. It emerges primarily in response to vibrations set up by the host. From what has been said, it is absolutely clear that fleas can dwell permanently only with those birds or mammals that have a "nest" (ungulates and monkeys, for example, have no fleas). Rabbits have fleas while hares do not. Bats are an exception, for they have fleas but no "nests".

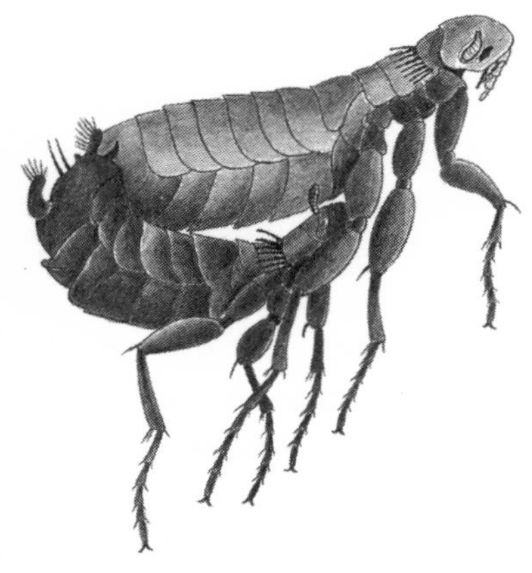

A Bird Flea (*Ceratophyllus* spec.) mating.

Early writers were clearly already familiar with the suctorial proboscis, which is a complicated structure consisting of the epipharynx and the laciniae, the sucking action of which is supported by other mouth parts. That the diet should consist exclusively and typically of blood was not considered surprising at that time, although not all writers supported this view. The fleas owe their considerable leaping capacity to the powerful muscles of the coxae and femora of the mid and especially of the hind legs. Aristophanes (445–386 B.C.) and Xenophon (*c.* 430–354 B.C.) report that Socrates (469–399 B.C.) feared the leaping of fleas. The capacity for jumping, however, varies greatly between species. Fleas, such as the Mole Flea, living on a host which is fairly immobile, usually possess a reduced jumping ability. Fleas suck blood voraciously, often gorging themselves to excess. The males are in fact usually smaller than the females.

"Wenn Frau und manche Maid
Über die Flöhe schreien,
Auch stark die Mücken stechen—
Bedeutet immer Naß."

When women and the maids
Wail about the fleas,
And sorely mosquitoes bite—
It is bound to be wet.

Hans Sachs (1494–1576),
from: Die Zeichen des Regenwetters
(Portents of rain)

In other cultures as well, knowledge about fleas was incomplete. Kamal al-Din al-Damiri's book *The Lives of Animals* was considered the leading zoological work of the early Arabian civilization. On the subject of fleas, we read:

"The flea is a creature of immense leaping capacity. It springs backwards in order to see who is trying to catch it; if it were to leap forwards, it would often have met its death." The flea is compared in its outward appearance to an elephant with "canine teeth" for biting and a rostrum for sucking blood. To combat fleas, a formula of exorcism is recommended, which, repeated twenty-five times, causes all the fleas to assemble on a Persian reed-cane that has been smeared with asses' milk and the fat of a he-goat and set up in the centre of the house. This staff is then carried to another place with all the fleas sitting upon it. But no flea may be killed or the remedy is ineffective. And finally comes a tip of real practical value: "Then wash through the house." In many areas, the human flea is virtually extinct today as a result of floor polish, vacuum cleaners and jointless flooring.

It is said that fleas appearing to someone in a dream signify that that person has slanderous enemies.

Al-Qazwini, quoting from another writer, says "that the flea is among those creatures that acquire the capacity for flight; it then becomes a fly, just as the caterpillar having acquired the capacity for flight becomes a butterfly". This statement is of course without foundation, although we know today that fleas and True Flies (Diptera) are closely related, and that the ancestors of the flea had wings. An indication of this is the presence of wing rudiments in the pupae of many species of flea.

Until the start of the modern era, fleas were an everyday phenomenon in all social spheres. In ancient and medieval times they must have been particularly troublesome. Although a number of details had been observed correctly, knowledge of their biology was still fragmentary and this made any effective control impossible. The annoyance had to be endured, and fleas found their way into the treasure-store of fairy tales, anecdotes, poems and stories.

In 1573, Johann Fischart (1547–1590) published his 4,000 line burlesque epic entitled *Flöh-Hatz—Weiber-Tratz*. The fleas complain of being unable to feed because of the relentless persecution they suffer at the hands of the women. (Fleas in fact show a definite preference for women, in positive reaction to the latters' ovarial hormones.) The same work also contains thirteen remedies for fleas. Many of them are based on the use of plants and extracts that are supposed to drive off or kill fleas: for example, it suggests gathering the plant green henbane which is also known as flea-bane. It also recommends the burning of fleas, since the smoke drives away other fleas. The blood of a she-goat and beef dripping are said to attract fleas, concentrating them in one place where they are then easily destroyed. The 13th remedy: "Smear hedgehog fat on a stick, place it in the middle of the room, then all the fleas assemble on the stick."

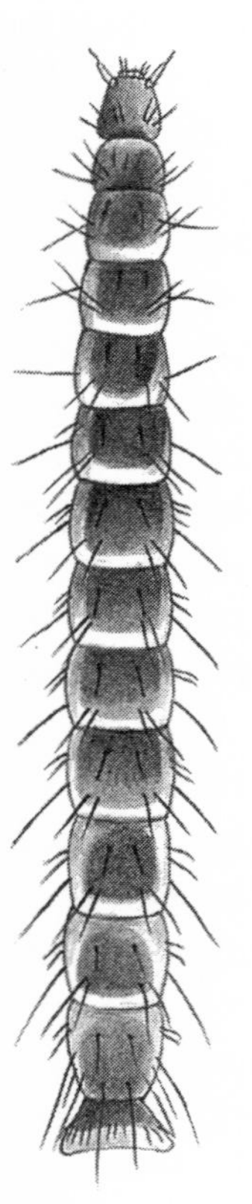

Flea larva *(Ctenophthalmus bisbidentatus)* from voles.

Johann Colerus makes a similar observation in his *Household Book*. "Flies and fleas bring tidings of rain when they sting and bite both man and beast more frequently and more severely than usual."

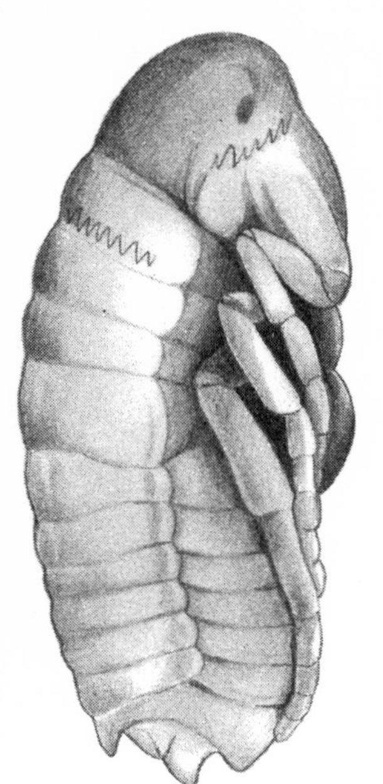

Pupa of the Dog Flea *(Ctenocephalides canis)*.

"The bravest warrior recoils in fright
When insects sting him in the night."

Wilhelm Busch

E. T. A. Hoffmann (1776–1822) wrote a novel entitled *Meister Floh* (Master Flea). Then there is Schmidt's *Flohkrieg* (Flea War) of 1790, *Der Stählerne Floh* (the Flea of Steel) by Nikolai Leskov (1831–1895), and the illustrated stories of Wilhelm Busch, in which fleas make a frequent appearance

The scene in Auerbach's Cellar in *Faust* (Part I) by Johann Wolfgang von Goethe contains a poem on fleas.

Fleas have even served as a subject for paintings and sculptures—or rather, less the insect itself than the attempts made to catch it. One example is "Searching for Fleas by Candle Light" by Gerrit van Honthorst (1590–1656). The flea is not shown, but the work portrays the beauty of a young woman in candle light. The old woman helping her remains in shadow, providing effective contrast. Another painter using the same motif is Georges de la Tour in his "Woman Searching for a Flea". And there is a porcelain statuette on the same theme that was designed by Luplau in 1773.

We are indebted to Antony van Leeuwenhoek for many valuable observations in early entomological research, including his accurate morphological description and illustration of a flea, showing the stages of its development, and copulation. (In the latter, the male is shown beneath the female, maintaining a firm hold with its specially developed antennae and the pincer-like appendages at the end of the abdomen.) Van Leeuwenhoek also notes the relationship between the capillary blood supply to the human skin and the sucking action of fleas: "It is certain that these insects do not pierce deeply into the skin, but position their piercing mouthparts exclusively on these blood vessels in the skin which are very numerous, and with a few shallow bites, they easily get to the blood and so to their food."

D'Jacinto Cestone (17th century) gives an equally precise account of the development of these insects which was frequently quoted in later works.

It comes as something of a set-back to read in an anatomical description of the flea by a Zurich physician Johann de Muralto (1718): "The tiny heart is suspended under the head in the thorax."

The physician Ernst Brückmann (1696–1753) who listed (admittedly with some hesitation) lunar fleas the size of elephants among the species of fleas, was nevertheless the inventor of an ingenious flea trap. It was described in the *Nutzbares, galantes und curiöses Frauenzimmer-Lexicon* (Useful, gallant and curious lexicon for women) published in Frankfurt and Leipzig in 1739. A small ivory cylinder is furnished with holes through which the fleas can enter. Inside the cylinder and closing off the top end was a rod. This was to be smeared with blood, to attract the fleas. They enter the trap, become stuck fast or cannot find their way out again. An improved method is recommended. "If the rod is smeared with a sweet, sticky substance such as, for example, honey instead of blood, and the trap suspended between the breasts or in another place, où vous savez, where fleas are especially troublesome, the latter would come jumping along eagerly after the sweet honey."

Flea traps became fashionable in a wide variety of designs, including some fitted with a small microscope with which to examine the captured enemy. Directions for their use, written in 1784, include the observation: "Many a demoiselle wears this gadget hung round her neck between the duplex genus feminum." Written on the case of a flea trap from Cologne are the lines "If you sting me, I will sting you in return" and on the base, "Revenge is sweet".

The Mole Flea, with a body length of 5.5 mm, is the largest indigenous flea and was used as a performer in flea circuses. It was dressed in clothes and made to pull minute carriages, arousing the curiosity and admiration of the spectators. It was easily "tamed", since the leaping capacity of this species is slight.

Finally a few words on the subject of the plague. Today we are aware of the role of certain species of flea in transmitting this dreadful disease. The Rat Flea *(Xenopsylla cheopis)* is the species primarily responsible for passing bubonic plague to humans, a disease originally restricted to rodent populations (particularly rats). But this link was unknown in the days when plague was rife. The plague has frequently entered the world of literature, and even of legend. In the *Decamerone*, Giovanni Boccaccio (1313–1375) gives an accurate and shocking account of the plague epidemic of 1348 in Florence. In the Middle Ages, almost all the cities of Europe were afflicted, usually several times, by this devastating disease which altered drastically the entire pattern of public life. In Vienna, a quarter of the population died in the epidemic of 1679 to 1680 and a fifth in that of 1713 to 1714. Conrad Gesner (1516–1556), one of the most eminent zoologists of his day, fell victim to the plague while working as a medical practitioner in Zurich. The epidemic of plague, known as the Black Death, that spread across Europe between 1347 and 1352, carried off about a quarter of the population of Europe. Inevitably, the "Great Pestilence", like Fire and Water, Sun and Moon, had a profound effect upon the intellectual life of the people. Today, reminders of the dread disease still exist in certain established customs, and as monuments, memorial stones, columns and plague cemeteries.

The outbreaks of the disease seemed inexplicable; superstition found an open door, and the belief became widespread that they were a divine punishment. People attempted early to protect themselves from the plague; there were numerous medicines. Doctors treating the plague victims wore thick clothing—and perhaps as a result were indeed less affected: the clothes afforded some protection from the dangerous fleas. Soon programmes of isolation and quarantine were introduced, probably as a result of the observation that, during epidemics, isolated settlements frequently remained free of plague. The Republic of Venice set up a "nazaretum" (called *lazaretto*) where strangers were obliged to reside for 40 days (a quaranta!) so that their state of health could be monitored. In 1422, a 14-day quarantine for ships was introduced.

It was only much later that the plague was effectively brought under control, by large-scale measures of rat extermination, once the chain of infection had been recognized.

Conclusion

It took at least 360 million years for insects to attain the wealth and variety of species that exist today. If we assume the number of species now living to be close on a million, it is still necessary to add that several million more species must have existed in the course of evolutionary history, which have long since disappeared in a natural process associated with radical environmental changes that have taken place on earth. We have evidence of only a fraction of the species in the form of fossils.

Important among the attributes that have contributed to the remarkable success of insects as a class is their small size and their outstanding adaptability. On the other hand, many species are highly specialized and so in greater danger of extinction than those with more generalized biological demands.

Man has been interested in insects for some three thousand years. At first it was necessity that drove him, but later on, the insects became increasingly a source of pleasure to him. Yet at no time has man's relationship to insects been an entirely positive one. Nor is it ever likely to be.

As natural conditions are increasingly altered by man, more and more insect species become endangered. Tens of thousands of species have already fallen victim to the advance of man, and every year, new ones are added. Many species die out before they have even been observed.

The following tale, told six hundred years ago by Kamal al-Din al-Damiri, might well serve as a warning to us to deal more carefully with the treasures of nature that, once lost, cannot be regained.

"Once upon a time, Caliph Umaiibu-el-Khattab was greatly troubled because the grasshoppers failed to come. He sent out messengers to Syria, to Yemen, to Iran. The last of the messengers brought back a few grasshoppers, upon which the caliph exclaimed joyfully: They still live! I have heard that Allah created a thousand species of animals, and the first of these that will become extinct is the grasshopper. But as soon as it has become extinct, all other species of animal will follow, as beads fall from a necklace when its string is broken."

Web-spinners (Embioptera) live on the ground, often beneath stones, in silken tunnels that they weave for themselves, using silk glands situated in the thickened fore-tarsi. The females are always wingless and the males of only certain species are winged. Here, male and female of *Embia major* from India.

Bibliography

BLÜTHGEN, P.: *Die Faltenwespen Mitteleuropas (Hymenoptera, Diploptera)*. Berlin, 1961.

BODENHEIMER, F. S.: *Materialien zur Geschichte der Entomologie bis Linné*. Vols. 1 and 2, Berlin, 1928, 1929.

BRANDT, H.: *Insekten als Rohstofflieferanten. Orion-Bücher,* vol. 135, Munich, 1960.

Die Neue Brehm-Bücherei. Leipzig, Wittenberg. Since 1949 approx. 60 monographs of species or groups of insects have been published in this series.

DUMPERT, K.: *Das Sozialleben der Ameisen*. Berlin (West), Hamburg, 1978.

EIDMANN, H.: *Lehrbuch der Entomologie*. 2nd edition edited by F. Kühlborn. Hamburg, Berlin (West), 1970.

EVANS, H. E.: *Das Trillionen Volk. Die unbekannte Welt der Insekten*. Bergisch Gladbach, 1969.

FABRE, J. H.: *Souvenirs entomologiques*. 10 vols., Paris 1879ff.

FARB, P. (Editor): *The Insects*. Time Life International (Nederland) N. V., 1964.

FORSTER, W.: *Knaurs Insektenbuch*. Munich, Zurich, 1968.

FROST, S. W.: *Insect Life and Insect Natural History*. New York, 1959.

GOETSCH, W.: *Vergleichende Biologie der Insekten-Staaten*. 2nd edition, Leipzig, 1953.

GRASSÉ. P. P. (Editor): *Traité de Zoologie*. Vols. 9 and 10, Paris, 1949 and 1951.

Group of authors: *Urania Tierreich Insekten*. Leipzig, Jena, Berlin, 1968.

GRZIMEK, B.: *Grzimeks Tierleben*. Vol. 3. *Insekten*. Munich, 1969.

HENNIG, W.: *Stammesgeschichte der Insekten*. Frankfurt/Main, 1969.

HERING, E. M.: *Biologie der Schmetterlinge*. Berlin, 1926.

IMMS, A. D.: *A General Textbook of Entomology including the Anatomy, Physiology, Development and Classification of Insects*. 9th edition edited by O. W. Richards and R. G. Davies, London, New York, 1964.

JACOBS, W., and M. RENNER: *Taschenbuch zur Biologie der Insekten*. Jena, 1974.

KAESTNER, A.: *Lehrbuch der Speziellen Zoologie*. Vols. 1, 3, Parts A and B, Jena, 1972 and 1973.

KEILBACH, R.: *Die tierischen Schädlinge Mitteleuropas*. Jena, 1966.

KÉLER, S. von: *Entomologisches Wörterbuch*. 3rd edition, Berlin, 1963.

KEMPER, H.: *Kurzgefasste Geschichte der tierischen Schädlinge, der Schädlingskunde und der Schädlingsbekämpfung*. Berlin, 1968.

KLAUSNITZER, B.: *Beetles*. New York, 1983.

LAMPEL, G.: *Biologie der Insekten*. Munich, 1973.

LINSENMAIER, W.: *Knaurs Grosses Insektenbuch*. Munich, Zurich, 1972.

MARTINI, E.: *Lehrbuch der medizinischen Entomologie*. 4th edition, Jena, 1952.

MATTHES, D.: *Vom Liebesleben der Insekten*. Stuttgart, 1972.

MATTHEWS, B. W. and J. R.: *Insect Behavior*. New York, 1978.

MILNE, L. and M.: *Insect Worlds*. New York, 1980.

OTTO, D.: *Ameisen—Leben im Tierstaat*. Leipzig, Jena, Berlin, 1971.

PRICE, P. W.: *Insect Ecology*. New York, 1984.

SCHIMITSCHEK, E.: "Insekten in Brauchtum, Kult und Kultur", in: *Handbuch der Zoologie*. Vol. 4, Berlin, 1968.

SCHIMITSCHEK, E.: *Insekten in der Bildenden Kunst*. Vienna, 1977.

SCHMIDT, H.: *Die Termiten*. Leipzig, 1955.

SCHRÖDER, C. (Editor): *Handbuch der Entomologie*. 3 vols., Jena, 1925 and 1929.

SEDLAG, U.: *Wunderbare Welt der Insekten*. Leipzig, Jena, Berlin, 1978.

STANEK, V. J.: *The Pictorial Encyclopedia of Insects*. London, New York, Sydney, Toronto, 1972.

STRONG, D. W. ET AL.: *Insects on* Plants. Cambridge, Mass., 1984.

TUXEN, L.: *Insektenstimmen*. Berlin (West), Heidelberg, New York, 1967.

WEBER, H.: *Biologie der Hemipteren*. Berlin, 1930.

WEBER, H.: *Lehrbuch der Entomologie*. Jena, 1933.

WEBER, H.: *Grundriss der Insektenkunde*. Jena, Stuttgart, 5th edition revised by H. WEIDNER, Stuttgart, 1974.

WESENBERG-LUND, C.: *Biologie der Süsswasserinsekten*. Copenhagen, Berlin, Vienna, 1943.

WIGGLESWORTH, V. B.: *The Life of Insects*. London, 1964.

WIGGLESWORTH, V. B.: *Insect Physiology*. London and New York, 1974.

WILLIAMS, C. B.: *Die Wanderflüge der Insekten*. Hamburg, Berlin (West), 1961.

Authors and works mentioned in the text (selection)

Aegineta, Paulus (16th century): *Opus de re medicina* (1534).

Aelianus, Claudius (A.D. 160–240): *Von den Eigenschaften der Tiere.—On the Characteristics of Animals*, translated by A. F. Scholfield, 1958.

Albertus Magnus (1193–1280): *De animalibus* (1255–1270); *Liber de natura rerum.*

Ulisse Aldrovandi (1522–1605): *De Animalibus insectis libri VII* (1602).

Aristotle (384–322 B.C.): *Historia animalium*, translated by D'Arcy Wentworth Thompson (1910).

Augustine, Saint, Bishop of Hippo: *De civitate Dei*, translated by J. Healey (1903).

Baldner, Leonhard (1612–1694).

Bartholomaeus Anglicus: *Medieval Lore*, edited by R. Stelle (1893).

The Bible, authorized King James Version.

Bauhin, Johann (16th century): *Historia fontis et Balnei admirabilis Bollensis Liber Quartus* (1598).

Bonnet, Charles (1720–1793): *Insectologie* (1744).

Borelli, Giovanni Alphonso (1608–1679): *De motu animalium* (1680/81).

Bowring, Edgar Alfred: *The Poems of Goethe* (1853).

Brückmann, Franz Ernst (1696–1753).

Cantimpré, Thomas of (1186–1263): *Liber de natura rerum.*

Caub, Johannes Wonnecke von: *Hortus sanitatis* (*c.* 1480).

Colerus, Johann (died 1639): *Haushaltsbuch* (Household Book), (1590).

Columella, Lucius Junius (A.D. 1–68): *De re rustica* (*c.* A.D. 50).

Crescentii, Petrus de (1230–1310): *Opus ruralium commodorum libri XII* (1304–1309).

Damiri, Kamal al-Din al- (1349 or 1341–1391): *Leben der Tiere* (The Lives of Animals).

Dioscorides, Pedanius (lst century A.D.): *The Greek Herbal of Dioscorides*, Book IV, Englished by John Goodyear, A.D. 1655; *Materia medica.*

Frisch, Johann Leonhard (1666–1743): *Beschreibung von allerley Insecten in Teutschland* (1720–1738).

Goedart, Jean (1620–1668): *Metamorphosis naturalis.*

Gould, William: *An Account of English Ants* (1747).

Herodotus (484–425 B.C.): Translations of his works by Henry Cary (1847).

Hildegard, Saint (1099–1179).

Homer (9th century B.C.): The *Iliad*, translated by A. T. Murray (1925).

Hooke, Robert (1635–1730): *Micrographia* (1665).

Imperato, Ferrante (16th century): *Natural History* (1599).

Hughes, Griffith: *Natural History of Barbados* (1750).

Isidore of Seville (died A.D. 636): *Origines sive entymologiae.*

Knox, Robert: Description of his Travels (1681).

Leeuwenhoek, Antony van (1632–1723): *Opera omnia sive Arcana naturae detecti microscopiorum* (1695–1722).

Linnaeus (Carl von Linné, 1707–1778): *Systema Naturae* (lst edition 1735, 10th edition 1758); *Fauna Suecica* (1746).

Lister, Martin (1638–1711).

Lonicer, Adam (1528–1586): *Naturaliae historiae opus novum* (1551).

Magnus, Olaus (1470–1558): *Historia de gentibus septentrionalibus* (1555); *Papyrus Ebers* (*c.* 1550).

Malpighi, Marcello (1628–1694): *Opera omnia* (1687).

Matthioli, Petro Andrea (born 1501).

Maurus, Rabanus (776–856): *De Universo.*

Merian, Maria Sibylla (1647–1717): *Der Raupen wunderbare Verwandlung* (1679, 1683; *Metamorphosis Insectorum Surinamensium* (1705).

Moufet, Thomas (1553–1604): *Insectorum sive minimorum animalium theatrum* (1634).

Paracelsus (Theophrastus Bombastus von Hohenheim, 1493–1541): *Physiologus* (15th century).

Pliny, Gaius Secundus Maior (A.D. 23–79): *The Naturall Historie*, translated by Philemon Holland (1634).

Pu Shang (born 507 B.C.): *Erh Ya.*

Ray, John (1628–1705): *Historia Insectorum* (1710).

Réaumur, Réné Antoine Ferchault (1683–1756): *Mémoires pour servir à l'histoire des insectes* (1734–1742).

Redi, Francesco (1626–1698): Esperienze intorno alla generazione degli insetti (1668).

Rondeletius, Guilelmus (16th century).

Rosenhof, August Johann Rösel von (1705–1759): *Insekten-Belustigungen.*

Schwenckfeld, Caspar (1563–1609): *Theriotropheum Silesiae in qo animalium vis, natura et usus sex libris perstringitur* (1603).

Sloane, Sir Hans: *A Voyage to the Islands of Madera and Jamaica* (1725).

Southall, John: *A Treatise of Buggs* (1730).

Sperling, Johann (17th century): *Zoologia physica*, (1661).

Swammerdam, Jan (1637–1685): *Historia insectorum generalis* (1669); *Bybel der natuure* (1737).

Vallisnieri, Antonio (1661–1730).

Wotton, Eduard (1492–1555): *De differentiis animalium* (1552).

Index

Numerals in Roman type refer to text pages, numerals in italics to numbers of illustrations.